CASPAR OLEVIAN
AND THE SUBSTANCE
OF THE COVENANT

REFORMED HISTORICAL-THEOLOGICAL STUDIES

General Editors
Joel R. Beeke and Jay T. Collier

Books in Series:

The Christology of John Owen
by Richard W. Daniels

The Covenant Theology of Caspar Olevianus
by Lyle D. Bierma

John Diodati's Doctrine of Holy Scripture
by Andrea Ferrari

Caspar Olevian and the Substance of the Covenant
by R. Scott Clark

CASPAR OLEVIAN AND THE SUBSTANCE OF THE COVENANT

The Double Benefit of Christ

R. Scott Clark

Reformation Heritage Books
Grand Rapids, Michigan

Published in 2008 by
Reformation Heritage Books
2965 Leonard St., NE
Grand Rapids, MI 49525
616-977-0599 / Fax 616-285-3246
e-mail: orders@heritagebooks.org
website: www.heritagebooks.org

Library of Congress Cataloging-in-Publication Data

Clark, R. Scott.
 Caspar Olevian and the substance of the Covenant : the double benefit
of Christ / by R. Scott Clark.
    p. cm.
 Originally published: Edinburgh, Scotland : Rutherford House, 2005.
 Includes bibliographical references (p.   ) and index.
 ISBN 978-1-60178-053-9 (pbk. : alk. paper)
 1. Olevian, Caspar, 1536-1587. I. Title.
 BX9419.O4C53 2008
 230'.42092--dc22
                                    2008032489

---

*For additional Reformed literature, both new and used, request a free
book list from Reformation Heritage Books at the above address.*

Through most of the twentieth century, my grandparents worked in the heat of the Kansas sun in the hope that their children might one day have the leisure to become scholars.
This book is dedicated to them.

CONTENTS

FOREWORD

I am very pleased to commend this book in which Dr Clark enters into an important ongoing discussion, namely the relationship between Reformers within the same confessional tradition and also the relationship between those Reformers and their heirs. Having already done extensive work in this area, including editing a book with Dr Carl Trueman (*Protestant Scholasticism: Essays in Reassessment*, Paternoster, Carlisle, 1999), in this work he contributes to an important discussion about how to assess the question of continuity and discontinuity as to doctrines, theological method, and historical contexts.

Since the 1940s and well into the 1980s with books such as R. T. Kendall's popular *Calvin and English Calvinism to 1648* (Oxford University Press, Oxford, 1979), the trend favoured the idea of discontinuity between Calvin and Calvinism, even to the point of seeing little relationship between those who claimed to be within the same confessional heritage. Reassessment began in the 1980s and through works like Dr Clark's, scholars and even the wider public have seen that some of the distinctions such as non-scholastic versus scholastic, humanist versus Aristotelian, and unilateral versus bilateral views of the covenant of grace often harbour simplistic dichotomies.

In the present book we find a thoughtful and reflective engagement with the original sources allowing the thought of Olevian to be seen in its own right as well as within the matrix of the other Reformers and even the catholic tradition. The book serves as a delightful symphony for the reader because the author allows for both discontinuity and continuity, while finding a harmony of concern from those within the Reformed expression of the catholic faith. Indeed, Olevian, a figure too often forgotten when considering the crucial thinkers involved in the sixteenth-century theological debates, comes alive within his historical milieu. The background of Olevian and the foreground of his own work in its particular setting helped shape the way he formulated his emphases within the Reformed confessional framework. This work reminds us of the necessity of viewing historical context as a step toward understanding theologians of the past and their relation to other thinkers.

Dr Clark has placed Olevian not only within the streams of thought arising from the Reformation debates but within the broader catholic context as well. This is also highly important and significant because it serves as a reminder that the Reformers and their heirs did not see their work as a divorce from the previous 1400 years of Christian history but as an integral part of it. They believed themselves to be reforming the one, holy, catholic, and apostolic church that arose from the apostolic preaching of the first century. Thus, Olevian and others like him always saw their work within this over-riding 'catholic' concern. Not only does such careful consideration provide a much needed reminder of the Reformers' desire but it also can aid in ecumenical discussions today, especially reminding those in the Reformed camp that their roots are not only 'reformational' but also 'catholic'.

I am pleased to be able to invite the reader into this book. I am sure the reader will find in it much upon which to reflect as well as a delightful read.

Paul R. Schaefer, Jr
Professor and Chair, Department of Religion and Philosophy
Grove City College, Pennsylvania
April 2005

ACKNOWLEDGEMENTS

Thanks are due to those who made this book possible. First of all to Barbara who endured her husband cloistered for an unreasonable number of years, and to Katie and Emily, who cannot remember when their father was not working on a book.

This research began as a doctoral thesis written under the supervision of the Reverend Doctor John E. Platt, Pembroke College, Oxford, who is a model of the scholarly virtues: industry, care and patience.

Thanks to all those who read and corrected the typescript in various stages of preparation including Carl R. Trueman, Paul R. Schaefer, Philip G. Ryken and Iain M. Duguid, and also to Brett Watson for his work on the index. Particular thanks are due to my colleagues W. Robert Godfrey, Stephen M. Baugh and Michael S. Horton and to Philip Henry, Gabriel Nave and Tom Wenger for their editorial help. Much gratitude is due to the editor of this series, David F. Wright, New College, Edinburgh, for his extraordinary labours on my behalf and to Lynn Quigley of Rutherford House for her gracious help. Any errors remaining, of course, are the author's sole responsibility.

Recognition is owed also to those institutions and libraries which supported this research, including Oxford University, St Anne's College, the Bodleian Library, Wheaton College, New Brunswick Theological Seminary and Westminster Seminary California.

Several families and individuals provided support for my research. Thanks especially to Mr and Mrs Robert L. Clark, Mr and Mrs Robert L. Northup, Mr and Mrs David Klaassen, Mr and Mrs Alan Mallory, Mr and Mrs Stephen Abery, Dr Thomas Martin and Mr and Mrs David Marsh for their generosity.

I am aware of a number of relevant volumes that have appeared since this work first went to the publisher. Of these, perhaps none is more significant than Philip Benedict, *Christ's Churches Purely Reformed: A Social History of Calvinism* (New Haven and London, 2002). This important work, however, does not affect the major conclusions of the present volume.

Finally, earlier versions of two chapters have appeared elsewhere. Part of chapter 3 of this book was first published as 'The Authority of Reason in the Later Reformation: Scholasticism in Caspar Olevian and Antoine de La Faye' in *Protestant Scholasticism: Essays in Reassessment*, ed. Carl R. Trueman and R. S. Clark (Carlisle, 1999). Part of the fourth chapter of this volume first appeared as 'The Catholic-Calvinist Trinitarianism of Caspar Olevian' in the *Westminster Theological Journal* 61 (1999), 15-39.

R. Scott Clark
Westminster Seminary California
April, 2005

Developer of.
Calvinism

INTRODUCTION
Heidelberg Calvinist

Caspar Olevian (1536–87) was a member of a distinctive *coetus*: the Heidelberg Calvinists, themselves part of a larger international society of theologians who were at work elaborating various themes in Calvin's theology according to their varied requirements. Olevian capitalised on theological concepts explicit and implicit in Calvin's theology such as trinity, covenant, predestination and double benefit (*duplex beneficium*) by which he unified his version of Calvinism, defended it against critics and taught it to students. There is no evidence in Olevian's own writings to support the contention that his theology was somehow a reaction to Calvinism. In fact, he taught all the elements of the Calvinist soteriology which critics found most objectionable: human depravity, the federal-forensic headship of Adam, double predestination, the prelapsarian covenant of works, limited atonement and conditions in the administration of the covenant of grace or the doctrine of sanctification. Olevian was therefore neither a repristination (Barth) nor repudiation of Calvin (Heppe) but rather a developer of Calvinism. It is the reader's prerogative to decide according to his own lights whether Olevian's appropriation of Calvin remains useful.

Caspar Olevian was a trinitarian, Protestant, federal, Calvinist theologian. As a leader among the influential Heidelberg theologians in the last quarter of the century, Olevian was one of the more significant Reformed theologians of the era. He was a student of and well regarded by such luminaries as Theodore Beza and Peter Martyr Vermigli.[1]

---

[1] In a letter of 12 March 1588 Beza wrote to Count Ludwig of Wittgenstein, 'Magnam in doctissimo et sincerae pietatis pleno theologo D. Oleviano beatae memoriae iacturam fecit ecclesia, istis praesertim temporibus, in quibus permulti sunt nomine re vero perpauci Theologi. Illius memoriae parentavi, ut et aliis maximis viris et mihi amicissimis, sicut ex versiculis quibusdam me is, si visum fuerit intelliges, quorum exemplar Gen. Domino Georgio mitto.' (G. Friedlander, ed. *Beiträge zür Reformationsgeschichte: Sammlung ungedruckter Briefe des Reuchlin, Beza und Bullinger, nebst einem Anhange zür Geschichte der Jesuiten* [Berlin, 1837], 167). (Peter Martyr Vermigli (1500–62) regarded Olevian as 'outstanding with respect to zeal' (*egregium studium*) possessing

In the late sixteenth and early seventeenth centuries, Olevian was considered a theologian, pastor, biblical scholar and one of the more outstanding Calvinist Reformers of the Palatinate. From the late seventeenth century, he came increasingly to be considered mainly in the light of his relations to the development of covenant or federal theology.

In the modern era, his importance for the development of covenant theology has been widely acknowledged. Heinrich Heppe, Karl Sudhoff, I. A. Dorner and T. M. Lindsay regarded Olevian as one of the primary sources of Reformed federalism.[2] Charles McCoy and J. Wayne Baker regard his covenant theology as of 'crucial' importance and originality.[3] Mark W. Karlberg describes Olevian's *De substantia* (1585) as 'perhaps the most important and influential treatise on the covenant to appear in the sixteenth century'.[4] J. F. G. Goeters declared that Olevian was the most important transmitter of 'genuine' Calvinism on German soil.[5] Most recently, D. A. Weir has pointed to Olevian as one of the four essential figures in the rise of the 'prelapsarian covenant idea' central to Reformed federalism.[6]

In the modern period, Olevian has received occasional treatment in the secondary literature. He has been regarded consistently in the light of his relations to Calvin and his role in

---

'uncommonly good doctrine' (suam non vulgarem doctrinam) 'Peter Martyr to de Bèze, 4 October 1559', *Correspondence de Théodore de Bèze*, ed. H. Aubert et al. [Geneva, 1983], 25, no.151).

[2] K. Sudhoff, *C. Olevian und Z. Ursinus: Leben und ausgewählte Schriften der Vater und Begründer der reformierten Kirche* (Elberfield, 1857), cited in L. D. Bierma, 'The Covenant Theology of Caspar Olevian', (Ph.D. Diss., Duke University, 1980), iii. See also Heinrich Heppe, *Geschichte des Pietismus und der Mystik in der Reformierten Kirche* (Leiden, 1879), 210; I. A. Dorner, *History of Protestant Theology*, trans. G. Robson and S. Taylor, 2 vols (Edinburgh, 1871), 2.36; T. M. Lindsay, 'The Covenant Theology', *British and Foreign Evangelical Review* 109 (1879), 531.

[3] C. S. McCoy and J. W. Baker, *Fountainhead of Federalism: Heinrich Bullinger and the Covenantal Tradition* (Louisville, 1991), 38.

[4] M. W. Karlberg, 'Reformed Interpretation of the Mosaic Covenant', *Westminster Theological Journal* 43 (1980), 19.

[5] 'Handelt es sich bei der Person und der Theologie des Olevian doch um nichts weniger als um den wichtigsten Vertreter des genuinen Calvinismus auf deutschem Boden' (J. F. G. Goeters, 'Caspar Olevian als Theologe', *Monatshefte für Evangelische Kirchengeschichte des Rheinlandes* [Bonn, 1988/9], 287).

[6] D. A. Weir, *The Origins of the Federal Theology in Sixteenth Century Reformation Thought* (Oxford, 1990), 36.

the development of Reformed covenant theology, e.g. Letham (1979), Karlberg (1980), Woolsey (1988), Weir (1990), Thomas (1997), Bierma (1997), Lillback (2001) and Van Asselt (2001).[7] It is the goal of this work to carry on the project begun by Bierma, the recovery of the earlier view of Olevian, and through him, a historical notion of the development of early Reformed orthodoxy.

As a pastor, university professor, and seminary instructor Olevian encountered hundreds of students during his 26 year teaching career. Some of those students themselves became influential and helped to transmit his ideas to other places and times. For example, it is nearly certain that Olevian directly influenced the English Presbyterian Thomas Cartwright (1535–1603) and, indirectly, Dudley Fenner (c.1558–87).[8] It was Olevian's covenant theology which was mediated to the founding professor of the University of Edinburgh, Robert Rollock (c.1555–99), via Robert Howie (c.1565–1645).[9]

---

[7] R. W. A. Letham, 'Saving Faith and Assurance in Reformed Theology: Zwingli to the Synod of Dort', 2 vols (Ph.D. Thesis, University of Aberdeen, 1979); Mark W. Karlberg, 'The Mosaic Covenant and the Concept of Works in Reformed Hermeneutics: A Historical–Critical Analysis with Particular Attention to Early Covenant Eschatology', (Ph.D. Diss., Westminster Theological Seminary, 1980); A. A. Woolsey, 'Unity and Continuity in Covenantal Thought: A Study in the Reformed Tradition to the Westminster Assembly', 2 vols (Ph.D. Thesis, Glasgow University, 1988); D. A. Weir, *The Origins of the Federal Theology in Sixteenth Century Reformation Thought* (Oxford, 1990); G. M. Thomas, *The Extent of the Atonement: A Dilemma for Reformed Theology from Calvin to the Consensus* (Carlisle, 1997), 113–14; Lyle D. Bierma, *German Calvinism in the Confessional Age* (Grand Rapids, 1997); Peter A. Lillback, *The Binding of God: Calvin's Role in the Development of Covenant Theology* (Grand Rapids, 2001); W. J. van Asselt, *The Federal Theology of Johannes Cocceius (1603–1669)*, trans. R. A. Blacketer (Leiden, 2001).

[8] Weir, *Origins*, 118–19; P. Collinson, *The Elizabethan Puritan Movement* (London, 1967), 152; Gustav Töpke records the name 'Thomas Cartirrightus' (ed., *Die Matrikel der Universität Heidelberg von 1386 bis 1662*, 7 vols [Heidelberg, 1886], 2.69, no. 8). On Cartwright in Heidelberg see A. F. S. Pearson, *Thomas Cartwright and Elizabethan Puritanism 1535–1603* (Cambridge, 1925), 131–55.

[9] G. D. Henderson, *The Burning Bush: Studies in Scottish Church History*, (Edinburgh, 1957), 67–9; A. A. Woolsey, 'Unity and Continuity in Covenant Thought', 2.258, 75; J. K. Cameron, ed., *The Letters of John Johnstone c.1565–1611 and Robert Howie c.1565–1645* (Edinburgh, 1963), 273; W. I. A. Hazlett, s.v. 'Rollock, Robert (c.1555–1599)', *Encyclopedia of the Reformed Faith*, ed. D. K. McKim (Edinburgh, 1992).

His influence as a theological writer was extensive in his own time and continues to the present. One can trace an intellectual connection to one of the chief formulators of the Reformed federal theology in the seventeenth century, Johannes Cocceius (1603–69), whose work influenced several generations of Reformed theologians and who himself claimed to be an heir of Olevian's federal theology.[10] In the twentieth century, Karl Barth made prominent use of Olevian as a sixteenth-century authority.[11] In his Göttingen lectures (1924–25), he looked to Olevian's theology of the covenant as a forerunner of his own theology.[12] Later, in his *Church Dogmatics*, he said that in Olevian he could hear 'the voice of Calvin'.[13]

International Calvinist Theologian

One important distinction between the first and second generations of the Reformation was the international character of the Calvinist Reformation. Olevian participated in the international propagation of Calvinism. Though Olevian produced much in the way of pamphlets and sermons during the 1560s as well as two popular books, *Firm Foundation* (*Vester Grund*) and *A Farmers' Catechism* (*Bawren Katechismus*), he was known to Europe, England and Scotland as a theologian with a Latin voice. Thus, his Latin works, e.g. his logic and rhetoric

---

[10] J. Cocceius, *Summa doctrina de foedere et testamento Dei* in *Opera theologica*, 8 vols (Amsterdam, 1673), 6:4; van Asselt, *Federal Theology*, 331, 340; C. S. McCoy, 'The Covenant Theology of Johannes Cocceius', (Ph.D. Diss., Yale University, 1956), 72, n. 3. The penetration or lack thereof, of Olevian's theology into the eighteenth and nineteenth centuries is an area for further research. My preliminary investigations into eighteenth-century uses of Olevian and the fact that so likely a source as H. Bavinck, in the nineteenth century, made no references to him in his *Gereformeerde Dogmatiek* (4 vols [Kampen, 1895]) suggest that Olevian may have become so closely identified with the origins of federal theology that he was not treated generally as a dogmatic theologian from the late seventeenth century until Heppe began to rehabilitate him by quoting him extensively in his *Die Dogmatik der evangelisch-reformierten Kirche* (Elberfeld, 1861).

[11] K. Barth, *Church Dogmatics*, 13 vols, ed. G. W. Bromiley and T. F. Torrance, trans. G. W. Bromiley (Edinburgh, 1956), 4/1.54–66.

[12] K. Barth, *The Göttingen Dogmatics: Instruction in the Christian Faith*, vol. 1, trans. G. W. Bromiley (Grand Rapids, 1991), 303.

[13] *CD* 4/1.59.

handbooks, his several biblical commentaries and two of his commentaries on the Apostles' Creed, were his most well-known and important publications and will therefore be the focus of this study.[14]

The Substance of the Covenant: The Double Benefit

Though we know Olevian primarily in relation to his role in the development of covenant theology, it is quite likely that he was known differently by his contemporaries and immediate successors. Judging by what was available in Thomas Bodley's library in 1605, Olevian would have been known not as a theologian of the covenant, but as a writer of handbooks on rhetoric, theological texts and commentaries on the Bible.[15] With the publication of Lyle Bierma's excellent work, there should be little doubt about exactly what Olevian taught about the covenant.[16] There remain, however, important unanswered questions about how, where and why he taught as he did. The

---

[14] G. Goeters' exhaustive '*Bibliographia Oleviana*' illustrates this bifurcation in Olevian's publishing career. His publications in the 1560s were nearly all in German, reflecting his attempt to influence his local situation. After the 1576 'Relutheranisierung' of the Palatinate, his publications were almost exclusively Latin (K. Müller, 'Caspar Olevian – Reformator aus Leidenschaft Zum 400. Todestag am 15. März 1987', *Monatshefte für Evangelische Kirchengeschichte des Rheinlandes*, 37/38 [1988–89], 64, 320–37).

[15] *The first printed catalogue of the Bodleian Library 1605*, a facsimile: *Catalogus librorum bibliothecae publicae quam ... Thomas Bodleius eques auratus in academia Oxoniensi nuper instituit* (Oxford, 1986).

[16] Bierma's research focused on Olevian's *Vester Grund* (1567). See Caspar Olevian, *A Firm Foundation*, trans. and ed. L. D. Bierma (Grand Rapids, 1995) for a complete English translation of the first edition of *Vester Grund*. A critical edition of the 1590 edition has been published in, Caspar Olevian, *Der Gnadenbund Gottes 1590*, ed. G. Franz, J. F. G. Goeters, W. Holtmann (Bonn, 1994). K. Sudhoff, 'Sudhoff's Olevianus', *Mercersburg Quarterly Review* 8 (1856), 163–98, contains an English translation of the first part of *Vester Grund*. *Der Gnadenbund Gottes* (Herborn, 1590), of which *Vester Grund* is a part, should not be confused with *De Substantia foederis gratuiti inter Deum et electos* (Geneva, 1585). This mistake was made by J. Ney, O. Ritschl, and F. Klooster (See J. Ney, s.v. 'Olevianus, Kaspar', *Realencyclopädie für Protestantische Theologie und Kirche*, ed. A. Hauck [Leipzig, 1896-1909]; O. Ritschl, *Dogmengeschichte des Protestantismus*, 4 vols [Göttingen, 1926], 3.417–18; F. Klooster, 'The Heidelberg Catechism: Origin and History', [Calvin Theological Seminary, 1989], 341.) Cf. Bierma, 'Covenant Theology', 10, n. 2.

present work is concerned to fill in that outline with a survey of the system of Olevian's theology, which he described as 'the substance of the covenant of grace'. Therefore, this work will trace the details of his theological system through a series of chapters describing his doctrines of God, Christ, salvation and the Christian life. These *loci* were chosen because they constitute the bulk of his own theological interests and serve to illustrate the main lines of his theology. Considerable attention, however, is also paid to the social and intellectual setting in which Olevian developed and taught his federal theology.

The covenant was a tool for, not the sum of, Olevian's theology. For example, it was closely related to his trinitarian doctrine of God. This aspect of his theology has been ignored, yet his trinitarianism was as significant as any other aspect for the structure and substance of his theology. His federalism also unified his trinitarian doctrine of God with his Christology and that with his soteriology and those doctrines with his Calvinist doctrine of sanctification and the sacraments. The first three of these *loci* were among those which comprised the first part of the double benefit (*duplex beneficium*) and his doctrine of sanctification (renewal in the image of Christ) was the second part of the double benefit. Considered together, these *loci* comprised what he called 'the substance of the covenant' (*substantia foederis*).

These two expressions, 'substance of the covenant' (*substantia foederis*) and 'double benefit' (*duplex beneficium*) summarised his soteriology. Considered objectively, the substance of the covenant is comprised of God's saving acts in Christ and the explanation of those acts in Christian theology. Considered subjectively, it refers to the Christian's personal apprehension of Christ's benefits. This phrase, double benefit, describes the two things which Christ has earned for his elect: justification and sanctification. Like the 'substance of the covenant', the double benefit has both objective and subjective elements. Justification concerns Christ's work *for* the sinner and sanctification concerns Christ's work *in* the sinner.

Though he used the expression only occasionally, 'double benefit' was one of the more significant expressions in Olevian's theological vocabulary. It seems rather certain that it was a revision of one found in the first paragraph of Calvin's discussion of justification in the *Institutes of the Christian Religion* (1559):

Christ was given to us by God's kindness to be apprehended and possessed by faith. By participation in him we receive chiefly a twofold grace (*duplex gratia*); namely that having been reconciled to God by his innocence we should have already in heaven a propitious Father instead of a judge; second that having been sanctified by his Spirit, we should pursue a life of innocence and purity.[17]

For 'twofold grace' Olevian substituted 'double benefit'.[18] In every other respect, this quotation could have come directly from Olevian's pen.[19] As it falls exactly in the middle of the *Institutes*, Olevian and his students in Herborn (c.1577–87) would have

---

[17] 'Christum nobis Dei benignitate datum, fide a nobis apprehendi ac possideri, cujus participatione duplicem potissimum gratiam recipiamus; nempe ut ejus innocentia Deo reconciliati pro judice jam propitium habeamus in coelis patrem: deinde ut ejus spiritu sanctificati innocentiam puritatemque vitae meditemur' (*Institutio Christianae Religionis* 1559, 3.11.1; *Joannis Calvini Opera Selecta*, ed. P. Barth and W. Niesel, 3rd edition, 5 vols [Munich, 1963–74], 4.182.4–8 (hereafter, *OS*).
The importance of the *duplex gratiae* for Calvin's theology has not always been well understood. In this regard the reader should consult the excellent work by Cornelis P. Venema, 'The Twofold Nature of the Gospel in Calvin's Theology: The *Duplex Gratia Dei and the Interpretation of Calvin's Theology*' (Ph.D. Diss., Princeton Theological Seminary, 1985). Venema's conclusions about the nature and function of the *duplex gratia Dei* in Calvin's theology are quite similar to my conclusions about the nature and function of the *duplex beneficium* in Olevian's theology.
[18] Henry Beveridge, in his 1845 edition of the *Institutes*, translated *duplex gratia* in 3.11.1 as 'twofold benefit'.
[19] Calvin used the term *beneficium* with some frequency, sometimes to describe general benefits (*Institutio*, 1.2.1; *OS*, 3.35.3–4), but more typically to describe the benefits of redemption, e.g. ibid. 4.10.23 (*OS*, 5.186.3–5) where he spoke of the *beneficium* of Christ's blood. Peter Martyr (*Loci communes* [1576]) also used the term in both senses, but not the expression *duplex beneficium*. The expression does not seem to have captured the imagination of the rest of the tradition. For example, though Wollebius spoke of the 'vocationis beneficium' regarding the visible communion in the church and addressed justification and sanctification in ways almost identical to Olevian, he did not speak of the *duplex beneficium* (idem, *Compendium theologiae Christianae* [Oxford, 1655]), 132, 202–13. Nor does the expression occur in P. van Mastricht, *Theoretico-practica theologia* (Utrecht, 1699). Nevertheless, the idea was used by other late-sixteenth-century writers. See for example, William Perkins, *The Foundation of the Christian Religion Gathered into Six Principles* (1558) reprinted in William Perkins, *The Work of William Perkins* (Appleford, 1970), 159. The use of the *duplex beneficium* theme in seventeenth-century Reformed orthodoxy bears further research.

encountered this passage in the middle of the academic year in his course of lectures through the *Institutes*. It seems most likely that, as he lectured through the *Institutes* each year, the significance of this passage, with its distinction between and correlation of justification and sanctification as twin benefits of Christ, penetrated his own theology. Additionally Olevian's use of this construct is a good example of how Calvin's students related to their teacher. Not content simply to repeat Calvin's *ipsissima verba*, they elaborated and reshaped his theology to meet the requirements of their own schools and parishes.

Olevian distinguished consistently the objective from the subjective elements of the faith because he was a Protestant theologian. This fact has not been disputed nor has it been fully appreciated. His Calvinism has been, however, the subject of dispute since Heinrich Heppe positioned him as a sort of proto-Cocceian antidote to Calvinist predestinarian dogmatism. As a 'preacher to the Germans', he was committed to propagating the Protestant message of justification by imputed grace through apprehensive faith in Christ alone.

Olevian's intention as a Calvinist theologian in the Later Reformation or Early Orthodox period was to unite a Protestant, predestinarian soteriology with more recent developments in the Protestant doctrine of God, namely Melanchthon and Calvin's trinitarianism, and those two topics with a Calvinist Christology.[20] He used the covenant to unify these topics with his Calvinist doctrine of sanctification and the sacraments.[21]

Method

Finally, a word is in order about the method of this book. It is the business of historical theology to discover in a responsible (i.e. historically critical and sensitive) fashion what a figure said as well as where and how he said it and most importantly, why.

---

[20] L. H. Zuck's comment that the 'Heidelberg approach sought to maintain continuity between the heart of Lutheranism and the heart of Calvinism' is equally true of Olevian (idem, 'Melanchthonianism and Reformed Theology in the Late Sixteenth Century', *Controversy and Conciliation: The Reformation and the Palatinate 1559–1583*, ed. D. Visser [Allison Park, PA, 1986], 181).

[21] He used three terms, *foedus*, *pactum* and *testamentum* synonymously.

Too many works of historical theology fail to answer these questions preferring to analyse theologians according to the author's own theological commitments. Such an approach invariably tells us more about the historian than about history. Such an approach also confuses dogmatic (or systematic) for historical theology. The latter is by nature descriptive not prescriptive. Its primary function is to provide the most accurate account of the past.

There is an approach to and version of the past on which interpreters from different backgrounds can agree. For example, Heiko Oberman, Richard Muller, G. R. Evans, David Steinmetz, Jill Raitt, Peter Stephens and David Bagchi have all written significant works helping us to interpret the theology of the sixteenth century from quite varied ecclesiastical, theological and institutional backgrounds. Yet, despite their varied situatedness, these authors, along with many others, have demonstrated an ability to illumine the past without allowing their personal theological convictions to overshadow it. Thus, it would seem that the work of writing history is not necessarily a war of competing agendas, but that, with all the attending hermeneutical and epistemological challenges, it is possible to tell something like the truth about the past.

I do not imagine that utter objectivity is a real possibility, or that historical theology is ever written without presuppositions or biases. Indeed, few books of interest are written by completely disinterested authors. My own interest in this topic was stimulated originally by the need to discover and examine critically my own theological heritage. Despite the potential dangers inherent in studying one's family tree, as it were, it is hoped that this work reflects faithful adherence to the principle of historical theology as a descriptive discipline.

According to this approach, then, Olevian's importance does not therefore lie primarily in what he has to say to us about our times or even about what one ought to believe, except perhaps inasmuch as one identifies with confessional Reformed theology, but rather in what he reveals to us about his own period, the nature of Reformed theology in the late sixteenth century and the way the story of Reformed theology has been told.

For these reasons, this book avoids making judgements about the correctness of Olevian's theology, choosing instead to consider his own history and times, in the hope that such a method will ultimately shed more light on why Olevian, with others like him, taught as he did, which should allow scholars and teachers to make clearer judgements about the nature and rise of Reformed theology.

CHAPTER 1

STRANGERS AND ALIENS:
International Calvinism in the Sixteenth Century

Writing in the first half of the 1560s, Olevian's eschatology was quite pessimistic.

> Now experience shows that, for the most part, things go badly for the godly in this life, whereas for the ungodly who oppress them they generally go better.[1]

Given the frequent textbook portrayal of triumphal Calvinism, one might expect Olevian to have been much more optimistic about the fortunes of the elect in this life.[2] A look at his circumstances, however, begins to explain his melancholy. The period of time from the Peace of Augsburg (1555) until the Peace of Westphalia (1648) is roughly the same period of time in which Calvinism arose and became for many (if not most Protestants of the period) the international face of Protestantism. Ironically, at this very same time, being neither Lutheranism nor Catholicism, Calvinism existed under the Imperial ban. That the Reformed Reformation had no legal standing in the Empire during the

---

[1] Caspar Olevian, *A Firm Foundation*, trans. and ed. L. D. Bierma (Grand Rapids, 1995), 82. 'Nun gibt es aber die erfahrung / daß es den gottseligen zum mehrern theil in disem leben ubelgehet / unnd den gottlosen die sie unterdructen / gemeiniglich besser geht' (*Vester Grund*, 114 in Caspar Olevian, *Der Gnadenbund Gottes 1590*, ed. G. Franz, J. F. G. Goeters, W. Holtmann [Bonn, 1994]).

[2] For a survey of North American textbooks see Thomas J. Davis, 'Images of Intolerance: John Calvin in Nineteenth-Century History Textbooks', *Church History* 65 (1996), 234–48.

[handwritten: 2nd Reformation - When Calvinism arose]

second half of the sixteenth century, is symbolic of Calvinism's political fortunes throughout Europe. Our task is to understand what it must have been like for Olevian to hold theological convictions, which were not only unpopular but also illegal, and then to understand what impact such a life situation had on his theology.

First, and most notably, the Lutheran and Catholic theological-political intolerance of Calvinism produced a Calvinist self-identity as 'strangers and aliens'. Whereas Lutheranism after 1530 was relatively secure in Saxony and in other Lutheran electorates under the protection of the *Pax Augustana*, Calvinism enjoyed no such protection. Second, the later Reformation was more Calvinist than it was Lutheran, if the latter is defined by its Christology and its sacramental theology. Those places which began with Lutheranism, in the 1530s and 1540s (e.g. England, Holland and the Palatinate), graduated, as it were, to Calvinism in the 1550s.[3]

The era in which Calvinism arose has been variously described as the Second Reformation, the Calvinist Reformation, as well as the Confessional Age and Early Orthodoxy.[4] Each of these labels is correct. Such distinctions however, would have been lost on Calvin and his successors in the late sixteenth century, for they saw themselves not as part of a Second Reformation or consolidation, but as part of a continuing or later reformation, heirs of the spirit and theological genius of the Lutheran reformation.[5]

---

[3] See Carl Trueman, *Luther's Legacy: Salvation and the Early English Reformers 1525–1556* (Oxford, 1994).

[4] Jill Raitt, ed., *Shapers of Religious Traditions in Germany, Switzerland and Poland, 1500–1600* (New Haven, 1981), xiii; Hajo Holborn, *A History of Modern Germany: The Reformation* (London, 1965), 249; James M. Kittelson, 'The Confessional Age: The Late Reformation in Germany', *Reformation Europe: A Guide to Research*, ed. Steven Ozment, (St Louis, 1982). Following Otto Weber (See *The Foundations of Dogmatics*, 2 vols, trans. Darrell L. Guder [Grand Rapids, 1981–82], 1.120–27), R. A. Muller distinguishes between the 'period of early orthodoxy (c.1570–c.1640)' and 'high orthodoxy (c.1640–c.1700)'. See 'The Debate over the Vowel Points and the Crisis in Orthodox Hermeneutics', *The Journal of Medieval and Renaissance Studies* 10 (1980), 70; see also idem, *Post-Reformation Reformed Dogmatics*, 2 vols (Grand Rapids, 1987–), 1.14.

[5] R. D. Linder, 'Early Calvinists and Martin Luther: A Study in Evangelical Solidarity' *Regnum, Religio et Ratio: Essays Presented to Robert M. Kingdon*, ed. Jerome Friedman (Kirksville, MO, 1987); Bodo Nischan 'Reformation or

In the 1550s, as Calvinism began to spread it also entered a profound and long-lasting conflict with Lutheranism, a conflict which peaked with the publication of the *Book of Concord* (1580). As the Calvinist-Lutheran theological conflict escalated, Roman Catholicism began to make resurgence in the wake of the conclusion of the Council of Trent in 1563. International Calvinism was profoundly aware of its religio-political alienation, not only from Rome but also from establishment Lutheranism. H. R. Trevor-Roper has described the Calvinism of this period as the 'ideological international' and 'that cosmopolitan fraternity of the persecuted Protestants of Europe'.[6] Anathema to the so-called 'Genuine' (*Gnesio*) Lutherans and Rome, Calvinists were frequently the target of persecution in this period and had good reason to feel at risk. The *Pax Augustana* provided little comfort to them and forced them to hide behind Melanchthon's *Augustana Variata* (1540) for legal standing within the Empire.[7] Indeed, Frederick III, Elector Palatine, was charged at the Diet of Augsburg on 14 May 1566 with violating the *Augsburg Confession* and threatened with expulsion from the Peace unless he repented of his Calvinism.

Despite these facts, international Calvinism of this period is sometimes portrayed as a uniformly successful movement. It has been said, for example, that Heidelberg was a Calvinist 'stronghold'.[8] This characterisation is an apparent attempt to extrapolate from widely held assumptions about the nature of Calvin's authority in Geneva to conclusions concerning international Calvinism generally. In the light of the extensive studies of Genevan city records conducted by Robert Kingdon,

---

Deformation? Lutheran and Reformed Views of Martin Luther in Brandenburg's "Second Reformation"', *Pietas et Societas: New Trends in Reformation Social History: Essays in Honor of Harold J. Grimm*, ed. Kyle C. Sessions and Phillip N. Bebb (Kirksville, MO, 1985), 7.

6 H. R. Trevor-Roper, *Religion, the Reformation and Social Change*, second edn (London, 1972), xiv.

7 C. P. Clasen, *The Palatinate in European History 1559–1660* (Oxford, 1963), 1–15; D. C. Davis, 'The Reformed Church of Germany: Calvinists as Influential Minority', *John Calvin: His Influence on the Western World*, ed. W. Stanford Reid (Grand Rapids, 1982).

8 H. C. Erik Midelfort, *Witch Hunting in Southwestern Germany 1562–1684. The Social and Intellectual Foundations* (Stanford, CA, 1972), 56; H. G. Koenigsberger and George L. Mosse, *Europe in the Sixteenth Century* (London, 1968), 277.

characterisations of Calvin as the 'unopposed dictator' of Geneva are no longer tenable.[9] In the same way, the caricature of a triumphalist international Calvinism is also no longer acceptable.[10] It is true that for a few years, in the last quarter of the sixteenth century, and for a part of the first quarter of the seventeenth century, Heidelberg was intermittently controlled by a Calvinist elite. For most of the period, however, from 1559 to 1576 Calvinism had only a tenuous hold on the Palatinate. For that entire time, Frederick was never able to bring his entire realm under one confession. His oldest son Ludwig, a devout Lutheran, had the right to rule the Upper Palatinate (*Oberpfalz*) from Amberg. Throughout his father's electorship, he thwarted Frederick's attempts to introduce Reformed theology and practice to the Upper Palatinate. Frederick tried to introduce reformed discipline in 1563 but was repelled by Ludwig. Unwilling to bring the full authority of his electorate to bear on his eldest son, Frederick tolerated this snub until 1566 when he travelled with Olevian to Amberg where he urged that the *Oberpfalz* be brought in line with Heidelberg. The second attempt produced a Calvinist academy, which was closed nevertheless immediately after Frederick's death in 1576. Frederick tried a third time to introduce the Calvinist reformation, but failed when the townsfolk locked his representatives out of the Church at Amberg and surrounded it with an armed guard.[11]

Calvin was himself the prototypical Reformed refugee.[12] Forced to flee Paris after the Affair of the Placards, he spent his life as an alien in a frequently hostile Geneva. He was sent packing by offended Genevans after his first two years only to be recalled in September 1541. Of his second tenure in Geneva, his

---

[9]   The entry s.v. 'Calvin, John' in the *Oxford Dictionary of the Christian Church*, 2nd edition revised (Oxford, 1983) describes him as such.

[10]   See R. M. Kingdon, *Geneva and the Coming Wars of Religion 1555–1563* (Geneva, 1956); and idem, *Geneva and the Consolidation of the French Protestant Movement 1564–1572* (Geneva, 1967); William Monter, *Calvin's Geneva* (New York, 1967); Gillian Lewis, 'Calvinism in Geneva in the Time of Calvin and Beza 1541–1605', *International Calvinism 1541–1715*, ed. M. Prestwich (Oxford, 1985); W. G. Naphy, *Calvin and the Consolidation of the Genevan Reformation* (Manchester, 1994).

[11]   Hendrik Alting, *Historia ecclesiae palatinae* (Amsterdam, 1646) repr. in *Monumenta pietatis*, ed. L. C. Mieg (Frankfurt, 1701), 217–22.

[12]   H. A. Oberman, 'Europa Afflicta: The Reformation of the Refugees', *Archiv für Reformationsgeschichte* 83 (1992), 91–111.

position can be considered to have been settled only in the last ten years. Even after his victory over his Perrinist opponents, he was unable to control the city completely.[13]

The 'churches under the Cross' in the Netherlands are another example of persecuted Calvinists. According to Andrew Pettegree, although the suffering of late sixteenth-century Dutch Calvinists was not unique, that their movement grew in spite of this suffering was.[14] The persecution of Calvinism was so widespread that even under Edward VI, English Protestants, despite the king's friendship to their cause, continued to think of themselves as God's 'poor persecuted little flock'.[15] Thus, it is not without reason that Willem Nijenhuis has described 'the earliest chapters of the Calvinist Reformation' (like those of Anabaptism) as having been 'written with the blood of the martyrs and tears of the refugees'.[16]

Even if international Calvinism can be said to have been successful early on (it was growing in popularity among pastors and theologians), the St Bartholomew's Day Massacre (1572) marked a shift in Calvinist fortunes throughout Europe.[17] R. J. W. Evans has described the massacre as the 'climax to the first decade following the Council of Trent', and noted that the 'aftermath of this was a fever of anxiety throughout Europe about similar plots'.[18] After 1572, Calvinism met with sporadic success and more often with serious and even violent resistance. Resurgent Catholicism, sparked by the foundation of the Society of Jesus (1540) and Spanish adventures in the Netherlands, was another cause for alarm for international Calvinism. Philip II demonstrated his commitment to prosecuting this improbable

---

[13] Naphy, *Calvin and the Consolidation*, 213–14.

[14] A. Pettegree, 'Coming to Terms with Victory: the Upbuilding of a Calvinist Church in Holland, 1572–1590', *Calvinism in Europe, 1540–1620*, ed. A. Pettegree, Alistair Duke and Gillian Lewis (Cambridge, 1994), 160.

[15] Catharine Davies, '"Poor Persecuted Little Flock" or "Commonwealth of Christians": Edwardian Protestant Concepts of the Church', *Protestantism and the National Church in Sixteenth Century England*, ed. P. Lake and M. Dowling (London, 1987).

[16] Willem Nijenhuis, *Ecclesia Reformata. Studies on the Reformation* (Leiden, 1994), 101.

[17] Michael Hughes, *Early Modern Germany, 1477–1806* (London, 1992), 66.

[18] R. J. W. Evans, *Rudolf II and His World, A Study in Intellectual History 1576–1612* (Oxford, 1973), 86.

war by bankrupting Spain three times in the sixteenth century. From 1567 to 1572, the Duke of Alva campaigned against Calvinism in the Netherlands, trying and convicting as many as twelve thousand persons.[19] Calvinists could also point to the aggressive measures adopted by Henry II (1547–59) to crush French Calvinism. Protestant Europe generally, and international Calvinism particularly, felt menaced by Philip's aggressive policies and the French Wars of Religion.[20] Peter Boquin wrote in the preface to his *Assertion of the Old and True Christianity, Against the New and False Jesuits or Society of Jesus* of his fear that 'the enemy has so recovered that same his citadel: that it may appear, that the whole crew of antichrist stands in great hope, shortly to recover their former authority, dignity, and power'.[21] John Field used the occasion of his 1581 dedication of his translation of Olevian's *Expositio Symboli Apostolici* (Frankfurt, 1576) to warn the Earl of Warwick about the dangerous Jesuits who 'have turned their rusty roughness into some smoothness' for no other purpose than to 'turn upside down the quiet peace the blessing of the Gospel has brought us, and drink up our blood'.[22]

Elizabeth I was the prime leader of the Protestant political response. From her accession to her death, she never stopped pressing for the formation of a Protestant League as a counterweight to the Holy Catholic league. To this end, she sent diplomats Sir Philip Sidney, Daniel Rogers, and Sir Thomas

---

[19] Among them, Guido de Bres (author of the *Confessio Belgica*), hanged in Belgium in 1567. H. G. Koenigsberger sees Philip's actions primarily as politically and ecclesiastically defensive (idem, 'The Politics of Philip II', *Politics, Religion and Democracy in Early Modern Europe*, ed. Malcolm R. Thorp and Arthur J. Slavin [Kirksville, MO, 1994]).

[20] Brian G. Armstrong, *Calvinism and the Amyraut Heresy. Protestant Scholasticism and Humanism in Seventeenth Century France* (Madison, 1969), 21; C. M. N. Eire, *War Against the Idols. The Reformation of Worship from Erasmus to Calvin* (Cambridge, 1986), 310.

[21] *Assertio veteris ac veri christianismi, adversus novum et fictum iesuitismum seu societatem Iesu* (London, 1576). Translated as *A Defence of the Olde, and True Profession of Christianitie, Against the New, and Counterfaite Secte of Jesuites* (London, 1581).

[22] Caspar Olevian, *An Exposition of the Symbole of the Apostles*, trans. John Fielde (London, 1581), 7, 8. See Henrie Parrie to the Earl of Pembroke, 'dedicatory epistle' in Zacharias Ursinus, *The Summe of Christian Religion*, H. Parrie, trans. (Oxford, 1587).

Bodley repeatedly to the Palatinate, Denmark and to the German Lutheran princes in her futile attempt to establish the federation. Because of the apparent Catholic military threat, Elector Palatine Frederick III (1515–76) and his second son, Prince John Casmir, co-operated closely with the Queen in this endeavour.[23]

Claus Peter Clasen's valuable study identified three common characteristics of those Calvinist refugees who found a home and provided leadership in Heidelberg: 1) They were all adult converts to Calvinism, persecuted and forced to flee abroad; 2) The focus of these refugees was European Calvinism; 3) Several of the most prominent leaders were quite young, which fed the militant spirit of Heidelberg.[24] With respect to Olevian, one should modify points two and three of Clasen's list. He did see his ministry to Germany as a divine vocation and it is not apparent that Heidelberg was any more 'militant' than Lutheran Württemberg or Roman Catholic Spain. At Naumberg (1561) and at the Diet of Augsburg (1566), Frederick III asked only for toleration of Calvinism within the terms of the Peace of Augsburg.[25] Beza was still making similar pleas twenty years later, in 1585, at the Colloquy of Montbéliard.[26]

---

[23] Jill Raitt, 'Elizabeth of England, John Casmir and the Protestant League', *Controversy and Conciliation: The Palatinate Reformation, 1559–1618*, ed. Derk Visser (Pittsburgh, 1986). See *Calvinism in Europe 1540–1610*, ed. A. Pettegree, Alistair Duke and Gillian Lewis (Manchester, 1992), 230–42.

[24] In support of point three it ought to be noted that Olevian was among these young scholars. Ursinus was a refugee from Silesian Lutheranism. Daniel Tossanus had left Montbéliard. See Jill Raitt, *The Colloquy of Montbéliard. Religion and Politics in the Sixteenth Century* (Oxford, 1993); Pierre Boquin and Peter Dathenus were refugees from French persecution; Hieronymus Zanchi and Immanuelo Tremelius were Italian refugees.

[25] Of course, Calvinists, like most other sixteenth-century groups, always asked for toleration so long as they were a minority.

[26] Clasen himself adds, 'Though Calvinist piety had an aggressive character, it cannot be finally proved that the militant policy of the Palatinate derived directly from religious concepts.' In fact, the doctrine of predestination could have a paralysing effect. Ursinus, for example, had condemned intervention in the French Wars in 1568 on 'theological grounds' that war was an act of providence which should not be challenged. On the other hand, Frederick rejected pleas for assistance from the Huguenots in 1562 in order to avoid a general European war. On this point see Clasen, *The Palatinate in European History 1559–1660*, 8, 9; Volker Press, *Calvinismus und Territorialstaat. Regierung und Zentralbehörden der Kurpfalz 1559–1619* (Stuttgart, 1970).

The popular image of Calvinism, that of theological 'storm troopers' marching across Europe, slaying enemies intellectual and political, simply does not corrclate to the evidence.[27] In fact, international Calvinism was struggling to survive. Indeed, it was a movement populated by true believers who thought of themselves as 'strangers and aliens' in the world.[28]

Caspar Olevian was one of those believers and a minister to the Calvinist strangers and aliens who found shelter in Heidelberg and Herborn for part of three decades in the late sixteenth century. He was a significant transitional figure who, by using the biblical language of covenant, helped to provide structure to the substance of Protestant and Reformed theology, i.e. the doctrines of God, man, Christ, salvation, church and sacraments. Most importantly, he used the doctrine of the covenant to establish stable relations between the Protestant doctrines of justification and sanctification without jeopardising either.

---

[27] Nicholas Tyacke uses this term to describe English Calvinists. See *Anti-Calvinists: The Rise of English Arminianism c.1590–1640* (Oxford, 1987), 1.

[28] See also Alistair Duke, 'Perspectives on International Calvinism', *Calvinism in Europe 1540–1620*, ed. A. Pettegree, Alistair Duke and Gillian Lewis (Cambridge, 1994), 1–9.

CHAPTER 2

CASPAR OLEVIAN: PREACHER TO THE GERMANS

O foolish Germans who has bewitched you so that you have fallen from the articles of the faith, so that you seek, in the mass, the body of Christ, which ascended to heaven, because of which you allow yourselves to be led away from the passion of Christ in which alone consists the remission of sins?[1]

Caspar von Olewig was born 10 August 1536 on *Olewiger Strasse* near the ruins of the Roman amphitheatre in the ancient Imperial city of Trier, notable for having hosted Athanasius in his banishment in 336-7 AD and for her ancient Imperial Roman relics dating to the city's foundation by the Emperor Augustus in 15 BC.[2] She also claimed dominical and apostolic relics which

---

[1] 'O insensati Germani quis fascinavit vos ut ab articulis fidei deficiatis, corpus Christi in Missa quaeratis, quod ascendit in caelum, quod patiamini vos à passione Christi abduci in qua sola remissio peccatorum consistit?' (Caspar Olevian, *In Epistolam d. Pauli apostoli ad Galatas notae, ex concionibus G. Oleviani excerptae, & T. Beza editae* [Geneva, 1578], 38-9).

[2] For a comprehensive modern bibliography of Olevian studies see the bibliography appended to K. Müller, 'Caspar Olevian - Reformator aus Leidenschaft Zum 400. Todestag am 15. März 1987', *Monatshefte für Evangelische Kirchengeschichte des Rheinlandes*, 37/38 (1988-89). The works which follow were omitted from Müller's bibliography or were published after his essay.

H. Scheible 'Olevian als Verteidiger der reformierten Abendmahlslehre', *Bibliotheca Palatina*, ed. E. Mittler et al., 2 vols (Heidelberg, 1986), 1:145-6; L. D. Bierma, 'Covenant Theology', 1-11; idem, *Encyclopedia of the Reformed Faith*, s.v. 'Olevianus, Caspar', ed. D. K. McKim (Louisville, 1992); idem, *Firm Foundation* (Grand Rapids, 1995), viii-xxv; F. H. Klooster, 'The Heidelberg Catechism: Origin and History' (Calvin Theological Seminary, 1989), 130-45; J. I. Good, *The Origin of the Reformed Church in Germany* (Reading, PA, 1887), 156-69; idem. *The Heidelberg Catechism in Its Newest Light* (Philadelphia, 1914);

continued to attract large numbers of pilgrims into the middle of this century.[3]

Caspar was born to privilege. His father, Gerhard, was a baker, a trades official, a city councillor, and a respected, wealthy citizen. His mother, Anna (nee Sinzig) was the daughter of the master of the butchers' guild.[4] He was baptised in the Church of St Lawrence and educated at home by his grandfather until he was old enough to attend school in St Lawrence and later at St Simon's and the Cathedral school. In a letter written to 'the youth devoted to true piety', he later testified that as a boy he was impressed with the teaching

> about God, the creation of man, about man's fall into sin, about reconciliation and his renewal through God's Son, the promised seed of the woman.... These seemed to me altogether holy and pious sayings, and it pleased the Lord by them to kindle in my soul sparks of a fervent desire to be taught and at length, to instruct others, either in the school, or in the Church.... Thereafter the Lord continually nourished these sparks in me, by his Holy Spirit, and by the reading of the holy scriptures.[5]

O. Thelemann, *An Aid to the Heidelberg Catechism*, trans. M. Peters (Philadelphia, 1896 [reprinted in Grand Rapids, 1959]); J. Ney, s.v. 'Olevianus, Kaspar', *The New Schaff-Herzogg Encyclopedia of Religious Knowledge*, ed. S. M. Jackson (Grand Rapids, 1969); J. G. G. Norman, s.v. 'Olevianus, Kaspar', *New International Dictionary of the Christian Church* (Exeter, 1978); M. Göbel, 'Dr. Caspar Olevianus 1535-1587', trans. H. Harbaugh, *Mercersburg Quarterly Review* 7 (1855), 294-306. R. W. A. Letham says incorrectly that Olevian was born in France ('Saving Faith and Assurance in Reformed Theology: Zwingli to the Synod of Dort', 2 vols [Ph.D. Thesis, University of Aberdeen, 1979] 1.196, 1.206). See also M. Turchetti, 'Olevianus, Kaspar', *The Oxford Encyclopedia of the Reformation*, 4 vols ed. H. J. Hillerbrand (New York, 1996), 3.174.

[3] Klooster, 'Origin and History', 131-2. Trier is also the birthplace of Ambrose (c.339-97) and one of the cities in which Jerome (c.347-420) received his education. In the modern period, Trier is famous as the birthplace of Karl Marx (1818-83).

[4] T. C. Porter, 'The Authors of the Heidelberg Catechism', Tercentenary Monument in Commemoration of the Three Hundredth Anniversary of the Heidelberg Catechism (Chambersburg, PA, 1863), 211.

[5] '...de Deo, de creatione generis humani, de lapsu in peccatum, de reconciliatione & instauratione per Filium Dei, semen illud mulieris promissum.... Haec mihi videbantur omnino sancte & pie dicta, & placuit Domino, illis verbis igniculos in me creare ardentis desiderii discendi & instituendi aliquando alios, vel in Schola, vel Ecclesia...Hos igniculos deinceps

These comments reflected the period before he left home for the University, where he came under the influence of *praeceptores* who

> in the school of Trier, according to its limits, were accustomed annually before Easter, to interpret the passion of our Lord Jesus Christ, to compare Old Testament types with their fulfillment by the passion of Christ (a quite happy practice, and which afterwards, by God's grace, opened the whole purpose of the Scriptures for me) nevertheless that hand-leading was rather obscured, because of the multitude human traditions, by which, Christ dead and raised up again was wrapped and obscured in Popery, so that, that same light, which I was seeing to shine from the comparison of types and fulfillment in Christ's passion, was not well able to produce fruit.[6]

Nevertheless, in time, with God's blessing, the instruction he received bore considerable fruit.[7]

At age thirteen he entered the college of St Germain, Trier. At the age of sixteen (1552) his parents sent young Caspar to the University of Paris to study languages. Later that year he moved to Orleans, a hotbed of Protestant sympathies, to begin his legal studies. While at University, he joined the underground Protestant 'churches under the Cross'.[8] Four years later, while at Bourges, in 1556, he befriended Prince Herman, the second son of Count Frederick of Simmern.[9] Olevian and the young prince were

---

Dominus continenter in animo meo fovit suum Spiritum, & sacrarum literarum lectionem' (*Expositio Symboli Apostolici* [Frankfurt, 1576] preface, 1, 2).

[6] '...qui quotannis ante Pascha, passionem Domini nostri Iesu Christi nobis in Schola Trevirorum interpretari, et typos veteris Testamenti, cum eorum per ipsam Christi passionem impletione, pro suo modulo conferre solebant (Res omnino salutaris: & quae scopum totius Scripturae mihi postea per Dei gratiam aperuit) tamen obscurior erat manuductio propter traditionum humanarum multitudinem, quibus Christus passus et excitatus in Papatu involuitur et obscuratur, ita, ut illa ipsa luce, quam ex collatione typorum et rerum impletarum in Christi passione elucere videbam, satis frui non possem' (*Expositio*, preface, 3).

[7] 'Sed tamen suo tempore illa πρόγνωσις eximio fructu, Deo benedicente, non caruit' (*Expositio*, preface, 3).

[8] F. J. R. Knetsch, 'Church Ordinances and Regulations of the Dutch Synods "Under the Cross" Compared with the French (1559–1563)', *Humanism and Reform: The Church in Europe, England, and Scotland, 1400–1643*, ed. J. Kirk (Oxford, 1991), 187–205.

[9] Frederick, of course, later became Frederick III, elector Palatine. On how the House of Simmern came by the Electorate see H. J. Cohn, *The Government of*

walking along the Auron River where they met a group of inebriated German students. These students asked the prince and Caspar to cross the river with them in a boat. For obvious reasons, he tried to dissuade Prince Herman from going along. Olevian, who remained on shore, failed to convince the prince, who with his court master Nicolas Judex, joined the other students in the boat. In middle of the river, the boys rocked the boat causing all passengers to fall out and drown.[10] Seeing the prince in danger, Olevian leapt into the river, in an attempt to rescue him. Unfortunately, he failed and only endangered himself and later confessed that, out of terror, he vowed that if God should save him, he would serve the Lord as a preacher to Germans. One of the prince's servants saved him, mistaking him for the prince. He took his *Juris Doctor* at the Université de Bourges, 6 June 1557, and returned home to practise law.

Olevian and Geneva

He left his law practice after eight months to visit Geneva. He then visited Zürich briefly, meeting Peter Martyr and Bullinger.[11] He wrote to Peter Martyr 6 May 1559 of his decision to remain in Geneva until Pentecost and he arrived in Trier in late June.[12] After Zürich, he returned to Geneva to read theology.[13] It has been said that he was one of the first students of the newly formed Genevan Academy.[14] This does not appear to be strictly accurate. According to the Academy register, Olevian's brother Anton was among the first one hundred students, but Caspar's name is not among them.[15] Rather, Olevian was among a group of students,

---

the *Rhine Palatinate in the Fifteenth Century* (Oxford, 1965).

[10] M. Adam, *Vitae Germanorum Theologorum* (Heidelberg, 1620), 598.

[11] Adam, ibid., 599; Göbel, 'Dr. Caspar Olevianus', 296; L. D. Bierma, 'Lutheran-Reformed Polemics in the Late Reformation: Olevianus' Conciliatory Proposal', *Controversy and Conciliation*, 52.

[12] *Corpus Reformatorum* (hereafter *CR*), ed. C. G. Bretschneider, 101 vols (Halle, 1834–1959), 45.513, no. 3049.

[13] *CR*, 45.513, no. 3049; Klooster, 'Origin and History', 134.

[14] E. W. Monter said Olevian was a student in the first three years of the Genevan Academy (*Calvin's Geneva* [New York, 1967], 113).

[15] S. Stelling-Michaud, *Le Livre du Recteur de L'Academie de Genéve*, 2 vols (Geneva, 1959), 1.19; 'Stamtafel Caspar Olevians', *Monatshefte für Evangelische Kirchengeschichte des Rheinlandes*, 37/38 (1988–89). G. Lewis

including young Thomas Bodley (the future Elizabethan diplomat who reorganised the now eponymous Oxford University library) who were involved in the transformation of the existing *Collège de la Rive* to what became the Academy of Geneva.[16] These students received instruction by the same men (i.e. Antoine Le Chevallier, François Bérauld, Jean Tagaut, and Beza), who had come from the Academy of Lausanne in March and May 1559 to compose the Academy faculty. This instruction took place both before and after the Academy was opened with a ceremony on 5 June 1559 and formally constituted on 9 November.[17]

In Geneva, he met the firebrand Guillaume Farel (1489-1565) who exhorted Caspar to cut short his studies and return to Trier to fulfil his vow to become a gospel preacher to the Germans.[18] Perhaps the most significant fact to keep in mind about his time in Geneva is that he studied in a city whose character was being transformed by sojourners and exiles. Those French, English, Polish, Scottish and German Calvinists who flocked to Geneva did so for mostly ideological reasons. Some of the brightest intellects in the Reformed world were gathered there to discuss and lecture on Scripture, theology and European (often French) politics. This educational and cultural milieu had a profound influence upon Caspar.[19]

---

mistakes Caspar's brother Anton for his son ('The Geneva Academy', *Calvinism in Europe 1540-1620*, ed. A. Pettegree, A. Duke, G. Lewis [Cambridge, 1994], 50).

[16] W. S. Reid, 'Calvin and the Founding of the Academy of Geneva', *Westminster Theological Journal* 18 (1955), 8-10; B. J. Kidd, *Documents Illustrative of the Continental Reformation* (Oxford, 1911), 594; Lewis, 'The Geneva Academy', 37-8; K. Maag, *Seminary or University? The Genevan Academy and Reformed Higher Education, 1560-1620* (Aldershot, 1995).

[17] Stelling-Michaud, op. cit. 1.61-64; K. Maag, 'Education and Training for the Calvinist Ministry: the Academy of Geneva, 1559-1620'. *The Reformation of the Parishes. The Ministry and Reformation in Town and Country*, ed. A. Pettegree (Manchester, 1993), 134.

[18] Adam, *Vitae*, 599; Klooster, 'Origin and History', 134.

[19] There was a reciprocal interest on the part of the Company of Pastors in the Palatinate. Of all extra-Genevan questions, after France of course, the Pastors spent the most time discussing the Rhenish Palatinate. See R. M. Kingdon, *Geneva and the Consolidation of the French Protestant Movement 1564-1572* (Geneva, 1967), 14; J. T. McNeill, *The History and Character of Calvinism* (Oxford, 1954), 178-88; E. W. Monter, *Calvin's Geneva*; G. Lewis, 'Calvinism in Geneva in the time of Calvin and of Beza (1541-1605)', *International Calvinism*, 39-70.

One evidence of that influence is the lasting relationship which he formed with the undisputed intellectual leader of post-Calvin Calvinism, Theodore Beza. Olevian corresponded regularly with Beza throughout his career. It is also worth noting that he frequently used Beza's 1565 Latin New Testament in his commentaries on the Pauline epistles.[20] Beza also edited and wrote the preface to Olevian's Commentaries on Galatians (1578 and 1581), Romans (1579),[21] and Philippians and Colossians (1580).[22] *De substantia* (1585) and *De inventione dialecticae* (1583) were both published in Geneva.[23] All these works were published after Olevian was exiled to the Wetterau district, where he published *Institutionis Christianae Religionis Epitome: E x Institutione Johannis Calvini excerpta, authoris methodo et verbis retentis* (1586) with Corvinus. His son-in-law Johannes Piscator edited and posthumously published Olevian's commentary on Ephesians (1588)[24] and Olevian's son Paul published his father's *Notae Gasparis Oleviani in Evangelia* posthumously in Herborn in 1587.[25] Olevian's *Homilia de vera et primaria causa errorum circa coenam Dominicam* was published in Heidelberg in 1617 and in German as *allem Streit des Abendmahls entrichten koenne* in Basel two years later.[26] Olevian, however, did not normally publish in Herborn, where he taught from 1584-87, rather he

---

[20] Theodore Beza, trans., *Iesu Christi D. n. novum testamentum sive novum foedus*, 2nd edn (Geneva, 1565).

[21] *In Epistolam d. Pauli apostoli ad Romanos notae, ex concionibus G. Oleviani excerptae, & a T. Beza editae: cum praefatione eiusdem Bezae* (Geneva, 1579).

[22] *In Epistolas d. Pauli apostoli ad Philippenses & Colossenses, notae, T. Beza editae: cum praefatione eiusdem Bezae* (Geneva, 1580).

[23] *De substantia foederis gratuiti inter Deum et electos* (Geneva, 1585). *De Inventione dialecticae liber, e praelectionibus G Oleviani excerptus* (Frankfurt, 1583).

[24] *In Epistolam d. Pauli apostoli ad Ephesios notae*. Olevian's other major work is a collection of German sermons and tracts, including the *Bauren Katechismus* and *Vester Grund*, (Heidelberg, 1567) published together as *Der Gnadenbund Gottes* in 1590 and 1593. See Caspar Olevian, *Der Gnadenbund Gottes 1590*, ed. G. Franz, J. F. G. Goeters, W. Holtmann (Bonn, 1994).

[25] Bierma, 'Covenant Theology', 9, n. 1; K. Dienst, s.v. 'Herborn', *Theologische Realenzyklopädie* v. 15 (Berlin, 1986). Little else is known of Paul except that he entered Heidelberg University in 1584 (G. Töpke, ed. *Die Matrikel der Universität Heidelberg von 1386 bis 1662*, 7 vols (Heidelberg, 1884-6), 2.115, no. 1).

[26] Klooster, 'Origin and History', 342.

published a substantial part of his work in Geneva, under Beza's oversight. Olevian's publisher was Eusthache Vignon, son-in-law and heir to Geneva's major publishing house, that of Jean Crespin (†1572).[27]

Reformation in Trier

That Olevian, with the rest of Calvinist Christendom, should think of himself as a stranger and alien in the earth, could be justified by a single episode in his life: his return home to fulfil his vow. While he was in Zürich, the Geneva Consistory wrote on his behalf to Otto Seel and Peter Sirkig (Sierck), evangelical members of the Trier city council. On 26 June 1559, ostensibly to fulfil his father's wishes – who had educated him for the purpose of serving the community – he applied to the city council for a position as a teacher. The council called him to teach philosophy and logic, in the secondary school, at a salary of one hundred gulden.

He passed a significant and tumultuous six months in his home town.[28] Initially, Caspar used Melanchthon's 1547 *Dialectices* to teach logic, in Latin, to a rather small group of auditors.[29] On 9 August, however, the day before St Lawrence's Day (the patron saint of Trier), he posted public notice at City Hall that he would begin, in the school, public worship services in

---

[27] R. M. Kingdon, *Myths about the St. Bartholomew's Day Massacres 1572-1576* (London, 1988), 13. See Hans Joachim Bremme, *Buchdrucker und Buchhändler zur Zeit der Glaubens-kämpfe: Studien Zur Genfer Druckgeschichte, 1565-1580* (Geneva, 1969), 238-9 for a biographical sketch of Vignon.

[28] Adam, *Vitae*, 599-600; J. I. Good, *Origin*, 161-8; idem, *The Heidelberg Catechism*, 201-41. See also J. Ney, *Die Reformation in Trier* (Halle, 1906-07); idem, s.v. 'Olevianus, Kaspar', *The New Schaff-Herzog Encyclopedia*; J. Marx, *Caspar Olevian oder der Calvinismus in Trier im Jahre 1559* (Mainz, 1846); J. F. G. Goeters, 'Der Trierer Reformationsversuch von 1559 im Rahmen der deutschen Reformationsgeschichte', *Monatshefte für Evangelische Kirchengeschichte des Rheinlandes*, 37/38 (1988-89).

[29] Sudhoff, *C. Olevianus und Z. Ursinus: Leben und ausgewählte Schriften der Vater und Begründer der reformierten Kirche*, (Elberfeld, 1857), 15-59; Bierma, 'Covenant Theology', 4; H. Heppe, *Geschichte des Deutschen Protestantismus in den Jahren 1555-81*, 4 vols (Marburg, 1852), 1.315-16. Olevian gave a *summa* of the episode in his letter to Calvin of 12 April 1560. *CR*, 46.46-9, no. 3178.

German on the next morning. He failed to obtain permission and the necessary support of the council for the new services beforehand, thus immediately jeopardising his reformation of Trier. It is hard to imagine that Olevian, *Juris Doctor*, formerly a practising lawyer in Trier, and son of a Trier city councillor, simply overlooked this requirement. Rather, it appears that he counted on the support of city councillors Sierck and Seel, the Burgomeister John Steuss, and perhaps also his father as well as other leading citizens. A large segment of the city, including the council secretary, turned out to hear him hold forth on justification by faith and against the invocation of saints, masses, and processions.[30] Olevian had become a preacher of the gospel to the Germans.

On the following Tuesday, based on the secretary's report of his preaching, an opposing councillor moved to have Olevian's services prohibited. Olevian said that he would submit to a council order to stop preaching. The order however, did not come. Instead, the council referred the question to the city's thirteen guilds. Three of them, including the powerful weavers' guild, supported Olevian outright, even offering to pay him if the council would not. Eight of the guilds said they would tolerate his

---

[30] Good, *Origins*, 161. It seems likely that there was significant support for these traditional rites in the community. The grocers and butchers undoubtedly profited from the various ecclesiastically sanctioned festivals. Thus, Olevian's criticisms were not well taken. Most of the city does not seem to have been weighed down by the 'burden of medieval religion'. Cf. S. E. Ozment, *The Reformation in the Cities. The Appeal of Protestantism to Sixteenth Century Germany and Switzerland* (New Haven and London, 1975), 23–150. Rather, the case of Trier seems partially to support the theory that the German townsfolk liked their amalgam of ancient rituals, traditional customs and folk Catholicism mixed with magic (G. Strauss, 'The Reformation and its Public', 211). R. W. Scribner gives parallel examples of this resentment of the reformation (idem, 'Ritual and Reformation', *The German People and the Reformation*, 122–46). See also A. E. McGrath, 'Justification and the Reformation Significance of the Doctrine of Justification to Sixteenth Century Urban Communities', *Archiv für Reformationsgeschichte* 81 (1990), 5–19; H. C. E. Midelfort, 'Toward a Social History of Ideas in the German Reformation', *Pietas et Societas: New Trends in Reformation Social History. Essays in Honor of Harold J. Grimm*, ed. K. C. Sessions and P. N. Bebb (Kirksville, MO, 1985), 11–21; H. Schilling, *Civic Calvinism in Northwestern Germany and the Netherlands* (Kirksville, MO, 1991); idem, 'Between the Territorial State and Urban Liberty: Lutheranism and Calvinism in the County of Lippe', trans. T. A. Brady Jr *The German People and the Reformation*, 263–83.

Latin instruction in the school. Only two guilds, the butchers (of which, ironically, Olevian's maternal grandfather had once been master) and the grocers, wanted him silenced.[31] On 20 August his preaching ministry was relocated to the council controlled St James' Church. Elector-Archbishop Johann VI (von den Leyden), was in Augsburg for the Imperial Diet on Olevian's first Sunday in the pulpit of St James.[32] Upon his return, the Elector sent a committee of five to find out who had authorised Olevian's preaching. The evangelicals on the council argued their right to worship according to the *Augsburg Confession*, under the *Pax Augustana* (1555). The Elector Trier, however, had forbidden the use of the *Augsburg Confession* in Trier.

Olevian's preaching met with enough popular approval so that the town was split between those who favoured him and those who opposed him. He tried to strengthen his position in the city by appealing directly to four of the guilds, in the guild houses, with one of the evangelical council members. The weavers, dyers, shoemakers and a majority of the smiths (among whom were Matthias and Mattheus, two of Olevian's five brothers) declared for the *Augsburg Confession* and for Olevian. There was a 'respectable Protestant minority' in Trier.[33] From the end of August until the early autumn, he fought a valiant battle for the hearts and minds of the citizens and city councillors of Trier. During the controversy, he (like Calvin) signed the *Confessio Augustana Variata* three times under oath to prove his adherence.[34] Such was not an unusual step for Calvinists in the

---

[31] Porter, 'Authors', 211.

[32] The Imperial Electoral College was composed of electors ecclesiastical and temporal. The Elector Palatine was a temporal electorate and theoretically the Emperor's closest electoral adviser.

[33] Good, *Heidelberg Catechism*, 214. Brother Friedrich was a physician. 'Stammtafel', *Monatshefte für Evangelische Kirchengeschichte des Rheinlandes*, 37/38 (1988–89).

[34] See O. Chadwick, 'The Making of a Reforming Prince: Frederick III, Elector Palatine', *Reformation Conformity and Dissent. Essays in Honor of Geoffrey Nuttall*, ed. R. B. Knox (London, 1977), 67, 68; D. B. Thompson, 'An Historical Reconstruction of Melanchthonianism and the German Reformed Church Based upon Confessional and Liturgical Evidence' (Ph.D. Diss., Columbia University, 1953)', 90; idem, 'The Palatinate Church Order of 1563', *Church History* 23 (1954), 341. Thompson notes with puzzlement (because of the synergism of Art. 18) that the *Variata* was accepted unquestioningly by Lutherans and others from 1540–60 ('Historical', 84). In

period. Olevian's future employer, Frederick III, consistently claimed fidelity to the *Variata*, and occasionally to the *Invariata*. Because of the scarcity of fair copies of the *Invariata*, only the 1540 *Variata* was available to sign. When Frederick signed a 1531 copy of the *Invariata* at Naumberg in 1561, it was with the understanding that he interpreted it according to the 1540 edition. How could Calvinists sign a document which could have been seen to bring their theological integrity into question? One answer is that the *Variata* became the *textus receptus* of the *Augsburg Confession* for two decades. Even the gnesio-Lutherans accepted it because they read it in light of the *Invariata*.[35] Calvinist signers of the *Variata* did something similar but for different reasons. Given the socially and politically precarious position in which international Calvinism existed, they saw in the *Variata* what they needed to see. In other words, they found the *Variata* to be a suitable vehicle for expressing simultaneously continuity with Luther on justification and the Calvinist development of the Protestant doctrine of the Supper.

Fearing the wrath of the Elector-Archbishop, the evangelicals appealed to Frederick III and Count Wolfgang of Zweibrucken for protection and another preacher to ease the load. The sympathetic count sent to help his Melanchthonian church superintendent, Cunemann Flinsbach (1527-71). The crisis came to a head in the late autumn when Olevian and his supporters were jailed by the Elector. Representatives from Zweibrucken, Hesse and the Palatinate arrived on 20 November to intercede for the evangelicals.[36] By 17 December, the Elector agreed to a fine of 3,000 gulden and five days later Olevian was freed and a few days later the rest of the evangelicals were allowed to leave the city two days after Christmas.[37] Some fled to Strasbourg while Olevian was

---

this period, however, Calvin signed both the *Invariata* and the *Variata* at different times. See W. Nijenhuis, 'Calvin and the Augsburg Confession', *Ecclesia Reformata. Studies on the Reformation*, trans. M. Foran (Leiden, 1972).

[35] Thompson, 'Historical', 84.

[36] On 1 January 1560, after Olevian had been released, Beza wrote to Bullinger about Olevian's imprisonment in Trier (*CR*, 45, No. 3151).

[37] Flinsbach was later poisoned, in Sponheim, by a priest (Good, *Origins*, 168).

repaid by Frederick III with a call to become Professor of Theology in the *Collegium Sapientiae*.[38]

His experience in Trier calls attention to an important psychological fact. Historically he was a second-generation reformer. Existentially, however, he experienced many of the same challenges of the first generation Protestants: popular acceptance, official rejection, and personal hardship for the sake of the gospel. In his attempted reformation of Trier, he was less a figure of the second reformation or consolidation than a part of the Later Reformation.[39] He identified with the struggle of international Calvinism to win a place as an accepted part of the *Pax Augustana*. To the extent this acceptance was withheld, he saw himself as part of a righteous, persecuted minority within Christendom. Undoubtedly he first came to this self-perception at Orleans and Bourges through his association with the underground Calvinist churches. This perception was reinforced through his unhappy experience in Trier.[40] In a letter written while in custody (11 December 1559), he described himself as a 'foot soldier in exile'.[41] In his letter to Calvin describing his experiences, he gave a detailed description of the political and military strategies of the Elector-Archbishop. He seems even to have perceived the struggle as one between himself and the Elector. He identified the Archbishop as 'Satan who seized all those who opposed him'. [42] He saw the reformation not primarily in political, but spiritual terms.

---

[38] On Frederick's personal and theological development see Owen Chadwick, 'The Making of a Reforming Prince'. See also Good, *The Heidelberg Catechism*, 123–72.

[39] In this sense, Olevian's experience of the Reformation parallels that of the Dutch *Nadere Reformatie*. J. R. Beeke says that there is no truly adequate English equivalent to this phrase though 'Second Reformation' has been adopted for the sake of convenience (*Assurance of Faith: Calvin, English Puritanism and the Dutch Second Reformation* [New York, 1991]).

[40] On the effect of the Trier experience see Goeters, 'Der Trierer Reformationsversuch'.

[41] *CR*, 45.701, no. 3145: 'pedem in exsilio'.

[42] 'Satanas rapiebat eos omnes plane transversos, ut nihil unquam visum sit horribilius: adeo ut qui antea fuissent pigerrimi et trunci, essent indefessi et vaferrimi, ut noctu etiam vix paululum temporis somno darent, quin continenter concurrerent, et nova singulis fere horis inirent consilia' (*CR*, 46.47, no. 3178).

Pastor and Professor in Heidelberg

After his release from prison he travelled immediately to Heidelberg to begin preparation to serve the Elector and the church. On 22 February he matriculated in the University of Heidelberg.[43] On 4 March 1561, he was made Professor of Dogmatics in the University of Heidelberg and on 9 July the faculty Senate received Olevian and promoted him, with Immanuel Tremellius, to the rank of *Doctor Theologiae*.[44] In the same year he married a widow, Philippine of Metz.[45]

He did not remain in the University. In 1562 he gave up his University post to be appointed to the Heidelberg Consistory and serve as preacher in St Peter's Church and in the Church of the Holy Spirit in Heidelberg.[46] During much of his tenure in Heidelberg he also served as superintendent of the Palatinate churches. Though this essay emphasises Olevian's academic work because of its theological and historical interest, it should be remembered that Olevian's chief desire was to be a preacher to the Germans. In 1566 his ministerial commitment was tested, as the plague afflicted the Electorate. The court withdrew and the University closed and most pastors fled, except Ursinus and Olevian. The latter stayed on amidst the tragedy and wrote two tender pastoral tracts to aid the ill and grieving.[47]

If it is true, as this work presupposes, that Olevian cannot be understood outside of his social-historical contexts (Trier, France, Geneva, and the Palatinate) it is equally true that the Palatinate of

---

[43] Töpke, *Die Matrikel*, 2.20. Franciscus Olevian, a relative of Caspar's was admitted into Heidelberg University from the *Collegium Sapientiae* on 7 March 1565 (idem, 2.35).

[44] Töpke, *Die Matrikel*, 2.25.

[45] Adam, *Vitae*, 600; Göbel, 'Dr. Caspar Olevianus', 304; Sudhoff, *C. Olevianus und Z. Ursinus*, 88–124; 'Stammtafel', *Monatshefte für Evangelische Kirchengeschichte des Rheinlandes*, 37/38 (1988–89), 9.

[46] F. H. Klooster said Olevian was replaced by Ursinus in both the *Collegium* and the University because the latter was more suited to the academy than Olevian ('The Priority of Ursinus in the Composition of the Heidelberg Catechism', *Controversy and Conciliation*, 90). Bierma implied that Olevian moved toward the ecclesiastical field voluntarily (idem, 'The Covenant Theology of Caspar Olevian', 6). That Olevian turned down a pastoral call from a church in Dordtrecht, in favour of serving as a private tutor (1577–84) then as a professor in academy as a productive professor in Herborn 1584–87, suggests that Klooster's theory is flawed.

[47] Porter, 'Authors', 220–21.

this period cannot be fairly interpreted without Caspar Olevian. In his 1953 thesis, however (working primarily under the influence of Heinrich Heppe), D. B. Thompson offered an interpretation of the Palatinate more or less ignoring Olevian.[48]

Thompson's thesis was that, having made his break with Luther on the matter of the bondage of the will in 1524–25 and on the matter of Christ's presence in the Eucharist by the writing of the 1535 edition of the *Loci Communes*, Philip Melanchthon became the father of a movement which was neither gnesio-Lutheran nor Calvinist and it was this movement which determined the unique character of theology and ecclesiology of the German Reformed church.

The first part of Thompson's thesis, that Melanchthon represents a type of Protestantism distinct from Geneva, Wittenberg, and Zürich, may be correct. His argument however, that Melanchthon's allegedly synergistic doctrine of justification and his ecclesiology controlled the Palatinate as reflected in the Palatine *Kirchenordnung* and the *Heidelberg Catechism*, is not correct as shall be shown.[49] This notion has much more to do with

---

[48] Thompson, 'Historical'.

[49] Thompson, ibid., 211 and passim. His *modus operandi* is to create the impression that the Palatinate was engulfed by a wave of Melanchthonian liturgical-confessional popularity which might tend to create the impression that the Palatinate also became Melanchthonian. For example, he appealed to the personal confession of John Sigismund (1608–09) as proof of this prevailing Melanchthonianism (ibid., 213). His interpretation, however, was flawed by his assumption that Sigismund was denying Calvinism. This was not correct. In fact, Sigismund's confession reflects standard Calvinist teaching. Second, Thompson's conclusions are rendered suspect by his method of reading the 1560s–80s using documents from the early seventeenth century. In addition, it should be remembered that what made the Palatinate outstanding is that it was perceived correctly by Lutherans and Melanchthonians alike – the latter were among the harshest critics of the Heidelberg Catechism – as a solitary bastion of Calvinism in 'evangelical' Germany (cf. ibid., 'Historical', 78–207). See also Lyle D. Bierma, 'Philip Melanchthon and the Heidelberg Catechism' K. Maag, ed., *Melanchthon in Europe: His Word and Influence Beyond Wittenberg* (Grand Rapids, 1999); and ibid. *The Doctrine of the Sacraments in the Heidelberg Catechism: Melanchthonian, Calvinist or Zwinglian? Studies in Reformed Theology and History* (Princeton Theological Seminary, 1999). In the latter, Bierma concluded that the Heidelberg Catechism should be described as a consensus document which deliberately passed over controversial matters in silence. In response it might be argued that, since a catechism is a naturally cumulative document, the questions addressing the sacraments directly should not be interpreted in isolation from earlier questions such as Q. 48 which clearly

Heinrich Heppe's desire to justify the union of Lutheran and Reformed churches in the nineteenth century than it does with what was happening in Heidelberg in the sixteenth century. Thompson's evidence for his contention was threefold.[50] First, that Frederick signed the *Confessio Augustana Variata*; second, that Frederick commissioned Melanchthon to write the *Responsio*; and third, Frederick's statement that

> What men understand by Calvinism, I do not know. I can say with a clear conscience that I have never read Calvin's writings. As for the agreement at Frankfort [i.e, the *Recess*, which he signed] and the *Augsburg Confession* that I signed, at Naumberg... I continue firmly in that faith, for no other reason except that I find it established in the Holy Scriptures contained in the Old and New Testaments.[51]

None of these three grounds, however, warrants such a conclusion. One has already observed that, like Calvin and Olevian, Frederick had a multitude of reasons to sign the *Augsburg Confession*. Most compelling among them: if he could not plausibly show some adherence to the *Confessio Augustana* he would almost certainly be forced to give up his electorate or face a potential war with the other Protestant princes. This explains his statement quoted above.

It was only slightly disingenuous for Frederick to claim that he had not read Calvin. This claim is best understood to be what contemporary politicians call deniability. Thompson admitted that 'Frederick was not as ignorant of the Reformed theologians as he pretended to be.'[52] In fact, Frederick had corresponded with both Calvin and Bullinger before the Augsburg Diet of 1566 when he denied knowing their views. Calvin himself had written to Frederick three years before the Diet where Frederick made his denial and Frederick himself wrote to Bullinger in 1565 seeking his support for his Catechism.[53] In reply, Bullinger sent a copy of

---

asserts and defends the *extra Calvinisticum* against the Melanchthonian and gnesio-Lutheran Christologies.

[50] Compare H. Heppe, 'The Character of the German Reformed Church', *Mercersburg Quarterly Review* 5 (1853), 194–7.

[51] A. Kluckhorn, *Briefe Fredrich des Frommen* 2 vols (Brunswick, 1868), 1.439. The translation is taken from Thompson, 'Historical', 273.

[52] Thompson, 'Historical', 326.

[53] Kluckhorn, *Briefe*, 1037–40.

the *Second Helvetic Confession* which Frederick undoubtedly read.[54] Frederick's denial becomes even more implausible if one accepts Fritz Büsser's suggestion that the *Second Helvetic* formed the substance of Frederick's defence at the Imperial Diet.[55] Calvin (and the Genevan theologians after him) certainly perceived Heidelberg to be sympathetic. Calvin was dissuaded from dedicating to the Elector the 1559 edition of the *Institutes* only because he wished to protect him from the wrath of the Lutheran princes.[56] Even if one ignores the correspondence, it cannot be ignored that the Elector had been thoroughly introduced to Calvinism through his theologians, whose writings were often dedicated to him and even if he did not read those, he certainly heard a great deal of Calvinism from the pulpit.[57] Nor can the Heppe-Thompson theory explain the vehemence with which Ludwig ejected all of his father's theologians on Frederick's death. Ludwig certainly believed that Ursinus, Olevian, Dathenus, Tossanus and Zanchi were Calvinists and he treated them accordingly.

In March 1559 after his accession to the Electorship, Frederick left to attend his ceremonial investiture. In his absence, a struggle for power broke out between the gnesio-Lutheran Superintendent Heshusius and the Zwinglian deacon Klebitz. The latter seized the moment to propose and successfully defend seven Reformed theses (for his M.A.) in the University. A furious and ugly row broke out. Legend has it that Heshusius and Klebitz even struggled physically for control of the communion chalice during a worship service. Whether factual or not, it serves as an apt metaphor for the power struggle which was taking place in Frederick's absence.[58] Upon his return, to settle the matter, the Elector sought on 1 November 1559 (and received) Melanchthon's

---

[54] Thompson said that Frederick kept Bullinger's *Confession* 'in reserve' to be used in an emergency at the Diet (ibid. 326–7).

[55] F. Büsser, 'Bullinger and 1566', *Conflict and Conciliation: The Palatinate Reformation, 1559–1618*, ed. Derk Visser (Pittsburgh, 1986).

[56] F. H. Klooster, 'Calvin's Attitude Toward the Heidelberg Catechism', *Later Calvinism. International Perspectives*, ed. W. F. Graham (Kirksville, MO, 1994), 316–18.

[57] Thompson argued that Olevianus and Ursinus were not the primary authors of the Heidelberg Catechism ('Historical', 277). He argued that it was a redaction by the committee mainly of Laski's catechisms (ibid. 285–8).

[58] Good, *Origins*, 140–45.

Responsio ad quaestionem de controversia Heidelbergensi. For Thompson, this is proof that Frederick III was self-consciously pursuing a synergistic *via media* between the Swiss Reformation and gnesio-Lutheranism.[59]

That Frederick commissioned Melanchthon to settle the quarrel shows nothing more than that the Elector had the good sense to ask a theologian respected by the German Princes, whose *Variata* Frederick had already found suitably vague, to arbitrate in a nasty ecclesiological-personal-theological dispute, the settlement of which had the potential to create serious problems for him among the other Princes. Thus it was natural that he should turn to Melanchthon for advice. After all, it was Melanchthon who had initially helped to create the crisis by recommending to Frederick that he hire the volatile Heshusius in the first place. Second, it was not as though Frederick had no idea what Melanchthon might say. At this late stage in Philip's career, there could have been little doubt about his views. In any case, Melanchthon simply advised that all the parties use only the *ipsissima verba* of Scripture – thus allowing each to interpret them as he wished. Third, Frederick could not afford to settle the dispute himself (he did eventually dismiss both of them) without the cover of Melanchthon's advice. If Frederick sided openly with the Zwinglian, he risked alienating the Princes. The alternative was even more unthinkable.[60]

Nor is it clear that, as Nevin, Heppe and Thompson have claimed, the *Heidelberg Catechism* is theologically 'Melanchthonian', if that means it was synergistic.[61] It is the second part of the claim that concerns us here. Though it has been widely assumed since Flaccius (from c.1555) attacked him as a synergist that Melanchthon really was such, at least one Melanchthon scholar has plausibly called this view into question.[62] Certainly Luther did not repudiate his theologian, even after Philip began to revise his strongly predestinarian

---

[59] Thompson, 'Historical', 1–49, 99–104, 229–40.

[60] Heshusius was so disliked that the Senate of the University refused to invite him to its meetings, though he was dean of the faculty of theology (Chadwick, 'The Making of a Reforming Prince', 61).

[61] Thompson, 'Historical', 289–300.

[62] See L. Green, 'The Three Causes of Conversion in Philip Melanchthon, Martin Chemnitz, David Chytraeus, and the Formula of Concord', *Lutherjahrbuch* 47 (1980), 89–114.

language from 1527 (in his commentary on Colossians and possibly as early as 1524 when he got hold of Erasmus' *De libero arbitrio*) and in the later editions of the *Loci Communes* where he emphasised the distinction between 'internal' and 'external' freedom.[63]

Even if it is determined that Philip was a synergist, it hardly follows that the Heidelberg reformation or the catechism was synergist in its soteriology. If it was, the Melanchthonian theologians certainly did not perceive it.[64] In fact, the Melanchthonian theologians were among the most vociferous critics of the catechism when it was first published. If the Heidelberg Catechism was Melanchthonian and even antithetical to Calvinism, it is hard to imagine why the Elector would have ordered it bound with a German translation of Calvin's Catechism.[65] Its alleged synergism was not obvious to Calvin, nor to the delegates to the Synod of Dort who read and approved it. Further, such an interpretation of the Catechism is impossible to square with the authorised exposition made by Ursinus or with that made by Olevian in his 1567 *Vester Grund.*[66]

The last point to be made in response to the Heppe-Thompson thesis is to consider the nature of the consciously reformed nature of the theologians and advisors with whom Frederick deliberately surrounded himself.[67] In fact, Frederick called no Melanchthonians to serve him, but Calvinists and

---

[63] R. Seeberg, *Textbook of the History of Doctrines*, trans. C. E. Hay, 2 vols (Philadelphia, 1905), 2.349. See *CR*, 1.688. He said that in the 1535 edition of the *Loci Communes*, Philip attributed 'to the human will an active, although small, part in producing conversion. He there recognizes three causes of conversion: the word, the Spirit and the human will.' In the 1543 edition he said, 'Cumque ordimur a verbo, hic concurrunt tres causae bonae actionis, verbum Dei, Spiritus sanctus et humana voluntas assentiens, nec repugnans verbo Dei' (*CR*, 21.658). Green notes appropriately that Melanchthon is not speaking here about the unregenerate but the regenerate (Spiritus sanctum efficacem esse per vocem Evangelii autitam...) and thus is discussing the struggle between sin and sanctification in the Christian life (idem, 'The Three Causes', 95).

[64] Good, *The Heidelberg Catechism*, 181.

[65] Good, *Origins*, 180–81. Cf. Thompson, 'Historical', 290–300.

[66] See the *Explicationes Catecheseos* in Zacharias Ursinus, *Opera theologica*, 3 vols, ed. Quirinus Reuter (Heidelberg, 1612); Caspar Olevian, *Vester Grund*, (Heidelberg, 1567).

[67] Thompson acknowledges this fact, but does not let it alter his theory ('Historical', 275).

Zwinglians. There were three Melanchthonians from Otto Heinrich's cabinet who continued to serve Frederick: Diller, Count Erbach, and Chancellor Probus.[68] Boquin was the only Calvinist among Frederick's early advisors. Thus it is significant that he chose to augment this cabinet exclusively with Calvinists. Frederick's decision to call Ursinus, Junius, Dathenus, Tossanus and Zanchi should be seen as strong *prima facie* evidence of the Elector's movement toward Calvinism.[69] If Frederick was not becoming a Calvinist, why would he bother to surround himself with Calvinists, a step which he surely knew would bring nothing but criticism from the other princes and their theologians? Thompson admitted that Frederick called Calvinist advisor-theologians because he found Peter Boquin's arguments 'cogent' but he failed to explain *why* Frederick was persuaded.[70] Actually, the Elector found Boquin's arguments cogent because he himself was moving toward Calvinism. Frederick was not duped into calling a group of advisors with whom he could have no sympathy. Nor is it likely that Frederick might have been confused about the theology of his new theologians. Though it was true that Olevian worked along side the Melanchthonian Flinsbach in Trier, there is little chance that the Elector might have confused Olevian's theology for Melanchthonianism.

Olevian's difficulties in Trier were well publicised. It was in fact his Calvinism which prevented him from convincing his

---

[68] Good, *Origins*, 136–7. Frederick also inherited a cabinet including the Gnesio-Lutheran Chancellor Minkwitz and the Zwinglians Erastus and Ehem (ibid.). In addition, Frederick's wife was strongly committed to Gnesio-Lutheranism.

[69] Thompson described Ursinus, his *Summa theologiae* and his *Catechesis minor* as 'Melanchthonian' ('Historical', 278–85). D. Visser argues that Ursinus was Melanchthonian in theology well into his tenure in Heidelberg (idem, *Zacharias Ursinus: The Reluctant Reformer: His Life and Times* [New York, 1983], 64–5, 154). This is partly true. From 1521, virtually all Protestant theology was indebted substantially and methodologically to Melanchthon in many respects. It is incorrect, however, to imply (if this is what Thompson and Visser intend) by the adjective Melanchthonian that Ursinus' soteriology moved in synergistic directions. See R. S. Clark and J. R. Beeke, 'Ursinus, Oxford and the Westminster Divines' in *The Westminster Confession into the 21st Century: Essays in Remembrance of the 350th Anniversary of the Publication of the Westminster Confession of Faith*, 3 vols, ed. J. L. Duncan (Fearn, Ross-shire, 2003–), 2.1–32.

[70] Thompson, 'Historical', 234. He apparently mistook Boquin for a Melanchthonian (ibid. 278).

opponents that he was really an adherent to the *Augustana Variata*.[71] Thompson would have done rather better to argue that the Palatinate in the period preceding Olevian's arrival, particularly under Otto Heinrich, was Melanchthonian – this is almost certainly the case and was a step in the transition of the Palatine theology from Lutheranism to Calvinism. As it stands, Thompson was forced to argue that despite the considerable evidence to the contrary, the Palatinate never 'switch[ed] to Calvinism' but was steadfastly Melanchthonian from 1559.[72]

Though Thompson undervalued it, Olevian's influence on the policies of the Palatinate was significant. One example of Olevian's Calvinistic influence on the Palatinate was his move as rector of the College to remodel the *Schulordnung* on the *Ordre du Collège de Genève*.[73] The same pattern is evident in his reformation of the Palatine *Kirchenordnung*. From (almost) the moment of Olevian's arrival, Frederick instituted a more rigorous, Genevan-style, church discipline requiring everyone to attend church on the Lord's Day except for illness.[74] The city of Heidelberg was divided into quarters. The minister with one elder attended to each district. Newcomers were discovered and examined as to their faith. Walking in parks, lanes or to taverns during worship was forbidden. Profanity, debauchery, drinking alcohol and fortune telling were forbidden generally. Mockery of those going to worship was punishable by fine. Each family was visited annually to prepare for communion.[75]

The discipline, though it might sound severe to modern ears, was relatively tempered. Doubtless, parishioners were grateful for that statute which limited sermons to one hour in length. Preachers were also restricted to the New Testament because it is 'most profitable to the common people and most edifying to the

---

[71] Thompson agreed (idem, 278).

[72] Thompson, idem, 273. These considerations make Thompson's claim incredible that 'It is clear, from this document and from the mass of other evidence, that Frederick III was never converted to Calvinism' (ibid., 328).

[73] Reid, 'Calvin and the Founding', 22–33; Sudhoff, *C. Olevianus und Z. Ursinus*, 505–6.

[74] A comparison of the Palatinate and Genevan Church Orders substantiates this claim. See E. W. Zeeden, 'Calvinistische Elemente in der Kurpfälzischen Kirchenordnung von 1563', *Existenz und Ordnung: Festschrift für Erik Wolf zum 60 Geburtsstag* (Frankfurt am Main, 1962).

[75] Sudhoff, *C. Olevianus und Z. Ursinus*, 124–39.

Churches'. Olevian had a significant influence over what parishioners heard each Sunday since sermons were to be reviewed by the Superintendents. Preaching became more frequent. Daily devotions were ordered and divine services were established on Wednesdays and Fridays, in which German Psalms and hymns were to be sung before and after the sermon.[76] Frederick instituted cultic reforms including the simplification of the Church calendar, *fractio panis* and removal of ornaments in Palatinate churches.[77] The *Augustana Variata* was imposed as the standard of discipline in the Palatinate.[78] Rather than reading this last move as paradigmatic (contra Thompson and Heppe), Frederick's use of the *Variata* should be seen as being driven by a pious pragmatism as much as anything. Those gnesio-Lutheran pastors who were unable to subscribe were effectively forced to leave. The first stages of the new Calvinist church order were consolidated with the publication of the fourth edition of the Heidelberg Catechism together with the *Kirchenordnung* of 1563. Olevian was the primary author of this Church Order.[79] He followed the advice given by Calvin in a 7 November 1560 letter and directed the Commission in 1562–63 which created the *Kirchenordnung* relying primarily on Genevan models.[80]

---

[76] H. Harbaugh, 'Creed and Cultus', *Tercentenary Monument*, 239–42.

[77] This was accomplished on 7 December 1561 according to a letter from Eusthathius Quercetanus to Calvin written 14 February 1562. *CR*, 47. 258, no. 3699.

[78] From 20 January to 8 February 1560 Frederick had been forced to defend his Calvinism before the Protestant princes at Naumberg. The conference was held to bring Frederick back from his Calvinist errors. At Naumberg, Frederick signed the *Augustana Invariata* of 1531 with the proviso that it was further explained in the *Variata* (1540). See Chadwick, 'The Making of a Reforming Prince', 67, 68, who sees this as the defining moment in Frederick's electorship; L. H. Zuck, 'Melanchthonianism and Reformed Theology in the Late 16th Century', *Controversy and Conciliation*, 175–82.

[79] Klooster, 'Origin and History', 189–92. Thompson admitted that Olevian headed the commission which drafted the new Church Order and that he used primarily Genevan style models ('Church Order', 348, n. 109). See also Good, *Origin*, 195–8 and P. Schaff, *History of the Christian Church*, 3rd edn, 8 vols (New York, 1910), 669, 810–11.

[80] *CR*, 46 235–7, no. 3272. Thompson admitted a significant Genevan influence on the Palatinate Church order from 1563 but denied that it had any theological significance since Calvin's church order was 'regulated by one principle – the eternal decrees' and Heidelberg's was (allegedly) not ('Historical',

The Heidelberg Catechism played a central role in the new regime. The new Church Order entailed a rigorous indoctrination. It directed that the Catechism should be read, from the pulpit, in worship, on nine Sundays.[81] The pastors were also to lace their sermons with references to the Catechism followed by sermons based on the Catechism and examination of catechumens each Lord's Day afternoon.[82]

Olevian and the Catechism

The one document for which Olevian is best known is also one in which his degree of involvement is most hotly debated. Most contemporary dictionary and encyclopædia entries on Olevian state categorically that he was one of the primary authors of the Heidelberg Catechism.[83] The earliest history of the Catechism was Hendrik Alting's *Historia de ecclesiis Palatiniis* (1644). He described a dual authorship by Olevian and Ursinus.[84] His father was co-worker with Olevian from 1561-75 and he himself was a student in Herborn and a professor of theology in Heidelberg University 1613-22. He also directed the *Collegium Sapientiae* after 1616. With such extensive personal experience, access to records which were lost in the Thirty Years War, and in the absence of contrary accounts, Alting's report should be

---

306-7; idem, 'The Palatinate Church Order', 342-54). This caricature of Calvin rests solely on the outdated 'central dogma' model of Calvin studies, the weakness of which has become apparent to contemporary Calvin scholars. There was a connection in theological method between Melanchthon, Heidelberg and Olevian that will be explored in chapter 5.

[81] Since the Catechism contains 129 Questions, each service likely read 14-15 questions.

[82] A. L. Richter, ed., *Die evangelischen Kirchenordnungen des sechszehnten Jahrhunderts* (Leipzig, 1871), 260-61. See also C. Allmann, 'Sketches from the History of the Heidelberg Catechism...'. *Tercentenary Monument in Commemoration of the Three Hundredth Anniversary of the Heidelberg Catechism* (Chambersburg, PA, 1863), 124-6.

[83] M. Turchetti's categorical claim, that Olevian 'wrote the Heidelberg Catechism' following Calvin's Catechism, is not supported by any evidence. Centuries of redaction criticism of the Catechism has discovered multiple sources, of which Calvin's catechism was but one (idem, s.v. 'Olevian, Kaspar', *The Oxford Encyclopedia of the Reformation*, 4 vols (New York, 1996), 3.174).

[84] H. Alting, op. cit. 189.

considered authoritative.[85] In the nineteenth century, J. W. Nevin argued that the substance of the Catechism was Olevian's while its form belonged to Ursinus.[86] Later historians argued the converse: its theology was Ursinus' and its form was Olevian's.[87] J. I. Good summarised numerous source critical studies and concluded that while the majority of the Catechism was Ursinus', Olevian had a substantial role in its formation.[88] More recently, G. A. Benrath and Walter Hollweg have disputed Olevian's role in the composition of the Catechism; '[a]ccording to this school, Ursinus is not to be regarded simply as co-author of the Heidelberg Catechism but as its main author'.[89]

In response, Lyle Bierma has shown a strong verbal identity between the Heidelberg Catechism and Olevian's *Vester Grund*. He contends that Olevian wrote *Vester Grund* in 1561 when he was teaching at *Collegium Sapientiae* and that it was to *Vester Grund* that Alting referred when he mentioned Olevian's preparatory book on the *foederis gratiae*.[90] If this dating of *Vester Grund* is correct, and Alting's early report is accurate, then it appears Olevian was, in fact, one of the Heidelberg Catechism's primary authors.[91] Though it is the case that the Catechism was

---

[85] Klooster, 'The Priority of Ursinus', 73, 74, discounted Alting's report, though he offered no reasons for doing so.

[86] J. W. Nevin, *History and Genius of the Heidelberg Catechism* (Philadelphia, 1847), 52.

[87] G. W. Richards, *The Heidelberg Catechism: Historical and Doctrinal Studies* (Philadelphia, 1913), 52, 53. Cf. J. I. Good, *The Heidelberg Catechism in Its Newest Light* (Philadelphia, 1914), 57.

[88] Good, *The Heidelberg Catechism*, 41–80. See also J. F. G. Goeters, 'Entstehung und Frühgeschichte des Katechismus', *Handbuch zum Heidelberger Katechismus*, ed. L. Coenen (Neukirchen-Vluyn, 1963).

[89] G. A. Benrath, '*Zacharias Ursinus als Mensch, Christ und Theolog*', *Reformierte Kirchenzeitung* 124 (1983), 155; Walter Hollweg, *Neue Untersuchung zur Geschichte des Heidelberger Katechismus* (Neukirchen, 1961), cited in F. H. Klooster, 'The Priority of Ursinus in the Composition of the Heidelberg Catechism', *Controversy and Conciliation*, 73; idem, Klooster, 'Origin and History', 159–79.

[90] Alting, op. cit. 189. G. W. Richards disputed that Alting referred to *Vester Grund*. Richards assumed that the date of publication was identical with the date of authorship (idem, *The Heidelberg Catechism*, 27, 28).

[91] L. D. Bierma, 'Olevianus and the Authorship of the Heidelberg Catechism: Another Look', *Sixteenth Century Journal* 13.4 (1982), 17–27; idem. '*Vester Grund* and the Origins of the Heidelberg Catechism', *Later Calvinism*; idem, *Firm Foundation*, ix–xxii..

mostly a revision of Ursinus' *Catechesis minor*, it is also the case the Olevian was presented as one of the Catechism's primary authors.[92] Whether *Vester Grund* was written before or after the catechism, it is clear that Olevian identified with the Catechism and one may read his theology in the light of the catechism.[93]

Frederick of Simmern became *Pfalzgraf* in 1559 in the midst of a violent quarrel between Klebitz, a Zwinglian deacon, and Tilemann Hesshusen (1527-88), the gnesio-Lutheran superintendent, over the nature of the Lord's presence in the Supper.[94] Olevian figured prominently in the Palatinate counter-attack against Hesshusen and the gnesio-Lutheran view of the supper.[95] Olevian continued to take an active part in the controversies over the nature of the Lord's Supper. Many of the tracts and sermons he wrote in this period were published posthumously in 1590 as *Gnadenbund Gottes.*[96]

There were other controversies. One of the first advisers whom Frederick appointed was Zwinglian physician-theologian Thomas Erastus.[97] Erastus shared Zürich's ecclesiology, that the

---

[92] See Bierma, *The Doctrine of the Sacraments*, 35.

[93] Zacharias Ursinus, *Opera Theologica*, 3 vols (Heidelberg, 1612).

[94] Alting, op. cit. 174-81, 191-2; Sudhoff, *C. Olevianus und Z. Ursinus*, 140-51, 184-240, 260-90; 'Olevianus à Bèze' 10 April 1561, *Correspondence de Théodore de Bèze*, vol. 3 (Geneva, 1963), 96, no. 170. Following Heshusius' dismissal from Heidelberg, he became infamous as a controversialist, even among fellow Lutheran scholastics. Against him Peter Boquin wrote *Examen libri quem d. Tilemannus Heshusius nuper scripsit, atque inscripsit de praesentia corporis Christi in coena Domini* (Basle, 1561) and toward him Calvin directed his *Dilucida explicatio sanae doctrinae de vera participatione carnis et sanguinis Christi in sacra coena ad discutiendas Heshusii nebulas* (1561) *CR*, 38.457-524. For Heshusius' relations to other Lutherans see R. E. Diener, 'Johann Wigand', *Shapers of Religious Traditions*, 29-31. R. Kolb, 'Luther, Augsburg, and the Concept of Authority in the Late Reformation: Ursinus vs. The Lutherans', *Controversy and Conciliation*, 44, 45.

[95] Olevian's theological position had personal consequences. He reported in a letter to Calvin, 22 September 1560, describing the Heidelberg Disputation, that early on in his stay in Heidelberg he was refused a bride because of his Calvinist faith. *CR*, 46.195, no. 3250.

[96] Bierma, 'Covenant Theology', 7, nn. 1-3, 8, nn. 1-2. Most of *Gnadenbund* is contained in Sudhoff, *C. Olevianus und Z. Ursinus*, 573-92.

[97] Alting, op. cit. 205. Sudhoff, *C. Olevianus und Z. Ursinus*, 339-70; Good, *Origins*, 217-28. This controversy reverberated well beyond the Palatinate. T. Maruyama, *The Ecclesiology of Theodore Beza* (Geneva, 1978), 108-22, shows that it substantially influenced Beza's doctrine of the church. Erastus' tracts and theses were later translated into English and used in Anglican ecclesiological

visible church ought to be subordinate to the civil authorities. Olevian brought to Heidelberg not only his unpleasant experience with a state-controlled church in Trier, but his Genevan ecclesiology.[98] Before long, Erastus and Olevian found themselves at loggerheads. The formal cause was the doctoral *disputatio* of the Englishman Thomas Withers, who had studied in the Genevan academy between 1559–61 and who joined the University in Heidelberg in March 1568.[99] He first submitted theses siding with the Puritans in the English vestiarian controversy. Professor Boquin, unwilling to offend the Palatinate's most valuable ally, Elizabeth I, returned the theses. Withers then presented theses on 10 June 1568 on church discipline and excommunication, arguing that, hypothetically, even princes could be excommunicated. His theses sparked a bitter pulpit war in St Peter's Church where Olevian shared the pulpit with the Zwinglian Adam Neuser. The issues had been smouldering, however, beneath the surface since 1562.[100] Bullinger wrote to Frederick in support of Erastus and the Zwinglians. Frederick was forced to take sides. On 13 July Frederick, with Ursinus and Boquin, supported Withers and Olevian.[101] Later, in correspondence with Bullinger, Beza also supported Olevian.[102]

---

controversies with Presbyterians. See also R. C. Walton, 'Der Streit zwischen Thomas Erastus und Caspar Olevian über die Kirchenzucht in der Kurpfalz in seiner Bedeutung für die internationale reformierte Bewegung', *Monatshefte für Evangelische Kirchengeschichte des Rheinlandes*, 37/38 (1988–89).

[98] Richard Hooker also interpreted this controversy as a struggle between Geneva and Zürich. See his *Ecclesiastical Polity*, preface, ch. ii.9 in Richard Hooker, *The Works of Mr. Richard Hooker*, ed. J. Keble, 6th edn, 3 vols (Oxford, 1874), 140–41. For a comparison of Olevian's political philosophy with Calvin's see H. H. Eßer, 'Die Staatsauffassung Johannes Calvins und Caspar Olevians', *Monatshefte für Evangelische Kirchengeschichte des Rheinlandes*, 37/38 (1988–89).

[99] *Le Livre du Recteur*, 82; Töpke, op. cit. 2.45, lists a Georgius Witherus, 22 March, who matriculated with three other 'nobiles Angli'.

[100] Olevian wrote to Calvin 24 September 1562 about the question of ecclesiastical discipline, describing the issues which were already present in Heidelberg. *CR*, 47.538–40, no. 3856.

[101] C. J. Burchill, 'Girolamo Zanchi: Portrait of a Reformed Theologian and His Work', *Sixteenth Century Journal* 15 (1984), 201, says that Zanchi and Ursinus agreed in principle with Olevian but sought to avoid personal discord with the Zurichers.

[102] See Klooster, 'Origin and History', 254–78, for a detailed discussion of the controversy.

This ecclesiological conflict brought to light tensions between the Calvinists of Heidelberg and Geneva, and the Zürich Zwinglians. In this episode, it is evident that whatever influence Zürich exercised over Olevian in his early theological training, eleven years later he was securely in the Genevan circle. Rudolph Gwalther (1519-86) undoubtedly spoke for the Zürichers when, in an otherwise irenic letter to Beza (attempting to smooth over the conflict on ecclesiology), he censured Olevian:

> There is, however, one thing, my brother, that I cannot let go unnoticed: not all those working with you are your likes, you who consider nothing more excellent or more precious than the peace of the Churches and the Glory of God. I, too, think Dom Olevianus is a good man, but I shall never approve the immoderate vehemence he has used against the most deserving men of the Church and the doctrine of truth – you yourself make no secret of your misgivings about it.[103]

The rhetoric in this dispute became overheated. In a letter to Bullinger, Erastus once referred to Olevian as a 'Pope'.[104]

---

[103] 'Hoc tamen, mi frater, non possum dissimulare, non omnes, qui illic agunt, tui similes esse, ut Ecclesiarum pace et gloria Dei nihil praestantius aut praetiosius habeant. D. Olevianum ego quoque virum bonum puto, sed vehementiam, qua in viros de Ecclesia et veritatis doctrina optime meritos absque omni animi moderatione usus est, nunquam probavero, et illam tibi quoque suspectam fuisse non diffiteris'. 'Gwalther à Bèze' Zürich 6 June 1570, *Correspondance de Théodore de Bèze*, vol. 11 (Geneva, 1983), 159. This translation is taken from 'Calvin and Calvinists in Europe 1550–1620', History Faculty Oxford University (Oxford, n.d.). The '*suspectam*' refers to Beza's letter of 13 February 1570 to Olevian in which he said, 'Ergo quae nuper ad te scripsi, mi frater, non eo spectant, ut hanc tuam acrimoniam in lentitudinem transformes, sed ut duntaxat eosque temperes, ut rem per se satis superque plerisque odiosam, amabilem potius quam terribilem et formidolosam reddas, quantam id quidem fieri potest ac debes. Necque vero mihi dubium est quin hoc ipsum spectes' (ibid., 46). Later Beza recalled counselling both Erastus and Olevian to moderation (Theodore Beza, *Tractatus pius et moderatus de vera excommunicatione* [Geneva, 1590], Praefatio, 1, 2). Gwalther complained about Olevian again three years later in a letter to Bishop Sandys (Hastings Robinson, trans. and ed., *The Zürich Letters* (Cambridge, 1845), 146, 238). Gwalther's source of information must have been (son?) Rodolphus Gualter and Rodolphus Zuinglius who joined the University of Heidelberg 25 March 1570. Topeke, *Matrikel*, 2.54.

[104] '...nisi quod praedicatas conditiones accipere voluerunt, quos etiam Papa acciperet, siquidem eo in loco res ipsius essent' ('Erast an Bullinger', 4 January

According to Gwalther, Erastus was a pacific, submissive theologian and Olevian a shark willing to use any legal means to achieve victory over his Zwinglian opponents.[105] This controversy also severely strained Olevian's relationship with Frederick's second son, Prince John Casmir (†1592), such that he would not allow Olevian to officiate at his wedding to a Lutheran woman. After the expulsion of the Calvinists from Heidelberg in 1576, Olevian was not invited to the prince's new Calvinist school in Neustadt, though Ursinus was.[106] Casmir also refused to call Olevian back to Heidelberg after the Reformed restoration in 1584.[107]

Olevian in Exile (1576-87)

The last years of Olevian's life are, paradoxically, the least well known, and yet it was the period during which he produced some of his most important books including commentaries on Galatians (1578), Romans (1579), Philippians and Colossians (1580), two handbooks on dialectics (1581 and 1583), a commentary on the Apostles' Creed (1585), a précis of Calvin's *Institutio* (1586), and, by writing the preface, helped produce a German edition of Calvin's sermons (1586).[108] It was for his Latin theology written or published in this period that Reformed theology later remembered him. Thus, the relative obscurity of these years is due more to the way the story of the Palatinate Reformation has been told than to any unimportance inherent to the period. The traditional focus on the Lutheran epoch (ca. 1517-

---

1567, Sudhoff, *C. Olevianus und Z. Ursinus*, 309, 10). One is not aware of like comments by Olevian about Erastus.

[105] R. Wesel-Roth, *Thomas Erastus* (Lahr-Baden, 1954), 48, 60, 92, seems to agree with Gwalther. This does not mean that there was an absolute divorce between Heidelberg and Zürich. Bullinger's *Second Helvetic Confession* supplied the substance of Frederick III's defence of the Catechism at the Imperial Diet in 1566. See F. Büsser, 'Bullinger and 1566', *Conflict and Conciliation: The Palatinate Reformation, 1559-1618*, ed. D. Visser (Pittsburgh, 1986).

[106] Alting, op. cit. 231-45, 245-50.

[107] Klooster, 'Origin and History', 355.

[108] *Predigten H. Johannis Calvini uber das buch Iob* (Herborn, 1587). For more bibliographic information see the appendix to J. F. G. Goeters' essay, 'Caspar Olevian als Theologe', in *Monatshefte für Evangelische Kirchengeschichte des Rheinlandes*, 37/38 (1988-89), 331.

55) has drawn scholarly attention away from the last quarter of the century.

Upon Frederick's death on 26 October 1576, Olevian became immediately *persona n o n grata* in Heidelberg. The Elector designate Ludwig VI (†1583), who was a devout and reactionary gnesio-Lutheran, had long resented Olevian's theology and his enthusiastic attempts at infiltrating Lutheran Amberg with Calvinism. Olevian was placed under house arrest and forbidden to talk, correspond or hold meetings. Upon his return to Heidelberg on 4 April, Elector Ludwig dispossessed the Reformed congregations of the city's major churches and on 21 April formally announced the re-introduction of Lutheranism.[109] The Reformed members of court were dismissed. Fortunately for Olevian, after Count Ludwig I of Wittgenstein (1532-1605) had gone to Berleberg, in the Wetterau District,[110] he received permission to take Olevian with him.[111] Once again, he was delivered from prison by benevolent nobility.[112]

Caspar and the Counts

With Count Ludwig zu Sayn-Wittgenstein's support, Olevian had a profound impact on the Wetterau Counties. He not only taught at Herborn, writing and publishing, but he continued implementing the Calvinist Reformation. Chief among the Wetterau counties was Wittgenstein. Count Ludwig appears to have been at Orleans at the same time as Count Herman Ludwig of the Palatinate. He had studied in Padua, with Count Philip of

---

[109] Alting, op. cit. 223–31; Sudhoff, *C. Olevianus und Z. Ursinus*, 419–28; Good, *Origin*, 235–40; Klooster, 'Origin and History', 284–331.

[110] The Wetterau District, near Frankfurt, east of the Rhine, was composed of a number of small counties each ruled by independent count. Those counties are: Sayn, Wittgenstein, Nassau, Wied, Solms and Hanau. G. Hinsburg likened Olevian's tenure in the district to the Apostle John's exile to Patmos (*Sayn-Wittgenstein-Berleburg. A History of the Counts of Wittgenstein* [Berleburg, 1920], 175). G. Menk, 'Caspar Olevian während der Berleburger und Herborner Zeit' (1577–87), *Monatshefte für Evangelische Kirchengeschichte des Rheinlandes*, 37/38 (1988–89), 139–204.

[111] John Casmir 'retired' to the estates, Bockenheim, Kaiserlautern and Neustadt, left to him in Frederick's will. Ursinus and Daniel Tossanus were called as professors to the academy founded at Neustadt.

[112] Adam, *Vitae*, 600–03.

Nassau. His first wife was daughter of the Count of Solms. His daughter married Count John VI of Nassau.

Within two years of his arrival in the Wetterau, Olevian succeeded in introducing there the Reformed practice of breaking the communion bread during the administration of the supper (*fractio panis*).[113] In the next four years, altars were transformed into communion tables and organs were replaced with Psalm singing from the Genevan Psalter. Private confession, absolution, Latin singing of the Scripture lessons, bowing at the name of Jesus, feast days, pictures, crosses, and crucifixes were all forbidden or removed. Ludwig and Olevian even managed to form a General Synod of the Wetterau counties, 13 July 1586, which the latter served as President. Under his leadership, the Synod adopted the Genevan Church order.[114] Between 1578 and 1618 the Wetterau Counties were followed by a 'wave of conversions' in twenty-two cities until the outbreak of the Thirty-Years War, including the imperial city of Bremen (1581), the deposed Archbishop of Cologne (1583), East-Friesland (1583), and Brandenburg (1613).[115] Caspar Olevian died at Herborn, 15 March 1587 of 'dropsy'.[116] He was buried in the choir of the church at Herborn.[117]

C. P. Clasen characterised Count Ludwig as 'militant' in his Calvinism and leader of one of the 'most restless and explosive social groups in the Empire'. Clasen alleged that the Counts of the Wetterau 'for purely economic reasons tried to force the secularisation of the ecclesiastical territories'.[118] R. Po-Chia Hsia has pursued this social analysis of the Reformed churches in the Wetterau counties. He has depicted them, correctly, as 'smaller

---

[113] On the significance of the *fractio panis* see B. Nischan 'The *Fractio Panis*, A Reformed Communion Practice in Late Reformation Germany', *Church History* 53 (1984), 17–29; O. K. Olson, 'The *Fractio Panis* in Heidelberg and Antwerp', *Controversy and Conciliation*.

[114] See W. Niesel, ed., *Bekenntnisschriften und Kirchenordnung der nach Gottes Wort reformierten Kirche* (Munich, 1937), 291–8.

[115] Hsia, *Social Discipline*, 26,7.

[116] Sudhoff, *C. Olevianus und Z. Ursinus*, 465–75. J. T. McNeill, op. cit. 270, mistakenly dated Olevian's death in 1585.

[117] Olevian's mother outlived him by nine years and was buried next to him.

[118] Clasen, *The Palatinate in European History 1559–1660*, 13; Sudhoff, *C. Olevianus und Z. Ursinus*, 458–65; Good, *Origins*, 254–6; Klooster, 'Origin and History', 332–44.

territories' often overlooked but which constituted 'an integral part of the mosaic of imperial politics'.[119] It is clear that 'threatened by territorialisation' these counts shored up their position within the empire and thus strengthened their relations with the House of Orange and worked for confessional uniformity among their subjects. The Second Reformation failed in that confessionalisation 'made uneven progress along the Rhine' failing to displace the folk religion of the shepherds, midwives, blacksmiths and peasants. The Reformed programme of desacralising nature was popularly rejected.[120]

The social analysis of the Reformation of the Wetterau District provides a useful balance to the earlier denominational hagiographies, yet Hsia overstates his case. The assertion, that the counts adopted Calvinism as part of a strategy to consolidate power, seems unlikely.[121] It is rather the case that the counts could not find support from Lutheran princes *because* they were Calvinist. Neither Clasen nor Hsia explained why the Wetterau counts chose to affiliate with an unpopular (and illegal) religion in an effort to fortify their position against hostile electors. Second, the Clasen-Hsia analysis assumed a model of economic determinism. Such a model fails to account for the fact that Count Ludwig apparently made an independent evaluation of the Reformed theology and cultus and made a principled, *theological* choice, not a self-serving religio-political calculation.[122] Third, the Clasen-Hsia theory of the Wetterau Reformation does not account for the undeniably strong personal relationship between Olevian and Ludwig which must have influenced the count in his decision. Evidence of this bond is that Olevian turned down a call to a

---

[119] R. Po-Chia Hsia, *Social Discipline in the Reformation: Central Europe 1550–1750* (London, 1989), 70.

[120] Hsia, *Social Discipline*, 152–3; cf. 26–38. H. A. Oberman, 'The Impact of the Reformation: Problems and Perspectives', *Politics and Society in Reformation Europe. Essays for Sir Geoffery Elton on his Sixty-Fifth Birthday*, ed. E. I. Kouri and T. Scott (London, 1987), has drawn attention to the 'loaded language' of the social analysis approach to Reformation studies.

[121] Hsia, *Social Discipline*, 70.

[122] In 1564 Ludwig evaluated the Heidelberg Catechism and queried Bullinger about the new Heidelberg Church order. By the time he was called to be *Großhofmeister* (1572–76) in Frederick's *Oberrat*, he was thoroughly Calvinist.

congregation in Dortrecht, the Netherlands, in order to serve Ludwig.[123]

The last quarter of the sixteenth century has usually been understood as a postlude to the Reformation and a prelude to seventeenth-century social and theological developments. As a result, Reformed federal theologians, such as Olevian, have been interpreted primarily in terms of their relations to the magisterial reformers and their relations to later Reformed dogmaticians. Such an approach, however, does not constitute a real advance in the understanding of an important period in Western history and the Reformed theology which it produced.

This analysis has sought to place Caspar Olevian in his context as a member of an influential but persecuted minority, international Calvinism. Far from departing from the Protestant tradition, Olevian saw himself as a part of the ongoing Reformation initiated by Luther and continued by Calvin.

•

---

[123] W. Nijenhuis, *Adrianus Saravia [c.1532–1613]*, trans. J. E. Platt (Leiden, 1980), 39, notes that both Olevian and Dathenus were called to Dort at the end of 1576. Boquin addressed his anti-Jesuit tract *Assertio Veteris Ac Veri Christianismi, Adversus Novum et Fictum Iesuitismum Seu Societatem Iesu* (London, 1576), to Ludwig I.

CHAPTER 3

OLEVIAN'S SCHOLASTIC
HUMANISM

When Olevian died, Theodore Beza (1519-1605) mourned his death
in verse, the significance of which is not literary but in the fact
that Olevian merited such verse. It was a small signal of his
inclusion in the Reformed republic of letters and suggests that he
was not just a Reformer and a theologian, but also a man of
letters: a Protestant humanist.[1] That is, he lived and worked in a
broadly humanist environment where learning and felicity of
expression were important values.

---

[1] R. J. W. Evans says membership in the republic was a means of
social mobility for scholars of common birth (idem, *The Making of the
Habsburg Monarchy 1550-1700* (Oxford, 1984), 38). See also G. H. M.
Posthumus Meyjes, 'Protestant Irenicism in the Sixteenth and Seventeenth
Centuries', *The End of Strife*, ed., David Loades (Edinburgh, 1984); idem,
'Charles Perrot (1541-1608): His Opinion on a Writing of Georg Cassander',
*Humanism and Reform: the Church in Europe, England, and Scotland,
1400-1643*, ed., J. Kirk (Oxford, 1991), 221-36; M. P. Fleischer, 'The Success of
Ursinus: A Triumph of Intellectual Friendship', *Controversy and Conciliation:
The Palatinate Reformation, 1559-1618*, ed., Derk Visser (Pittsburgh, 1986);
idem, *Späthumanismus in Schleisen* (Munich, 1984); Menna Prestwich, 'The
Changing Face of Calvinism', *International Calvinism 1541-1715*, ed. M.
Prestwich (Oxford, 1985), 1-14. See also D. R. Kelley, *Foundations of Modern
Historical Scholarship* (New York, 1970); P. E. Hughes, *Lefèvre: Pioneer of
Ecclesiastical Reform in France* (Grand Rapids, 1984); Q. Skinner, *The
Foundations of Modern Political Thought*, 2 vols (Cambridge, 1978), 2.189-238;
A. E. McGrath, *Intellectual Origins*, 33-57; L. W. Spitz, *The Renaissance and
Reformation Movements. Vol. 1: The Renaissance* (St Louis, 1971), 284-5. On the
relation of the reformation to humanism see R. D. Linder, 'Calvinism and
Humanism: The First Generation', *Church History* 44 (1975), 167-81; E.
Cameron, 'The Late Renaissance and the Unfolding Reformation in Europe',
Humanism and Reform, 15-36.

Olevian did not, however, experience humanism in stark opposition to scholasticism, but rather he experienced humanism and scholasticism as two branches of the same academic tree. One sees their close relations in the intellectual and stylistic connections between his logic handbooks and his second commentary on the Creed. Olevian's *Exposition of the Apostles' Creed* (*Expositio symbolici apostolici*), based on his catechetical lectures in the *Collegium Sapientiae*, went through five editions between 1576 and 1618, in the Wechel Press, Frankfurt. He also published his first logic handbook, *Fundamentals of Dialectic* (*Fundamenta dialecticae*, 1581) at the same press.

By the time he matriculated in university, humanism was a fact of academic life. Erasmus and Lefèvre had been dead for two decades and François Rabelais (1490-1553) died whilst Olevian was a student. He was roughly contemporary with the generation(s) which produced Theodore Beza (1519-1605), Michel de Montaigne (1533-92), Jean Bodin (c.1529-96), François Hotman (1524-90) under whom he studied at university, Sir Philip Sidney (1554-86) the English diplomat and poet, and Crato of Crafftheim (1519-86). He also taught in the theology faculty in the University of Heidelberg (founded 1386) which had a long history of support for the liberal arts.[2]

Proper consideration of his humanism ought to relieve an overly narrow conception of Olevian as only a theologian of the covenant or cohort in the development of the Heidelberg Catechism. Rather, his exposure to humanism was an important component of his preparation for his ministry. Further, there are several reasons to think that Olevian's relations to humanism illustrate the way many Calvinists of the period related their religion to the rising challenge posed by the late renaissance.

At the same time, to many historians of doctrine, scholasticism has often appeared to be one of the dangers which Protestant theologians had to navigate in order to remain truly Protestant. Scholasticism is usually said to entail a certain amount of rationalism, i.e. a system of thought in which human

---

[2] Johannes Reuchlin (1455–1522) translated Greek authors in Heidelberg and gave private tuition. Rudolf Agricola (1443–85) taught for three years at Heidelberg. Melanchthon read classics there from 1509–12. His petition for an M.A. was rejected on account of his youth.

reason is supreme, the fulcrum by which all other authority is levered.[3]

Like humanism, scholasticism was a method and not an anti-Protestant rationalising movement. Olevian made deliberate use of Protestant scholastic methods and synthesised them with his humanist training, in order to adapt the gains of the earlier Protestants to the demands of the late-sixteenth-century Calvinist schools.[4] One would do well to describe his scholasticism as Reformed humanist-scholasticism.

One reason earlier scholarship did not see Olevian's scholasticism is that it missed the synthesis which Protestant orthodoxy achieved between scholasticism and humanism with the onset of the Reformation. This blind spot was itself the result of the assumption that humanism was entirely opposed to scholasticism. In fact, it is becoming clear that such was not the case.

Erika Rummel says that many of the traditional criteria used to distinguish scholasticism from humanism fail because the debate between humanists and scholastics was actually an argument between two university faculties, which developed in stages. In the late fourteenth century the debate was rather unfocused. By the late fifteenth and early sixteenth centuries the arts and theology faculties were competing for territory and students and they were arguing about method. In the third stage, by the middle of the sixteenth century, the terms of the debate had shifted to the question of which faculty was contributing more to the decline of the faith: the aesthetically motivated

---

[3] M. E. Osterhaven's comments are typical: 'History has demonstrated the futility of that kind of [scholastic] Christianity. An orthodoxy whose chief assets are theological precision, logical consistency, and formalism, one which delights in itself but sells short the life within, is bound to fail.... Cold and uninteresting except to the few, it led to rationalism and unbelief' ('The Experientialism of the Heidelberg Catechism', D. Visser, ed., *Controversy and Conciliation: The Palatinate Reformation, 1559–1618* [Pittsburgh, 1986], 199). More recently C. Lindberg has described the entire late-sixteenth-century confessional period as a time of 'rationalistic and creed-bound Protestantism and Catholicism'. See, idem, *The European Reformations* (Oxford, 1996), 359. For a response to this approach see C. R. Trueman and R. S. Clark, eds, *Protestant Scholasticism: Essays in Reassessment* (Carlisle, 1999); W. J. Van Asselt, and E. Dekker, eds, *Reformation and Scholasticism* (Grand Rapids, 2001).

[4] W. J. Bouwsma, 'The Two Faces of Humanism', *Itinerarium Italicum*, ed. H. A. Oberman and T. A. Brady (Leiden, 1975), 3–61.

humanists in the arts faculty or the dogmatically motivated scholastics in the theology faculty?[5] Yet, in the last stage, scholastics could be found quoting the classics to show they were not illiterate and humanists produced syllogisms to show that they were not intellectually sloppy.[6]

One observes this intellectual and methodological overlap in Protestant humanist-scholastics such as Melanchthon.[7] Under his influence, the 1558 statutes of Heidelberg University were re-drafted to require the arts faculty to lecture on Aristotle.[8] Whether this was a humanist or scholastic move seems difficult to say. To complicate matters further, he also criticised the later scholastics not for using the *quaestio disputata*, but for allowing it to fall into disrepair. For all the rhetorical missiles which Luther and the humanists launched against it, scholasticism as a method, albeit revised by evangelical theology and political necessity, flourished throughout the sixteenth century.[9]

---

[5] E. Rummel, *The Humanist-Scholastic Debate in the Renaissance and Reformation* (Cambridge, MA, 1995), 9–10.

[6] Rummel, *The Humanist-Scholastic Debate*, 14.

[7] Q. Breen, 'Three Renaissance Humanists on the Relation of Philosophy and Rhetoric', *Christianity and Humanism* (Grand Rapids, 1968), 1–68. E. F. Rice Jr distinguished three uses of Aristotle in the late medieval period (idem, ed., *The Prefatory Epistles of Jacques Lefèvre d'Etaples and Related Texts* [New York, 1972], xvi, xvii).

[8] See D. Sinnema, 'The Discipline of Ethics in Early Reformed Orthodoxy', *Calvin Theological Journal* 28 (1993), 16–18.

[9] J. P. Donnelly, *Calvinism and Scholasticism in Vermigli's Doctrine of Man and Grace* (Leiden, 1976), 29–41. Donnelly has observed that the scholastic method persisted throughout the sixteenth century in part because of the continued use of Aristotle in undergraduate training. He says 'to think as an educated person was virtually to think as an Aristotelian'. These comments conflict, however, with his approach (ibid., 10, 11) where, following Armstrong, he divides the biblical humanism of Calvin from the 'embryonic Protestant Scholasticism' of Peter Martyr, Beza and Zanchi. He does so by counting Calvin's citation use of medieval scholastic authors (ibid., 7). This is not an accurate barometer of Calvin's relationship to scholasticism since he typically cited an author only when it was to his rhetorical benefit. In another context Donnelly acknowledges how difficult it can be to trace the influence of one author on another (idem, 'Italian Influences on the Development of Calvinist Scholasticism', *Sixteenth Century Journal* 7 (1976), 83–5; idem, *Calvinism and Scholasticism*, 192, 173).

Olevian's Humanism

There is little doubt that humanism exercised massive influence on the Reformation.[10] It is a remarkable fact, however, that despite the well-documented connections between humanism and the Reformation, there is no scholarly consensus on the exact nature of humanism or its relations to the Reformation.[11] Was the Reformation influenced by the Renaissance *messages* or *methods*? More precisely, did Calvinism maintain the 'Lutheran' doctrine of justification or did its dalliance with humanism entice it away from the Reformation to a sub-Protestant moralism? According to H. R. Trevor-Roper, this is exactly what happened. Calvinism became the suit of armour which Erasmianism put on to survive the sixteenth century.[12]

---

[10] A. E. McGrath has argued that Protestantism's central insight, i.e. justification as *actus forensis* derived not from the Church's theologians, but from humanism. See idem, 'Humanist Elements in the Early Reformed Doctrine of Justification', *Archiv Für Reformationsgeschichte*, 73 (1982), 5, 17–19. See also his argument in '*Mira et nova diffinitio iustitiae*: Luther and Scholastic Doctrines of Justification', *Achiv für Reformationsgeschicte* 74 (1983), 37–60 and J. Mackinnon, *Luther and the Reformation*, 4 vols (London, 1925), 1.161–8. See also L. C. Green's valuable study, 'The Influence of Erasmus upon Melanchthon, Luther and the Formula of Concord in the Doctrine of Justification', *Church History* 43 (1974), 183–200. McGrath observed that where the Vulgate had '*credidit Abraham Deo et reputatum est illi ad iustitiam*' Erasmus had '*Credidit autem Abraham Deo et imputatam est ei ad iustitiam*'. Beza followed this translation in his influential translation *Novum testamentum sive foedus* (Geneva, 1565), '*Credidit autem Abrahamus Deo, et imputatum est ei ad iustitiam*'. Beza's Latin testament along with Tremellius' and Junius' *Testamenti veteris biblia sacra* (Frankfurt, 1579) became more or less the received text of Scripture used by Reformed orthodoxy.

[11] See A. E. McGrath, *The Intellectual Origins of the European Reformation* (Oxford, 1987), 32–43, for a summary of some of the historiographical issues.

[12] H. R. Trevor-Roper, *Religion, the Reformation and Social Change*, 2nd edn (London, 1972), 234–6. F. Büsser suggests that Erasmus was the 'father of Reformed theology generally'. See idem, 'Zwingli the Exegete: A Contribution to the 450th Anniversary of the Death of Erasmus', *Probing the Reformed Tradition*, ed., E. A. McKee and B. G. Armstrong (Louisville, 1989), 192.

Others have argued Reformed theology was moralist in that orthodox Calvinism's use of federal theology marked a regression to Gabriel Biel's *pactum Dei* theology. See McGrath, 'Mira et Nova', 59; idem, *Iustitia Dei*, 2.40; S. Strehle, *Calvinism, Federalism and Scholasticism: A Study of the Reformed Doctrine of the Covenant* (Bern, 1988), 2.

Scholastics valued the classics for their

usefulness in advancing theology.

Pace Trevor-Roper and others, this chapter contends that what was fundamentally true of Luther with respect to humanism – that he was glad to use its philological advances and appreciated the movement *ad fontes* – was also fundamentally true of Olevian. He drank deeply from the well of humanist-inspired liberal arts education and shared the concern of humanists about the reform of manners. He made use of the rhetoric of humanism, but always he made his learning a servant of his theology.

One's definition of humanism must be qualified by the reasons for and the context in which one's subject studied the liberal arts.[13] Calvin and Olevian were not marked by any speculative or rationalising intellectual curiosity. They were not pursuing the new learning for its own sake, but rather they put their training in the arts faculties into the service of Protestant theology. In this way, they were not humanists, but shared the primary characteristic of the scholastics: they valued the classics for their usefulness in advancing theology.[14] Though educated in the Arts faculties, they spent their lives as theologians.

> Paul Oskar Kristeller defines the *studia humanitatis* as a
>
> cycle of scholarly disciplines, namely grammar, rhetoric, history, poetry, and moral philosophy.... Renaissance humanism was not as such a philosophical tendency or system, but rather a cultural and educational program which emphasized and developed an important but limited area of studies.[15]

To say that Olevian was a humanist, given Kristeller's definition, is to say more about *how* he conducted his studies than *what* he actually believed. In this way then, for Olevian, as for Calvin and Beza, humanism was primarily a set of tools which he used to advance his theological program.[16]

---

[13] See Rummel, *The Humanist-Scholastic Debate*, 12–13.

[14] Rummel, *The Humanist-Scholastic Debate*, 14.

[15] P. O. Kristeller, *Renaissance Thought and its Sources*, ed., M. Mooney (New York, 1979), 22. See also Q. Breen, *John Calvin: A Study in French Humanism* (Grand Rapids, 1931).

[16] McGrath, *Intellectual Origins*, 66. If so, then Bouwsma's argument that Calvin's goal was not to set forth a 'true theology' as much as to remedy the evils of his age, is not correct, because it has made Calvin more humanist than he really was. See W. J. Bouwsma, 'Calvin as Renaissance Artifact', *John Calvin and*

As a counter-balance to Kristeller, some scholars have drawn attention to moral and intellectual concerns which united humanists. For example, R. D. Linder says that humanism was also marked by 'concern for the potentials and actions of men as men'.[17] D. R. Kelley has called attention to the 'sense of history' which marked the humanist movement as a whole.[18] Hanna-Barbara Gerl and Erika Rummel have suggested a third distinguishing mark of the humanists: intellectual curiosity, unbridled by concerns for theological orthodoxy.[19] The humanist,

---

the Church. *A Prism of Reform*, ed., T. George (Louisville, 1990), 35. See also idem, *John Calvin: A Sixteenth Century Portrait* (New York, 1988), 113–27. R. W. Battenhouse and C. M. N. Eire have seen strong evidence of Erasmian influence on Calvin's theology in the form of a neo-Platonist anthropology. Eire's reading of Calvin helps to explain his antipathy toward material representations of the Deity in worship. Battenhouse has overstated Calvin's debt to neo-Platonism. See R. W. Battenhouse, 'The Doctrine of Man in Renaissance Humanism', *The Journal of the History of Ideas* 9 (1948), 447–71; C. M. N. Eire, *War Against the Idols: The Reformation of Worship from Erasmus to Calvin* (Cambridge, 1986), 3. P. W. Butin has challenged this characterisation by arguing that it is one thing to assume a connection between Calvin and neo-Platonic dualism, it is quite another to prove it. He argues that most of the apparently dualist passages in Calvin do not refer to a Greek spirit-flesh dichotomy but a Pauline Holy Spirit-sinful flesh dualism. See P. W. Butin, *Revelation, Redemption and Response: Calvin's Trinitarian Understanding of the Divine-Human Relationship* (New York, 1994). Butin's thesis is summarised in 'John Calvin's Humanist Image of Popular Late-Medieval Piety and its Contribution to Reformed Worship', *Calvin Theological Journal 29* (1994), 419–31.

[17] R. D. Linder, 'Calvinism and Humanism: The First Generation', *Church History* 44 (1975), 169.

[18] D. R. Kelley, *Foundations of Modern Historical Scholarship: Language, Law, and History in the French Renaissance* (New York, 1970), 21. W. J. Bouwsma seeks to revise what he describes as Kristeller's 'lowest common denominator' approach to humanism. Humanism was not empty of philosophical content but rather the rhetorical tradition appropriated by the Renaissance 'was also the vehicle of a set of basic intellectual conflicts crucial to the development of European culture in the early modern period'. Instead, Bouwsma wants us to see that humanism was 'engaged in an internal struggle between two poles: Augustinianism and Stoicism' ('The Two Faces of Humanism', *Itinerarium Italicum: The Profile of the Italian Renaissance in the Mirror of its European Transformations*, ed., H. A. Oberman and T. A. Brady [Leiden, 1975], 3–61. Reprinted in W. J. Bouwsma, *A Usable Past* [Berkeley, 1990], 3–4).

[19] Hanna-Barbara Gerl, *Philosophie und Philologie* (Munich, 1981), 32–3, cited in Rummel, *The Humanist-Scholastic Debate*, 12–13.

unlike the scholastic, was willing to consider a wider range of questions and authorities.

Because Olevian's humanism was mainly a means to an end, these three marks of humanism do not fit him well. Additionally, it is important to remember that one must compare him with later not earlier Renaissance humanism. R. J. W. Evans describes the humanism of this period as

> a cultural Renaissance, uniform in its essentials, but operating on several levels of complexity. It embraced both active and passive members of the *Respublica litteraria*: from the pinnacle of recognized authors who might hope to correspond with Lipsius down to the ranks of those who were just – though in a double sense – fellow-travellers.[20]

Olevian had ambivalent relations to this cultural Renaissance. He was a man of letters – hence a 'fellow-traveller' – and yet he had a different agenda from many of his humanist contemporaries.

In the first half of the sixteenth century, Protestant reformers and humanists were often the same people. It is not apparent that being a humanist was a cause of much tension for the earlier reformers. Olevian's relations to late humanism were complicated, however, by the fact that the nature of the Renaissance was changing. Like the Reformation, it was evolving toward institutionalization.[21] The trajectory of late humanism was not entirely friendly to Calvinists such as Olevian.

For these reasons, scholars of the Reformation and humanism have had difficulty agreeing on the relations between the rise and development of Protestant theology and the renewal of learning. The fact is that the Protestants themselves were ambivalent about the new learning. Calvin said:

> Read Demosthenes or Cicero; read Plato, Aristotle, and others of that tribe. They will, I admit, allure you, delight you, move you, enrapture you in wonderful measure. But betake yourself from them to this sacred reading. Then, in spite of yourself, so deeply will

---

[20] Evans, *The Making*, 31–2.

[21] C. S. Lewis linked the English humanism of the late sixteenth century with Puritanism. 'In reality, the puritans and the humanists were quite often the same people. When they were not, they were united by strong antipathies and by certain affinities of temper' (idem, *English Literature in the Sixteenth Century* [Oxford, 1954], 18).

Calvin – enjoy the great works of literature but scripture is divine!

it affect you, so penetrate your heart, so fix itself in your very marrow, that, compared with its deep impression, such vigor as the orators and philosophers have will nearly vanish. Consequently, it is easy to see that the Sacred Scriptures, which so far surpass all gifts and graces of human endeavor, breathe something divine.[22]

In this passage Calvin himself displayed four humanist characteristics: affection for the classics, a passion for good letters, a concern for personal renewal, and an excellent mastery of style and metre. Yet, as this passage also illustrates, his primary source was not Seneca, but *sacra scriptura*. For all their beauties, the classics were not *verbum Dei*.[23] He made his humanism a servant to his Protestant theology. R. R. Bolgar has described these Protestant humanists as proponents of *pietas litterata*, revisers of the classical humanist agenda, interested in writing correct Latin, whose Christianity 'checked men's curiosity and set bounds to their zeal to learn from the pagan past'.[24]

---

[22] John Calvin, *Institutes of the Christian Religion*, trans. F. L. Battles, ed., J. T. McNeill (London, 1961), 1.8.1. 'Lege Demosthenem, aut Ciceronem: lege Platonem, Aristotelem, aut alios quosvis ex illa cohorte: mirum in modum, fateor, te allicient, oblectabunt, movebunt, rapient: verum inde si ad sacram istam lectionem te conferas, velis nolis ita vivide te afficiet, ita cor tuum penetrabit, ita medullis insidebit, ut prae istius sensus efficacia, vis illa Rhetorum ac Philosophorum prope evanescat; ut promptum sit, perspicere, divinum quiddam spirare sacras Scripturas, quae omnes humanae industriae dotes ac gratias tanto intervallo superent' (idem, *Institutio Christianae Religionis* 1559; *Joannis Calvini Opera Selecta*, ed., P. Barth and W. Niesel, 3rd edn, 5 vols [Munich, 1963–74], 3.72.32–40 [hereafter, *OS*]).

[23] L. W. Spitz says that 'Luther gave enthusiastic support to humanist culture in its sphere, but sharply rebuffed its encroachments in the domain of theology where God's Word and not human letters reigns supreme' (idem, *The Religious Renaissance of the German Humanists* [Cambridge, MA, 1963], 238). H. A. Oberman says that in Luther's case, humanism was 'put into the service of a new Augustinian theology' (idem, 'Headwaters of the Reformation: *Initia Lutheri-Initia Reformationis*', *Dawn of the Reformation* [Edinburgh, 1992], 78). A. Ganoczy has also noticed the change in Calvin's relations to humanism brought about by his conversion to the evangelical faith. From the publication of *Psychopannychia* (1534) Calvin adopted the same relations to humanism as Luther. Though strongly influenced by its methods, his humanism was 'entirely subordinate to the demands of the radical reform' (A. Ganoczy, *The Young Calvin*, trans. D. Foxgrover and W. Provo [Edinburgh, 1987], 179, 80). See also McGrath, 'Humanist Elements', 14–15; idem, *Iustitia Dei*, 2.36–9, idem, *Intellectual Origins*, 59–68.

[24] R. R. Bolgar, *The Classical Heritage and its Beneficiaries*, 352, 356, 369.

This theory explains why Olevian, like Calvin, does not fit well under the Gerl-Rummel rubric. He was opposed to fruitless speculation, whether pursued for the sake of art or theology. Neither, however, was he fully scholastic, in the medieval pattern. He synthesised aspects of both movements. He, like many other early orthodox Protestant theologians, represents a tertium quid. He was a Reformed humanist-scholastic. It was his Protestant theology which distinguished him from the humanist mainstream.[25]

Unlike Luther, for example, Olevian was not educated in university as a theologian, and so was not a product of the Theology faculty and its competitive suspicions of the Arts faculty. He received a liberal education which certainly included the rudiments of theology, but the focus was elsewhere. Because of his background in French legal humanism, he interacted much more closely with classics in a traditional humanist fashion than Luther did.[26] He took his remedial theological training in a study tour to Zürich and Geneva.

See also L. Jardine, 'Humanism and Dialectic in Sixteenth Century Cambridge: A Preliminary Investigation', in R. R. Bolgar, ed., *Classical Influences on European Culture A. D. 1500–1700* (Cambridge, 1976), 141–54. P. R. Schaefer's description of the Reformed humanism of the early seventeenth-century Cambridge Puritans well describes Olevian and the Continental Reformed theologians: 'While the puritans had an extremely high regard for biblical authority, even at times seemingly making their "precisenesse" overshadow their use of present epistemic practices, they in fact never denied the usefulness of "humane learning" in the Arts' (idem, 'The Spiritual Brotherhood on the Habits of the Heart: Cambridge Protestants and the Doctrine of Sanctification from William Perkins to Thomas Shepard' [D.Phil. Thesis, Oxford University, 1994], 20).

[25] The Protestants mainly followed Augustine's anthropology not Erasmus', at least regarding the results of the Fall on human rationality. Budé and Lefèvre were, however, less sanguine *de libero arbitrio* than Erasmus. See J. D. Tracy, 'Humanism and the Reformation', *Reformation Europe: A Guide to Research*, ed., S. Ozment (St Louis, 1982), 33, 43. See also P. O. Kristeller, *Renaissance Thought*, 169–98; P. E. Hughes argued that Calvin was heir to Lefèvre's humanism and theology (idem, 'Jacques Lefèvre d'Etaples (c.1455–1536)', *Calvinus Reformator: His Contribution to Theology, Church and State* [Pochestroom, 1982], 93–108; See also idem, *Lefèvre: Pioneer of Ecclesiastical Renewal in France* [Grand Rapids, 1984]). Olevian's soteriology will be discussed in chapter 6.

[26] B. Hall says, 'to be a student of civil law at Bourges and Orléans was to be intimately drawn to the study of classical literature' ('John Calvin, the Jurisconsults and the *Ius Civile*', *Studies in Church History*, vol. 3 [Oxford, 1966], 203).

Education reform was one of the most prominent elements of the humanist intellectual.[27] Teaching as a noble vocation was a weighty humanist influence on Olevian. The Heidelberg Catechism was directed education for the masses and his commentaries on the Creed and on the Gospels and Pauline epistles were the product of his lectures to divinity students. This background helps to illumine Olevian's few autobiographical comments about his education. As a schoolboy in the early 1550s, he was influenced by the humanist movement. In his early education he was

> wonderfully kindled with a desire both to learn and teach others about God...for I happened upon the writing of a very learned man, where nearly in this same opinion he exhorted young men: 'there is nothing more excellent,' he said, 'than for men to teach others...'.[28]

As a humanist Olevian hoped to pass on his own passion for learning to his students:

> I speak as a young man, to young men: hoping it will be, so that those things having no small moment in my soul, will likewise kindle sparks in your souls, that may engender the earnest desire to learn as well as to teach. Moreover, you might feel yourselves not only challenged by my example but also helped by my little work, God granting.[29]

These brief passages witness to his deep gratitude for the learning he acquired as a boy and to his genuine desire not only to train ministers, but learned young men.

---

[27] E. Cameron, 'The Late Renaissance and the Unfolding Reformation in Europe', *Humanism and Reform: The Church in Europe, England and Scotland* (Oxford, 1991).

[28] 'Certe accensus sum ego, admodum puer, desiderio discendi et docendi alios de Deo, occasione in speciem exigua, re ipsa autem magna: incidebam enim in doctissimi cuiusdam viri scriptum, ubi in hanc fere sententiam iuventutem hortabatur: Nihil praeclarius, aiebat, quam homines docere...' (*Expositio Symboli Apostolici* [Frankfurt, 1576], preface). The name of the 'certain excellent learned man' would appear to be lost.

[29] 'Loquor cum iuvenibus ut iuvenis: sperans fore, ut quae non parum momenti habuerunt in animo meo, in vestris quoque animis scintillas excitent, quae ardens desiderium, tum discendi, tum docendi ex se generent. Et quidem eo magis, cum non tantum exemplo invitatos, sed etiam opella mea, Deo dante, adiutos vos senseritis' (*Expositio*, preface).

Olevian's Legal Humanism

At age thirteen he entered the college of St Germain, in Trier. At age sixteen (1552) his parents sent him to the University of Paris to study languages.[30] Later that year he moved to Orleans, a hotbed of Protestant sympathies, to begin his legal studies. As a student in three major French universities, he came into contact with the renaissance. As a law student, he came under the influence of French legal humanism.

Though it is well known that Olevian was a law student, it has not been appreciated until recently what that legal training entailed. Basil Hall noted in 1966, however, that when John Calvin's father forced him into the study of the law, these 'were humanist studies'.[31] So too, as a student in Paris, Orleans, and Bourges, Olevian received extensive exposure to the tradition of Guillaume Budé (c.1467-1540).[32]

Legal humanism had its roots in the work of Lorenzo Valla (1406-57) and was continued by Guillame Budé and Andrea Alciato (1492-1550).[33] Born in Paris, Budé studied law, probably from 1483-86, at the Université de Orleans.[34] He was instrumental in the foundation of the *Collegium Trilinguae* (later the College de France) and the Bibliotheque Nationale. At the Université de Bourges and in Orleans, Olevian, like Calvin and Beza before him, studied Budé's two most influential works, the Commentary on the Greek Language (*Commentarii linguae graecae*, 1529) and the elegant *Annotations on the Pandectae in Twenty-Four Books* (*Annotationes in quatuor et viginti Pandectarum libros*, 1508). The *Commentarii* set new standards in the study of Greek as the *Annotationes* did for the study of Latin.[35]

---

[30] *Expositio*, 12.

[31] Hall, 'Jurisconsults', 204.

[32] On Budé see D. O. McNeil, *Guillame Budé and Humanism in the Reign of Francis I* (Geneva, 1975).

[33] Calvin studied with the latter at Bourges.

[34] Rudolf Agricola (1443–85), Johannes Reuchlin (1455–1522) and Erasmus (1466–1536) all taught at the University of Orleans. By papal order (1219) the University of Paris was forbidden to teach the *Corpus Iuris*. Thus Budé had to go to Orleans. The ban was lifted in 1679.

[35] The *Annotationes* was not the end, but rather the beginning of the renaissance of Latin. R. J. W. Evans, *The Making of the Habsburg Monarchy 1550–1700* (Oxford, [reprinted] 1984), 25, says the period 1550–1600 is marked by thirst for education and high quality neo-Ciceronian Latin.

The legal humanists applied the principles of classical humanism to jurisprudence, rejecting the medieval scholastic applications of the Justinian Digest by Accursius (†1260) and Bartholus of Sassoferrato (1314-57), in favour of a text-critical, grammatico-historical approach to the Digest itself.[36] Olevian's education was very similar to Calvin's with the exception that at Orleans and Bourges, he was taught by the famous humanists François Hotman, François Baudoin, Charles DuMoulin and François Le Douaren, who themselves had come under Calvin's influence.[37]

After his university education and brief career at law, Olevian returned to school in Geneva. His theological education there was not, however, a complete break from his humanist training in France.[38] Gillian Lewis has recently noted that Beza's rectoral address 'was a manifesto of an evangelical position' which justified the study of classic authors not 'merely as a prolegomenon to Scriptural philology, but more liberally, in terms of the wisdom it may provide'.[39]

Olevian's interests were, however, overwhelmingly theological and his theology was thoroughly Calvinist. In his preface to his *Expositio* (1576) in which he addressed his students, 'youth zealous of true piety' (*iuventuiti verae pietatis studiosae*), he commended learning to them but more frequently the 'fervent study of the holy Scriptures'.[40] So he was urging them on in their studies not merely for the sake of study, but that they might be of some benefit to the church. There was even a sort of democratic vision of education. He advocated study to the end of teaching both 'young folk, and white headed farmers'.[41] Such instruction might occur 'either in school or in the church'.[42]

---

[36] Hall, 'Jurisconsults', 205–11; McNeil, *Guillame Budé*, 16–22; Q. Breen, *John Calvin: A Study in French Humanism* (Grand Rapids, 1931), 100–145. The *Digesta* was the major part of the Corpus *iuris civilis*. The other two parts are the *Institutio* and *Codex Iustinianus*.

[37] Kelley, *Foundations*, 103–36.

[38] Maag, 'Education and Training', 134–7; Lewis, 'The Academy of Geneva', 41–5; Reid, 'Calvin and the Founding of the Academy of Geneva', *Westminster Theological Journal* 18 (1955), 12–21.

[39] Lewis, 'The Geneva Academy', 40.

[40] '...ardens sacrarum litterarum studium' (*Expositio*, preface).

[41] '...habere ibi in conspectu, non tantum iuvenes, sed etiam agricolas canos' (*Exposito*, preface).

[42] '...vel in Schola, vel Ecclesia' (*Expositio*, preface).

His preparation of future students was realistic. After describing his own training, he spoke frankly of the pecuniary deprivations of participating in the learned ministry:

> Finally, for as much as the ingratitude of the world drives away and frightens many both from learning and teaching, so too, shall not Christ punish the world for this ingratitude? If he remains faithful, ought not this satisfy us? Christ the Lord of heaven and earth will not allow you who serve him to be completely destitute of necessities: but he that provides seed to the flower, he also will provide bread for food.... Let us, we, our wives and our children, in our calling, content ourselves with ordinary things, and surrender our selves to our heavenly Father to be fed through Christ at his hands: for he is the true Father, and will never be unmindful of compassion, and a fatherly care over us....[43]

The studies to which he exhorted his pupils were harnessed to the needs of the Church. Like Luther and Calvin, he was committed to the principle *sola scriptura* and his message was *sola gratia, sola fide.*

The Epistle Dedicatory to *De Substantia* (1585)

Preceding the text of *De substantia* is a dedicatory epistle written by Antoine de La Faye (c.1540-c.1617). This epistle is of interest to us for three reasons. It is likely that the text of *De substantia* arrived at the publisher's shop whilst La Faye was rector of the Academy or shortly thereafter. Olevian's fame and the significance of the book warranted a preface by someone of La Faye's position. It is apparent as well that, in Vignon's estimation, Olevian and La Faye were united by their Calvinist humanism. Second, this epistle is also of interest to us as it provides valuable insights into the intellectual, cultural, and social milieu of the

---

[43] 'Postremo cum ingratitudo mundi multos a discendo & docendo deterreat, agite, an Christus ingratitudinis mundi poenas luet? Su ipse fidelis manet, an non sufficere nobis debet? Non patietur Christus, coeli & terrae Dominus, vos ipsi servientes, rebus necessariis omnino destituti: sed qui suppeditat semen seminanti, is & panem in cibum suppeditabit.... Simus igitur in vocatione contenti mediocribus, & tradamus Patri coelesti per Christum nutriendos nos uxores, & liberos nostros: ipse enim solus vere pater est, & affectus & officii sui paterni nunquam erit immemor, & eo minus immemor...' (*Expositio*, preface).

Wetterau District, in which Olevian studied and ministered. Third, this epistle also provides a good example of the way Calvinist-humanist-Protestants, such as Olevian and La Faye applied their humanism to their students. La Faye fled from France to Geneva in 1561. He was appointed regent of the Academy and made a citizen of Geneva in 1568. In 1570, he was made principal of the Academy. In 1574 and 1575 he pursued medical training in Italy. Widely published over a fifty-year period, he taught philosophy and law in the Genevan Academy and was its ninth Rector (1580-84).[44] He also served as pastor in village churches around Geneva.[45] He assisted as one of Beza's team members at the Colloquy of Montbeliard in the spring of 1585 and was a delegate to the national synod of Montauban in 1594. He was not completely subservient to Beza since he opposed several of Beza's handpicked replacements in his own unsuccessful attempt to replace him as the president of the *Compagnie des Pasteurs*. He did, however, capture the title, *Premier Docteur en Théologie* in 1584.[46] The date of his death is uncertain.[47]

La Faye dedicated *De substantia* to 'the illustrious and noble *Graf* Georg, Lord of Sayn, Junker Count in Wittgenstein and Lord

---

[44] J. Raitt, *The Colloquy*, 73. Haag credited to La Faye 19 books (*La France Protestante, ou Vies des protestants français qui se sont fait un nom dans l'histoire*, 9 vols [Paris, 1846–59], s.v. La Faye, Antoine de). Among them are *Disputatio de verbo Dei* (1591); *Disputatio de traditionibus adversus earum defensores pontificios* (1592); *Disputatio de Christo Mediatore* (1597); *De legitima et falsa sanctorum spirituum adoratione* (1601); *Disputatio de bonis operibus* (1601); *Geneva Liberata* (1603); *Enchiridion theologicum aphorista methodo compositum ex deiputationibus* (1605); *De vera Christi ecclesia* (1606); ὑπομνημάτιον *de vita et obitu clarissimi viri D. Theodori Bezae* (1606); *Emblemata et epigrammata miscellanea selecta ex stromatis peripateticis* (1610). La Faye also wrote commentaries on Romans (1608–09); 1 Timothy (1609) and Ecclesiastes (1609).

[45] Haag, op. cit. P. F. Geisendorf characterised La Faye as 'ambitious', 'scheming', and 'mediocre' (*Theodore de Bèze* [Geneva, 1967], 395–7).

[46] S. Stelling-Michaud, editor, *Le Livre Du Recteur de L'Académie de Genève* (1559–1878), 2 vols (Geneva, 1959), 1.78. It does not appear that La Faye was ever a student in Geneva. Haag, op. cit.; P. F. Geisendorf, *Théodore de Bèze* (Geneva, 1967), 395–7; J. Raitt, *The Colloquy of Montbéliard*, 73.

[47] It is not certain when La Faye was born and Haag says that he died of the plague in 1615, 1616, or perhaps as late as 1618 (Eugene Haag, *La France Protestante*).

in Homburg'.[48] Duke Georg (1565-1631) was the eldest son of Ludwig zu Sayn-Wittgenstein, who initially arranged for Olevian to come to the Wetterau Counties.[49] La Faye also mentioned a certain relative (*cognatus*) to Georg, Graf Philips, a 'Junker Baron in Winneberg and Lord in Beilstein'.[50] This Junker Baron was most probably Philips zu Winneburg-Beilstein (1564-1634). La Faye dedicated the book to them for three reasons. First, both Graf Georg and Graf Philipp were matriculated in the Geneva Academy on 5 October 1581, three months after La Faye became Rector;[51] Second, because both Georg and Philip were Olevian's students at Herborn. Third, because both were, like Ludwig zu Sayn-Wittgenstein, staunch supporters of Olevian's Calvinism in the Wetterau Counties.[52]

From 1568 until the turn of the century, a steady stream of students, noble and commoner travelled from Heidelberg, Neustadt, and the Wetterau to study in Geneva. As early as the 1570s, however, there was a certain cross-pollination as the glory began to fade from the Genevan Academy and students from

---

[48] Epistle Dedicatory, 3. To my knowledge, this is the first analysis of the seven-page Epistle Dedicatory to *De substantia foederis gratuiti inter Deum et electos* (Geneva, 1585).

[49] *Allgemeine Deutsche Biographie auf Veranlassung und mit Unterstützung seiner Majestaat des König von Bayern Maximillian II* (Leipzig, 1875) 24.624–6.

[50] Epistle Dedicatory, 6. See also F. Baron von Freytag Loringhoven, *Europäische Stammtafeln, Stammtafeln zur Geschicte der Europäschen Staaten*, ed., Detlev Schwennicke, vol. 5 (Marburg, 1978), Table 106.

[51] S. Stelling-Michaud, ibid., 1.108.

[52] Counts Georg and Philip were just two of a number of young men who studied in Geneva. Philip Fettius, William When, David Dryander and Christopher Vulteius from the Wetterau district were all studying at the Academy in 1568 (*Le Livre Du Recteur*, 1.98–103). In 1581, there were several other counts, including three from Solms: Philip, John Albert and George Eberhard (ibid., 1.104). In 1576 Counts Ludwig Gulielmus, Johannes, George, and Philipp 'fratres, comites Nassoviae, Cattorum, Vianden et Dietz, domini in Beilstein...' were matriculated in Heidelberg University. This Philip should not be confused with Graf Philipp of Winnenburg-Beilstein who entered Heidelberg University on 19 August 1587, after Olevian's death. See Töpke, *Die Matrikel*, 2.75, nos 8–11; 2.135, no. 142. Henry J. Cohn has characterised these sorts of academic communities as 'pinnacles of Calvinist late humanist achievement' (idem, 'The Territorial Princes in Germany's Second Reformation, 1559–1622', *International Calvinism*, 151).

Geneva moved to Heidelberg to study.[53] H. C. Eric Midelfort explains that as Europe moved toward a rational economy, the Wetterau nobility, under humanist criticism, were forced to defend their inherited social position. The nobles, said their humanist critics, were bestial, the worst Sabbath breakers and blasphemers. In the face of this attack, the nobility established rigorous *Ritterakademien* 'in order to learn to live up to the high standards they had long claimed for themselves'.[54] The counts who moved between Germany and Geneva, however, did not do so to preserve their social position. In fact, given the minority position which they occupied among German nobility generally, they should have availed themselves of Lutheran, instead of Calvinist education and contacts. Against this background one can understand, then, why La Faye commended his former students, not only as 'select nobles' and 'pious auditors'[55] but as those 'uncommonly steeped in piety and doctrine'[56] and possessing those virtues which La Faye and Olevian sought to inculcate in their students: amiable disposition, modesty, sound doctrine, and piety.[57] Most nobles wish by nature to be happy, but 'a true few know the way of blessedness'.[58] In contrast to 'all men' (*omnes homines*), he congratulated the *Grafen* because, they 'in the flower of youth', pursued the knowledge of four languages,[59]

---

[53] Lewis, 'The Geneva Academy', 54-6, 62-3; C. P. Clasen, *The Palatinate in European History 1559-1660* (Oxford, 1963), 39.

[54] H. C. E. Midelfort, 'Curious Georgics: The German Nobility and Their Crisis of Legitimacy in the Late Sixteenth Century', *Germania Illustrata: Essays on Early Modern Germany Presented to Gerald Strauss*, ed., A. C. Fix and S. C. Karant-Nunn (Kirksville, MO, 1992), 239.

[55] '...selectis quibusdam nobilibus & piis auditoribus...' (*Epistola*, 6).

[56] '...pietate et doctrina non vulgarito tincto...' (*Epistola*, 6).

[57] '...amabiles mores, modestia, doctrinam, pietatem...' (*Epistola*, 6).

[58] '...pauci verae foelicitatis viam norunt...' (*Epistola*, 3). La Faye was probably drawing a contrast with passages in Aristotle regarding εὐδαιμονία, e.g. *Ethica Nichomachea*, book I; *Ethica Eudemia*, book I.

[59] Epistola, 3. '...in hoc aetatis flore...linguarum quattuor cognitionem consecutum esse...' (*Epistola*, 6, 7). He probably had in mind Latin, Greek, French and possibly Hebrew. See Göbel, 'Dr. Caspar Olevianus', 302). It is possible that Olevian learned enough Hebrew in Geneva and Zürich to teach it in Heidelberg and Herborn. La Faye, however, probably did not know Hebrew. In his commentary on Ecclesiastes, *In Librum Salomonis qui inscribitur Ecclesiastes, commentarius Antonii Fayii* (Geneva 1610), he made no use of Hebrew. La Faye was not shy about demonstrating his linguistic skills. In his commentaries on Romans, *In D. Pauli Apostoli epistolam ad Romanos* (Geneva,

and despite their noble birth – he regarded it as a moral handicap – they have made progress in philosophy, history and civil law.[60] He treated the counts as representatives of the Calvinist republic of letters when he said, 'and we all praise you, who have renewed these same virtues...'.[61]

As a Protestant humanist, his interests extended, however, beyond moral renewal and good letters. So one ought to note how he qualified Olevian's '*humanitas et fraternitas*' as being '*in Christo*'.[62] His strongest praise for the counts was reserved for their enthusiasm 'for the knowing and worshipping of God'.[63] It was godliness, not letters, which moved him to 'inscribe this epitome of Christian piety' to the counts.[64] For La Faye, as for Beza and Olevian, the way to felicity is to listen to the 'divine voice' (*divina vox*), 'following God's light' rather than 'human decisions'. He feared that most of George and Philip's contemporaries had missed the 'legitimate goal': peace with God.[65]

La Faye warned that the counts should not congratulate themselves because they exist, live, move, have sentience or historical consciousness.[66] These gifts are common to believers and reprobate alike. Complete blessedness consists in drawing near to God.[67] In good Calvinist fashion he argued: 'clearly, the human condition is in many respects deplorable, indeed no less in this respect, that not only our appetite, but the very 'mind of the flesh' is 'at enmity with God''.[68] To rectify the situation is

---

1608) and 1 Timothy, *In divi Pauli Apostoli epistolam priorem ad Timotheum* (Geneva, 1609) he made extensive use of the Greek text. Had he known Hebrew, he probably would have demonstrated it.

[60] *Epistola*, 7.

[61] '...et nos omnes, qui haec ipsa in te novimus, laudamus' (*Epistola*, 6).

[62] *Epistola*, 7.

[63] '...quod Dei cognoscendi et colendi sis valde studiosus'. Piety also consists in reading books such as De substantia (*Epistola*, 7). '...ac sane is in pietate multum profecisse censendus est, cui unice scriptura illa placuerint, quique in iis evoluendis dies noctesque collocat legendo, audiendo, meditando, loquendo, scribendo' (*Epistola*, 5).

[64] *Epistola*, 7.

[65] 'Dei lucem sequentes...hominum decretis' (*Epistola*, 3).

[66] A prominent humanist theme, e.g. of Petrarch (1304–74), is that one's own existence and feelings are the proper subject of celebration (*Epistola*, 3–4).

[67] *Epistola*, 4.

[68] 'Deploranda sane est generis humani conditio multis in rebus, sed nonparum in eo, quod non appetitus solum noster, sed ipsum τῆς σαρκὸς φρόνημα sit ἔχθρα εἰς θεόν, ut ait Apostolus' ([Romans 8:7] *Epistola*, 4).

humanly impossible, nor will it do to blame God for our state. We were not so constituted by God. This enmity is the product of the struggle of earth-loving body against a heaven-directed mind.[69] The image of God has been 'erased in us, painted over by Satan's brush' and it 'retains hardly anything of its primeval beauty'.[70] Sin-induced darkness occupies our minds as a tyrant occupies a citadel, such that, *post lapsum*, we are no more able to see the light, apart from God's grace, than, as that ignorant (*ignarus*) Aristotle said, an owl is able to look at the sun.[71] Our appetites though created good, have been corrupted by sin and deflected toward disorder.[72]

In the resulting moral chaos, however, 'God's righteousness and mercy have shone most brightly' because by his covenant treaty he restrained the rebel and vanquished the vast separation between himself and humanity and threw open the entrance to true happiness. The foundation of the covenant is God's unique mercy exhibited in Christ, whose blood ratified the covenant.[73] This was Olevian's achievement, to have 'firmly and clearly embraced the chief point of sacred doctrine, that is, that covenant

---

[69] 'Nec vero inimicitia illa ex eo proficiscitur, quod terrena corporis mole semper deorsum vergente, et mente coelum versus tendente constemus'. It would seem almost certain that he has in mind neo-Platonism (*Epistola*, 4).

[70] '...obliterata nobis et Satanae penicillo inducta, vix quicquam primaevae illius suae pulchritudinis retineat' (*Epistola*, 4). This is virtually the same image Calvin used in *Institutio* 1.15.4; *OS*, 3.179.8–14.

[71] '...videamus, quam solis noctua lucem intueri potest, ut ipse quoque veri boni ignarus Aristoteles dixit' (*Epistola*, 4–5). The reference ad nocturam (ἡ γλαύξ) is probably to Aristotle, *Metaphysics*, 2.1 (993b10). Thomas commented on this passage in *Summa Theologiae*, 1a,5. See also Aristotle, Περι τα ζωια ιστοριων (*Historia animalium*), *Aristotelis Opera* vol. 1, ed., I. Bekker (Berlin, 1960), 619 b.18–23. Nicolas of Cusa also made a nearly identical remark in *De docta ignorantia*, *Opera Omnia* ed., E. Hoffmann and R. Klibansky, vol.1 (Lippe, 1932), 1.1.14–18.

[72] La Faye also commented on human disorder in his commentary on Ecclesiastes 7.21, *In Liber Salomonis*, 189. Aristotle used ἀταξία routinely. In *Aristotelis Opera*, it occurs in *De partibus animalium*, 641.b.23; *De caelo / Περι ουρανου* 301.a.3, 5; *Physica / Φυσικης* 190.b.15; *Metaphysica / Μετα τα φυσικα* 985.a.1, 1070.b.28; *Politica / Πολιτικων* 1302.b.28, 31. The most likely parallel, however, is in Περι αρετων και κακων 1251.a.22.

[73] 'Dei iustitia clarissime fulsit, et clementia eluxit...beneficium pacto foedere aeternum promisit' (*Epistola*, 5).

(*hoc est foedus illius*), by which God binds to himself all his reconciled elect and blesses them'.[74]

Olevian's Aristotelianism

[handwritten annotation: Aristotelian philosophical commitment- sign of Reformed Scholasticism]

According to Armstrong, 'Aristotelian philosophical commitments' are a defining mark of Reformed scholasticism.[75] Use of or dependence upon Aristotelian language or categories has also been used as an indicator of a certain degree of rationalism. In order to remove Olevian from suspicion of such rationalism, some scholars have made much of Olevian's intellectual debts to the French educational reformer Peter Ramus, arguing that Olevian's Ramism proves that he was an anti-Aristotelian and that he was reacting to harsh, Bezan, metaphysical, predestinarianism.[76] The attempt to pit certain Reformed theologians as rationalist Aristotelians (e.g. Beza) against Ramists (e.g. Olevian) fails in this case, however. In the case of Olevian's *On the Discovery of Dialectic* (*De inventione dialecticae*, 1583), it is impossible to distinguish sharply between his Ramism and Aristotelianism. There is abundant evidence of Aristotle's influence as well as Ramus' in Olevian's thought. For example, in *De inventione*, Olevian made use of all of the categories of Aristotle's *Organon*: Substance, Quantity, Quality, Relation, Place, Time, Posture/Position, State/Condition, Action, and Affection.[77]

---

[74] 'Hic enim paucis, solide et perspicue summum complexus est doctrinae sacrae, hoc est foedus illius, quo Deus sibi reconciliatos electos omnes suos devincit, eosdemque beat' (*Epistola*, 6).

[75] Armstrong, *Calvinism*, 32.

[76] See Jürgen Moltmann, '*Zur Bedeutung des Petrus Ramus für Philosphie und Theologie im Calvinismus*', *Zeitschrift für Kirchengeschicte* 68 (1957), 295–318. See also J. I. Good, *The Heidelberg Catechism in Its Newest Light* (Philadelphia, 1914); J. T. McNeill, *History and Character of Calvinism*, 391. For a refutation of this argument see L. D. Bierma, *German Calvinism in the Confessional Age: The Covenant Theology of Caspar Olevianus* (Grand Rapids, 1996), 162–8. See also idem, 'The Role of Covenant Theology in Early Reformed Orthodoxy', *The Sixteenth Century Journal* 21 (1990), 458–9; W. J. van Asselt, *The Federal Theology of Johannes Cocceius (1603-1669)*, trans. R. A. Blacketer (Leiden, 2001), 75, 330–31; W. J. Ong, *Ramus: Method and the Decay of Dialogue* (Cambridge, MA, 1958).

[77] Aristotle, *The Organon*, 2 vols, trans. Harold P. Cooke (London, 1949), 13–17; See *Aristotelis Opera, Organon, Categoriae*, 2.11ᵃ–4.19ᵇ. L. D. Bierma has recently made this same observation in *German Calvinism in the Confessional Age* (Grand Rapids, 1997), 162–5.

He translated Aristotle's οὐσία with *substantia* and followed the definition of 'being' in the *Organon*.[78]

It is true that he used obviously Ramist charts and his arrangement of the material was nearly identical with book one of Piscator's Ramist *Corrections* (*Animadversiones*).[79] Further, he did use the same bipartite definition of dialectic, *inventio* (discovery) and *iudicium* (arrangement) as the Ramist Piscator and followed Ramus in defining method as *doctrina* or teaching.[80]

Nevertheless, it would be mistaken to conclude too much from these connections. For instance, his definition of *doctrina* was not substantially different from that Melanchthon's.[81] For both, dialectic is the art of teaching clearly and making proper distinctions.[82] Olevian was an Aristotelian whose theology was controlled neither by his Aristotelianism nor by his Ramism, but by his Calvinism.[83]

Throughout *De inventione*, Olevian mixed obviously Aristotelian substance with Ramist presentation. He followed Aristotle by dividing each question into *simplex* and *coniuncta* parts, distinguishing between cause and effect and between

---

[78] Aristotle, *The Organon*, 20–35; Bierma, 'The Covenant Theology of Caspar Olevian', 232. This definition is discussed in detail in chapters 5 and 6.

[79] J. Piscator, *Animadversiones argumentum in dialecticam P. Rami*, 2nd edn (London, 1583); *De inventione*, 168.

[80] *De inventione*, 3, 167–70. W. Ong translates '*iudicium*' in this context as 'arrangement' (idem, *Ramus*, 183–4; see also, 15, 240; *Animadversiones*, 12). See also, idem, *Ramus*, 162.

[81] *CR*, 12.513.

[82] Rudolf Agricola had the same basic pedagogical concern. He 'sought to demonstrate the true function of logic as an element basic to rhetoric which through straight thinking and effective style produces conviction' (Spitz, *The Religious Renaissance*, 28).

It is possible that this Ramist influence on Olevian's rhetoric manifested itself in the way he expressed his theology. He often used bipartite categories. The *duplex beneficium* structure of his theology is the most obvious example. See Caspar Olevian, *In Epistolam d. Pauli apostoli ad Romanos notae* (Geneva, 1579), 128. He often made bipartite distinctions as for example in his definition of justification and sin (idem, *De substantia*, 2.10, 69; idem, *Ad Romanos*, 6–7). The preaching of the gospel itself consists of two parts.

[83] W. R. Godfrey, noting that the Aristotelian Gomarus defended the Ramist Perkins against the Ramist Arminius, says that for many Calvinists '[t]he methodology of Ramism often yielded the same theological conclusions as the methodology of Aristotle' ('Biblical Authority in the Sixteenth and Seventeenth Centuries: A Question of Transition', *Scripture and Truth*, ed., D. A. Carson and J. D. Woodbridge [Grand Rapids, 1983], 235).

substance and accidents. At the same time, under each head he also included 'rules for argument' (*regulae argumentandi*) and the 'light of arguments' (*lumen argumentorum*) and the *usus*, each pedagogical devices supplied by Ramus.

Though Ramus affected Olevian's method of presentation his philosophical language was Aristotelian, as illustrated by his discussion of the nature of substance.[84] 'Substance is being' and being is proper to it.[85] 'Primary and secondary substances are distinguished by Aristotle. He calls 'particulars' primary substances, such as 'this man, that tree'. He calls 'classes' (*species*) and 'kinds' (*genera*) secondary substances'.[86] Such distinctions are necessary, he continued, to understand the nature of being and to avoid both the error of the 'impious Manichaeans' (imagining two gods, one evil and one good) and confounding 'the works of God with the works of the Devil'.[87] Whatever is must be 'either creator or creature' and whatever has been created is good. Sin, on the other hand, is 'not a creature, nor a thing created', but the 'destruction by Satan of the image of God'. Sin is not being but the corruption of being'.[88]

From this definition of *substantia* and the distinction entailed in it, between primary and secondary substances, Olevian concluded that primary substances, being indivisible, were *extra intellectum*. Secondary substances are not, however, and from

---

[84] As part of his explanation he provided an '*ordo substantiarum*' in which he distinguished 'corporea substantia' from 'incorporea'. Under the latter he distinguished 'infinita' (Deus) from 'finita' (angeli, animae). Under 'corporea' he listed a series of bipartite distinctions between simplex and mixta and below the latter he distinguished between 'perfecte' and 'imperfecte'. He continued by making more detailed distinctions under 'perfecte mixta' between animate and inanimate, sentient and non-sentient, rational and irrational substances (*De inventione*, 168).

[85] 'Substantia est ens, quod proprium esse habet' (*De inventione*, 167).

[86] 'Differunt primae substantiae et secundae substantiae apud Aristotelem. Primas substantias vocat individua, ut hunc hominem, hanc arborem. Secundas substantias vocat species et genera' (*De inventione*, 167).

[87] 'In hunc finem discernendum est ENS a non Ente, ne aut cum impiis Manichaeis duos creatores fingamus, bonum & malum, aut ne confundamus opera Dei cum operibus Diaboli' (*De inventione*, 168).

[88] 'Quicquid enim esse habet est aut creator aut creatura: & creaturae sunt res bonae Genes. 1.... Peccatum quod accessit non est creatura, seu res creata, sed destructio imaginis Dei & corruptio a Sathana & hominis voluntate inducta: non Ens, but corruptio Entis' (*De inventione*, 168).

them one can discern, according to God's eternal will, God's existence.[89]

Similarly, he used the substance/accidents distinction, as an occasion for teaching theology. If one prudently distinguishes substance from accidents, one will distinguish between the promised and eternal indwelling of the Holy Spirit and Aristotle's 'good motion' (*bonus motus*). Thus Christ promised to us the Paraclete, not 'good motions of the heart or consolation'– that would be confusing effect for cause – as much as the author of them himself. When Scripture says the same about angels, it speaks not about 'good motions', but about 'good spiritual subsistences, i.e. Christ'. Thus the 'insanity' of the Sadducees is apparent, who imagined angels to be the good movements of the heart.[90]

From these examples, one may fairly conclude that Olevian was a critical, Christian reader of Aristotle. The question is whether these categories, as Olevian used them, were mainly formal or whether they also entailed beliefs about the nature of the created order and God, i.e. what were Olevian's relations to Aristotelian metaphysics? The answer to that question depends upon how one defines the word metaphysics. Considered broadly the term is a synonym for 'natural theology' but used more narrowly it refers to ontology.[91] Olevian was indebted to

Metaphysics

---

[89] 'Etsi autem secundae substantiae extra intellectum nihil sint: tamen utile est videre seriem in hac tota universitate rerum, quam intellectu seu mente circumferentis discernimus Deum a rebus creatis, a quibus in aeternum discerni vult' (*De inventione*, 169, art.3; 170, art.4).

[90] 'Inter Entia etiam ipsa prudenter discernendae substantiae ab accidentibus, ut cum Christus promittit, se nobis Paracletum missurum, qui in nobis sit, & maneat nobiscum in aeternum, non promittit tantum bonos motus cordis seu consolatione, sed ipsum authorem, omnis consolationis fontem, nempe causam cum effectu. Item cum Scriptura loquitur de Angelis, non loquitur de bonis motibus, sed spiritibus bonis subsistentibus. Christus.... Hic apparet insania Saducaeorum, qui angelos fingebant esse bonos motus cordis' (*De inventione*, 169, Art. 2). See R. A. Muller, *Dictionary of Latin and Greek Terms* (Grand Rapids, 1985), s.v. '*motus*'.

[91] There is a long history of using the term metaphysics to mean the study of transcendent final causes or natural theology. See the *Oxford English Dictionary* (Oxford, 1971), s.v. 'Metaphysic'. See also F. Copleston, *A History of Philosophy*, 9 vols (New York, 1962), 1.20); J. Barnes, 'Metaphysics', *The Cambridge Companion to Aristotle*, ed., J. Barnes (Cambridge, 1995), 66. Some, however, treat metaphysics as though it refers to pure ontology only. See M. V.

Aristotelian metaphysics only in the latter, narrow sense of the term. Thus Olevian regarded the categories as more than just linguistic conventions; rather, he thought that the categories describe accurately the world as God has created it.[92] The way Olevian used the categories to advance his theology is more important, however, than the mere fact that he relied on them. For example, in the case of the substance/accidents distinction, he argued that Christ, through his Spirit, is the substance who moves us. That is, Christ and the Spirit form the substance of the covenant as distinguished from Christian consolation which is the effect of justification.

Nevertheless, Olevian's epistemology was not Aristotelian. He did not begin with Aristotle's categories as a fundamental starting point and then move to Scripture. Rather, having begun with Scripture and the Christian faith summarised in the creeds, he found use for the Aristotelian categories to express his theology. For Olevian, without the light of the Word of God, Aristotle was unable to interpret properly his own observations.

Thus, the meaning which Olevian attached to the substance/accidents distinction was quite within the tradition of Christian Aristotelianism. He recognised that Aristotelian philosophical language had been transformed by Christian theological and ecclesiastical usage. He understood that the Church seized the Aristotelian term οὐσία, translated it with *essentia* and used it to explain the doctrine of the Trinity.[93] He understood that Aristotle did not intend to teach the doctrine of the Trinity, but the Church has found Aristotelian language flexible enough to bear Christian usage.[94] He used Aristotle's language of 'being' not to consider being in itself, but to consider how it testifies to the Creator. In the same manner, he argued that sin is a moral (the corruption of creation), not ontological (the

---

Wedin, *The Cambridge Dictionary of Philosophy*, ed., R. Audi (Cambridge, 1995), s.v. 'Aristotle'.

[92] There is also uncertainty concerning whether his logical categories are to be regarded 'as ontological or as purely linguistic' (C. Lejewski, s.v. 'Logic, History of', *Encyclopedia of Philosophy*, ed., P. Edwards, 8 vols (New York, 1967).

[93] *De inventione*, 170, art. 5.

[94] J. Owens makes this same point in regard to Thomas' use of Aristotle. See idem, 'Aristotle and Aquinas', *The Cambridge Companion to Aquinas*, ed., N. Kretzmann and E. Stump (Cambridge, 1993), 46.

Sin moral (corruption of creation) not problem, an ontological

lack of being), problem, and as a catholic Trinitarian Calvinist rejected Aristotle's doctrine of God.

Olevian's Scholasticism

Caspar Olevian has never been described as a Protestant scholastic. Indeed, he has been used in both the nineteenth (by Heppe) and twentieth centuries (by J. Moltmann) as a buffer to Calvin's predestinarian dogmatism. He has also been distinguished by Barth from the Protestant scholastics as an heir of Calvin's gracious, covenant theology.[95] More recently, Olevian has been used as a foil to Ursinus' scholastic villain.[96] This perception of Olevian as an anti-scholastic theologian exists for two reasons. First, because the definition of scholasticism has been too narrow and second because he has been read selectively and too narrowly as only a covenant theologian.

In this context, it is useful to read Antoine de La Faye's clever defence of the necessity of the system of the *disputatio* as a means of propagating and preserving the truth. His defence of the scholastic method is relevant to the present study for two reasons. First, it is contemporary with Olevian's tenure in Herborn, and provides a unique insight into the workings of the Reformed academy in the late sixteenth century. Second, it is a reasonable assumption that La Faye speaks for Olevian (and others like him)

---

[95] K. Barth, *Church Dogmatics*, 4/1 ed., G. W. Bromiley and T. F. Torrance, trans. G. W. Bromiley, (Edinburgh, 1956), 58–9; O. Gründler, 'Thomism and Calvinism in the Theology of Girolamo Zanchi' (Th.D. Diss., Princeton Theological Seminary, 1961); idem, 'From Seed to Fruition: Calvin's Notion of the *semen fidei* and Its Aftermath in Reformed Orthodoxy', *Probing the Reformed Tradition*, 109; B. G. Armstrong, *Calvinism and the Amyraut Heresy* (Madison, 1969); J. S. Bray, *Theodore Beza's Doctrine of Predestination* (Nieuwkoop, 1975); W. Klempa, 'The Concept of the Covenant in Sixteenth and Seventeenth-Century Continental and British Reformed Theology', *Major Themes in the Reformed Tradition* ed., D. K. McKim (Grand Rapids, 1992), 98.

[96] See R. W. A. Letham, 'Saving Faith and Assurance in Reformed Theology: Zwingli to the Synod of Dort', 2 vols (Ph.D. Thesis, University of Aberdeen, 1979); idem, 'The *Foedus Operum*: Some Factors Accounting For Its Development', *The Sixteenth Century Journal* 14 (1983), 457–67; D. A. Weir, *The Origins of the Federal Theology in Sixteenth Century Reformation Thought* (Oxford, 1990); C. S. McCoy and J. W. Baker, *Fountainhead of Federalism: Heinrich Bullinger and the Covenantal Tradition* (Louisville, 1991); G. M. Thomas, *The Extent of the Atonement: A Dilemma for Reformed Theology from Calvin to the Consensus* (Carlisle, 1997), 114 .

since the Genevan academy was Olevian's theological college and he deliberately patterned the Herborn Academy on the Genevan model. As a result, the *curricula* of the two academies were virtually identical.

The *Theological Theses Proposed and Disputed in the Genevan Academy Under Theodore Beza and Anthony La Faye* (*Theses theologicae in schola Genevensi sub Theodoro Beza et Antonio Fayo propositae et disputae*, Geneva, 1586) contain an impressive example of Reformed pedagogical sophistication.[97] La Faye said,

> It has long been the complaint of very many, that those, whom they call the Schoolmen and Disputers, have given the study of the holy Scriptures, not only a great injury, but even a death wound. And therefore it may seem wonderful to some, that the custom of disputing divine matters is retained in these Churches and Schools, which are reformed according to the pure word of God....[98]

In this passage, La Faye began to confront the fundamental questions surrounding the adoption by Reformed theology in this period of the scholastic method of theology. Can theology be scholastic and biblical or are the two naturally antithetical?[99] Is it not true, in the nature of the case, that by disputing matters of

---

[97] *Theses theologicae in schola Genevensi ab aliquot sacrarum literarum studiosis sub DD. theol. Beza & Antonio Fayo S.S. theologiae professoribus propositae & disputatae. In quibus methodica locorum communium S.S. theologiae epitome continetur* (Geneva, 1586). Translated and published in English as *Propositions and Principles of Divinitie propounded and disputed in the universitie of Geneva, by certaine students of Divinitie there, vnder M. Theod. Beza, and M. Anthonie Faius, professors of Divinitie* (Edinburgh, 1591). La Faye wrote the epistle dedicatory for the *Theses Theologicae* in June 1586, just nine months after writing the preface to *De substantia*.

[98] *Propositions*, ii. 'Queruntur iam diu non pauci, sacrarum literarum studiis labem maximam & velut interitum allatum esse ab iis, qui Scholastici & Disputatores sunt appellati. Mirum ergo fortasse videbitur alicui, cur in Ecclesiis & scholis ex puro Dei verbo restitutis, de rebus divinis disputandi consuetudo retineatur' (*Epistola*, 1).

[99] J. H. Alsted (1588–1638) and Johannes Maccovius (1578–1644), for example, deliberately distinguished their scholasticism from medieval scholasticism. See Richard Muller, *Post-Reformation Reformed Dogmatics*, 2 vols (Grand Rapids, 1987), 1.81. On Maccovius see M. I. Klauber, 'The Use of Philosophy in the Theology of Johannes Maccovius (1578-1644)', *Calvin Theological Journal* 30 (1995), 376–91.

sacred doctrine one places them in the realm of philosophy thus thereby making them less than certain?

La Faye conceded that the medieval scholastics, using some of the very same theological and pedagogical methods, did corrupt theology. '[I]n the very first beginning of the Church there was a very sore blow given to religion, by those who being swollen up by the pride of human arguments, would rather submit Christ unto their judgements, than themselves unto his majesty'.[100] Too often the Schoolmen have consumed 'the moisture and life of piety, so that there remained nothing for them, but the dry and withered bark...'.[101] Scholasticism *per se*, however, does not necessarily lead to rationalism or bad theology. La Faye's plan for preserving orthodoxy from whatever dangers are associated with scholasticism was based on a sharp distinction between that which belongs to Pythagoras and that which has been spoken by 'Jehovah by his Prophets and Apostles in his word written...'.[102] The blame for the association of the disputation with the corruption of the gospel lies not with the disputation itself, but rather with the medieval theologians who confused opinion and revelation.[103] Because they were 'over diligent (which is not to be commended)' it does not follow that 'therefore careful diligence should be disliked'.[104]

He gave four reasons why the disputation system ought to be used by reformed theological students. 1) Because divinity consists of holy things, care is required. 2) The writings of Scripture are full of sharp disputations (especially the Pauline

---

[100] *Propositions*, iii. 'Nec vero negandum est, ipsis Ecclesiae primis temporibus non vulgarem plagam illatam esse religioni, ab iis qui typho ratiocinationum humanarum turgentes, Christum sibi, quam se Christo subiicere malverunt' (*Epistola*, 2).

[101] *Propositions*, iv. '...correpta & apprehensa vitalem pietatis succum exhausit & absumpsit, arido tabenteque remanente cortice' (*Epistola*, 3).

[102] *Propositions*, ii. '...sed Iehova per Prophetas & Apostolos suos in verbo suo per ipsos scriptos' (*Epistola*, 1).

[103] La Faye's contemporaries (e.g. Polanus) as well as later Reformed theology (e.g. Alsted and Turretin) would describe this as a confusion between *theologia ectypa* and *theologia viatorum*. See R. A, Muller, *Dictionary of Latin and Greek Theological Terms* (Grand Rapids, 1985), s.v. *theologia ectypa*; idem, *Post-Reformation*, 1.126-36.

[104] *Propositions*, v. *Epistola*, 'Nec enim si illi nimium diligentes fuerunt, (quod in laude ponendum non est) solers idcirco diligentia viturperanda est' (*Epistola*, 3-4).

epistles). The only way biblical disputations can be discussed is by the 'use of reasoning'. 3) Our Lord himself disputed with 'Doctors, Pharisees, Sadducees, & c.' as Paul disputed with 'the Jews, with the Philosophers, with the brethren'. 4) The Fathers also disputed, e.g. Irenaeus against the 'Gnostics', Tertullian against the Marcionites, Athanasius against the 'Arians' and Nazianzen, Cyril, Theodoret, Hilary, Augustine and many others, 'almost against innumerable heresies...'.[105]

His list shows that he was aware that by using and defending the *disputatio* he and the Academy might be identified with the medieval schoolmen and therefore he was at pains to cast himself and his students as heirs of the patristic polemical tradition. It was not the method, but its subversion which was the problem. He proposed a three-step remedy for the disease which ailed the medieval scholastic system. Disputations become profitable, when 'nothing else is considered in them but...': 1) the ways of the Lord which are mercy and truth; 2) deceit, subtlety, self-love and desire of victory is removed; 3) the desire of the truth, the love and reverence of God's majesty joined with modesty and singleness is used therein.[106] In effect, he was arguing that the medievals abused the disputation because they lacked sanctification.

In his mind, the Reformed disputation system was envisioned as a gathering for fraternal, theological, and moral correction.[107] All Christian teachers have a responsibility to 'frame and fashion their scholars' so that they

> timely season them with the juice of these virtues in such sort, as when afterwards they shall come abroad from their private studies, to any public calling, they may perpetually retain those virtues.[108]

Though it was a mild exaggeration to equate the more informal biblical disputes (e.g. Jesus and the Pharisees) with the classroom

---

[105] *Propositions*, v. *Epistola*, 4.

[106] *Propositions*, v, vi. *Epistola*, 4.

[107] Melanchthon made a similar argument in *De coniunctione scholarum cum ecclesiis, CR*, 11.613. See P. Fraenkel, *Testimonia Patrum. The Function of the Patristic Argument in the Theology of Philip Melanchthon* (Geneva, 1961), 144.

[108] *Propositions*, vi. 'Sic ergo suos discipulos fingere & formare Christiani omnes doctores debent, ut eos mature in scholis harum virtutum succo sic imbuant, ut postea, cum ex umbra in aciem veniendum erit, tota vita eundem retineant ac conservent' (*Epistola*, 5).

Objective truths of the Christian faith summarized by the articles of the Apostles' Creed

disputatio, La Faye's defence of the use of the scholastic method in the Calvinist academy shows that he was aware of the increasing need for doctrinal and apologetic precision required by the changing ecclesiastical and political circumstances in which the academy existed.[109]

Olevian on Substance and God

Olevian's debt to the standard Aristotelian logical categories was signalled in the title of one his major works, *On the Substance of the Covenant of Grace Between God and the Elect* (*De substantia foederis gratuiti inter Deum et electos*, 1585). By 'substance of the covenant' Olevian meant the objective truths of the Christian religion summarised by the articles of the Apostles' Creed.[110] If, however, there is a substance, that without which Christianity is not, there are also accidents, things not of the essence of the Christian religion. This basic Aristotelian distinction was implied throughout his survey of federal theology.[111]

Olevian's associations with Protestant scholasticism are also evident in his doctrine of God. In fact, a comparison of Olevian with Ursinus and Polanus on the doctrine of God shows that though there were noticeable rhetorical differences between Ursinus' *Compendium of Christian Doctrine* (*Compendium Christianae doctrinae*, 1584) and Olevian's creedal commentaries, the substance of their doctrines of God was virtually identical. For example, in the *Compendium*, Ursinus gave an exposition, followed by a series of proofs, then a statement of objection and finally a refutation of those objections. This was the method of the disputation and Melanchthon's *Common Places* (*Loci*

---

[109] Among the disputants were Jacobus Arminius (*Theses Theologiae*, 147) and the Remonstrant Johannes Uutenbogaert (ibid. 64, 117). Among La Faye's later students were two sons of Daniel Tossanus, and Ludwig, Olevian's son. *Enchiridion Theologicum Aphoristica Methodo Compositum ex disputationibus* (Geneva, 1605).

[110] *De substantia*, 1.1.2, 13; 2.1.

[111] Peter Martyr Vermigli used these exact same categories in a similar way in his explanation of the relations between the old and new covenants. Whatever differences exist between the old and new covenants are accidental, not substantial. 'In summa quicquid est discriminis inter utrunque Testamentum, totum id non in substantia foederis, verum in accidentibus versatur: Nam antiquitus foederis caput summum erat, Deum verum fore nobis vere Deum' (idem, *Loci communes* [London, 1583], 2.27.16).

communes).[112] Though Olevian did not follow this pattern consistently in his creedal commentaries, he made significant use of exactly this scholastic pattern of discourse in his biblical commentaries. As has already been shown, all one may conclude from the formal differences, where they occur, is that sometimes Olevian found it more advantageous to lecture discursively, and, at other times, he lectured in the moral formally academic style.

In his three commentaries on the Apostles' Creed, *Vester Grund* (1567), *Expositio symbolici apostolici* (1576) and *D e substantia* (1585), after establishing the theme for which his exposition of the creed was a vehicle, he moved directly to his doctrine of God. In comparison, Amandus Polanus (1561-1610), in his *Theological Distinctions* (*Partitiones Theologicae*, 1590), began with revelation and then moved to the doctrine of God, the divine attributes and the persons and works of the Trinity.[113] His prolegomena was headed *de fide*, which he used synonymously with 'the knowledge of God' (*cognitionis Dei*) and outlined the relations of faith to revelation, the parts of Scripture (two, on faith and good works).[114] The knowledge of God is in two parts, first regarding the divine essence and attributes, second, regarding his works.[115]

This was quite like the pattern which Olevian followed in *De substantia* and the *Expositio*. In the latter, he addressed matters preparatory to the Creed: the nature of Christ's kingdom (*regnum*), faith (*fides*), and the covenant (*foedus*). The eleventh heading, 'Description of God' (*Descriptio Dei*), resembled Polanus' and Ursinus' summary of the divine attributes. It is noteworthy, given the anti-scholastic use to which Olevian has been put, that he placed his discussion of providence and his

---

[112] Zacharias Ursinus, *Doctrinae Christianae Compendium* (Geneva, 1584). The *Compendium* was translated by H. Parrie as *The Summe of Christian Doctrine* (Oxford, 1587). For a detailed discussion of the various editions of Ursinus' *Compendium* see J. E. Platt, *Reformed Thought and Protestant Scholasticism* (Leiden, 1982), 49-56. For a detailed discussion of his methodological debt to Melanchthon see Platt, ibid., 51-9.

[113] Amandus Polanus, *Partitiones theologicae iuxta naturalis methodi leges conformatae duobus libris, quorum primus est de fide: alter de bonis operibus* (London, 1591).

[114] *Partitiones*, 1.1.

[115] 'Cognitionis Dei seu fidei de Deo duae sunt partes, prima de essentia Dei, secunda de operibus ipsius. Essentia Dei, est natura Dei, per quam Deus revera est & subsistit' (*Partitiones*, 1.1).

description of the divine nature not under Christology, but after his partition of the Creed and before his exposition of the article 'I Believe in God the Father' and his discussion of the Trinity. He said,

> God is a spiritual essence, eternal, good, pure, of an incomprehensible glory, wisdom, infinite power, immutable justice, ineffable mercy, unchangeable truth, in short, the highest good: and he is the eternal Father, the Son, the coeternal image of the Father and the Holy Spirit proceeding from both.[116]

Compare Olevian's *descriptio* with Question 42 from Ursinus' *Summa*:

Who is God?

> God is one spiritual essence, intelligent, eternal, infinite, distinct from all creatures, true, righteous, pure, merciful, beneficent, free, the source and cause of all things, immense with respect to power and wisdom, angry with sin, that is, eternal Father, who begat from eternity the Son his image and Son, the image of the co-eternal Father, and Holy Spirit proceeding from the Father and the Son, as the Divinity was revealed in the sure Word and divine testimonies, that the eternal Father with the Son and Holy Spirit created, conserved and govern heaven and earth and all creatures by his providence, in humanity in general, he gathers to himself an eternal Church for the sake of his Son and for himself, and he will judge the just and the unjust.[117]

---

[116] 'Deus est essentia spiritualis, aeterna, bona, pura, incomprehensibilis tum gloriae, tum sapientiae, infinitae potentiae, immutabilis iustitiae, ineffabilis misericordiae, veritatis constantissimae, denique solum & summum bonum: & est Pater aeternus, Filius imago Patris coaeterna & Spiritus sanctus ab utroque procedens' (*Expositio*, 19).

[117] Q.42 Quis est Deus? Est essentia unica spiritualis; intelligens, aeterna, infinita, alia a creaturis omnibus, verax, bona, iusta, casta, misericors, benefica, liberrima, fons & causa bonorum omnium, immensae potentiae & sapientiae, irascens peccatis quae est pater aeternus, qui Filum imaginem suam ab aeterno genuit, & Filius, imago Patris coaeterna, & Spiritus sanctus procedens a Patre & Filio, sicut patefacta est Divinitas certo verbo & testimoniis divinis, quod Pater aeternus cum Filio & Spiritu sancto creaverit conservet & gubernet sua providentia coelum & terram & omnes creaturas & in genere humano sibi colligat aeternam Ecclesiam propter Filium & per eum, & sit iudex iustorum &

The verbal similarities are striking. Like Ursinus, Olevian gave a standard, if brief, list of the divine attributes. From these attributes, he moved to the divine persons and from them to revelation and salvation.

He began with the attributes because he assumed the primacy of Scripture, in which, he believed, God reveals himself as having these attributes and treated them as corollaries to the divine persons. That is, it is as true of God that he is incomprehensible as it is that he is Father, Son and Spirit. The order and structure of Olevian's *descriptio* suggests a reciprocity between the divine persons and the divine attributes. To say that God is merciful or just necessarily entails the triune God. Because, for Olevian and Ursinus, there is no other God than the triune God incarnate in Jesus Christ, to answer the question, 'who is God' meant to discuss the nature of God proper, the Trinity, as a prelude to addressing the incarnation. Therefore, framed and grounded as it was by divine self-revelation, the *descriptio* cannot be fairly described as speculative. Further, one concludes that Olevian regarded it as quite natural to begin teaching the doctrine of God by beginning with the attributes as a precursor to his more developed discussion of the Trinity and Christology. That is, if one is to teach that Christ is God, and from that affirm the Trinity, one must have a clear idea of what the word God means.

It should also be noticed that near the end of his description of the divine nature, Ursinus spoke of divine providence generally, thence he moved to God's 'gathering' (*colligat*) of his elect. This was the traditional way of considering the relations between the decrees of providence and election. The latter was considered special and the former general (*in genere*). That Ursinus related the decrees this way is not surprising. That Olevian did the same thing might be. In his 'first use or fruit' (*primus usus sive fructus*) of the doctrine of divine providence, Olevian argued that the God who redeems us is the same God who created and sustains us.[118] Part of the Father's universal government includes the gathering of the church 'by the voice of

---

iniustorum (Zacharias Ursinus, *Opera Theologica*, 3 vols, ed. Q. Reuter [Heidelberg, 1612], 1, 14).

[118] '...certo statuet quotidie mane & vesperi non minorem potentiam in conservatione & gubernatione rerum omnium Deum exerere, quam in prima creatione' (*Expositio*, 59).

the Gospel' (*voce Euangelii*) and 'the internal voice of the Son' (*interna voce filii*).[119] Therefore, the *foedus* is a source of comfort for the elect only because the God who made the *foedus* is omnipotent and his electing power and decree are but subsets of his universal 'power' (*potentia*) over all things.[120] Indeed, the Christian must understand that suffering is the product of divine providence and one of the 'benefits of God' (*Dei beneficia*) and resign himself to the divine wisdom.[121]

If the dominant scholarly descriptions of Ursinus and Olevian were accurate, one should hardly expect such theological identity between them.[122] After all, Ursinus and Olevian taught their doctrines of God in the context of two distinct genres: Olevian, following his usual method, proceeding through the heads of doctrine in the Creed and Ursinus following his usual method of proposition, analysis, objection and refutation. After all, neither the Heidelberg Catechism (which was itself commenting on the Creed) nor the Apostles' Creed itself require this sort of exposition of this head of doctrine, yet both scholars, writing in different genres, were compelled so to describe God. Why? Olevian defended the 'utility' (*utilitas*) of his description of God:

> The use of this description is this: that we might know the nature of God and by true faith embrace him as our one and only highest good, and that we should fear to offend him and honour him so that by true faith and fear or repentance he might be glorified by us.[123]

---

[119] *Expositio*, 59.

[120] 'Credo me habere foedus cum Deo omnipotente, qui & omnipotentia sua omnia quae vult in toto mundo efficiat, & quaecunque non vult sive non decrevit, impediat' (*Expositio*, 48).

[121] *Expositio*, 61.

[122] For a survey of recent scholarship on Ursinus see J. R. Beeke and R. S. Clark, 'Ursinus, Oxford and the Westminster Divines'. *The Westminster Confession into the 21st Century: Essays in Remembrance of the 350th Anniversary of the Publication of the Westminster Confession of Faith*, 3 vols, ed. J. L. Duncan (Fearn, Ross-shire, 2004), 2.1–32.

[123] 'Usus descriptionis huius est, ut cognita Dei natura, vera fide ipsum amplectamur ut unicum et summum nostrum bonum, eumque offendere metuamus: quo vera fide et timore seu resipiscentia a nobis glorificetur' (Olevian, *Expositio*, 20).

He believed that Christians must know and embrace certain truths about God in order to believe in him savingly.[124] There were certain propositions about the divine nature, which, with the western theological tradition, he accepted as properly belonging to the conception of God. He regarded the *descriptio* as a fitting means of propagating Protestant truth and argued that it is only when one knows who God is that one can appreciate the magnitude of his grace in condescending to promise 'by an everlasting covenant that he will be a God unto us'.[125]

He resorted to a *descriptio Dei* for other reasons as well. First, following the pattern of *inventio* and *iudicium*, he harvested the results of his biblical exegesis in a systematic order, under the headings of the creed, in order to present a coherent and compelling account of the Christian faith to his students in Heidelberg and Herborn. The second reason was internal to Olevian's doctrine of God. His trinitarian doctrine of God was foundational to the rest of his theology. For example, his predestinarian soteriology was premised on divine immutability and his explanation of providence was premised on his belief in divine goodness. Therefore, in order to teach those doctrines, he had first to establish his doctrine of God.

Considering the western theological tradition, Olevian had two likely answers to the problem of divine sovereignty and evil. The first was the Augustinian, neo-Platonist turn to ontology by considering evil the absence of being and the second being an Aristotelian turn to a series of causalities. He chose the latter. As we have already seen, Olevian believed divine providence to be omnipotent relative to all things created, controlling good and evil. Obviously, he had to face the question of God's relations to evil ('*An igitur Deus autor peccati?*').[126] The only way he could

---

[124] 'Est autem Dei natura immutabilis, quamobrem certo ea a nobis auseret, modo credamus. Haec Dei natura, lucet in facie Christi: cum dicit: Confide filii, reittuntur tibi peccatua tua' (*Expositio*, 25).

[125] 'Primum enim dum audimus Deum, qui promisit foedere sempiterno se fore nobis in Deum, esse intelligentem, sapientem, aeternum, bonum, iustum, misericordem et c. rectissime inde concludimus, ex formula nimirum foederis gratuiti: eum non modo natura sua talem esse, verum etiam nobis credentibus talem se exhibere velle, & quidem foedere sempiterno, etsi ominis creaturae diversum suadere videantur. Qui naturam hanc Dei cognovit, a quo in foedus receptus est: is amplam habet ei fidendi materiam, & ex fide viatam suam secundum Dei voluntatem instituendi' (*Expositio*, 20).

[126] *Expositio*, 51–3.

avoid making God directly liable for evil was to suggest some distance between God and evil by calling attention to the agents or secondary causes of evil. Thus, on the question of the relations between providence and sin Olevian's theodicy did not take immediate refuge in paradox but argued that God is properly free from sin. Not God, he said, but the devil (*Diabolus*) put malice into Adam's heart. Sin belongs properly to him and to corrupted humans. It is true, he conceded, that God uses sin, but his intention is distinct from that of the devil. The devil instigates sin but God uses the instrument of sin 'to his own glory' (*ad suam gloriam*).[127] This line of argumentation is identical to that used by Ursinus in his *Compendium Doctrinae* on *Heidelberg Catechism* Question 27. Both theologians supported their arguments by appealing to many of the same biblical passages.[128]

Olevian was educated in French universities not primarily as a theologian, but as a Calvinist humanist. He was treated as a learned man by his colleagues in the Calvinist Republic of Letters. His education put him in the company of influential counts and princes whom he served as tutor and pastor. He valued learning and spent his life as a teacher and as an educational reformer. As an undergraduate he learned basic humanist techniques for reading texts in their original languages. Later he put those same skills to use as a Calvinist theologian.

His Aristotelianism was subordinated to and interpreted by his Christianity. By thus placing Aristotle within a Christian framework, Olevian re-interpreted the categories in ways that served his theological and pedagogical interests.

Thus, Caspar Olevian was a part of the scholastic development of Reformed orthodoxy in the late sixteenth century. He synthesised humanism and scholasticism producing a *tertium quid*: a transitional stage in Reformed orthodoxy between the earlier stages of Protestant theology and the more highly developed dogmatic theology of the seventeenth century.

---

[127] Olevian, *Expositio*, 51–3.

[128] Olevian cited and argued from Genesis 50:30, 1 Samuel 16:11, 1 Kings 2:8, 36, 44, and 2 Samuel 19:19. This appeal to causalities was virtually the uniform Calvinist scholastic approach to the problem of evil.

CHAPTER 4

OLEVIAN'S TRINITARIAN DOCTRINE OF GOD

Since Johannes Cocceius (1603-69) laid claim to the heritage of Caspar Olevian's covenant or federal theology, the interpretation of Olevian's theology has been inextricably bound to larger issues.[1] Whether in the interests of Heppe's ecumenism or Barth's neo-orthodoxy, Olevian has been interpreted almost solely as a covenant theologian, but this view needs to be challenged. In fact, Olevian was as much a theologian of the Trinity as he was a federal or covenant theologian. Indeed, he was a federal theologian because he was a trinitarian theologian. In his mind, to exposit the Trinity, or the ancient trinitarian creeds, was to teach the doctrine of the covenant, since the covenant is nothing more than a way of describing the relations which obtain between the triune God and his people.

Olevian wrote his theology in a pedagogical, controversial, and creedal context. His use of the doctrine of the Trinity allowed him to accomplish several things simultaneously: the education of youth in catholic truth; the demonstration of the catholic orthodoxy of Reformed theology; and a theological justification of Calvin's structural revision of Protestant theology.

In March 1576, looking back over 15 years of controversial ministry in Heidelberg, Olevian wrote to the Elector Frederick of the 'storm which in many places is agitated against this Church'.[2]

---

[1] 'Exemplum huius disquisitionis alii quoque viri docti praebuerunt: imprimis laudatissimae memoriae vir, Gaspar Olevianus' (J. Cocceius, *Summa doctrina de foedere et testamento Dei* in *Opera theologica*, 8 vols [Amsterdam, 1673], 6:4).

[2] '...adversus tempestatem illam quae multis in locis adversus hanc Ecclesiam excitatur' (Caspar Olevian, *Expositio symbolic apostolici* [Frankfurt,

Many are in tumult, as if horrendous doctrine is preached in the congregation of the Church, and rumours of such are spread far and wide. One might say that a sea of insults is vomited forth against us.[3]

The broadest circle of Olevian's difficulties was his participation in the Protestant struggle to define himself as an orthodox catholic and yet repudiate the Roman claim to primacy. Within that circle, however, there were other equally intense struggles. To his right, he argued with the gnesio-Lutherans over numerous theological *loci*. To his left, he was engaged in ecclesiological arguments with Zwinglian Erastians.[4]

This latter controversy became strangely connected with another and potentially more damaging controversy when some of the Zwinglian party became associated with the growing anti-trinitarian movement as it moved into the Palatinate.[5] That he found himself at odds with anti-trinitarians was nothing new. Virtually from the moment Calvin arrived in Geneva, he battled against radicals such as Peter Caroli (1537), Miguel Servetus (1545-53), as well as the Italian anti-Nicenes, and Polish unitarians (1550s-60s).[6] The problem did not disappear with

---

1576 repr. 1584], *Epistola*, 3).

[3] 'Tumultuantur multi, quasi horrenda doctrina sonet in coetu huius ecclesiae, illique; rumores longe lateque sparguntur. Dictat aliquis, mare convitiorum in nos...' (*Expositio, Epistola*, 4).

[4] Gnesio is derived from the Greek adjective γνήσιος, i.e. genuine.

[5] H. Alting, *Historia ecclesii Palatinae* (Amsterdam, 1646) 205-12.

[6] *Defensio orthodoxae fidei de sacra Trinitate contra prodigiosos errores Michaelis Serveti* (1554), *Corpus Reformatorum*, ed. C. G. Bretschneider, 101 vols (Halle, 1834-1959), 36.453-453-644 (hereafter *CR*); *Responsum ad quaestiones Georgii Blandratae* (1558), *CR*, 37.321-32; *Responsum ad fratres Polonos, quomodo mediator sit Christus, ad refutandum Stancaro errorem* (1560), *CR*, 37.333-42; *Ministrorum ecclesiae Genevensis responsio ad nobiles Polonos et Franciscum Stancarum Mantuanum de controversia mediatoris* (1561), *CR*, 37.345-58; *Brevis admonitio Ioannis Calvini ad fratres Polonos, ne triplicem in Deo essentiam pro tribus personis imaginando, tres sibi deos fabricent* (1563), *CR*, 37.629-38; *Epistola Ioannis Calvini qua fidem admonitionis ab eo nuper editae apud Polonos confirmat* (1563), *CR*, 37.641-50. See B. B. Warfield, 'Calvin's Doctrine of the Trinity', *The Princeton Theological Review* 7 (1909), 553-652, repr. in *Calvin and Calvinism* (New York, 1931). The latter edition is used here. See also Philip W. Butin, *Revelation, Redemption and Response. Calvin's Trinitarian Understanding of the Divine-Human Relationship* (New York, 1995), 29-38; Antonio Rotondò, *Calvin and the Italian Anti-Trinitarians*, trans. John and Anne Tedeschi (St Louis, 1968), 11-28; J. N. Tylenda, 'The Controversy on

Calvin's death in 1564, but only intensified, thus increasing pressure on Calvinist Protestants to distinguish themselves from the heretics.[7]

Geneva was not alone. By the summer of 1570, several of the Zwinglian theologians who had sided with Erastus in the discipline controversy were advocating what appeared to the Heidelberg Calvinists to be a form of Arianism.[8] Adam Neuser, Johann Sylvan, with Matthias Vehe, Jacob Suter, and Johann Hasler (all part of Erastus' circle of anti-disciplinarian dissent) stood accused of heresy. Though it seems unlikely that he was ever really anti-trinitarian, Erastus himself was excommunicated for five years on account of his association with the radicals until he was able to demonstrate that he was not a heretic.

The presence of anti-trinitarianism in Heidelberg presented special problems for Frederick III. Because the Calvinists denied the sharing of properties (*communicatio idiomatum*) as defined by the Lutherans, and thus the ubiquity of Christ's humanity and his local-physical presence in the eucharist, they were subject to charges of rationalism by the gnesio-Lutherans. If they were rationalists on the eucharist, the argument went, then perhaps they were also secretly anti-trinitarian? Frederick's position within the Empire was precarious enough without having to answer charges of tolerating heresy against catholic doctrine. For example, Adam Neuser fled to Turkey, became alcoholic, dabbled in the occult, died there of dysentery (in 1576) and was cremated. His actions allowed Lutheran critics to charge that Calvinism leads to Islamic fatalism and provided Frederick's critics with even more ammunition.[9] The conflict became so intense that the

---

Christ the Mediator: Calvin's Second Reply to Stancaro', *Calvin Theological Journal* 8 (1973), 131–57.

[7]   Rotondò, *Italian Anti-Trinitarians*, 2–10.

[8]   J. I. Good represents the traditional interpretation of the Heidelberg Antitrinitarians (idem, *The Origin of the Reformed Church in Germany* [Reading, PA, 1887], 221–5). This interpretation has been challenged by C. J. Burchill, *Bibliotheca Bibliographica Aureliana: Bibliotheca Dissidentium: Répertoire des Non-Conformistes Religieux de Seizième et Dix-Septième Siècles*, ed. A. Seguenny, I. Backus, J. Rott, vol. 11 *The Heidelberg Antitrinitarians: Johann Sylvan, Adam Neuser, Matthias Vehe, Jacob Suter, Johann Hasler* (Baden-Baden, 1989). See also idem, 'Aristotle and the Trinity: The Case of Johann Hasler in Strasbourg 1574–1575', *Archiv für Reformationsgeschichte* 79 (1988), 282–310.

[9]   Burchill, *Antitrinitarians*, 110–11.

Emperor Maximilian II was forced to convene the Imperial Reichstag in 1570 to address the Unitarian heresy. The affair ended unhappily. One of the anti-trinitarians, Sylvan, was arrested for 'defaming the Elector'. Heidelberg's civil judges favoured corporal not capital punishment for heretics. The theologians, however, including Olevian, argued persuasively for the latter.[10] On 23 December 1572, Frederick ordered Sylvan beheaded in the marketplace near the Church of the Holy Spirit.[11] In the light of his conflicts with some of his former Zwinglian allies, his Lutheran critics, and most importantly, the anti-trinitarian radicals, it is easier to see Olevian's immediate political and rhetorical need to demonstrate his continuity with Luther's Reformation and a genuine trinitarian catholicity.

The Sources of Olevian's Trinitarianism

Like most sixteenth-century authors, Olevian cited his sources or influences only when it was to his rhetorical advantage. Even then, one finds only occasional references to Athanasius and Augustine or Tertullian.[12] Additionally, his personal library has never been discovered and he had access to the University library in Heidelberg for 15 years. Therefore, it is difficult to know exactly all the literary sources of his trinitarianism. Nevertheless, it is possible to make some informed guesses about some of his immediate sources.

His use of the doctrine of the Trinity was, in fact, the continuation of a trend which began in the 1520s during Zwingli's Christological and eucharistic disputes with Luther. The trend continued into the 1550s with Calvin's *Institutio* and Melanchthon's final revision of his *Loci Communes*.

Olevian had two connections with Zwingli. The first was indirect. Inasmuch as Zwingli was the first major Protestant

---

[10] On 2 December 1572 Olevian wrote to Beza of his agreement with the punishment of Sylvan. *Correspondance de Théodore de Bèze*, vol. 13 (Geneva, 1988), 225–7, no. 958.

[11] Burchill says that Sylvan was executed even though he recanted in jail and convinced Zanchi of his orthodoxy on the Trinity (*Antitrinitarians*, 99, 100).

[12] He cited Augustine most often. He cited Athanasius as an authority in support of his Christology (*De substantia*, 2.104) and referred once to Tertullian's *De resurrectione carnis* (ca. 207). See Caspar Olevian, *In epistolam D. Pauli apostoli ad Galatas notae* (Geneva, 1578), 90.

alternative to Luther's Christology, and given that Olevian spent his entire adult life in controversy with Lutherans on Christology (and the eucharist) and was regarded by Lutherans as another 'sacramentarian', it seems nearly impossible that he would have been unaware of at least the general outlines of Zwingli's doctrine of God.[13] Second and more directly, he studied briefly in Zürich where he had a firsthand introduction to Zwinglianism via Bullinger. He also later solicited the support of the Zürichers for his reform programme in Heidelberg.

For Zwingli, to speak of Father, Son or Holy Spirit was to 'speak of all three'.[14] Against Luther's doctrine of the *communicatio idiomatum*, Zwingli argued that the Creed says 'he ascended' (*ascendit*). For him, the idea of Christ's human ubiquity constituted a denial of the local ascension. If consubstantiation is true, then Pentecost was superfluous. It is the Spirit who quickens, draws to Christ, assures of salvation, and applies salvation to sinners. It is he who writes the law on our hearts.[15]

Melanchthon was another likely source for Olevian's trinitarianism. Olevian's relations to Melanchthon have been disputed since Heppe first claimed that Olevian was part of a Melanchthonian reaction to predestinarian Calvinism. At issue has always been whether Olevian was influenced by Melanchthon's apparent move to synergism. Some Calvinist scholars have denied any connection between Olevian and Melanchthon. Both positions are, however, overstated. It is reasonable to think that Olevian was influenced not only by Melanchthon's rhetoric but also in part by the structure of his theology, particularly as it developed in the 1540s and 1550s. There is however no evidence that he was influenced by Melanchthon's developing doctrine regarding the freedom of the will (*de libero arbitrio*), at least as measured by Melanchthon's writings in the later editions of the *Loci communes* (1533 *et seq.*).

In 1559 Olevian was using Melanchthon's *Dialectices* as a textbook so one is certain that he was familiar with the 'Teacher of Germany' (*Praeceptor Germaniae*). There are several other

---

[13] 'Sacramentarian' was a pejorative Lutheran reference to the Zwinglian etymological definition of the eucharist as an 'oath' or 'pledge' by the believer to God rather than the *locus* of Christ's physical presence by virtue of his ubiquity.

[14] W. P. Stephens, *The Theology of Huldrych Zwingli* (Oxford, 1984), 80.

[15] Stephens, *Huldrych Zwingli*, 129–32.

reasons to suppose that he was aware of, and used the *Loci Communes*. They were, after all, the Systematic Theology for Protestants from 1521 until the publication of the first edition of Calvin's *Institutio* in 1536. Even after the *Loci* faced competition they hardly retired from the field. Because they were in constant demand, Melanchthon revised them until his death in 1560.[16] Certainly, among Lutherans, with Luther's strong approval, they carried enormous authority. It is a fact that during his Heidelberg period Olevian spent much time interacting with Lutheran criticisms of the Calvinist Christology, soteriology and sacramental theology and it is unlikely he could have taught formerly Lutheran students without having read the *Loci communes*.

In the first edition of the *Loci* Melanchthon determined to make a radical break with the traditional form of the medieval systematics. He refused to begin with the doctrine of God and the Trinity. In his Epistle Dedicatory, he listed the usual order of theology but said that some of these, such as the Trinity, are better adored than investigated.[17] Instead, like Luther, eschewing all speculation, he began with law and gospel.

The most outstanding difference between the first edition of the *Loci* and those which followed is that the later editions begin not with predestination, sin and grace, but with the very topics he once labelled 'things incomprehensible' (*incomprehensibiles*) namely, the doctrine of God and the Trinity.[18] There are several explanations for Melanchthon's reorganisation of the *Loci*. First, from 1521 he developed a growing appreciation of patristic theology, in large part out of Luther's need for a Patristic precedent for his eucharistic theology.[19] Second, like most

---

[16] Chemnitz lectured on the *Loci Communes* for 30 years from 1553. See Martin Chemnitz, *Loci theologici*, trans. J. A. O. Preus, 2 vols (St Louis, 1989), 13–16.

[17] 'In his ut non licet per humanam imbecillitatem quosdam assequi ita rursum sunt quidam quos repuderit plane universum vulgus christianum tenere. Mysteria divinitatis rectius adoraverimus quam investigaverimus' (P. Melanchthon, *Loci theologici*, CR, 21.13–23 and *Loci communes* [1521 edn], CR, 21.84, 'Mysteria divinitatis rectius adoraverimus, quam investigaverimus').

[18] *CR*, 21.84

[19] On Melanchthon's use of the Fathers see P. Fraenkel, *Testimonia Patrum: The Function of the Patristic Argument in the Theology of Philip Melanchthon* (Geneva, 1961) and E. P. Meijering, *Melanchthon and Patristic*

theologians he discovered that theology is more than soteriology. It is well to teach justification *sola gratia, sola fide*, but by whom? God, of course, but who is he? Obviously, such central questions cannot long go unanswered. Third, like Calvin and Olevian after him, Melanchthon, from 1529, faced anti-trinitarian radicalism and was forced to develop a more thorough doctrine of God and the Trinity in response.[20]

The 1533 revision began with the heading 'Concerning God' (*de Deo*) and contained nearly nineteen columns on the divine unity, the three persons, the Holy Spirit, creation and the problem of evil.[21] Now his treatment of the doctrine of the Trinity was one of the most extensive and was the longest part of his doctrine of God. This trinitarian emphasis did not mark a departure – for Luther was unquestionably a trinitarian theologian – but an area of advance or development.[22] Luther's Christology and eucharistic theology forced him to focus on the Son and it does not appear that he really integrated the doctrine of the Trinity into theology. Whilst his treatment of it was sincere, it did not structure his theology the way it would Olevian's.[23]

Calvin's trinitarianism has often been discounted in the scholarly literature. B. B. Warfield noted that since F. C. Baur,

---

Thought: The Doctrines of Christ, Grace, the Trinity and the Creation (Leiden, 1983).

[20] M. Rogness, *Philip Melanchthon: Prophet Without Honor* (Minneapolis, 1969), 75–81.

[21] *CR*, 21.255–74. The 1543 edition is translated in *Loci Communes*, trans. J. A. O. Preus (St Louis, 1992), hereafter, Preus. The 1555 edition is translated in *Melanchthon on Christian Doctrine. Loci Communes 1555*. trans. and ed. C. L. Manschreck (Oxford, 1965). See chapters 1–3.

[22] Luther's theology of the Trinity does not appear to have developed during his life. See G. Rupp, *The Righteousness of God: Luther Studies* (London, 1953), 88. Althaus' survey of Luther's theology spent only two pages on Luther's doctrine of the Trinity. See idem, *The Theology of Martin Luther*, trans. R. C. Schultz (Philadelphia, 1966), 199–200. B. de Margerie characterises Luther's theology of the Trinity as a reaction to Scotus and notes his reluctance to discuss the interior relations of the trinitarian persons (*The Christian Trinity in History*, trans. E. J. Fortman [Still River, MA, 1982], 199–204). K. Hagen, however, claims that 'the Trinity is implicit and explicit in all of Luther's theology'. See K. Hagen, 'Did Peter Err? The Text is the Best Judge', *Augustine, The Harvest, and Theology (1300–1650)*, ed. K. Hagen (Leiden, 1990), 124.

[23] *De servo*, however, shows a well-developed and thoughtful doctrine of God. His defence of divine impassability and immutability was a central part of his criticism of Erasmus.

Calvin's interest in the doctrine of the Trinity has been portrayed as 'remote and purely traditional' because he was thought to have followed Melanchthon in subordinating the doctrine of the Trinity to the doctrine of justification.[24] Baur was correct to notice the relative absence of the doctrine of the Trinity from Melanchthon's early theology. He pursued the question improperly, however, by failing to observe Melanchthon's theological development and the growing prominence of the doctrine of the Trinity in Protestant theology from 1525.

There are several pertinent observations to be made about Calvin's trinitarianism. First, he was thoroughly committed to and defended vigorously the catholic creeds and language of the church, but not only because it was such, but because it was biblical.[25]

Second, he emphasised the Trinity in its external operations, that is, the economic Trinity or the distinct roles which each of the divine persons played in the history of redemption.[26] For example, in the 1559 *Institutio*, most of 1.13 was devoted to his defence of Christ's Deity. For Calvin, the anti-trinitarians were not only attacking catholic Christianity as an institution and tradition, but salvation itself.[27] His emphasis on external trinitarian operations was partly in reaction to perceived fruitless medieval speculations. He acknowledged that those 'who intemperately delight in speculations will not be at all satisfied' with his account.[28] He rebuked Lombard for pursuing (in *Sententiae*, 1.9) the question of eternal generation.[29] The dispute, he argued, dissolves (*liquet*) when one considers that 'from eternity three persons have subsisted in God'.[30] Thus, in his

---

[24] B. B. Warfield, 'Trinity', 195. J. Thompson has repeated Baur's view. See idem, *Modern Trinitarian Perspectives* (Oxford, 1994), 81.

[25] Warfield, 'Trinity', 206–11. See *Institutio Christianae Religionis 1559*, 1.13.5; *Joannis Calvini Opera Selecta*, ed. P. Barth and W. Niesel, 3rd edn 5 vols (Munich, 1963–74), 3.113–6 (hereafter, *OS*).

[26] Butin, *Revelation*, 39.

[27] *Institutio*, 1.13.8–13, 19, 21–7; *OS*, 3.118–27, 132–3, 135–48.

[28] *Institutio*, 1.13.29. 'Nam quos oblectat speculandi intemperies, minime placandos suscipio'; *OS*, 3.151.12–4.

[29] Though Calvin did not cite it, he was apparently referring to chapter 4. See Peter Lombard, *Sententiae in IV Libris Distinctae*, 3rd edn (Rome, 1971), 1.9.4.

[30] '...ab aeterno tres in Deo personas substitisse' (*Institutio*, 1.13.29; *OS*, 3.151.19–20).

doctrine of the Trinity, as elsewhere, his focus was on God's ordained power and revealed will.

Nevertheless, in at least one section (1.13.25), he engaged in a fairly nuanced discussion of intra-trinitarian relations. God is 'essentially one'.[31] The Spirit and Son are essentially 'unbegotten' (*ingenitus*). At the time the Father is first in order and the 'beginning and source of divinity' (*principium et fons divinitatis*), the distinction being personal, not essential.[32] Deity, considered absolutely, exists of itself.[33] So the Son may be said to exist 'of himself' (*ex se ipso*) considering his Deity and not his person. Considering his Sonship, he is 'of the Father' (*ex patre*), but not so that the Father is 'deifier' (*deificator*) of the Son and Spirit.

Third, Calvin's trinitarianism was integral to his conception of God, his nature, revelation and redemption.[34] It was impossible for him to think of God without thinking of the trinitarian persons and them in unity.[35]

Fourth, Calvin's trinitarianism was structural, i.e. it influenced strongly the structure and organisation of his theology. From 1536, he progressively integrated the doctrine of the Trinity into his theology and reciprocally the doctrine increasingly influenced his theology. The prominence of the Trinity can be marked simply by observing the development of his *Institutio*. The 1536 edition was arranged in two parts, on Lutheran lines. The first chapter exposited the law and chapters two through five exposited the gospel. The Creed occupied only one of those chapters.[36] On the whole, the first edition of the *Institutio* was quite similar to Melanchthon's 1521 *Loci Communes*.

As a result of his controversy with Caroli, he developed greatly his doctrine of the Trinity in the second edition. From 1539 the formal structure of his theology was threefold: Book One deals mainly with the Father, and our guilt before the law; Book Two deals mainly with God's grace to sinners in Christ so that the

---

[31] '...unum essentialiter Deum esse' (*Institutio*, 1.13.25; *OS*, 3.145.14).

[32] *Institutio*, 1.13.25; *OS*, 3.145.16.

[33] 'Deitatem ergo absolute ex se ipsa esse dicimus' (*Institutio*, 1.13.25; *OS*, 3.146.6).

[34] Butin, *Revelation*, passim, has also noticed this phenomenon.

[35] *Institutio*, 1.13.17; *OS*, 3.131.2–7.

[36] See Jean-Daniel Benoît, 'The History and Development of the *Institutio*: How Calvin Worked', *John Calvin*, ed. G. Duffield (Grand Rapids, 1966).

[handwritten annotation: Calvin: Subsequent to justification, the Spirit infuses elect w/ grace of sanctification]

basic law/gospel structure of the earlier edition remains. Books Three and Four focus on the Holy Spirit's work in uniting sinners to Christ and sanctifying them in the church through the means of grace. By 1559, he expanded his discussion to nearly six times its original size.[37] Additionally, the final edition of the *Institutio* was divided into four books, and fully one half of it was controlled by his theology of God the Spirit, which is fundamentally a trinitarian move.[38]

Fifth, through Calvin's trinitarianism, he retained the Lutheran law/gospel dichotomy in justification while answering the central methodological question: If justification is not the result of sanctification what should one do with the doctrine of sanctification? After the first edition of the *Institutio*, he made sanctification the place for Christian gratitude in response to the forensic, objective event of justification and the product of one's mystical union (*unio mystica*) with Christ through the Holy Spirit.[39] Where the medieval soteriology (both the *Via Antiqua* and *Via Moderna*, for different reasons) thought of infused grace (*gratia infusa*) as the means to final justification, Calvin made it the office of God the Spirit to infuse the elect, subsequent to justification, with the grace of sanctification.

In his scheme, the decalogue, summarised in the golden rule, is the norm of the Christian life as the structure of the grateful response to imputed justice (*iustitia imputata*). It is not as if this

---

[37] Warfield, 'Trinity', 219–23.

[38] *Pace* Dowey, who treats the structure of the *Institutes* more as an impediment to their interpretation than as a guide (*The Knowledge of God in Calvin's Theology*, New York, 1952, 41).

[39] See *Institutio* 3.1.1; *OS*, 4.1–2. Both W. Elert and G. Ebeling denied that Luther taught the *tertius usus legis*. G. Ebeling notes that it was Melanchthon who first used the terms *usus legis* and that Luther did not use the terminology (W. Elert, 'The Third Use of the Law', *Lutheran World Review* 1 [1949] 38–48; G. Ebeling, 'On the Doctrine of the *Triplex Usus Legis* in the Theology of the Reformation', *Word and Faith*, trans. J. W. Leitch [London, 1963]). Nevertheless, it seems to me that Luther taught the substance of the *tertius usus legis*, particularly in the Larger Catechism. In order to distinguish Luther from Calvin, Elert particularly was forced to caricature Calvin's theology of law and gospel. For a superior account of Calvin's use of the law see I. J. Hesselink, *Calvin's Concept of the Law* (Allison Park, PA, 1992), ch. 5, and M. S. Johnson, 'Calvin's Handling of the Third Use of the Law and its Problems', *Calviniana: Ideas and Influence of Jean Calvin*, ed. R. V. Schnucker (Kirksville, MO, 1988). See also B. A. Gerrish, 'John Calvin on Luther', *Interpreters of Luther*, ed. J. Pelikan (Philadelphia, 1968).

were a novelty. This was a basic Protestant instinct. Luther turned to the normative aspect and regulating function of the law in the Christian life when confronted with antinomianism. Melanchthon taught the importance of Spirit-infused sanctification under the head 'Concerning good works' (*de bonis operibus*) and five sub-heads, as the proper response to grace.[40] Martin Chemnitz (1522-86) and the *Formula of Concord* followed him.[41] In short, Calvin only formalised what already existed in principle in the Protestant re-arrangement of justification to sanctification. Why did he and not the Lutherans take this developmental-structural step? The most satisfactory explanation is that his soteriology was the product of a more highly developed and theologically integrated doctrine of the Trinity.[42] A good illustration of this integration is the fact that he did not simply repeat catholic doctrine in response to the anti-trinitarians, but also defended various aspects of his soteriology. Against the Polish anti-trinitarians, he defended Christ's mediatorial office and work precisely because Christ's saving work and ongoing priestly intercession is contingent upon his consubstantiality with the Father and the Spirit and upon his eternal filiation.

Calvin's name does not often appear in Olevian's writings. Nevertheless, each of Olevian's three commentaries on the Creed reveals significant similarity to Calvin's treatment of the Trinity in the *Institutio*. This was no coincidence. It must be remembered that Olevian was Calvin's student and he lectured, in three terms, through Calvin's *Institutio* at Herborn and published his own *Epitome* of the *Institutio* in 1586.[43] The *Epitome* was designed as an aid for his students to enable them to read Calvin more easily. He eliminated from his lectures Calvin's dated polemics, which might distract the reader from the master's positive theological

---

[40] 1. Quae opera sint facienda. 2. Quomodo fieri possint. 3. Quomodo placeant. 4. Cur facienda sint. 5. Quod sit discrimen peccatorum, cum necesse sit fateri, quod in hac vita maneant peccata in Sanctis (*Loci Theologici* (1543) *locus* 9. *CR*, 21.762–800).

[41] *Loci theologici*, loci 8–9. *Formula of Concord*, *Solid Declaration*, 6.

[42] See A. Ganoczy, 'Observations on Calvin's Trinitarian Doctrine of Grace', trans. K. Crim, *Probing the Reformed Tradition: Historical Studies in Honor of Edward A. Dowey, Jr*, ed. E. A. McKee and B. G. Armstrong (Louisville, 1989).

[43] Caspar Olevian, *Institutionis Christianae Religionis Epitome. Ex institutione Johannis Calvini excerpta, authoris methodo et verbis retentis* (Herborn, 1587).

point. It was, as Oliver Fatio notes, a rather successful 'scissors and paste' affair.[44] The *Epitome* reminds us that the *Institutes* functioned at Herborn as Lombard's *Sententiae* did in the Middle Ages and as Melanchthon's *Loci* in the Lutheran academies.[45] It became a primary text on which Calvin's students commented. In these circumstances one may be certain that the content of the *Institutes* coloured Olevian's pedagogy including his theology of the Trinity.

The Creedal Context

Given his reputation as an early federal theologian, one might be surprised to find that Olevian cast his theology as nothing more than an exposition of the Apostles' Creed. In fact, he wrote three distinct commentaries on the Creed in his programme to show that his Calvinism was nothing more than a recovery of the ancient Christian faith.

Is this a new faith?

It is the old, true, undoubted Christian faith that the apostles confessed and preached. And this short confession of faith is a reliable guide for recognizing and judging whether something is orthodox or not. For whatever is contrary to one or more of the Articles of Faith must be false. If one simply sticks to the Articles of Faith, one cannot go wrong.[46]

---

[44] 'Avec des ciseau et de la colle, Olevianus a ingenieusement composé son *Epitome* qui se lit, il faut le dire, agréablement' (O. Fatio, 'Présence de Calvin à l'époque de l'órthodoxie reformée. Les abregés de Calvin à la fin du 16e et au 17e Siècle', *Calvinus Ecclesiae Doctor*, ed. W. Neuser [Kampen, 1978], 191). This writer is grateful to Daniel and Frederique Lackner (Pembroke College, Oxford) for their assistance with this essay. See also B. B. Warfield, 'On the Literary History of Calvin's *Institutes*', *Calvin and Calvinism* (New York, 1931) and John Platt, *Reformed Thought and Scholasticism. The Arguments for the Existence of God in Dutch Theology, 1575-1650* (Leiden, 1982), 35-6. Olevian's *Epitome* was soon replaced in popularity by his son-in-law Piscator's *Aphorisimi Christianae Doctrinae* (Herborn, 1594). Piscator's relations and reaction to Olevian's theology is an area which requires further study.

[45] Fatio, 'Presence', 197.

[46] Caspar Olevianus, *Firm Foundation. An Aid to Interpreting the Heidelberg Catechism*, trans. and ed. Lyle. D. Bierma (Grand Rapids, 1995), 12. 'Is diß ein newer Glaub? Es ist der alte / mahre / ungezweisselte / Christliche

If one is to be faithful to the Apostle's teaching in Romans 12, any interpretation of Scripture must be 'according to the analogy of faith' (*secundum analogiam fidei*). No interpretation must contradict the foundation or any article of the faith.[47]

Though it was typical for Protestants to discuss the Creed under the heading 'gospel', few linked their message so explicitly to the Creed. To confess the Creed was no formal rite, but a source of gospel comfort. To say 'I believe' is to trust God's providence and to remember Christ's passion.[48] The question arises: why did he write so many commentaries on this one Creed? It is not obvious why the Apostles' Creed, and not the Nicene (perhaps the most important of the catholic trinitarian Creeds) would be the most useful vehicle to facilitate his move to an explicitly trinitarian structure for his theology. After all, the latter contained no 'he descended into hell' (*descendit ad inferna*) which Reformed Christology found so troubling.[49] The Chalcedonian definition would have been a more suitable vehicle for carrying on controversy with his Lutheran opponents.

There are several explanations for this phenomenon. First, there was an established tradition of using the Creed this way. Second, it is rhetorically simpler than the Nicene and more comprehensive than the Chalcedonian Definition or the Athanasian Creed. Third, unlike the others the Creed was not clearly linked with any controversy (e.g. there was no *filioque* controversy attached to it) and thus served as a more universal vehicle for the exposition of Calvinism as a catholic faith. Fourth, though it is clear that Olevian did not regard it as actually written by the Apostles, it retained an aura of apostolic authority.[50]

Glaub / den die Aposteln bekant und geprediget haben. Und ist dise turke bekkanntnis des Glaubens / ein gewisse richtschnur / darben man erkennen und urtheilen sol / welche lehr vot Gott / ob sie recht sen oder nicht. Dann was einem oder mehr Artiklein des Glaubens zu wider ist / muß salch senn / Bund wenn man einsältig ben den Artiklein des Glaubens bleibt / so kan man nicht irz gehen' (Caspar Olevian, *Vester Grund* [Herborn, 1590], repr. in *Der Gnadenbund Gottes 1590* ed. G. Franz, J. F. G. Goeters, W. Holtmann [Bonn, 1994], 13).

[47] 'Ne igitur fides a voluntate Dei aberret, danda erit opera, ut quemadmodum ad Rom 12 praecipit Apostolus, omnis prophetia sive interpretatio scripturae sit secundum analogiam fidei: ne interpretatio pugnet cum fundamento, aut ullo articulo fidei' (*Expositio*, 15).

[48] *Firm Foundation*, Q. 15. *Vester Grund*, 13–14.

[49] Also sometimes 'descendit ad infernos', e.g. *De substantia*, 1.5.1.

[50] 'Iam vero cum articuli fidei, summum contineant doctrinae a Rege

Finally, it was also useful because the bulk of the Creed focussed on the second person of the Trinity, his incarnation and redemptive work. This Creedal emphasis allowed Olevian to propound his gospel and refute his opponents simultaneously. Olevian's creedal commentaries belonged to an established literary genre. By the time Rufinus (c.345-410) wrote his *Commentarius in symbolum Apostolorum* (c.404) 'the literary genre to which Rufinus' essay belonged was familiar to his contemporaries. He remarked in his opening paragraphs that he had 'forerunners in the same field'.[51] His commentary continued to be published, often under Jerome's name, into the Middle Ages.[52] Ambrose (c.339-97) published his *Explanation of the Creed for Beginners* (*Explanatio symboli ad initiandos*)[53] and Augustine published a collection of sermons as *On the Faith and the Creed in One Book* (*De fide et symbolo liber unus*) in 393.[54] Lombard's *Sententiae* (1148-58) were structured on the Creed.[55] In the late medieval period both Alexander of Hales (c.1186-1245) and Bonaventure (c.1217-74) wrote on the Creed. Aquinas preached a series of sermons which he published in 1273 as *Sermons on 'I Believe in God'* (*Collationes credo in Deum*).[56] Following Alexander of Hale's commentary on Lombard's *Sententiae*, the attention of medieval theologians (e.g. Duns Scotus and Ockham) moved away from the Creed as such toward commentaries on the *Sententiae* and their own *Quodlibeta*.

Christo Apostolis traditae...' (*Expositio*, 2). The Belgic Confession (1561), Art. 9, refers ambiguously to the 'three creeds, namely, that of the Apostles, of Nice and of Athanasius' ('les trois symboles, celui des Apôtres...'. See Philip Schaff, ed., *The Creeds of Christendom*, 3 vols, 6th edn (Grand Rapids, 1983), 3.393.

[51] Rufinus, *A Commentary on the Apostles' Creed by Rufinus*, trans. J. N. D. Kelly (London, 1955), 9, 10; J. N. D. Kelly, *Early Christian Creeds*, 2nd edn (London, 1960).

[52] Schaff, *Creeds of Christendom*, 1.14–23.

[53] J. P. Migne, ed., *Patrologia Latina*, 221 vols (Paris, 1844-66), 17.1155–60 (hereafter MPL).

[54] MPL, 40.181–96.

[55] Book one is on the Trinity; book two on creation and sin; book three on the incarnation and the virtues; book four on the sacraments and last things.

[56] Thomas Aquinas, *The Sermon Conferences of St. Thomas Aquinas on the Apostles' Creed*, trans. N. Ayo (Notre Dame, IN, 1988). See *De articulis fidei et ecclesiae sacramentalis, S. Thomae Aquino, Opera Omnia*, Leonine edn, vol. 42 (Rome, 1979).

Protestants, anxious to demonstrate as clearly as possible the catholicity of their faith, seized on the Creed as an apologetic vehicle. Such commentaries were a way of introducing their views and demonstrating continuity with the apostolic faith. That there was but one holy apostolic faith was a notion held universally by Protestants in the sixteenth century and, for them, it was a matter of mustering the appropriate sources to show their continuity with this faith.[57]

Urbanus Rhegius' *Die Zwölff artikel unsers christliche glaubens* (1523) and Zwingli's *Exposition of the Articles* (*Expositio articulis*, 1523), Explanation of the Faith (*Fidei Ratio*, 1530) and his *Exposition of the Faith* (*Expositio fidei*, 1531) marked the beginning of sixteenth-century interest in and polemical use of the Creed.[58] Luther's treatment of the Creed is found in both the Larger and Smaller (1529) Catechisms. Erasmus' 1524 *Investigation Concerning the Faith* (*Inquisitio de fide*) and 1533 *Clear and Pious Explanation of the Apostles'* Creed (*Dilucida e t pia explanatio symboli quod Apostolorum*) consolidated the new attention to the Creed.[59]

Protestants, of course, were not the only ones casting their faith in Creedal terms. Johann Gropper published a pre-Tridentine *Enchiridion* (1536).[60] In 1566 the Tridentine catechism was published in which the first third (*pars prima*) was devoted to

---

[57] J. Pelikan, *Historical Theology: Continuity and Change in Christian Doctrine* (London, 1971), 38–9, 42–3.

[58] Urbanus Rhegius, *Die Zwölff artikel unsers christliche Glaubens...* (1523), translated as, *A Declararation* [sic] *of the Twelue Articles of the Christen Faythe* (London, 1548). H. Zwingli, *Christianae fidei a Huldrico Zuinglio praedicatae brevis et clara expositio...* (Zürich, 1536) is in M. Schuler and J. Schultess, eds, *Huldrici Zuinglii opera completa editio*, 8 vols (Zürich, 1828/9–42), 4.42–78. *Expositio articulis* and *Fidei ratio* are in *Huldreich Zwinglis sämtliche Werke*, ed. E. Egli *et al.* (Berlin et al. 1905–). The *Fidei ratio* is also in H. A. Niemeyer, ed., *Collectio confessionum in Ecclesiis reformatis publicorum* (Leipzig, 1840). The last edition was used in this essay.

[59] *Erasmus: Inquisitio d e fide*, ed. C. R. Thompson (New Haven, 1950). *Dilucida et pia explanatio...* in *Opera Omnia Desiderii Erasmi Rotterdami* 5–1, ed. J. N. Bakhuizen van den Brink (Oxford, 1977). The English translation of the *Explanatio* was published as *A Playne and Godly Exposition or Declaration of the Commune Crede* (London, c.1533). A. von Harnack attributed to Luther the genesis of the sixteenth-century interest in the Creed (idem, *The Apostles' Creed*, trans. S. Means (London, 1901).

[60] H. Jedin, *A History of the Council of Trent*, trans. E. Graf, 2 vols (St Louis, 1957), 406.

a defence of the Roman interpretation of the Creed.[61] In the same year Joannes Hessels, professor of theology in Louvain, published his *Brief and Catholic Explication of the Apostles' Creed* (*Brevis et catholica symboli apostolici explicatio*, 1562) and four years later Bishop Jean du Tillet published a French commentary. The Jesuit 'apostle to Germany', Peter Canisius (1521-97), whose *Summa doctrinae Christianae* (1555) became one of the most significant catechisms defending the Roman faith as it was steadily revised, expanded, translated and republished over the next three decades, exposited the Creed in the first chapter.[62]

Olevian took an active part in the Reformed response to Rome. As early as 1561 he had told Beza that he intended to defend Calvinism against the 'German papists' by writing his own articles on the Lord's Prayer and the Apostles' Creed.[63] In the preface to his *Expositio*, he wrote that he hoped this 'simple and plain declaration of the grounds of our religion' might serve as a 'testimony of doctrine' by which God might 'oppose' (*opponere*) and 'curb' (*reprimere*) the critics of the Palatinate church.[64] 'Gentlemen, why are you so upset?' asked Olevian,

> Consider each of the articles of our Christian faith, will you discover the upsetting stuff? Are not all things done to the rule of God's word, and are they not directed to edification in true and sound godliness? If you do not feel in your consciences that same consolation of this doctrine, I will concede to you, that there is merit in your attack against us. Be careful, however, I beg, that you do not attack your own conscience, God himself, who has set up his tribunal in your conscience.[65]

---

[61] *Catechismus ex decreto concilii Tridentini* (Leipzig, 1862).

[62] The edition used in this work is *Summa doctrinae Christianae* (Antwerp, 1574).

[63] 'Quare cogitavi de refutandi sexaginta articulis papisticis ex oratione Dominica et Symbolo Apostolico dumtaxat sumptis argumentis, idque germanice.... Quare, cum certo mihi constet de donis Dei in te collatis, rogo ut lingua gallica me in hoc genere iuves, et argumenta perspicua et brevia quae vulgus [in]telligat, quibus detegatur turpidito p[apa]tus, et quibus omnino decadenda p[ro]ponatur omnibus eorum religio, in brevia capita coniicias, et prima occasione oblata ad me mittas' (*Olevianus à Bèze*, 10 April 1561 *Correspondance de Théodore de Bèze*, vol. 3 [Geneva, 1963], 97).

[64] '...ut esset testimonium doctrinae.... Ei hanc arcanam opponere volui...in aliis nonnihil reprimere...' (*Expositio*, Dedicatory Epistle, 3).

[65] 'Sed quid tumultuamini ô boni?... Considerate singulos Christianae

This heavy Reformed reliance on the Creed meant more detailed treatment of it throughout the century. In his 1531 *Expositio fidei* Zwingli spent a mere 33 columns on the Creed.[66] Olevian's treatment, particularly in the first two commentaries dedicated exclusively to the Creed, was expansive by comparison. Calvin's *Institutio* from 1539 grew markedly and the pattern of the later editions was shaped partly by the Creed. Book One corresponds to 'I believe in God' (*Credo in Deum*); Book Two, 'And in Jesus Christ' (*Et in Iesum Christum*); Book Three, 'I Believe in the Holy Spirit' (*Credo in Spiritum sanctum*); Book Four, 'Holy Catholic Church' (*Sanctam ecclesiam catholicam*). As Calvin's student, Olevian followed his teacher's example and his exegesis of the Creed. His three commentaries certainly witness to the Reformed desire to demonstrate a catholic and creedal basis for Reformed Protestantism.

The variety of form of these Reformed commentaries was limited. Pierre Viret's (1511-71) was a dialogic exposition written c.1548.[67] Olevian's *Firm Foundation* (*Vester Grund*, 1567) was also catechetical. More typically, they were a straightforward, article by article exposition of the Creed. To this sort of exposition belong four sermons in Bullinger's *Decades* (1552), Olevian's other two commentaries and one by Peter Martyr Vermigli.[68]

---

nostare fidei articulos, an in ullo invenietis ita tumultuandi materiam? Anon ad verbi dei regulam omnia exiguntur et ad aedificationem om vera et solida pietate diriguntur? Sinon ipsimet consolationem in conscientiis vestris ex hac doctrina sentietis, dabo vobis ultro vos merito in nos innsurgere: At videte quaeso, ne adversus conscientiam vestram, adversus Deum ipsum, qui in conscientia tribunal suum erexit, insurgatis' (*Expositio*, 4-5).

[66] In both *CR*, 4.45-78 and in the Schuler-Schultess editions.

[67] Pierre Viret, *Exposition Familiere des Principaux Poincts du Catechisme & la doctrine Chrestienne, fait en forme de dialogue Instruction Chrestienne* (Geneva, 1563), 22-98. It was translated into English as *A Verie Familiare and Fruitful Exposition of the xii Articles of the Christian Faieth Conteined in the Commune Crede, called the Apostles Crede, made in dialoges* (London, c.1548).

[68] Heinrich Bullinger, *Decades* (Zürich, 1552). The Parker Society translation (Cambridge, 1849) was based on the 1587 edition. Peter Martyr Vermigli, '*Simplex duodecim fidei articulorum expositio*', *Loci Communes* (London, 1576), 467-93. The English translation was published as *A Briefe and most excellent exposition of the xii articles of our Fayth commonly called the Apostles' Creed*, trans. H. Jackson (London, 1578). Cf. Jean Garnier, *A Briefe and Plane Confession of the Christian Faithe, Conteinyng 100 Articles after the Order of the Simbole or Crede of the Apostlelles*, trans. N. Malbie (London, 1562). Frederick III also structured his personal confession of faith around the Creed. It

Beza's 1558 *Confession de la foi Chrestienne*, written just before Olevian arrived in Geneva, was structured around the Creed. Part of Ursinus' *Summa theologiae* (1561/2) is a commentary on the Creed and of course the middle section of the Heidelberg Catechism (Questions 22-59) was itself a commentary on the Creed and an attempt to position the Palatinate Reformation squarely within catholic orthodoxy.[69] Question 22 asked,

> What then are these things which it is necessary for the Christian to believe?

> Everything, which is promised to us in the Gospel, the sum of which is comprehended in the Apostles' Creed, or all in the heads of our catholic and undoubted Christian faith.[70]

The Heidelberg ubiquitarian and Arian controversies also served to intensify Olevian's need to demonstrate Reformed orthodoxy. By using the Creed, Calvinist reformers, though still a minority within the broader evangelical church, established their orthodox credentials.

The Development of Olevian's Trinitarianism

Olevian cannot be understood apart from the pervasive influence of the growing Protestant turn to the doctrine of the Trinity. It was a driving force and structuring influence in nearly all his writing and teaching from the early 1560s.

Though it was more extensive than that of early Protestantism, his treatment of the doctrine of the Trinity was not nearly as detailed as Peter Lombard's.[71] Like Calvin, he was careful to avoid speculation. In this respect, it was also quite

---

was translated as '*A Christian Confession of the late most noble and mightie Prince, Friedrich of that name the third Count Palatine by Rhein*' (London, 1577).

[69] Bierma says that Ursinus' *Summa Theologiae* was patterned on Calvin's 1542 Genevan Catechism ('Covenant Theology', 78).

[70] '*Quaenam sunt illa, quae necesse est hominem Christianum credere? Omnia, quae nobis in Evangelio promittuntur, quorum summa in Symbolo Apostolico, seu in capitibus catholicae et indubitatae omnium Christianorum fidei, breviter comprehenditur.*' See Niemeyer, *Collectio*, 434.

[71] Lombard, *Sententiae*, Liber primus, De mysterio Trinitatis, is in 210 '*distinctiones*', each with a number of sub-heads.

similar to other Protestant scholastics such as Amandus Polanus, who in his *Theological Divisions* (*Partitiones theologicae*, 1590) moved quickly from a general discussion of the divine nature and attributes and the benefits of such knowledge, to a discussion of the Trinity.[72]

Lyle Bierma has attempted to demonstrate the link between *Vester Grund* (1567) and the Heidelberg Catechism. This link, though probable, is not certain, and given that the authorship of the catechism was deliberately obscured, will probably remain uncertain.[73] It is certain, however, that Olevian conceived of *Vester Grund* as an explanation of the 'articles of the old, true, undoubted Christian faith'.[74] The title itself, *Firm Foundation*, speaks simultaneously to the circumstances in which it was written and its intent. Heidelberg in the mid-1560s was disturbed by a number of theological and political controversies, pitting Reformed Protestants against Lutheran. In *Vester Grund* Olevian intended to communicate to troubled parishioners, who must have wondered whom to trust, that the Reformed theology offered assurance of salvation for doubting souls.

What is also striking about *Vester Grund* is that, judging only by its form and structure, it might have been written well before the early 1560s. Despite the elaboration of the locus *de Deo* by Melanchthon and Calvin, *Vester Grund* began with soteriology, almost as if (considered formally) the previous 30 years had not occurred.[75] Further, *Vester Grund* concluded with 22 questions on the benefits (*Wohlthaten*) of forensic justification and the assurance of salvation which flows from

---

[72] Amandus Polanus, *Partitiones theologicae iuxta naturalis methodi leges conformatae duobus libris, quorum primus est de fide: alter de bonis operibus* (London, 1591), 1.4–5.

[73] He has argued this in 'Olevianus and the Authorship of the Heidelberg Catechism: Another Look', *Sixteenth Century Journal* 13 (1982), 26–7 and in the 'General Introduction' to Caspar Olevianus, *A Firm Foundation*.

[74] 'Vester Grund / Das ist / Die Artikel des alten / wahren / ungezweisselten Christlichen Glaubens', *Vester Grund*, title page.

[75] *Vester Grund*, 2–15. Butin's claim that, despite the fact that he headed Book I of the *Institutes*: *de cognitione Dei creatoris*, Calvin really did not mean to identify God as Creator or that he did not mean to suggest that there is any 'genuine' knowledge of God in creation must be regarded as special pleading (*Revelation*, 55–6). For a superior account of Calvin's theology of nature see S. E. Schreiner, *The Theater of his Glory: Nature and the Natural Order in the Thought of John Calvin* (Grand Rapids, 1995).

it.[76] His discussion of the Trinity was, as it were, sandwiched between two largely practical sections demonstrating that his doctrine of the Trinity was, in his own mind, closely connected to one's personal spirituality and therefore it was not an esoteric but rather central doctrine to the Christian faith.

This connection between his trinitarianism and his doctrine of the Christian life explains why he addressed the doctrine of the Trinity primarily in economic terms, i.e. there was a strong emphasis on the divine economy of salvation and the Protestant doctrines of justification and sanctification. For example, in his Christology he taught the Son's consubstantiality with the Father, and the personal distinction between Father and Son, but stressed Christ's 'submissive, obedient humiliation' to the Father.[77] He tended to treat God the Father as creator, God the Son as redeemer and God the Spirit as sanctifier since these are principal ways in which the Christian relates to God.

Olevian defined the gospel itself as 'a revelation of the fatherly and immutable will of God', Christ's voluntary sacrifice and the free gift of the Holy Spirit.[78] It was the merciful Father who approached rebellious humanity, who gave the gospel promise to sinners and it was the God-Man who bore their sins.[79] The Father binds himself to sinners by oath. God the Son fulfilled the terms of the oath. The covenant blessings are imparted by God the Spirit.[80]

The Trinity nearly always conditioned Olevian's definition of God.[81] To know God as Triune is to know the true God.[82] Indeed, there is no other God to be known than the God who has revealed

---

[76] *Vester Grund,* 146.

[77] *Firm Foundation,* Q.85. 'die underthenige gehorsame nidrigung' (*Vester Grund,* 73).

[78] *Firm Foundation,* Q.9. 'Das Euangelium ist ein offenbarung des vätterlichen unnd unwandelbaren willen Gottes' (*Vester Grund,* 8).

[79] Ibid., Q.2. *Vester Grund,* 3.

[80] Ibid., Q. 4. *Vester Grund,* 4.

[81] Though his doctrine of God remained stable, his *ordo docendi* was flexible. In *Vester Grund,* like the Heidelberg Catechism (1563) Q.25, he began his doctrine of God with the Trinity, in the *Expositio* (1576) he opened his doctrine of God with a generic definition before moving to the Trinity. In *De substantia* (1585) he emphasised the fact (1.1.3–5) that the God of the covenant is Father, Son and Spirit.

[82] Ibid., Q.17. *Vester Grund,* 15.

himself to be Triune.[83] When defending the uniqueness of Christianity among world religions, he first appealed explicitly not to the Trinity, but to his doctrine of God and the sufficiency of Christ's atonement. Jews and Muslims, he argued, do not really believe in both God's absolute justice and mercy because they believe the deity may be bribed.[84] The Trinity, however, served as the background for his argument. He made his trinitarian apologetic explicit a few questions hence. 'The Turks and Jews say, of course, that they worship the God of heaven and earth. But there is no other God who created heaven and earth than the Father, Son, and Holy Spirit into whose name we are baptised.' And since they 'neither believe in this Father, Son and Holy Spirit, it follows that they do not believe in God, because there is no other God'.[85] It is not mere formal, but true and hearty adherence to the Articles which sets the Protestants apart from them. It is quite possible to profess a trinitarian faith yet be an idolater. Christians too, whether in popery or 'half-evangelicals' (*halb Evangelisch*), must flee idolatry.[86]

---

[83] Ibid., Q. 20. *Vester Grund*, 18.

[84] Ibid., Q.7. *Vester Grund*, 6–7. This was standard Protestant anti-Muslim rhetoric. See Belgic Confession, Art. 9; Second Helvetic Confession, Art. 3.

[85] *Firm Foundation*, Q.18. 'Sagen doch die Türken und Juden / daß sie den Gott Himmels und der Erden anbeten. Die weil sein ander Gott ist der himmel und Erden erschaffen hat / dann der Vatter / Sohn und H. Geist / in welches namen wir getauffe senn: Und aber die Türken und Juden an denselbigen Vatter / Sohn und heiligen Geist mit glauben und in nicht anbeten / So Glauben sie auch nicht an Gott / Dann es ist sein ander Gott' (*Vester Grund*, 17).

[86] *Firm Foundation*, Q.19. *Vester Grund*, 17–18. Bierma says that that 'half-evangelicals' likely refers to his ubiquitarian gnesio-Lutheran opponents (*Firm Foundation*, 126, n. 32). This view is confirmed by Olevian's comments in his *Brevis admonitio de re Eucharistica* published with his *Notae in evangelia* in which he distinguished between 'Evangelicals' (Evangelicorum), 'Majestics' (Maiesticorum) and 'Catholics' (Catholicorum). These he regarded more precise categories than the more common 'Pontificos, Lutheranos, & Ubiquitarianos'. He considered his position 'evangelical', i.e. truly Protestant. The 'Majestics', i.e. those teaching the doctrine *genus maiestaticum* in Christology are the same *genus* (Olevian spoke of three *genera*) as the Ubiquitarians and Lutherans (*Admonitio*, [Herborn, 1587], 14–15). In *Vester Grund* he spoke of those '*im Papsthum*' (in Popery) 'and the half-evangelicals'. Thus, the latter refers to those whom he regarded as being essentially Roman in doctrine but who called themselves 'Evangelical', i.e. the Lutherans. Given this correlation, C. Gunnoe's hypothesis advanced in his review of *Firm Foundation* that '*halb-evangelisch*' may refer to Nicodemites seems incorrect (*Sixteenth Century Journal* 27 [1996], 1090). Olevian never discussed explicitly the Nicodemite problem.

In the early 1560s, his explanation of trinitarian doctrine proper was restrained and Calvinist. If God is one, why say Father, Son and Spirit? Because God has so revealed himself in his Word. A Christian therefore ought to be satisfied with God's self-revelation that 'these three distinct persons are the one, true, eternal God'.[87] Following hard on this abbreviated answer Olevian supplied a number of classical biblical proofs with little explanation.

His first proof for the doctrine of the Trinity was from the Son's co-eternality and consubstantiality with the Father. He also argued the Son's pre-existence and mediatorial role in creation, his pre-incarnate ministry to the Patriarchs and finally from the fact that the Son is the proper object of saving faith.[88] The Spirit was present at creation, hovering over the waters. It was he who moved the prophets. Olevian noted the biblical *loci* in which the Spirit was identified with Yahweh. Negatively, to deny the deity of the Spirit is to deny the deity of the Son and the Father, since it is through the Spirit that the Father and Son reveal themselves to us.[89]

In 1576 Olevian published a second creedal commentary, *Expositio symbolici apostolici*. Substantially the material in the first two commentaries was nearly identical. There were, however, formal differences. The second commentary began with a briefer introduction. What required 26 questions and answers in *Vester Grund* required 19 in the *Expositio*. Where in *Vester Grund* he was addressing individual persons about the Protestant gospel and about assurance of faith, in the *Expositio* he addressed the Creed primarily in terms of the two kingdoms: Christ's eschatological kingdom and the kingdom of darkness.[90] In *Vester Grund* the Creed was circumscribed by more obvious pastoral

---

[87] *Firm Foundation*, Q.20. 'daß dise dren unterscheidliche personen / der eineig / warhafftig / ewig Gott seind' (*Vester Grund*, 18). This turn to the mystery of the trinitarian faith was the general Protestant approach in the late sixteenth century. For example, Chemnitz' discussion of the relations between the persons, though rather more elaborate, did not attempt to offer any resolution of the tension. See *Loci Theologici*, 1.2–7.

[88] *Firm Foundation*, Q.22. *Vester Grund*, 19.

[89] Ibid., Q.24–5. *Vester Grund*, 20–21.

[90] See R. W. A. Letham, 'Saving Faith and Assurance in Reformed Theology: Zwingli to the Synod of Dort', 2 vols (Ph.D. Thesis, University of Aberdeen, 1979), 1.197–99.

concerns, e.g. assurance of faith. It is clear that in the *Expositio* the real concern was Christological. His commentary on the second part of the Creed comprised 55 percent of the book. By contrast, he spent 33 percent of the book on the first part of the Creed and in the remaining few pages he dispensed with the Spirit and the Church visible.

One explanation for the difference between *Expositio* and *Vester Grund* is that the latter was done shortly after arriving in Heidelberg. *Vester Grund* was more a defence of the soteriological Protestantism of the Calvinist reformation in Heidelberg, written in German and addressed to a literate but confused church-going population. The *Expositio* was a more academic reaction to years of controversy with Lutheran critics and was written in Latin, the language of the academy. It was originally a series of lectures given to divinity students in the seminary in Heidelberg. In his dedicatory epistle to Frederick III, he reminded the Elector that his lectures were nothing more than what he had taught publicly for the previous 15 years.[91] In that case he appears to have published it as a defence and a summary of his handling of the Creed.

His identification of the covenant (*foedus*) with Christ's Spiritual reign (*regnum*) in his elect led naturally to a certain Christocentrism. 'Christ the priest and King of the Church has ratified this covenant to eternity, by his merit, between God and us, and daily administers it efficaciously among us.'[92] Christ was the Mediator. 'God' in this context might refer to the divine substance or more likely to the Father, since it is he who 'out of mere mercy elected us in Christ before the foundation of the world'.[93] Certainly 'efficacy' (*efficacia*) refers to God the Spirit, through whom Christ reigns in us by leading our hearts to the knowledge of our evil and consideration of the divine

---

[91] 'Multos, imo innumeros habemus syncerae huius expositionis capitum doctrinae testes, imo celsitudinem tuam, quae eadem hic leget quae publice saepe audivit annis iam quindecim, quibus Domino placuit ut Catechetica fidei Christianae fundamenta Ecclesiae suae hic traderem' (*Expositio*, Dedicatory Epistle, 5–6).

[92] 'Hoc foedus Christus sacerdos & Rex Ecclesiae inter Deum & nos merito suo in aeternum sancivit, & efficacia sua quotide in nobis administrat' (*Expositio*, 4).

[93] '...qui ut ex mera misericordia ante iacta fundamenta mundi, in Christo nos elegit' (*Expositio*, 16).

justice.[94] It is by the work of the Spirit that consciences are illuminated so that by faith the converted may receive the double benefit (*duplex beneficium*) in Christ.[95] The locus of Christ's work is 'in us' (*in nobis*), which is the visible congregation.

As with Calvin, there is no other way to think or talk about the divine being apart from the Trinity. To say 'I believe in God' is to profess faith in God who has revealed himself in Scripture to be one in three persons.[96] God is tri-personal. 'Person or hypostasis' (*Persona sive* ὑπόστασις) has reference to an 'individuated thing' (*res individua*), i.e. a thing 'knowing, willing', yet incommunicable to another, unsustained by any other.[97] Each trinitarian person has unique properties (*propria*) which distinguishes him from the other persons. The Father, Son and Holy Spirit are three distinct persons, nevertheless the same essence, each subsisting of himself.[98] As proof, he appealed to the Creation narrative:

> In the beginning God created the heavens and the earth and the Spirit of God hovered over the face of the deep and God said 'Let there be light' and there was light (Genesis 1:1).[99]

The 'Trinity of persons' (*Trinitas personarum*) were present at Jesus' baptism (Matthew 3): The Son incarnate, the Spirit 'in the form of a dove' (*specie quasi columba*), the Father speaking from heaven 'with a clear voice' (*clara voce*).[100] The Father can only be an eternal Father if he has a co-essential Son begotten from eternity. Only if the Spirit is co-essential with the Father and the Son can the *filioque* be true.[101]

---

[94] '...per quem ipse in nobis regnet, impetrat. Efficacia vero, qua ut Rex Ecclesiae, primum corda ad agnitionem sui mali, & divinae iustitiae considerationem adducit...'(*Expositio*, 4–5).

[95] '...per Spiritum sanctum illuminatur eorum conscientia...ut se ad Deum, in Christo duplex beneficium accipiant...' (*Expositio*, 5).

[96] *Expositio*, 27–8.

[97] 'Est autem persona sive ὑπόστασις res individua, intelligens, volens, incommunicabilis, nonsustentata ab alia...' (*Expositio*, 28).

[98] 'Patrem, Filium, et Spiritum sanctum esse tres personas distinctas, unam tamen eandem essentiam' (*Expositio*, 43).

[99] 'In principio, creavit Deus, coelum et terram, & Spiritus Dei movebat se super faciem aquarum, dixitque Deus, fiat lux & facta lux' (Genesis 1:1). *Expositio*, 43–4.

[100] *Expositio*, 44.

[101] Ibid., 45.

God is in three distinct, co-eternal subsistences, but he is one essence. In support, Olevian took Deuteronomy 6:4 as proof of the 'one...divine essence' (*unam...divinam essentiam*). Predictably, he appealed to the dominical mandate of Matthew 28:18-20 and more interestingly he took the trisagion of Isaiah 6:3 as proof of the Trinity.[102]

In the section of the *Expositio* in which Olevian explained his trinitarian theology most explicitly, he produced a commentary on the Creed in approximately ten and a half columns. Here his defence of the Trinity was cumulative moving from the Deity of Father, to the Son, to the Spirit. Even the worst heretics (presumably Muslims and Jews) do not deny the deity of the God the Father.[103] If, therefore, the Son has the same divine nature, then his deity must follow. With the Father, the Son is creator of heaven and earth, possessing immutable justice, mercy and everlasting truth. As the only begotten Son (*Filium unigenitum*), he is the co-eternal image of the Father.[104] To deny the consubstantiality of the Son with the Father is to place oneself in 'extreme jeopardy' (*periculum praestantissimum*).[105] As a microcosm of the *Expositio* he was most thorough on Christ's deity. Though on the deity of the Spirit, he was adamant that whoever denies the Spirit, in effect, denies the Father and Son, since apart from the Spirit it is impossible to believe in them.[106]

As with the first two commentaries, in his third and most famous work, *De substantia foederis gratuiti inter Deum et electos* (1585), Olevian explained the Creed as a means of

---

[102] Calvin appealed to the same passage in defence of Christ's deity – only implicitly a trinitarian interpretation – not as a trinitarian proof (*Institutio* 1.13.11, 23; *OS*, 3.123.32–5). In his commentary on Isaiah, he downplayed it as a proof of the Trinity but seems to have thought that it was a Patristic commonplace for the Trinity (*CR*, 36.129). Among the most likely Patristic sources on the Trinity, Gregory of Nazianzus used it as such in *Oratio* 34.13 (J. P. Migne, ed., *Patrologia Graeca*, 161 vols [Paris, 1857–66], 36.253–4). Ambrose used it as a trinitarian proof, in *De fide*, 2.12.106–7 (MPL, 16.582–3) and in *De Spiritu sancto*, 3.15.110 (MPL, 16.803). If it was not clearly a patristic commonplace, it was so for some influential medieval academic theologians such as Peter Abelard (*Theologia summi boni*, 91, 132–4). On the latter see M. T. Clanchy, *Abelard: A Medieval Life* (Oxford, 1997), 271.

[103] *Expositio*, 28.

[104] Ibid., 29.

[105] Ibid., 38.

[106] Ibid., 41.

advancing his doctrine of the covenant. This commentary, however, marked a significant structural development in Olevian's relation of Creed and covenant. Unlike the previous two commentaries, this work was in two parts. The first part was an exposition of the Creed nearly identical to the first two. The second part was devoted entirely to the development of his theology of the covenant. Having said that, it would be a mistake to consider *De substantia* only a third commentary on the Creed with an appendix on the covenant. From its first lines, Olevian was clearly using the Creed as a vehicle to expound his theology of the covenant. Where *Vester Grund* had opened with an explanation of the gospel, and the *Expositio* with Christ's Lordship, *De substantia* began with an exposition of the substance of the covenant between God and man.

The focus of *De substantia* was on the gracious nature of the covenant. Still it was necessary for him to establish the nature of God, from which theology flowed the rest of his theology. In his description of God, he moved from a list of the divine attributes to the Trinity. He regarded the term Trinity as theological shorthand for the divine attributes.[107] He considered creation and sustaining providence to be an external operation of all three persons of the Trinity.[108]

For the first time in his commentaries on the Creed he quoted extensively the 'Athanasian Creed', which he regarded as 'taken from the pure word of God'.[109] It is interesting that Olevian, in the course of developing his federal theology, should turn to the Athanasian Creed. It signals that, in the period of his exile from Heidelberg, he had turned to the Athanasian as a more elaborate and suitable expression of his trinitarianism. Why? First, there is the obvious rhetorical advantage to be gained by the rather stronger language of the Athanasian. The trinitarian faith is the 'Catholic' faith, the universal faith of the Christian church. Thus, his exposition of the covenant (*foedus*) was not a Calvinist or

---

[107] '...denique solum & summum bonum: & est Pater aeternus, Filius imago Patris coaeterna & Spiritus sanctus ab utroque procedens' (*Expositio*, 19). 'Pater aeternus, qui Filium characterem suae hypostaseos ab aeterno genuit è sua substantia' (*De substantia*, 1.1.4).

[108] '...pater aeternus cum Filio et Spiritu sancto condiderit, sustentet et gubernet caelum et terram et omnes creaturas' (*De substantia*, 1.1.4).

[109] 'Huc etiam pertinet prior pars Symboli Athanasii è puro verbo Dei desumti' (*De substantia*, 1.1.4).

Protestant novelty, but nothing less than a catholic move. Second, the Athanasian Creed's use of *substantia* ('neither separating the substance' [*neque substantiam separantes*]) formed an obvious verbal link between Olevian's theology and his trinitarianism. Following on from the language of the Athanasian Creed ('For there is one person of the Father: another of the Son: and another of the Holy Spirit'),[110] he affirmed a distinction between the three persons based on their 'unique properties'.[111] This tri-personal distinction was necessary to the divine being.[112]

The Trinity was so central to his conception of Christianity that he interpreted the original temptation as an offer by Satan to Adam of the privileges of intra-trinitarian communion which belong alone to the divine subsistences.[113]

Trinity, Creation and Substance

For Olevian, as already noted, both creation and providence are trinitarian operations. He embraced the medieval view that Scripture, by using the plural *Elohim*, implied the trinitarian persons.[114] He developed his doctrine of providence under his doctrine of God. Because of the creedal structure of his theology this trinitarianism led naturally to an extended consideration of the work of the Father. Nevertheless, under providence he also included the Son, and the Spirit. Because the Spirit is eternal God, he also 'upholds all things'.[115] Interestingly, under the rubric of kingship, in *Vester Grund*, he did not discuss the Son's role in creation. He did, however, discuss providence, a topic most

---

[110] 'Alia est enim persona Patris: alia Filii: alia Spiritus Sancti' (*The Creeds of Christendom*, ed. P. Schaff, 3 vols [Grand Rapids, 1983], 2.66).

[111] 'Adhaec singulas personas peculiaribus proprietatibus...' (*De substantia*, 1.1.6).

[112] '...nulla enim creatura est quae ab aeterno genuerit Filium...' (*De substantia*, 1.1.6).

[113] 'Quia Sathan suadens Evae mandati divini transgressionem non tam coecus [sic; caecus] erat ut personas in Deitate negaret, sed et personas ipsas ut Evae cognitas et earum gloriam etiam probe notam ei proponit, asserens, Elohim, id est personas illas in Deitate scire, qua die ederint ex illa arbore, fore ut ipsorum oculi aperiantur, et sint sicut Elohim scientes bonum et malum: pro ut nempe personae in Deitate scientes sunt boni et mali' (*De substantia*, 1.1.7).

[114] *De substantia*, 1.1.7.

[115] *Firm Foundation*, Q.127.

closely related in Olevian's mind to creation.[116] In his *Expositio*, however, he elaborated on the Son's agency in creation where he discussed creation in federal terms. Like Calvin, he sometimes used God synonymously with the Father. His preserving grace, his good creation and his providence are corollaries.[117] 'We do not have a covenant with an unknown God.'[118]

Obviously, one of the more significant terms which emerges from the *pars prima* of *De substantia*, is the term *substantia* itself. Why did he include the term in the title of the work and what did he mean by it?

Not surprisingly, *substantia* was an important concept in Calvin's trinitarian theology.[119] He headed his discussion of the incarnation, 'Christ clothed with the true substance of human flesh' (*Christum veram humanae carnis substantiam induisse*).[120] He allowed that *substantia* could be used synonymously with *subsistentia*.[121] By subsistence he meant a person resident in the Godhead distinct by incommunicable attributes from the other persons.[122] Thus when he said that to the faithful is 'exhibited' a 'true and substantial communication' of Christ's body and blood under the signs of the holy supper, he was actually saying that in the supper the believer communicates with God himself.[123]

Substantia is equally important in Olevian's theology. What is the *substance* of the covenant? The answer comes partly in *De substantia* itself, but also partly in his earlier work, *De inventione*, where he gave his generic definition of *substantia* in six articles.[124] In the opening remarks he defined substance as 'being' because 'being proper' belongs to it. Both God (incorporeal, infinite and

---

[116] Ibid., Q. 34. *Vester Grund*, 34–6.

[117] Ibid., Q.28–43. *Vester Grund*, 30–41.

[118] Ibid., Q.29. 'Das wir nicht mit einem unbekanten Gott einen Bund haben' (*Vester Grund*, 30).

[119] See D. Willis, 'Calvin's Use of *Substantia*', *Calvinus Ecclesiae Genevenesis Custos*, ed. W. Neuser (New York, 1982).

[120] *Institutio*, 2.13; *OS*, 3.447.15–16.

[121] 'Si verbum de verbo transferre libeat, subsistentia dicetur. Multi eodem sensu substantiam dixerunt' (*Institutio* 1.13.2; *OS*, 3.111.2–9).

[122] See J. Raitt, 'Calvin's Use of *Persona*', *Custos*, 275.

[123] '...veram substantialemque corporis ac sanguinis Domini communicationem, quae sub sacris coenae symbolis fidelibus exhibetur...' (*Institutio* 4.17.19; *OS*, 5.365.18–366.1).

[124] Caspar Olevian, *De inventione dialecticae liber, è praelectionibus Gasp. Oleviani excerptus* (Geneva, 1583), Cap. 39, Articles 1–6, 167–170.

indivisible substance) and created substances share this definition. In the 'order of substances' (*ordo substantiarum*) there were corporeal and incorporeal substances. Among corporeal and incorporeal substances there are perfectly and imperfectly mixed substances. Among perfectly mixed corporeal substances are included animate and inanimate substances. Among animate substances there are sentient and non-sentient. Among sentient there are 'rational' (*rationalis*) e.g. humans and 'irrational' (*irrationalis*) e.g. horses. It was most important for Olevian that one distinguish properly between 'primary substances' (*primas substantias*) and 'secondary substances' (*secundas substantias*). Primary substances are indivisible and 'secondary substances' are composite. God alone is a primary, simple substance and creatures are secondary, complex substances.

Olevian also used substance in a broader sense to include all that God has done for us in Christ. It was shorthand for the twofold benefit (*duplex beneficium*): justification and sanctification. Moses was speaking of the substance of the covenant when he promised, 'God will circumcise your heart and that of your children.'[125] 'Certainly the very substance of the covenant was not in their flesh', since not everyone who heard the promise spoken verbally had a circumcised heart.[126]

> Therefore, the covenant of grace, if you see its essence, is a sworn oath promised by God, a gift to you by God who is never angry with you (Isaiah 54) and by our adoption in God's Son we have been made heirs of eternal life with Jesus Christ the eternal and only begotten Son of God....[127]

Substantia described relations between the Son and the Father. Analogously, The 'substance of the covenant' (*substantia foederis*) described the special relations between God and his

---

[125] 'Sic de substantia foederis loquitur Moses Deuter.30 'Circuncidet Deus cor tuum et seminis tui' (*De substantia*, 1.1.2).

[126] 'Certe ipsa foederis substantia non erat in ipsorum carne. Nec eorum etiam omnium corda fuerunt circumcisa, quibus foedus administratum seu oblatum fuit per circumcisionem' (*De substantia*, 1.1.2).

[127] 'Foedus itaque gratuitum, si essentiam eius spectes, est promissa et iurata à Deo donatio suimet in Deum nunquam nobis irascentem Isai.54. et assumtio nostri in filios Dei et haeredes vitae aeternae in Iesu Christo aeterno et unigenito Dei Filio...' (*De substantia*, 1.1.2).

elect.[128] God the Son, who is consubstantial with the Father and the Spirit, has become incarnate, and thus consubstantial with us for the sake our redemption and subsequent sanctification. So closely connected was Olevian's notion of *substantia* to his conception of the Trinity, the covenant, and double benefit he even identified the person of the Holy Spirit as the *substantia*.[129]

Caspar Olevian was a Calvinist, catholic and creedal trinitarian theologian. The doctrine of the Trinity not only supported and coloured the substance of this theology, but also structured it. Several external *stimuli* pushed him in a trinitarian trajectory. First, this was the direction of much of Protestant theology (including Melanchthon and Calvin) from the 1540s. Second, the rise of anti-trinitarianism by association with the Heidelberg Calvinists threatened to bring the Reformation there into disrepute. Third, by using the Creed to express his theology he joined an ancient Christian tradition and moved naturally to a more highly developed notion of the Trinity. Chief among the internal, structural stimuli for his trinitarianism was his need to relate his doctrines of creation, Christ, salvation, and sanctification in a coherent fashion.

---

[128] '...unius est cum Patre substantiae & gloriae...' (*Expositio*, 66).

[129] 'Item cum scriptura loquitur de Angelis, non loquitur de bonis motibis, sed spiritibus bonis subsistentibus' (*De inventione*, 169, Art. 2). On the role of Aristotelian physics in Protestant orthodoxy see R. A. Muller, *Dictionary of Latin and Greek Theological Terms* (Grand Rapids, 1985) s.v. '*motus*'.

CHAPTER 5

OLEVIAN'S FEDERALIST CHRISTOLOGY

From Luther's death in 1546 Protestantism entered into a period of intense struggle over the question who were the proper heirs to Luther's theological legacy. In the wake of his death, evangelical theology was convulsed by a series of disputes over the nature of justification, sanctification and worship. One faction, the *gnesio-*Lutherans, laid exclusive claim to Luther's legacy.[1]

Otto Heinrich's reformation of the Palatinate in 1556 was not theologically beholden to the gnesio-Lutherans, but to Philip Melanchthon. Since the gnesio-Lutherans suspected Melanchthon of being a compromiser with the hated Zwinglians on the eucharist and therefore on Christology, they also now considered the Palatinate to be a rebel territory. This perception was only strengthened after Frederick III's accession in 1559, when he inaugurated a Calvinist second Reformation of the electorate.

From the moment Olevian arrived in Heidelberg, he was deeply involved in the defence of the Reformed Christology and theology of the eucharist against Lutheran criticisms. In early June 1560, he defended the Calvinist theology of the eucharist in the Heidelberg disputation. Again, in 1564 with Boquin, Ursinus, and Dathenus, he defended the Reformed Christology at the Maulbronn Colloquy (10–15 April) against Jakob Andrae (1528–90), Johann Brenz (1499–1570), and the other Wittenberg theologians.[2] They spent the first eight sessions on Christology

---

[1] See Robert Kolb, *Martin Luther as Prophet, Teacher and Hero* (Grand Rapids, 1999), 17–74, 103–20.

[2] Johannes Brenz, *Epitome colloquii inter illustrissimorum principum D. Frederici Palatini Electoris, et D. Christophori Wirtenbergensis theologos, de maiestate hominis Christi, deque vera eius in Eucharistia praesentia,*

and the second eight on the eucharist. This arrangement was not mere happenstance. In the minds of both parties, the two issues were inseparable.[3] This chapter contends that Olevian considered his Reformed Christology to be necessary to a right understanding of the eucharist and a part of the substance of the covenant of grace, and therefore a central part of true Protestant religion.[4] His Christology followed from his trinitarian doctrine of God and was the point of contact between it, his Protestant soteriology, and his Calvinist doctrine of sanctification. He therefore explained his Christology in federal terms in order to unify his theology and respond to his Lutheran critics.

Behind the eucharistic and Christological controversies in which Olevian was involved lay decades of rancour between Luther and the 'sacramentarian' Zwinglians.[5] From the mid-1520s Luther and the Lutherans rejected Zwingli's Christology and eucharistic theology as rationalist. Zwingli's refusal to accept what Luther regarded as the clear teaching of Scripture: *hoc est corpus meum*, was really a refusal to accept the (Protestant) gospel of grace.[6]

Maulbrunniae instituti (Wittenberg, 1564). For a Reformed account see Zacharis Ursinus, *Opera Theologica*, 3 vols, ed. Q. Reuter (Heidelberg, 1612), 2.84–167; H. Alting, *Historia ecclesii Palatinae* (Amsterdam, 1646), 192–3. See also K. C. Sudhoff, *C. Olevianus und Z. Ursinus: Leben und ausgewählte Schriften der Vater und Begründer der reformierten Kirche*, vol. 8 (Elberfeld, 1857), 160–90. The most recent history of the colloquy is contained in P. Biel, 'Colloquy or Cul de Sac at Maulbronn in 1564', a paper delivered at the American Society of Church History in Chicago, 28–30 December, 1991 (Portland: Theological Research Exchange Network, 1992).

[3] In his account of the colloquy, Brenz made the questions of Christology and the eucharist parallel (Johannes Brenz, *Epitome colloquii...Maulbrunniae instituti* [Wittenberg, 1564], 9). Proportionally, however, if Brenz' account is an accurate indicator, two-thirds of the discussion centred on Christology (ibid., 1–59), and the final third on the eucharist (ibid., 59–88).

[4] In this regard it is interesting that H. Scheible entitled his 1986 biographical essay on Olevian: 'Olevian als Vereteidiger der reformierten Abendmahlslehre'. See *Bibliotheca Palatina*, ed. E. Mittler et al., 2 vols (Heidelberg, 1986), 1:145–6.

[5] See M. U. Edwards Jr, *Luther and the False Brethren* (Stanford, CA, 1975), 82–144.

[6] B. A. Gerrish, 'The Lord's Supper in the Reformed Confessions', *Major Themes in the Reformed Tradition*, ed. D. K. McKim (Grand Rapids, 1992), 254.

For Luther, the eucharist was primarily a mystery, the gospel incarnate: Christ for us to be received by faith. Thus, he discussed the sacraments under justification. Zwingli, however, emphasised the etymology of *sacramentum*, i.e. oath or pledge. The sacrament was one's believing response to Christ, one's pledge of loyalty, so he tended to discuss it under sanctification.[7] To Luther, of course, Zwingli's views sounded necessarily like the moralism (i.e. the confusion of law and gospel) he had just abandoned. Hence the Zwinglians became, in Lutheran rhetoric, 'Sacramentarians', and rejected as sub-Protestant.[8]

Zwingli, however, regarded Luther, on the eucharist at least, as someone not yet delivered fully from the clutches of Popery. The enmity between Luther and the Zürichers was not ended at Marburg (1529), but became more intense. For his part, Luther doubted Zwingli's salvation and the genuineness of the Christianity of Bullinger et al. who continued to publish his works.[9]

The *Consensus Tigurinus* (1549) between the Genevans and the Zürichers served only to confirm in the minds of the gnesio-Lutherans that Calvinism, though it attempted to cloak itself with Luther, was really nothing more than a cleverly disguised Zwinglianism.[10] Lutheran suspicion of Calvinism, for example, was at the heart of the controversy between Joachim Westphal (c.1510/11–74) and Calvin from 1552, when Westphal attacked the *Consensus Tigurinus* with his pamphlet, *A Confused Mixture of Dissenting Opinions of the Sacramentarians on the Lord's Supper Gathered from Their Books*.[11] He followed this with two other

---

[7] For recent treatments of Zwingli's Christology and eucharistic theology see W. P. Stephens, 'Zwingli on John 6:63: "*Spiritus est qui vivificat, caro nihil prodest*"', R. A. Muller and J. L. Thompson, eds, *Biblical Interpretation in the Era of the Reformation* (Grand Rapids, 1996); R. Cross, '*Alloiosis* in the Christology of Zwingli', *Journal of Theological Studies* 47 (1995), 105–22.

[8] *Formula of Concord* (1580), Art. 7, *De coena Domini*: 'Etsi Cingliani Doctores non in eorum Theologorum numero, qui Augustanam Confessionem agnoscunt et profitentur' (P. Schaff, ed., *The Creeds of Christendom*, 3 vols, 6th edn (Grand Rapids, 1931), 3.135.

[9] Edwards, 190–96.

[10] I. A. Dorner, *History and Development of the doctrine of the Person of Christ*, trans. W. L. Alexander and D. W. Simon, 5 vols (Edinburgh, 1866–70), 4.175.

[11] *Farrago confusanearum et inter se dissidentium opinionum de coena Domini, ex sacramentariorum libris congesta* (Magdeburg, 1552). On Lutheran

similar tracts assaulting the Calvinist position. Calvin responded, in 1555, to which Westphal replied. Calvin's 1556 response was followed by a barrage of literature by Westphal lasting until 1558.[12] Westphal's intent was to demonstrate that Calvin was nothing more than a crypto-sacramentarian, hiding in Protestant garb. In the late 1570s even Martin Chemnitz (1522–86), who was much more irenic than Westphal, Johannes Brenz, or Andrae, was prosecuting the sacramentarians for hiding their errors in orthodox-sounding language.[13]

The eucharistic controversy vitiated the remnant of visible Protestant unity in a period when Tridentine Romanism was ascending. Another result, even more dangerous to those Calvinists not in a free city-state such as Geneva, was that they were vulnerable to charges of being outside the *Pax Augustana*.[14]

At a Lutheran synod in Stuttgart (19 December, 1559) the Wittenberg divines declared for the majestic genus (*genus maiestaticum*), i.e. as a result of the incarnation, Christ's humanity was transformed by personal union with his deity. The transformation of Christ's humanity was at the heart also of the Maulbronn colloquy. The twin Lutheran concerns about the Calvinist Christology were clearly portrayed in the title of Johannes Brenz' summary of Maulbronn: *On the Majesty of Christ's Humanity and his True Presence in the Eucharist.*[15] For the gnesio-Lutherans, the Reformed were guilty of Nestorianism (separating the two natures), failing to appreciate the nature of the incarnation, the true relations between Christ's natures, and therefore, the nature of Christ's presence in the eucharist. In sum, they were blaspheming Christ's majesty.[16]

---

hostility toward Calvin see D. Steinmetz, 'Calvin and His Lutheran Critics', *Lutheran Quarterly* 4 (1990), 179–94.

[12] For a review of the primary literature see G. Kawerau, s.v. 'Westphal, Joachim', *The New Schaff-Herzogg Encyclopedia of Religious Knowledge*, ed. S. M. Jackson, 13 vols (New York, 1908–12; repr. Grand Rapids, 1977), 12.328–9.

[13] 'Sicut Sacramentarii concedunt, corpus Christi vere esse in Coena, quia existimant sub illa voce, se posse opiniones suas occultare' (Martin Chemnitz, *De duabus naturis in Christo de hypostatica earum unione, de communicatione idiomatum et aliis quaestionibus inde dependentibus etc* [Leipzig, 1580], 332).

[14] Brenz cast the debate as one in a series between critics and defenders of the Protestant religion, including the Leipzig Disputation between Luther and Eck (*Epitome colloquii*, 7).

[15] *De maiestate hominis Christi, deque vera eius in Eucharistia praesentia.*

[16] Brenz, *Epitome*, 36, 81. The German Reformed were particularly

In his tract, *On the Personal Union of the Two Natures in Christ*, Brenz argued that the expression *unio hypostatica* is relatively meaningless since God is omnipresent and can only be so personally.[17] Additionally, there is in all humans a duality of natures, such that this sort of language is not sufficiently exalted to describe Christ. Further, given the necessary communication of properties (*communicatio idiomatum*) between Christ's two natures, the Logos cannot be said to have ever worked beyond Christ's humanity.[18] This assertion, of course, was his refutation of the *extra Calvinisticum*.

At Maulbronn, the Wittenberg theologians followed Jacob Andrae's argument that Christ's humanity was, with his deity, omnipresent and immense, so that he was seated at the right of the Father at conception *in utero*.[19] In his glorification, Christ shed whatever limitations to which he temporarily subjected himself on earth.[20] They offered a *triplex modus* of the divine presence in creatures. The first mode is 'of power and virtue' which is present in all creatures. The second is his gracious presence in angels and blessed humans. The third mode is that by which he dwells in Christ the man, with whom God communicates all his wisdom, knowledge, and power in heaven and on earth, such that, in his humanity Christ knows, hears, works, and is

---

sensitive to this criticism. Both Q.47 and Q.48 of the *Heidelberg Catechism* were devoted to answering the charge of Nestorianism.

[17] Dorner, 4.178. Johannes Brenz, *De personali unione duarum naturarum in Christo* (Tübingen, 1571), 44. Though it is not certain just which books Olevian was reading, it seems reasonable to assume that he was familiar with Brenz' Christology since they were across the table from one another at Maulbronn. Therefore, his Christology provides a suitable background against which to evaluate Olevian's.

[18] Dorner, 4.180–6.

[19] J. Brenz, 'Antithesis doctrinae Palatinorum et Vuirtenbergisium theologorum de persona Christ et Eucharistia', Art. 6, in *Epitome*, 91–2. He also argued this in *De personali*, 43–4.

[20] Though Dorner (4.186–7) regarded Andrae's position as extreme, it is not evident that his colleagues at Maulbronn thought so. 'Quia vero in hoc utero matris cum filio Dei personaliter unitus fuit...filium Dei esse ipsam dexteram Dei...Christum hominem in utero matris ad dexteram Dei collocatum, et tum temporis in possessionem huius Maiestatis pervenisse, qua cum filio Dei potest ubique praesens adesse, a quo in unitatem personae assumptus, et in hanc maiestatem collocatus est' (*Epitome*, 33). Biel ('Colloquy', 5) notes that Lutheran position at the colloquy bore a close resemblance to Andrae's *Brevis et modesta apologia* (Tübingen, 1564).

present with all things.[21] In Christ's *status maiestaticus* it was not as if, for Brenz, his humanity was 'being stretched out and diffused in space'. Rather, his transformation took him beyond time and space.[22] For Brenz, this was no denial of Christ's humanity, since he did not consider it essential to humanity to be bound by time and space. Humanity cannot become deity but deity can 'pour itself into' humanity.[23]

According to Brenz and Andrae the only way truly to keep Christ's two natures in personal union (*unio personalis*) was to affirm his *status maiestaticus*. The trajectory of this Christology was toward a doctrine of θέωσις, or the absorption of the human into the divine.[24] Yet for Brenz, the Reformed doctrine that Christ's humanity is substantially unchanged in the ascension constituted a denial of Christ's majesty.[25] The Lutheran theologians correctly recognised that the Palatinate theologians were arguing that it is not possible for human nature *per se* to share in 'the substantial or essential quality of God' (*proprietatem Dei substantialem sive essentialem*).[26] Though the Palatinate theologians were affirming the divinity of Christ's *person*, nevertheless, to Lutheran ears, the Calvinist denial of the *status maiestaticus* sounded like an assault on Christ's deity.[27]

At the Colloquy, the Lutherans affirmed a Chalcedonian distinction between Christ's two natures. They agreed with the Palatinate theologians that his deity was eternal (*ab aeterno*) and *spiritus* and in no way commuted to creaturehood.[28] His humanity, they agreed, had a beginning and was *ex substantia* of the virgin Mary, by virtue of the Holy Spirit, according to which

---

[21] Brenz, *Epitome*, 17.

[22] Dorner, ibid., 4.181. Brenz, *De personali*, 49–50; ibid., *Epitome*, 21.

[23] Dorner, ibid., 4.182.

[24] Dorner, ibid., 4.179.

[25] Dorner, ibid., 4.178.

[26] Brenz, *Epitome*, 23. 'Palatini Theologi asseverant, hanc transfusionem proprietatum Divinae naturae in humanam fieri non posse, sine humanam naturae cum Divina confusione, aut abolitione' ('*Anthesis*', Art. 5, *Epitome*, 91).

[27] *Formula of Concord*, Art. 7, Negativa. Contrariae et damnatae Sacramentariorum doctrinae rejectio, 12, rejected the Reformed notion that 'Christum substantialem corporis et sanguinis sui praesentiam neque promittere neque exhibere' and (Art. 13) 'Deum ne quidem...efficere posse, ut corpus Christi, uno eodemque tempore in pluribus, quam uno tantum loco, substantialiter praesens sit' (Schaff, *Creeds*, 3.144).

[28] Brenz, *Epitome*, 18.

Christ is true man. His *substantia*, in body and soul, consists with us humans in every respect, sin excepted. Further, they agreed that, for all eternity, he will remain true man (*verus homo*).[29] They explicitly denied that Christ's humanity will ever be absorbed into the deity. Rather God assumed this true and natural man in personal union in order that, by such means, he might communicate all his majesty to it.[30]

Here lay the core of the issue which Olevian would address in his Christology. What is the *substantia* of Christ's humanity and deity after the personal union, and how does he relate to his people?

Olevian's Exegetical Christology

Like most Protestant theologians of the age, Olevian was first of all an exegetical theologian. His *notae* on Philippians 2 and Colossians 1 illustrate his mature interaction with biblical texts on Christology.

His exegesis of Philippians 2:5–11 was spread over eight pages of his commentary on the epistle.[31] He observed the moral intent (*scopus*) of the chapter (vv.1–6) but his real interest lay in the meaning (*sententia*) of the text (vv.7–11).[32] When Scripture used the term μορφή it referred properly to the Son's 'image or pattern' (*figura aut typus*) rather than to his essence or nature. The incarnate Son retained his membership in the Godhead and his 'identity of glory' (*identitatem gloriae*).[33] God will not transfer

---

[29] See also Brenz, *Epitome*, 21.

[30] Brenz, *Epitome*, 18.

[31] Caspar Olevian, *In Epistolas D. Pauli Apostoli ad Philippenses et Colossenses*, ed. Theodore Beza (Geneva, 1580), 17–25. In this commentary he followed Beza's Latin text of the New Testament, first published in 1556 as *Novum Domini Nostri Iesu Christi Testamentum* by R. Stephanus. It was revised and republished in 1565, 1567, and in conjunction with Immanuel Tremellius and Franciscus Junius, ed., *Testamenti Veteris Biblia Sacra* (Frankfurt, 1579) and in London in 1580, 1581, 1582, and 1598. It was in print through much of the seventeenth century. This research has used the 1565 and 1582 editions, and a later reprint *Novum Testamentum Domini Nostri Jesu Christi* (London, 1834).

[32] 'Scopus Pauli est, exhortari ad concordiam et humilitatem. Explicemus verba, et textus sententiam' (*Ad Philippenses*, 18). His text of 2.7 reads: 'Sed ipse se exinanivit, forma servi accepta, similis hominibus factus' (*Ad Philippenses*, 18).

[33] *Ad Philippenses*, 18–19.

his glory to humanity, even in the incarnation. He grounded this latter proposition, it should be noted, not in a philosophical *a priori*, but in his reading of Isaiah 42:8.[34] Respecting Christ's humanity, in direct contradiction to the gnesio-Lutheran position, he contended that Christ 'was constituted as any other human'.[35] The words 'assumed the form of a servant' (*forma servi assumpta*) require evangelicals to confess that Jesus assumed a 'truly human nature with all the human frailties, and in it he was obedient unto death for us, even the death of the cross'.[36] His commentary on the remaining verses in the passage make it clear that for Olevian any diminution of the true humanity jeopardises the very purpose of the incarnation: the redemption of sinners by the incarnate Son's active (i.e. the humiliation of an incarnate life) and passive (i.e. his suffering and death) obedience to the Father.[37]

Olevian's gospel, however, did not end with the crucifixion. His reformed Christology was evident in his discussion of the ascension under Philippians 2:9–11. In his exaltation at the right hand of God (*ad dextram Dei*) Christ did not put away (*deposuit*) the same humanity in which he emptied (*exinaniverat*) himself for us but retained it when he assumed his office as exalted high priest and king.[38] His glorious heavenly session demonstrates that the Jesus who was crucified was himself the eternal and essential Son of God.[39] 'Therefore we believe both in Christ seated at the

---

[34] 'Μορφὴν potius converti debet natura seu ingenium, quam figura aut typus: ita ut essentiam seu naturam referatur in utroque membro, tam in forma Dei quam in forma servi. Nam attributa seu proprietates utrobique continentur in adiunctis verbis, ut aequalem esse Deo innuat, qui apud Isaiam 42 ait: Ego Dominus et hoc nomen meum, gloriam meam alteri non dabo' (*Ad Philippenses*, 18).

[35] '...constitutus ut quivis alius homo' (*Ad Philippenses*, 18).

[36] '...natura vere humana cum omnibus calamitibus, in eaque fieri pro nobis usque ad mortem, mortem autem crucis' (*Ad Philippenses*, 19).

[37] 'Observa quantum malum sit peccatum, quod non nisi obedientia Filii expiari potuit' (*Ad Philippenses*, 19). 'Obedientia. Humiliavit se factus obediens Patri. Primus homo superbia summa se extulit, ut non obediret Deo' (ibid., 20).

[38] *Ad Philippenses*, 20. 'Ad gloriam Dei Patris. Tam gloria, quam adiectione *Dei Patris* quod de exaltatione huius Iesu dixerat, declarat scilicet hanc personam, quae assumpsit humanam naturam ex Maria virgine, declaratam esse in summa gloria, quod sit aeternus et essentalis Patris Filius, quod ex summa gloria sit conspicuum: quam ut nulli creaturae communicat, Isa. 42' (ibid., 23).

[39] '...hic Iesus crucifixus ostendat se aeternum et essentialem esse Dei Filium' (*Ad Philippenses*, 21).

right hand of God, and we believe him to be nearer to us in power, to reign in us, than he should be with his body on the earth'.[40] In effect, he was arguing that the Calvinist Christology does not remove Christ from God's people.[41] Rather, by virtue of his trinitarian theology and use of redemptive-historical (rather than ontological) categories, the ascension and outpouring of the Spirit brings Christ to the elect in a way not hitherto possible.

For Olevian, Christ was omnipresent in his deity. That is, the Son, being fully God, consubstantial with the Godhead, shares those properties common to the deity. Hence, if God is immense, then God the Son is immense, yet in his deity not his humanity. The Lutherans called the Calvinist resolution of this particular Christological problem, the *extra Calvinisticum.*[42]

In this scheme the Son was understood to operate both in personal union, in the incarnation, but also beyond the incarnation, hence the Calvinistic *extra.* According to Olevian, Satan has operated most efficaciously through the doctrine of *genus maiestaticum*, in which Christ was ascended in majesty at conception, *in utero*, and present in all creatures whether good or evil.[43] Interestingly, he also believed that Christ was seated *ad dextram*

---

[40] 'Ergo tum credimus in Christum sedentem ad dextram Dei, cum propiore virtute nobis adesse credimus, in nobis regnare, quam cum in terris corpore suo esset' (*Ad Philippenses*, 23).

[41] That is, he was not teaching the doctrine of the so-called 'real absence' of Christ.

[42] The most outstanding treatment of the *extra Calvinisticum* is D. E. Willis, *Calvin's Catholic Christology. The Function of the So-Called Extra Calvinisticum in Calvin's Theology* (Leiden, 1966). See also H. A. Oberman, 'The "Extra" Dimension in the Theology of Calvin', *Journal of Ecclesiastical History* 21 (1970), 43–64.

[43] 'Reliquum est genus tertium eorum, qui Maiestatis hominis Christi assertores videri volunt: Horum haec est sententia, carnem Christi in ipsa conceptione in eam maiestatem esse subuectam, ut et in utero in coelum ascendit, et ad dextram Dei consederit, et sit (horresco eorum verba et scripta referens) in omnibus bonis et malis creaturis. Per hoc Satan efficacissme operatur, ad evertendum Dei consilium' (*Admonitio*, 18; see also, 25). He frequently proposed a diabolical cause for the Lutheran Christology. See Caspar Olevian, *Firm Foundation*, trans. and ed. L. D. Bierma (Grand Rapids, 1995), Q.77; idem, *Vester Grund* (Herborn, 1590) repr. in *Der Gnadenbund Gottes 1590*, ed. G. Franz, J. F. G. Goeters, W. Holtmann [Bonn, 1994], 68. N.B. Quotations from *Vester Grund* have followed the Sudhoff edition (Frankfurt, 1854) in the use of capital letters. See also, idem, *Expositio symboli apostolici* [Frankfurt, 1576, repr. 1584], 89.

Dei while in the uterus. Again, the question was not *whether* Christ was glorious and ubiquitous, but *how*. His answer was that the Son operates by virtue of his deity, which he shared with the other trinitarian persons. Considered ontologically, to say that God the Spirit is at work, is to say that God the Son is also at work.

Where his focus in the commentary on Philippians was on Christ's humanity, in Colossians the accent fell on his deity. From this verse, he deduced two doctrines. First, that the Son of God had not beginning and existed before all creatures; second, that he has always existed as the only begotten from all eternity.[44] As in his commentary on Philippians, Olevian was primarily interested in propagating his soteriology by establishing his Christology. He reminded his readers that redemption and the knowledge of God are found only in Christ, 'who is the image of the invisible God' (*qui est imago Dei inconspicui*).[45]

> It is certain that God communicates himself to his own in no other way than...through knowledge of this sort, through which man ought not flee God, but draw near to him, trust him, and expect every good thing from him.[46]

Such intimate knowledge of God was promised by the prophets.[47] 'Nevertheless, this New Covenant knowledge, given to God's people in Christ, cannot be considered to penetrate beyond the veil of God's hiddenness.

> God in his bare essence, considered outside of Christ, is hidden from us that is, it is not possible to see him either with the body's or with the mind's eye.[48]

---

[44] *Ad Colossense*, 90–91. The pagination in this commentary is consecutive from the notes on Philippians. See also Caspar Olevian, *De substantia foederis gratuiti inter Deum et electos* (Geneva, 1585), 1.3.1: 'Quamobrem quod Filius ab aeterno est a Patre genitus, (quae generatio scaturigo est si ordinem respicias reliquarum proprietatum divinarum quas λόγος ab aeterno habet)...'.

[45] *Ad Colossense*, 85–6.

[46] 'Certum est Deum non aliter se communicare suis quam per cognitionem et quidem eiusmodi cognitionem, qua homo non fugiat Deum, sed ad eum accedat, ipsi fidat, ab eo omnia bona expectat' (*Ad Colossense*, 86).

[47] He quoted Jeremiah 31:34 'Cognoscent me a minimo usque ad maximum' and Hosea 2:20 'Et cognosces Jehovam' (*Ad Colossense*, 86), passages to which he referred quite frequently throughout his writings.

[48] 'Atqui Deus in sua essentia nuda extra Christum est nobis inconspicuus,

Doubtless Luther's distinction between *Deus absconditus et revelatus* formed the background of these comments.

These comments should not be misconstrued to mean, however, that Olevian believed that it is impossible to talk about God *extra Christum*. He began the next paragraph saying, 'Clearly it is not possible to see God' which proposition was followed by the quotation of Exodus 33:20.[49] It is not that God does not have bare essence (*essentia nuda*) but rather that it cannot be seen. He was discussing divine invisibility and incomprehensibility rather than the doctrine of the knowledge of God.[50]

In the light of the arguments one finds Olevian making elsewhere about the natural knowledge of God, he cannot be understood to be denying the relative efficacy or existence of general revelation. Rather, he was doing Christology under the larger rubric of soteriology. Thus, he argued, because of the divine holiness and justice, any such revelation by God would only serve further to prosecute us sinners for our unrighteousness.[51]

> How is God made visible in Christ? God was made visible in the flesh. For he also is God who assumed flesh, and in his flesh he offers the knowledge of his justice, goodness, mercy, φιλανθρωπία, truth, omnipotence.[52]

Here one sees the synthesis of his doctrine of God with his Christology. Olevian's Christ should be understood as the saving revelation of the triune God.

Trinity and Christology

Olevian began with a traditional, Protestant doctrine of God, which he applied to the Son and the Spirit. He did not derive his

---

hoc est, neque corporis, neque mentis oculis conspici potest' (*Ad Colossense*, 86).

[49] 'Non posse Deum conspici perspicuum est Ex.33' (*Ad Colossense*, 86). See also *De substantia* 1.6.30.

[50] 'Tanta tamque incomprehensa est ipsius maiestas. Locus est Esa. 6' (*Ad Colossenses*, 86). The expression *Deus manifestatus in carne* is regular in Olevian's theology, e.g. *De substantia*, 1.6.1-2.

[51] *Ad Colossense*, 86.

[52] 'Quomodo ergo in Christo est conspicuus? I. Tim 3. Deus conspicuus factus est in carne. Nam et Deus est is qui carnem assumpsit, et in carne iustitiam suam, bonitatem, misericordiam, φιλανθρωπίαν, veritatem, omnipotentiam suam cognoscendam praebet' (*Ad Colossense*, 87).

notion of the deity from his experience of Christ, but from his doctrine of the Trinity and his broader doctrine of God which supported his Christology.[53] For example, his appeal to John 10:28, 'no one shall snatch my little sheep out of my hand', was predicated on Christ's consubstantiality with the Father.[54] Against his gnesio-Lutheran opponents, he stressed Christ's humanity by ascribing to the Spirit the work of Christ's virgin conception and birth. It was the Spirit who endowed the God-Man with a 'truly human nature with a body and soul from the substance of the virgin'.[55] Thus, his trinitarian doctrine of God served as the backbone of his Christology.

He conceived the eternal generative relations between the Father and Son as a sort of spring, 'the Son was begotten, from eternity, of the Father'.[56] At the same time the divine persons are distinct subsistences. Each person possesses incommunicable properties, which distinguish him from the others.[57] Each trinitarian person knows and wills in a way which distinguishes him from the other trinitarian persons. There is 'one and the same infinite, integral, and perfect essence in each person'.[58] It follows, then, given Olevian's premises, that if there is a certain lack of communication of properties in the Godhead, then it is not problematic to assert an analogous lack of communication in the personal union of the God-Man. It was appropriate, therefore, that only God the Son should assume humanity. It seemed to

---

[53] W. E. Korn made a similar argument regarding the Christology of the Heidelberg Catechism. See idem, 'Die Lehre von Christi Person und Werk', *Handbuch zum Heidelberger Katechismus*, ed. L. Coenen (Neukirchen-Vluyn, 1963). More recently, however, G. Zimmerman has argued that the Catechism is a document driven primarily by personal religious experience. See idem, 'Der Heidelberger Katechismus als Dokument des subjektiven Spiritualismus', *Archiv für Reformationsgeschichte* 85 (1994), 180–204.

[54] *Firm Foundation*, trans. L. D. Bierma (Grand Rapids, 1995), Q.28. *Vester Grund*, in *Gnadenbund Gottes* (Heidelberg, 1567; repr. Bonn, 1994), 29–30. According to Olevian, the heresiarch Arius did not so much deny the Son's deity, as his consubstantiality with the Father (*Firm Foundation*, Q.78; *Vester Grund*, 69).

[55] *Firm Foundation*, Q.67. *Vester Grund*, 56–7.

[56] *De substantia*, 1.3.1: 'Quamobrem quod Filius ab aeterno est a Patre genitus, (quae generatio scaturigo est si ordinem respicias reliquarum proprietatum divinarum quas λόγος ab aeterno habet)...'.

[57] *De inventione*, 170.

[58] '...una est infinita in singulis personis, integra, perfecta et eadem essentia' (*De inventione*, 170).

Olevian that, in the Lutheran Christology, there was not a sufficient distinction between the divine subsistences, nor a sufficient appreciation of the distinct roles of the divine persons in the economy of salvation and sanctification.[59] For example, κοινωνία does not consist so much in receiving 'the true and palpable body of Christ' or receiving his divine nature, but rather that in the supper one is joined to 'the whole Christ, God and Man, offered for us'.[60]

It has already been observed that the term *substantia* played no small part in the gnesio-Lutheran Christology and in Olevian's doctrine of God. It was conspicuous in his Christology as well. For example, in *Vester Grund* he began by assuming the immutability of divine justice.[61] That being so, God the Son must become consubstantial with us to accomplish redemption.[62] In each restatement of his Christology, in 1576 and in 1585, he repeated the same argument.[63]

As shown previously, he followed Aristotle's definition of substance. For Olevian, God is *the* 'primary substance'; all others are secondary, being created. Humans were created good, such that sin is not essential to humanity. Sin is not *ens* (being) but the *corruptio* of the divine image and God's good creation.[64] Therefore, he considered sin morally not ontologically. Nevertheless, He did consider the relations between God and man in ontological terms. Though humanity's being is analogous to

---

[59] Chemnitz, however, did recognise that it was not necessary for the entire Trinity to become incarnate. 'Ut ideo non sit opus, totam Trinitatem contra analogiam fidei, incarnari.... Qua enim ratione tota plenitudo Deitatis in assumpta natura Christi inhabitat personaliter, ita, ut tamen, nec Pater, nec Spiritus Sanctus, sed solus Filius sit incarnatus' (*De duabus naturis*, 326).

[60] 'Tum facile animadvertes, non in receptione unici illius veri et palpabilis corporis Christi intra nostra coropora κοινωνια consistere, sed in vinculo artissimo spiritus Christi, non cum divina tantum eius natura, sed toto Christo Deo et homine pro nobis oblato nos coniungentis: et quidem multo firmus, quam si omnes creaturae nos cum eo unirent: quoniam Creator ipse vinculum huius coniunctionis est'. (*Admonitio*, 23–24).

[61] *Vester Grund*, 60.

[62] *Vester Grund*, 61.

[63] See *Expositio*, 91–2; *De substantia*, 1.3.6–7.

[64] 'Et vidit Deus quicquid fecerat, et erat valde bonum Itaque homo bonus à Deo fuit conditus et esse habet bonum: Peccatum quod accessit non est creatura, seu res creata sed destructio imaginis Dei et corruptio a Sathana et hominis voluntate inducta: non Ens, sed corruptio Entis' (Caspar Olevian, *De inventione dialecticae* [Geneva, 1583], 168).

the divine existence, there is not an exact correspondence. Olevian distinguished between Creator and creature. That which is from eternity is distinct from that which belongs to the species of created things.[65] Further, he regarded any refusal to embrace his Christology as an attempt to overturn the substance of the covenant (*substantia foederis*) itself which is comprehended in all the other articles.[66] Olevian was no more Christocentric than his scholastic contemporaries and successors. Though he regarded his Christology as central to his theology, he tied its welfare to the entirety of the faith of which his Christology was but a single article. Therefore, it is not possible to identify Olevian's idea of *substantia* entirely with his Christology. The incarnation was of the *substantia* of the faith, but it was not the whole substance of the faith. Rather he considered the entire Christian faith as summarised in the Apostles' Creed to be the *substantia*.[67]

For Olevian, there is also a continuity of substance between Christ and the redeemed. What makes us human is what makes Christ human. The contrast with Brenz and Andrae on this point was quite sharp. For Olevian, Christ's humanity is significant *because* it is not transformed by and yet remains personally united to his deity. In order to emphasise his conception of Christ's humanity he said that the Son was

---

[65] 'Etsi autem secundae substantiae extra intellectum nihil sint: tamen utile est videre seriem in hac tota universitate rerum, quam intellecu seu mente circumferentes discernimus DEUM a rebus creatis, a quibus in aeternum discerni vult: et cum species creatas enumeramus, magis acquiescimus, quasi fines et metas naturae intuentes, multarum etiam usum simul consideramus' (*De inventione*, 169).

[66] 'Verba, HOC EST NOVUM TESTAMENTUM requirunt, ut tantum de corpore eum discipulis loquente praecedentia verba accipiamus, nisi velimus substantiam foederis in 2.3.4.5.6.7.8. articulo comprehensam evertere, nec admittit omnium articulorum illorum natura, ut tertium quid inter panem & Christum substituatur vel admisceatur' (*De substantia*, 2.70).

[67] The opening sentence of the second part of *De substantia* summarises the first half, which was a commentary on the Creed. 'Adhuc de tota substantiae foederis dictum est omnibus & solis electis, seu iis qui fide donantur, in hac, & aeterna vita communi' (*De substantia*, 2.1). See also ibid., 1.9.1 and 2.62.

not begotten of the substance of the Father, but of the substance of the Virgin by the Holy Spirit, and that was born united to the eternal and only begotten Son of God.[68]

He was not denying the consubstantiality of the Son with the Father.[69] Rather, with the incarnation in view, he was emphasising Christ's consubstantiality with our humanity. Both Christ's humanity and deity so belong to his 'substance and being' that they simultaneously form the person yet they retain their distinctive attributes.[70] This was the doctrine of *unio hypostatica* which Brenz and Andrae had rejected.[71]

It was Olevian's notion of our common *substantia* with Christ's humanity which underlay his understanding of the eucharist, Christ's body and blood as 'food' and 'drink for our souls'.[72] This union was a mystical notion closely related to his idea of *unio Christo*. This was an important notion for Olevian and he returned to it often. Unlike Calvin, however, he offered neither detailed discussions of the nature of the *unio mystica* nor its relations to the eucharist.[73] Rather he focussed on the objective

---

[68] '...non e substantia Patris gignatur, sed de Spiritu sancto e substantia virginis, eaque aeterno et unigenito Dei filio unita nascatur' (*De substantia*, 1.3.1).

[69] In his commentary on Romans 1.3 he affirmed that 'Christus non est factus filius Dei, sed ab aeterno ex substantia Patris genitus' (Caspar Olevian, *In epistolam D. Pauli apostoli ad Romanos notae ex Gasparis Oleviani concionibus excerptae* [Geneva, 1579], 5). See also *De substantia*, 1.6.9. where he clearly affirmed Jesus' consubstantiality with the Father.

[70] *Firm Foundation*, Q.71. *Vester Grund*, 58–9.

[71] Chemnitz, however, was much closer to Olevian in his explanation of the *unio hypostatica* in *De duabus naturis*, cap. VIII. He also denied that the Lutherans defined it as the communication of attributes, but rather he argued, the *communicatio* follows from the hypostatic union. 'Nos in nostris Ecclesiis hypostaticam unionem, non definire communicatione, sicut cap. 4. de unionis descriptione exposuimus. Sed illam oriri et sequi ex unione, eo modo, sicut in hoc capite explicatum est' (*De duabus naturis*, 325). The expression *personalis unio* occurs frequently in Olevian's Christology. For example, see idem, *Expositio*, 98–100.

[72] 'In sacra Eucharistia diserte annunciatur atque promittitur corpus Domini pro nobis esse traditum, atque ita esse cibum nostrarum animarum sanguinem novi testamenti pro nobis & pro multis esse effusam in remissionem peccatorum, atque ita esse potum nostrarum animarum' (*De substantia* 2.50). See also *Vester Grund*, 61.

[73] In his second response to Westphal, Calvin had defined what he meant by *substantia*. 'Should anyone raise a dispute as to the word substance, we assert

facts of redemption with a view to affirming the certainty of the salvation of the elect.[74] For example, he reasoned that since Christ was consubstantial with us, and since his resurrection body remained consubstantial with ours, and since God has taken our 'whole man' (*totum hominem*) into his covenant (*foedus*) and made us 'confederates' (*confoederati*), he will also resurrect substantially our same body.[75] Calvin's doctrine of the *extra carnem* and his mystical notion of the eucharist, however, provided Olevian with a middle ground between the gnesio-Lutheran and early Zwinglian poles. It retained Luther's emphasis on the gospel (in which the sacrament is the means of help to needy sinners) whilst maintaining a Reformed Christology. Given that Calvin and Olevian worked out their Christologies in similar circumstances (in dialogue with the same sort of Lutheran Christologies) it is surprising that the latter missed the opportunity to exploit his teacher's position on the eucharist to his own rhetorical and theological advantage.

At the Maulbronn colloquy, Olevian was one of the leading Reformed spokesmen, making the opening statement for his side and answering the only question put to the colloquy by Frederick III.[76] He was an appropriate representative for the Palatinate

---

that Christ, from the substance of his flesh, breathes life into our souls; nay, infuses his own life into us, provided always that no transfusion of substance be imagined' (idem, *Second Defense of the Pious and Orthodox Faith Concerning the Sacraments in Answer to the Calumnies of Joachim Westphalia*, trans. Henry Beveridge, *Selected Works of John Calvin*, 5 vols [Edinburgh, 1849; repr. Grand Rapids, 1983], 2.248). 'De voce substantiae si quis litem moveat, Christum asserimus a carnis suae substantia vitam in animas nostras spirare: imo propriam in nos vitam diffundere, modo ne qua substantiae transfusio fingatur' (*Secunda defensio piae et orthodoxae de sacramentis fidei* [Geneva, 1556] in *Corpus Reformatorum*, ed. C. G. Bretschneider, 101 vols [Halle, 1834–1959], 37.47). Clearly this was a mystical conception of *substantia*. The believer benefits from the *substantia* of the ascended and glorified Christ. The question was not whether believers share in Christ's substance, but how and where. It is by faith that one receives the benefits of union with Christ. In the Christian life, however, with the Word and by the Spirit, the Lord's Supper becomes a means of the inspiration of the substance of Christ's flesh into the believer.

[74] This forensic emphasis might be considered a Lutheran move, in contrast to the more interior types of Reformed theology which developed later.

[75] 'Haec ipsa & non alia corpora, quod ad substantiam attinet, resurgent. Deus enim fons vitae qui non dimidium, sed totum hominem in foedus recepit, vivificabit quoque corpora sibi confoederata' (*Expositio*, 186).

[76] Ursinus, *Opera*, 2.93–5. According to Brenz, Boquin was the leading

theologians because he was developing a coherent response to their Lutheran critics beginning with a very Protestant discussion of law and gospel. He developed the Protestant soteriology by using the rubric of the covenant in which Christ was considered as '*Mittler*'.[77] Only a few years earlier he had learned from Calvin that the Lord's Supper (*coena Domini*) is Christ's covenant feast with his people in which God's people meet and are drawn to their ascended Lord.[78] In the supper, Christ communes with, strengthens and confirms them in the covenant. Therefore one finds a correct understanding of Christ's two natures only in the covenant and it becomes a prelude to the correct understanding of salvation and the Supper.

Brevis Admonitio: Christological Federalism

The gnesio-Lutheran Christology was formulated partly in reaction to Calvinism. Reciprocally, Olevian's doctrine was affected by the gnesio-Lutheran doctrine. One observes the effect of this dialogue with the gnesio-Lutherans in an anonymous, undated tract on the eucharist which has not hitherto received scholarly attention.

Appended to Olevian's Commentary on the Gospels (*Notae in Evangelia*, 1587) was *A Brief Admonition Regarding the Matter of Eucharist* (*Brevis Admonitio de re Eucharistica*), which was in three parts, and which may have grown out of his leadership of

---

spokesman for the Palatinate theologians on Christology and Olevian took the lead in the second part of the colloquy in which the eucharist was considered. According to Ursinus' more detailed account, however, Olevian played a leading role throughout the colloquy, participating significantly on four of the six days. There are other interesting differences between the Reformed and Lutheran accounts as well. For example, Ursinus attributed to Olevian the famous and provocative syllogism from *Actio secunda*, 11 April: 'Oceanus ambit universam terram. Antwerpia sita est ad Oceanum, Ergo Antwerpia ambit universam terram' (Ursinus, *Opera*, 2.106). Brenz, however, ascribed the syllogism to the entire Reformed team (idem, *Epitome*, 40). The different ways in which the two parties reported the colloquy to their constituents was due to their ideological commitments, but also to the difference in genre of the reports. Ursinus' report was virtually a transcript and Brenz wrote a summary.

[77]   *Vester Grund*, 2.

[78]   E.g. Joannis Calvini, *Institutio Christianae Religionis 1559*, 4.17.10; *Opera Selecta*, ed. P. Barth and W. Niesel, 3rd edn 5 vols [Munich, 1963–74], 5.351–2.

the General Synod of the Wetterau counties.[79] Since it was published posthumously by his son Paul, with the *Notae in Evangelia*, which were lectures which he delivered in the Herborn Academy one suspects that the *Admonitio* was likely a lecture delivered in the Academy.[80] On either hypothesis, the *Admonitio* provides an interesting glimpse into what Calvinists were telling one another about the eucharist and their opponents.[81]

Both Olevian and the gnesio-Lutheran theologians regarded Scripture as the *fons* of all theology and they both read Scripture within a decidedly Aristotelian framework which informed the sorts of distinctions they made. For example, both assumed the correctness of Boethius' definition of *persona*, i.e. an individual substance of a rational nature.[82] Olevian, however, assumed a distinction between deity and humanity on the basis of his understanding of *natura*. Chemnitz, on the other hand, assumed the possibility of different relations between Christ's humanity and divinity on the basis of his understanding of degree (*gradus*) and class (*genus*).[83] Both also made reference to external

---

[79] Caspar Olevian, *Brevis admonitio de re eucharistica* (Herborn, 1587). This document is distinct from his *Fürschlag* to be discussed below. He began by addressing '*fratres in Christo dilecto*' which suggests that it might have been used at a synod or classis meeting. The General Synod of 1586 which met at Herborn discussed the theology and administration of the sacraments, linking them closely with the covenant ('Synodus Generalis Herbornae Habita', in W. Niesel, ed. *Bekenntnisschriften und Kirchenordnung der nach Gottes Wort reformierten Kirchen* [Munich, 1937], 296–7).

[80] Inside the title page, (page 1) the *Admonitio*, is described as a '*concio*' (lecture).

[81] The *Admonitio* is in three parts, two thirds of which are polemic. Part one: on Christ's institution of the eucharist (2–14); Satan's attempt to overturn the divine counsel (14–20); and the means by which one might obviate Satan's counsel (20–8).

[82] Olevian and Calvin seemed to assume this definition, but Chemnitz cited it explicitly. 'Illam vero Boëtius ita definit: Persona est naturae rationalibis individua substantia' (*De duabus naturis*, 81).

[83] There does not seem to have been a direct connection between Chemnitz and Olevian. There was an indirect connection, however, through Z. Ursinus who wrote *Responsio ad argumenta Martinii Kemnicii et al. de coena Domini*, probably in the early 1580s. See idem, *Tractationum theologicarum*, 2 vols (Neustadt, 1587-9), 2.635–52. It seems likely that Olevian was aware of Chemnitz' Christology, if only through Ursinus. Chemnitz serves as a useful third party in this discussion since, where Brenz and Andrae might be considered somewhat extreme in their views, his may be considered quite representative of the mainstream of Lutheran orthodoxy. He was Luther's

authorities. Martin Chemnitz, for example, provided extensive quotations and explanation of Patristic authorities with some reference to but little explanation of Scripture.[84] Olevian, however, tended to appeal to and explain Scripture and occasionally referred to a Patristic authority.

The *Admonitio* illustrates well Olevian's Reformed Christology. He, like the Lutherans, began with the Supper and worked back to Christology. Nevertheless, he arrived at quite different conclusions. In his mind, the gnesio-Lutheran doctrine of 'real communication or transfusion of properties of the divine nature in the human' violated the distinction between creator and creature by effectively replacing Christ's humanity with his deity.[85]

This confusion of creature with the creator was at the core of his anti-papal polemic. In the Roman mass, folk are led away from God their creator and redeemer by a perverse celebration of the eucharist. In it, Satan has converted to a means of merit that which ought to be a sign of God's munificence.[86]

In his commentary on Romans he also extirpated the 'false opinion of all times' that the sacraments produce justice 'on the grounds of the performance of the rite without faith and the conversion of the heart' (*ex opere operato sine fide et conversione cordis*).[87] The Roman mass was a propitiatory sacrifice, a rite of

---

student, Melanchthon's colleague and an influential commentator on the *Loci Communes*. First presented publicly in 1576, and published in 1578, the Latin text used here appears to have been a second edition. In citing Chemnitz, J. A. O. Preus' translation, *The Two Natures in Christ* (St Louis, 1971), has been consulted but not quoted.

[84] On Chemnitz' use of the Fathers see A. L. Olsen, 'The Hermeneutical Vision of Martin Chemnitz. The Role of Scripture, and Tradition in the Teaching Church', *Augustine, The Harvest, and Theology (1300–1650)*, ed. K. Hagen (Leiden, 1990); R. A. Kelly, 'Tradition and Innovation: The Use of Theodoret's *Eranistes* in Martin Chemnitz' *De Duabus Naturis in Christo*', *Perspectives on Christology: Essays in Honor of Paul K. Jewett*, ed. M. Shuster and R. A. Muller (Grand Rapids, 1991).

[85] 'In definitione autem unionis personalis, quid sit, dissentimus. Palatini enim Theologi docent...quod humana natura non sit particeps facta omnium proprietatum Divinae naturae, reali communicatione, vel transfusione proprietatum Divinae naturae in humanam' (J. Brenz, '*Antithesis*, Art. 3', in *Epitome*, 89).

[86] *Admonitio*, 15.

[87] This translation of 'ex opere...' is suggested by H. A. Oberman, *The Harvest of Medieval Theology* (Cambridge, MA, 1963), 467. 'Extirpanda falsa

the Antichrist in which the eucharistic bread is substituted for God and the fulfilment of Paul's warning (in Romans) about honouring the creature in place of the creator.[88] Though he certainly agreed with the Lutheran critique of the mass –that it perverted justification – it is significant that he considered idolatry to be the chief Roman error. Reformed theologians, beginning with Zwingli, were concerned about the evil of idolatry.[89] Olevian's attack on Rome, however, was quite brief relative to his treatment of the Lutherans. His strategy was to portray the Lutheran errors as slightly less offensive than Rome's. Thus, his treatment of Christology should be read largely as an extended anti-Lutheran argument.[90]

Though obviously concerned about Christ's majesty, the gnesio-Lutherans were more concerned about connecting the eucharist with the promises of gospel such that they argued Christ's objective presence in the eucharist and consequently, the 'eating by the unworthy' (*manducatio indignorum*).[91] Moreover, when Chemnitz said,

---

opinio omnium temporum: quod Sacramenta putarunt prodesse ex opere operato sine fide & conversione cordis' (*In Epistolam d. Pauli apostoli ad Romanos notae, ex concionibus G. Oleviani excerptae*, ed. Theodore Beza (Geneva, 1579), 108.

[88] *Admonitio*, 15. 'Antichristus panem Eucharisticum sanctificatum in monumentum corporis Filii Dei, quo redempti sumus, in locum ipsius Christi agnoscendum honorandumque substituit.... An non hoc est prorsus transformare gloriam τοῦ λόγου incorruptibilis, in similitudinem elementi corruptibilis? Ad Rom. I. An non hoc est honorare creaturam loco Creatoris? (*Admonitio*, 16). He rejected the doctrine of transubstantiation explicitly as the lying of 'Antichrist rabble' (*De substantia*, 2.76).

[89] For an example of the Lutheran critique of the Roman mass see the *Confessio Augustana* (1530), Art. 3 (Schaff, *Creeds*, 3.34–9). For an example of an early Reformed response to the same see Huldrych Zwingli, *Commentarius de vera et falsa religione* in *Huldrici Zuinglii opera completa editio*, 8 vols ed. M. Schuler and J. Schultess (Zürich, 1828/9–42), 1.239–72.

[90] Even in *pars tertia* of the *Admonitio* which he began positively concluded with quite overheated rhetoric, attacking Lutheran 'scorpions' and Satanic errors (*Admonitio*, 26–8).

[91] Brenz, *Epitome*, 71–2; ibid. *De personali*, 51–4. The *manducatio indignorum* taught that Christ is physically and objectively present, by sacramental union with the elements, so that he will be eaten (*manducatio*) by the 'unworthy' (*indignorum*). See *Formula of Concord*, Art. 7, 16. *Negativa. Contrariae et damnatae Sacramentariorum doctrinae rejectio* (Schaff, *Creeds*, 145).

And I repeat the warning I gave before, in the first genus as we call it, we say that God was crucified and dead, that the communication is real, but we add that this was in the person, not in the second, i.e. in the divine nature,[92]

he was distinguishing between 'real communication' and 'essential transfusion or physical confusion' so as to protect the Chalcedonian distinction between the two natures.[93] Nevertheless, Olevian read this sort of language to imply everything which Chemnitz intended to deny. In Olevian's doctrine of God, it was impossible to concede that 'God was crucified', even under the locus of Christology.

Like Chemnitz et al., Olevian was also concerned to maintain a conception of the divine majesty, but one which prohibited the *manducatio* and he was singled out by Brenz for his opposition to the same.[94] Rather, in teaching a Calvinist particularity, he was careful to point out that Christ 'gave himself for the Church' (quoting Ephesians 5:25) '[w]herefore the Apostles in Acts admitted none to the breaking of bread, except the believing and baptised'. He envisioned mixed congregations, but was concerned about their state and, like the Lutherans, the admission of unbelievers to the eucharist.[95] In distinction to his Lutheran counterparts, he argued that the Supper is not a means of justification. 'As Peter says in Acts 10: "Who believes in [Christ] is justified."'[96]

Another difference between Olevian's Christology and that of the gnesio-Lutherans was the context in which he worked out his

---

[92] 'Repeto autem commonefactionem antea etiam traditam, In primo scilicet genere, sicut usitate appellamus, quando dicimus Deum crucifixum et mortuum, communicationem quidem esse realem, sed addimus eam fieri in persona, non in altera etiam divina scilicet natura' (Chemnitz, *De duabus naturis*, 333).

[93] 'Quod vero dicitur, Nos sub appellatione realis communicationis essentialem transfusionem aut physicam confusionem...' (*De duabus naturis*, 333).

[94] Brenz, *Epitome*, 71–3.

[95] 'Viri diligite uxores vestras, sicut Christus dilexit Ecclesiam, et exposuit semetipsum pro ea.... Ideo Apostoli in Actis non alios admittebant ad fractionem panis, quam credentes et baptizatos' (*Admonitio*, 2). Olevian's ecclesiology will be discussed in chapter 7.

[96] '...sicut Actor [sic]. 10. ait Petrus, Qui in hunc credit, iustificatus est' (*Admonitio*, 2). He probably had in mind Acts 13.39, which, in the Vulgate reads: 'in hoc omnis qui credit iustificatur'.

Christology and eucharistic theology. He understood Christ's work and hence the Supper in a *federal* context, i.e. considering Adam to have been the first corporate, legal, or federal representative of all humanity and Christ the second federal head of (redeemed) humanity. In such a scheme the parallels between the first Adam and Christ are most important since the intent of the incarnation is that the God-man should obey where Adam did not and more he must be able to satisfy the divine wrath. Hence, in Olevian's Christology, Christ's consubstantiality with Adam was at the heart of the matter because it was one of the organising principles of his soteriology.

As part of his federalism, he also placed Christ's work in an Anselmic scheme. God having willed to save sinners, 'it was necessary that a certain person with a *mandatum...à patre* be raised up in the human race'. For this reason, he says that Paul (in Romans 1:3) taught about Christ's two natures (*de duabus in Christo naturis*): '[t]hrough man sin has entered into the world and death through sin'.[97] Therefore he placed great stress on Christ's humanity.

> Because he was born of the seed of man he is true man. Therefore Christ's flesh was not brought forth from heaven (*ergo caro Christi non ex coelis allata*), but having been born from the blood of the virgin, David's daughter, so that he might be true man.[98]

The Lutherans agreed that Jesus was true man, and for the same reason, that he was born of the virgin. His remark, '*ergo caro Christi non ex coelis allata*' reveals, however, how he viewed the Lutheran Christology. By teaching the *communicatio* and the

---

[97] 'Oportebat certam esse personam quae instauraret genus humanum: (de qua Euangelium tractat) quae mandatum haberet a patre et ad hoc ordinata esset. Quemadmodum enim per hominem peccatum ingressum est in mundum et per peccatum mors: ita oportebat certum esse personam, quae salvaret, ad Rom. 5. Personam autem Deus promiserat certam, filium suum, qui propter nostram salutem homo factus est. Itaque docet de duabus in Christo naturis (Caspar Olevian, *In epistolam D. Pauli ad Romanos notae* [Geneva, 1579], 5). For the relations between Calvin's soteriology and Anselm's see R. B. Strimple, 'St Anselm's *Cur Deus homo* and John Calvin's Doctrine of the Atonement', *Aoasta, Bec and Canterbury*, ed. D. E. Luscombe and G. R. Evans (Sheffield, 1996).

[98] 'Quod ex semine hominis nascitur verus est homo. Ergo caro Christi non ex coelis allata, sed ex virginis sanguine, quae est filia Davidis, nata est, ut esset verus homo' (Caspar Olevian, *In Romanos*, 5).

genus maiestaticum, though they affirmed Christ's virgin conception, they implied a sort of docetism in which a heavenly, deified humanity overwhelmed natural humanity as if one nature were sufficient for redemption.

Where the gnesio-Lutherans stressed the 'real communication' of the two natures, Olevian was emphasising the reality of Christ's sufferings.[99] The Lutherans assigned to Christ's flesh what was proper to his deity. Olevian agreed that the deity operated on Christ's humanity, not to transform it, but to make it suitable for the accomplishment of redemption. Christ's deity 'sanctified Christ's flesh and vivified it hypostatically in unity'.[100] By his strong emphasis on Christ's humanity and the personal union of the two natures, he may be read as having positioned himself, ironically, as the true champion of Luther's *theologia crucis* relative to the gnesio-Lutheran *theologia gloriae*.[101] More than that, he was positioning his Christology as the more Chalcedonian of the two.[102]

Like other Reformed theologians of his era, Olevian used the biblical analogy of marriage to express both his federalism and particularism.[103] In his view, Christ died for his *sponsa* (bride).

> The Lord instituted the eucharist for none other than his bride, that is, for those who believe and who are baptised, those professing faith and repentance. The reason is that he yielded not his body for others, but for his bride (Ephesians 5:23).[104]

---

[99] For example, see Chemnitz, *De duabus*, 315.

[100] 'Deitas ipsam Christi carnem sanctificat et vivificat hypostatice ei unita' (*In Romanos*, 6).

[101] *In Romanos*, 6.

[102] See Dorner, 4.225–7. J. Brenz, however, opened his argument by quoting Chalcedon (*De personali*, 6–7). Thus it is not as if the Definition was not in the Lutheran consciousness.

[103] For example see J. L. Farthing, '*De Coniugio Spirituali*: Jerome Zanchi on Ephesians 5:22–33', *Sixteenth Century Journal* 24 (1993), 621–52; idem, 'Holy Harlotry: Jerome Zanchi and the Exegetical History of Gomer (Hosea 1–3). *Biblical Interpretation in the Era of the Reformation*, ed. R. A. Muller and J. L. Thompson (Grand Rapids, 1996).

[104] 'Eucharistiam non aliis instituit Dominus, quam suae sponsae, hoc est, credentibus et baptizatis, sive profitentibus fidem et poenitentiam. Ratio est, qua corpus suum non tradidit pro aliis, quam pro sponsa, ad Ephe. 5.v.23' (*Admonitio*, 2).

This implied a particularist soteriology. This notion was, in turn, grounded in Olevian's idea of the nature of Christ's death and its purpose. He consistently described Christ's death in substitutionary categories.[105] Only in the case that Christ's humanity is preserved can he be said to have accomplished obedience and satisfied the divine wrath.

In Olevian's scheme, sin was not considered an ontological but moral problem. Thus, his solution was framed in moral, forensic, soteriological, and covenantal terms. In the case that all Adam's children are conceived and born in sin, there is none except the God-Man capable of rendering sufficient obedience to turn away the divine wrath. Therefore, the two natures must be united but distinct, so that he remains the God-Man and not some *tertium quid*. Where the Lutherans began with the *communicatio*, Olevian began with the necessity of a mediator between sinful flesh and a transcendent, holy God. A mediator necessarily implies parties in legal relations requiring someone to represent sinners to God and him to sinners. Hence, Olevian conceived Christ's work as obtaining salvation which was the outworking of the eternal covenant (*foedus aeternum*) between God and the Church.[106]

For Olevian the eucharist is a symbolic representation of the 'special benefit', that is, the Christ's 'sacrificial offering of his body and blood, by which the Bridegroom redeemed her from Satan's power, and ratified the eternal covenant with the Father'.[107] Through Christ's death the *foedus* was renewed (*renovetur*) and the fellowship (κοινωνία) between Christ and his bride was strengthened (*augeatur*).[108]

For Olevian, the primary function of the supper was to serve as the means of covenant renewal and confirmation of God's gracious intent toward his people. This concept of covenant renewal also indicates how Olevian's Christology differed from

---

[105] *Admonitio*, 25.

[106] *Admonitio*, 3. '...ut sit cultus Eucharisticus pro sancito foedere aeterno erga Patrem...' (op. cit. 4). See also *De substantia* 2.73: 'Cum enim in substantia foederis demonstratum sit Christum pro omnibus & solis electis...'. Olevian's soteriology will be discussed, in detail, in the next chapter.

[107] '...pro beneficio speciali his symbolis repraesentato, nempe unico illo corporis et sanguinis sui in cruce oblato sacrificio, quo sponsus a potestate Satanae eam redemit, et foedus aeternum cum Patre sancivit' (*Admonitio*, 3).

[108] *Admonitio*, 3, 22. See also *De inventione*, 190–91.

both his gnesio-Lutheran opponents and the Zwinglians. Among the latter, in its earlier manifestations, the supper was treated primarily under sanctification and there was no notion of mystical union with Christ in the Supper. Even though in later Zwinglianism there was movement toward the more overtly mystical position, Bullinger's Second Helvetic Confession (1561/66) treated the supper in Article 19, under the broader head of the church, which is to say under sanctification.[109] On the other hand, for the gnesio-Lutherans the supper was treated under justification.[110]

Like Calvin, Olevian occupied a mediating position. Though he denied that the eucharist communicates justifying grace, he also did not treat it primarily under sanctification. Rather, its primary function was said to be to renew the covenant promise of redemption in Christ. Therefore, in his *Notae* in the gospels he said that the sacraments are promises from God of the justification of God's people.[111] Nevertheless, the Protestant law-gospel dichotomy was fundamental to his soteriology and it coloured his eucharistic theology.[112] Therefore he also considered the supper an act of gratitude which is a means to sanctification.[113] Thus, the eucharist is to be celebrated in 'worship and honour of Christ' in gratitude for the 'dear imputed righteousness' which is the ground of the Christian's justification. 'I strongly insist about this,' he lectured, 'that *iustitia imputata* is received even before the sacraments' and the commemoration of Christ's death does not contribute to one's justification. The eucharist is, however, part of the public celebration of our union

---

[109] The *Consensus Tigurinus* shows movement by the Zürich theologians from their earlier positions. Articles 6 and 7 teach that believers have a spiritual communication with Christ in the Supper. See H. A. Niemeyer, ed., *Collectio confessionum in Ecclesiis reformatis publicatorum* (Leipzig, 1840), 193. See also *Confessio Helvetica Posterior*, Art. XIX, in P. Schaff, ed. *The Creeds of Christendom*, 3 vols, 6th edn (Grand Rapids, [repr.] 1983), 3.285–9;

[110] *Formula concordiae*, Art. 7 in P. Schaff, ed., *Creeds*, 3.135. Martin Chemnitz said, 'Ostendendum est etiam, cibum ac potum illum, esse vivificum et saluitiferum, quod certe non est naturale Idioma humani corporis, sed Christi corpus ex hypostatica cum Divinitate unione praerogativam illam accepit et habet' (idem, *Epistola Dedicatoria, De duabus naturis*, 13).

[111] *Notae in Evangelia*, 218.

[112] Olevian's law-gospel dichotomy in justification is discussed at length in chapter 6.

[113] *Admonitio*, 20.

with Christ's death and resurrection, 'through the Gospel, sealed in baptism, that you and your household might offer inwardly and outwardly worship to Christ the Redeemer'.[114] It is the function of the supper to call attention to Christ, 'God revealed in the flesh' (*Deus manifestatus in carne*) and his redemption, represented by the breaking of the bread (*fractio panis*).[115] Therefore his eucharistic theology was closely related to his doctrines of justification and sanctification.[116] His connection of the supper with justification distinguished him from the Zwinglians and his federal or covenantal approach to the eucharist distinguished his treatment of the supper from the gnesio-Lutherans.

His use of 'κοινωνία' was another indicator of the way federalism functioned in his Christology. He used it consistently to describe the ministry of the ascended Christ, through the Holy Spirit, among his people. This reflected his concern to affirm the Christian's mystical union with Christ. In contrast, Martin Chemnitz used 'κοινωνία' just as consistently in *On the Two Natures* (*De duabus naturis*, 1580) to describe relations between the two natures of Christ.[117] Olevian's application of it reflected his need to protect his conception of the special relations between the two natures.

In response to the gnesio-Lutheran doctrine, Olevian alleged that the Lutheran version of the *communicatio idiomatum* and their doctrine of Christ's *genus maiestaticum* constituted nothing

---

[114] 'Ac primum quidem ad cultum honoremque Christi quod attinet, quam cara tibi est Christi mortui et excitati gloria, quam cara gratuita fidei etiam ante usum sacramentorum imputata iustitia, tam fortiter huic rei insistito, ut non iustitiam primum in opere commemorationis mortis Domini quaeras: sed publica laetitia pro iam ante ipsius morte parta et resurrectione in lucem producta, patefacta vero per Euangelium, Baptismo obsignata, tu, domusque tua Christo redemptori cultum hunc Eucharisticum interne et externe exhibeas' (*Admonitio*, 20).

[115] *Admonitio*, 22.

[116] The Heidelberg Catechism treated the supper in the second part of the catechism (Q.75–82) not under the third part (Q.86–129). See *The Heidelberg Catechism in German, Latin and English with an Historical Introduction* (New York, 1863).

[117] Martin Chemnitz, *De duabus naturis*, 216–17, 254, 265, 331. He was following Cyril of Alexandria and John of Damascus' expression ἰδιωμάτων κοινωνία. For references see John Calvin, *Institutes of the Christian Religion*, trans. F. L. Battles, ed. J. T. McNeill (Philadelphia, 1961), 2.14.1. n. 4.

less than a denial Christ's true humanity. In Olevian's mind, for Christ to be truly and fully human, he must share the natural limitations which humans experience. To be consubstantial with us, Christ must remain in the same humanity with which he was conceived, in which he suffered, and with which he ascended. Olevian's remedy to the problems he perceived in both the Lutheran and Roman Christologies was to place his Christology in the context of the *foedus*, which required both a distinction of the two natures and their personal union in Christ.[118]

His first reason for asserting and defending the Calvinist conception of Christ's true humanity and deity was to be able to teach Christ's vicarious substitutionary death. The first work of the *sponsio* was that Christ should die as '*Sponsor* (guarantor) of the New Testament, that he might justify his bride, the elect Church...from all sins'.[119] Another motive was his desire to be able to speak meaningfully, from a Reformed Christology, about the 'second part of the promise' (*altera pars sponsionis*): Christ's priestly, mediatorial work in his ascension. Part of the Christian's assurance is that one has a mediator who is consubstantial with one, who has not only died as the expiation of sins, and the propitiation of the divine wrath, but who also carries on a ministry of intercession before the Father.[120]

In *De substantia* he discussed Christ's intercessory ministry in tandem with his reign over the Church.[121] Working primarily from Psalm 110, Olevian conceived the incarnate Son conducting his Melchizedekian priesthood 'in the heavenly Sanctuary where is light inaccessible...without interruption' (*in coeleste*

---

[118] *Admonitio*, 20–8.

[119] 'Primum enim cum Christus sponsor esset novi testamenti, qui sponsam suam Ecclesiam electam iustificaret...ab omnibus peccatis' (*De substantia*, 1.6.11).

[120] See his reflections on 1 John 2:1–2 in *De substantia*, 1.6.13. Olevian's practical and pastoral concerns are even more evident in his earlier *Expositio symboli apostolici* (89, 97), where he explained the *consolatio* of hypostatic union.

[121] 'Deinde et alterum e descriptione ex scripturae verbis posita non minus est manifestum, sessionem Christi ad dextram Patris omnipotentis esse exaltationem λογου incarnati in sacerdotio et regno: et continere duas partes: prior est locus honorificentissimus in quem exaltatus est: altera est coram Angelis et beatis hominibus palam declarata potestas officii, sistendi se in conspectu Patris ut aeternum Sacerdotem et administrandi omnia in coelo et in terra ut aeternum Regem Ecclesiae' (*De substantia*, 1.6.10).

Sanctuarium ubi est lux inaccessa...sine interruptione).[122] One may be assured that, because one has a priest continually before the Father, 'all memory of our sin has been abolished'.[123] His continual ministry is evidence that Christ's *oblatio* is efficacious.[124] Behind these grounds for confidence is the certainty that all of this is the result of God's 'immutable divine decree'.[125]

Olevian's Pastoral Response: his 'Fürschlag'

Olevian's capacity for polemic has been observed already. He was, however, also capable of irenicism, particularly in the context of his parish ministry. He preached regularly in Holy Spirit Church (*Heiliggeistkirche*) and taught catechumens as well as seminary and university students. His pastoral ministry began almost from the moment he arrived in Heidelberg. He also preached regularly on Sunday evening in conjunction with the administration of the Supper. As he taught catechism or looked out over his pulpit he saw folk whom he could hardly regard as being fully Reformed. Though there had been a sharp change in Palatinate administration, the eucharist was still a central part of both Calvinist and Lutheran worship and parishioners expected to receive the supper regularly.

Yet Olevian faced some thorny practical problems. Most of his congregation, particularly in the early days of the Calvinist Reformation of Heidelberg, probably did not appreciate the differences between the Calvinist and Lutheran ideas of the eucharist or if they did, having been instructed with Luther's Smaller Catechism, they were likely hostile to the new teaching. On the one hand, he needed to lead his congregation more fully into the truth, and on the other to defend the new Calvinist teaching.[126]

---

[122] *De substantia*, 1.6.12.

[123] '[P]ropter ipsum omnis peccatorum nostrorum memoria abolita maneret' (*De substantia*, 1.6.12).

[124] *De substantia*, 1.6.14.

[125] *De substantia*, 1.6.14. This expression occurs quite frequently in sections 14–18.

[126] Bierma, 'Lutheran Reformed Polemics in the Late Reformation: Olevianus' Conciliatory "Proposal",' *Controversy and Conciliation: the Palatinate Reformation, 1559–1618*, ed. D. Visser (Pittsburgh, 1986), 53, characterises Olevian's preaching on the eucharist as a broadside against

Thus, his sermons set out to correct the Lutheran theology of the eucharist, which was grounded in the Lutheran Christology, and to present the correct understanding of both.[127] Thus, whether in pulpit or at conference table, the questions of eucharist and Christology were ever before him. He was not interested, however, in simply scoring debating points against the opposition. Rather, his Reformed Christology, including a correct understanding of the eucharist and Christ's substantial and continuing humanity, was the ground of the Christian's assurance of faith which itself was the result of appropriating Christ's twofold benefits of justification and sanctification.[128] 'I am confident' (*Ich gewiß*), he said, because Christ was born '*im Fleisch*'.[129]

In the 1590 edition of *Gnadenbund Gottes* his collection of sermons on the eucharist was followed by an interesting, anonymous tract, *Proposal, How Doctor Luther's Doctrine of the Holy Sacraments (Contained in his Small Catechism) Can be Shown from the Word of God to Be Compatible with the Reformed Churches.*[130] The exact date and occasion of his *Fürschlag* is uncertain. Bierma surveys three possibilities: first, that it was Olevian's contribution to the Frankfurt Recess of 1558; second that it was written during his Heidelberg period (1560–76); third, that it was written after his exile from Heidelberg

---

ubiquity and the *manducatio infidelium*. In February 1564, M. Flaccius responded to Olevian in *Widerlegung vier predigten eines Sakramentierers, mit Zunamen Olevianus*. The wealth of material in these sermons would be a fruitful area of research, but one which is beyond the scope of this work. See the 1590 edition of *Gnadenbund Gottes* (Herborn, 1590; repr. Bonn, 1994), 225–411.

[127] In the 1590 edition of *Gnadenbund Gottes*, *Vester Grund* was 163 pages long and the collection of sermons on the Lord's Supper was just slightly shorter at 157 pages.

[128] *Firm Foundation*, Q.72. *Vester Grund*, 61–2.

[129] *Vester Grund*, 43.

[130] *Fürschlag, Wie Doctor Luthers Lehr von den Heiligen Sacramenten (so in seinem kleinen Catechismo begrissen) auß Gottes Wort mit den reformirten Kirchen zu vereinigen seye* was appended to his sermons on the Lord's Supper ('Predigt...in dem H. Abendmal unsers Herrn Jesu Christi'), published in the facsimile reprint of the 1590 edition of *Gnadenbund Gottes* (Bonn, 1994). L. D. Bierma's English translation of the *Fürschlag* is in *Controversy and Conciliation*, 63–71. This tract is anonymous, but its inclusion in *Gnadenbund Gottes* makes it probable that Olevian was its author. In the light of his 16-year Christological and eucharistic controversy with the gnesio-Lutherans and Ludwig's antipathy for Olevian, his anonymity in this tract is understandable.

ca.1577–80.[131] He rejects the first two options as implausible. The Recess came before Olevian's theological training in Geneva and Zürich and the heat of the Lutheran-Calvinist controversy (1560–76) makes the second unlikely. He concludes in favour of the third on the strength of the expression, in the preface, 'woefully banished Christians' (*'den jammerlich verjagien Christen'*) which he takes to refer to the expulsion of 1576.[132]

This reconstruction, though probable, requires a minor revision. The *Fürschlag* was actually little more an outline rather than a fully developed argument. Therefore, though it was published after the exile, it probably reflects his parish and classroom teaching as he led students and catechumens from the Lutheran to the Calvinist view.

Both the gnesio-Lutherans and the Heidelberg Calvinists considered themselves Luther's heirs. The Calvinists laid claim to Luther's doctrine of predestination.[133] In his account of the colloquy, Brenz portrayed the Lutherans as Luther's true heirs on the basis primarily of their unity with his Christology and eucharistic theology.[134] Because the Wittenberg spokesman represented an important segment of an established religion in the Empire his (the Lutheran) characterisation of the Calvinist Christology was quite influential, controlling the received story of Calvinism for centuries after. Not only had the Calvinists fallen from the Protestant religion, indeed, the Calvinist Christology was blasphemous, 'Talmudic' and 'Alcoranic' (i.e. from the Koran).[135]

In the light of such a portrayal, it was incumbent upon Olevian to establish his Protestant credentials and, by extension, those of his Palatinate colleagues. This explains his solicitous language. He needed to achieve a measure of acceptance for

---

[131] Bierma, 'Lutheran-Reformed', 51–3.

[132] Caspar Olevian, 'Fürschlag', 188. See L. D. Bierma, 'Lutheran-Reformed Polemics in the Late Reformation: Olevianus' Conciliatory Proposal',' *Controversy and Conciliation*, 51–62. Bierma's English translation of the *Fürschlag* is in *Controversy and Conciliation*, 63–71.

[133] At the Colloquy of Montbéliard (1585) Theodore Beza claimed repeatedly to follow Luther on predestination. See J. Raitt, *The Colloquy of Montbéliard* (Oxford, 1993), 154, 207–10.

[134] Brenz, *Epitome*, 30, 80. Brenz also appended to *De personali* a collection of sentences from Luther on the eucharist.

[135] Brenz, *Epitome*, 49. See also Raitt, *Colloquy*, 9.

German Calvinists as Protestant brothers, which the Wittenberg theologians had been most reluctant to grant.[136]

> Furthermore, I herewith plainly acknowledge that I do not think of the late Dr. Luther in any other way than as a great servant of God, whom I, too, love from the heart and speak of only in honor.[137]

He also had to establish his Protestant credentials by demonstrating a correlation between the Calvinist Christology and eucharistic theology with Luther's.

> I also have no doubt that if the right honorable man were still living and should see this meditation, he would be satisfied that it is in accord with Scripture....[138]

He continued by quoting Luther's own warning, from the preface to the 1545 Latin edition of works, that his writings should be read carefully.[139] By implication, Olevian was saying that the gnesio-Lutherans were slavish in their devotion to Luther and that it was actually the German Calvinists who were carrying on his Protestant hermeneutical program, *sola Scriptura*. He was not claiming that his Christology agreed with Luther's but that he was following the Doctor's own method (*'Diß seind Doctor Luthers*

---

[136] Brenz admitted that the Wittenberg theologians were unwilling to call '*frater*' those who denied Christ's '*summam Maiestatem*' and who made 'empty and mendacious' ('*vanum et mendacem*') his promises (*Epitome*, 82–3). Calvinists had long been more solicitous of their older brothers. See B. A. Gerrish, 'John Calvin on Luther', *Interpreters of Luther*, ed. J. Pelikan (Philadelphia, 1968). On the Reformed view of Luther generally see R. Kolb, 'Luther, Augsburg, and the Concept of Authority'; Bodo Nischan, 'Reformation or Deformation? Lutheran and Reformed Views of Martin Luther in Brandenburg's 'Second Reformation', *Pietas e t Societas: New Trends i n Reformation Social History. Essays in Honor of Harold J. Grimm*, ed. K. C. Sessions and P. N. Bebb (Kirksville, MO, 1985), 203–15.

[137] '*Proposal*', 63–4. 'Für's ander bekenn ich hiemit rund / Daß ich von Doctor Luther seligen anders nicht halte / denn von einem großen diener Gottes / den ich auch von hertzen liebe / und anders nicht dann in Ehren von im rede' ('Fürschlag', 189).

[138] 'Proposal', 64. 'Ich zweiffel auch nicht, da der gute ehrliche Mann noch hie leben / und dise betrachtung sehen solte / er würde mit derselben als schriftmässigen zu friden senn...' ('Fürschlag', 189).

[139] Olevian translated Luther's remarks into German for his readers. See Martin Luther, *Luthers Werke Kritische Gesamtausgabe*, ed. J. K. F. Knaake, G. Kawerau et al. (Weimar, 1883–), 54, 179–87.

seligen Wort'), deriving his theology from Scripture and reading Luther critically.[140] 'If now God has given grace so that the persecuted Christians in the school of the cross have been graced with somewhat more light, who would wish wantonly to douse such light?'[141] According to Olevian, the Calvinist Christology was not only in the trajectory of Luther's own method and principles but it was also an advance over Luther's own conclusions, delivered by the hand of providence.

It is not hard to imagine that few of Olevian's Lutheran opponents found this sort of argument compelling. That he made this sort of connection is more important, however, than whether it actually existed, because it says something important about not only Olevian, but also the German Calvinists of the period: they were not theological radicals, but consciously reforming an existing Protestant tradition.

This chapter has argued that Olevian developed and defended his Christology in the context of a 27-year dialogue with gnesio-Lutheran theology.[142] In response to his critics, he defended a Reformed Christology, the basic outlines of which were developed by Calvin. Though both the gnesio-Lutherans and the Calvinists shared several concerns, Olevian's Christology was distinguished from the Lutherans by his federalism, and his more highly developed trinitarianism.

He regarded his Reformed Christology and particularly Christ's continuing consubstantiality with us (against the Lutheran doctrine of ubiquity) as part of the *substantia* of the *foedus* between God and the elect. To Olevian, it appeared that in the Lutheran Christology, Christ's deity swallowed up his humanity, effectively denying the Chalcedonian distinction between the two natures.

Both Olevian and his Lutheran opponents reasoned primarily from Scripture but often expressed their Christologies using Aristotelian categories. Nevertheless, Given the Lutheran charges

---

[140] Ursinus made a similar argument in 1581, in chapter 6 ('*De authoritate Lutheri*') of his *Admonitio Christiana de libero concordiae*. See idem, *Opera*, 2.574–95.

[141] 'Proposal', 64. 'Da nun Gott Gnad gegeben hette / daß die versolgten Schriften in der Creutzschulen mit etwas weiterm liecht von Christo weren begnadet worden: Wer wolte solches liecht muttwillig dämpffen...' ('Fürschlag', 189).

[142] This was almost half of Olevian's life.

of rationalism against the Reformed Christology, it is ironic that Olevian positioned himself as Luther's true heir, over against his more philosophically inclined adversaries.

His Christology was, however, more than a reaction to Lutheran opposition. It is evident throughout his literary corpus that he wanted to provide a federalist, particularist Christology coherent with his soteriology and pastoral concerns. He wanted his students and parishioners to believe in the Christ who died for them, and who was raised for their justification, and who is locally ascended at the right hand of God where he conducts his priestly ministry for them. Hence, one finds in Olevian an emphasis on the necessity of Christ's consubstantiality with God and us in order to offer assurance of justification to his parishioners.

CHAPTER 6

JUSTIFICATION:

The First Benefit of the Covenant of Grace

The doctrine of salvation and particularly the question of how men are justified before God was at the centre of the sixteenth-century controversy between Protestants and Rome. Yet, it was also a cause of contention between the Protestants themselves. Like all the other theological topics, the Protestant soteriologies developed throughout the sixteenth century and were still under revision in the age of orthodoxy, scholasticism, and confessionalism.[1] By the time Olevian was working out his

---

[1] For a bibliography of the modern secondary literature through the mid 1980s on the doctrine of justification see A. E. McGrath, *Iustitia Dei: A History of the Christian Doctrine of Justification*, 2 vols (Cambridge, 1986). The following is a supplementary bibliography of monographs and essays not listed in McGrath's bibliography or published since 1986. B. Hägglund, *The Background of Luther's Doctrine of Justification in Late Medieval Theology* (Philadelphia, 1971); L. C. Green, 'Faith, Righteousness, and Justification: New Light on their Development Under Luther and Melanchthon', *Sixteenth Century Journal* 4 (1973), 65–86; idem, 'The Influence of Erasmus upon Melanchthon, Luther and the Formula of Concord in the Doctrine of Justification', *Church History* 43 (1974), 183–200; C. P. Carlson, Jr, *Justification in Earlier Medieval Theology* (The Hague, 1975); J. Heinz, *Justification and Merit: Luther vs. Catholicism* (Berrien Springs, MI, 1984); A. Zumkeller, 'Der Terminus "*sola fides*" bei Augustinus', *Christian Authority: Essays in Honour of Henry Chadwick*, ed. G. R. Evans (Oxford, 1988); E. Yarnold, '*Duplex Iustitia*: The Sixteenth Century and the Twentieth', ibid.; S. Strehle, '*Fides aut foedus*: Wittenberg and Zürich in Conflict Over the Gospel', *Sixteenth Century Journal* 23 (1992), 3–20; idem, '*Imputatio iustitiae*: Its Origin in Melanchthon, its Opposition in Osiander', *Theologische Zeitschrift* 50 (1994), 201–19; C. P. Bammel, 'Justification By Faith in Augustine and Origen', *Journal of Ecclesiastical History* 47 (1996), 223–35; Lowell C. Green, 'Luther's Understanding of the Freedom of God and the Salvation of Man: His Interpretation of 1 Timothy 2:4', *Archiv für Reformationsgeschichte* 87 (1996), 57–73.

doctrines of faith, justification, and predestination, Protestantism had been convulsed by serious internal controversies over the relations between faith and works (e.g. the Majorist controversy, 1551–2) with the result that stability in the various Protestant soteriologies was shaken. Moreover, from Olevian's point of view, Reformed theologians laboured under the constant suspicion that they were 'crafty and hot', i.e. they pretended to be Protestant but were really sub-Protestant fanatics.[2] For these external reasons, Olevian had good reason to reconsider the doctrine of salvation he received from his teachers Calvin, Beza, and Martyr.

There were also internal reasons in Protestant theology which caused Olevian to recast the received soteriology in more

---

This chapter assumes that the forensic doctrine of justification (*iustitia imputata aliena*) as expressed in the magisterial Protestant confessions was the fruit of Luther and Melanchthon's theological collaboration and the result of Luther's theological development from 1513–19. It is further assumed that the forensic doctrine of justification is a fixed part of the definition of the word Protestant. Cf. S. Strehle who argues that the Protestant doctrine of justification was derived primarily from Melanchthon's 1532 commentary on Romans (*Imputatio Iustitiae*, 201–7). His reading of the *Confessio Augustana* (Art. 3) as well as the earlier writings of Melanchthon and Luther seems strained, however. For a more careful and convincing account of the Protestant development of the doctrine see A. E. McGrath, '*Mira et Nova Diffinitio Iustitiae*: Luther and Scholastic Doctrines of Justification', *Archiv für Reformationsgeschichte* 74 (1983), 37–60; idem, *Iustitia Dei*, 2:1–32; H. A. Oberman, '*Iustitia Christi* and *Iustitia Dei*: Luther and the Scholastic Doctrines of Justification', *Harvard Theological Review* (1966), 1–26; L. C. Green, 'The Influence of Erasmus'; Hägglund, *The Background*; J. L. Farthing, *Thomas Aquinas and Gabriel Biel: Interpretations of St. Thomas Aquinas in German Nominalism on the Eve of the Reformation* (Durham, NC, and London, 1988), 150–80.

There is a considerable variety of opinions on exactly when Luther became a Protestant. A. E. McGrath argues that Luther made his Protestant breakthrough during his lectures on the Psalms in 1513–14 so that he was armed with a substantially new (i.e. Protestant) definition of justification when he came to his lectures on Romans ('Mira et Nova', 42–6; idem, ' "The Righteousness of God" from Augustine to Luther', *Studia Theologica* 36 [1982], 73–4). H. A. Oberman says, however, that not until Easter, 1518, did Luther have in place the 'three principles of the Reformation', i.e. *sola gratia, sola scriptura* and *sola fide* (idem, *Luther: Man Between God and the Devil* [London, 1993], 192). L. C. Green argues that Luther did not re-define his doctrine of faith and fundamentally re-interpret Romans 1:17 until 1518–19 ('Faith, Righteousness, and Justification').

[2] 'Alii autem sunt versuti et calidi et quidem omnium nocentissimi Sacramentarii' (*Formula Concordiae, Epitome*, Art. 7 in *Die Bekenntnisschriften der evangelisch-lutherischen Kirche*, 2 vols (Göttingen, 1956–9), 2.796.

explicitly federal terms.[3] Earlier Protestant theology had taught, more or less uniformly, the importance of sanctification, but in its theological organisation, it had created no ready place for a more mature doctrine of Christian renewal.

Olevian's Protestant, federal, predestinarian soteriology was an attempt to address that lacuna by adding to the established Protestant law-gospel dichotomy a formal place for a more developed doctrine of sanctification without jeopardising the forensic doctrine of justification.[4] He did so by using his doctrine

---

[3] A. A. Woolsey has shown that the federal impulses which found expression in Reformed scholasticism were latent in earlier Protestant theology. See idem, 'Unity and Continuity in Covenantal Thought: A Study in the Reformed Tradition to the Westminster Assembly', 2 vols (Ph.D. Thesis, Glasgow University, 1988).

[4] In his preface to Olevian's notes on Galatians, Beza observed how by explaining the nature of the covenant Olevian was explaining and defending the Protestant gospel against Rome. See *In epistolam D. Pauli apostoli ad Galatas notae* (Geneva, 1578), *Epistola*, 2 (hereafter *Ad Galatas*). The threefold structure (Guilt, Grace, and Gratitude) structure of the Heidelberg Catechism was one of the more obvious examples of this restructuring by Reformed theologians.

Olevian's federalism should be said to unify, rather than dominate, his theology. In this regard, some of the critics of Reformed federalism seem to have misunderstood it theologically and historically. Judging by the literature from the nineteenth and early twentieth centuries, many scholars appear to have drawn their conclusions from H. Heppe's *Die Dogmatik der evangelisch-reformierten Kirche* (Elberfeld, 1861), *loci*, 13–14, which drew almost solely from Cocceius. Hence, the discussion tended to ask whether Cocceius was the progenitor of Reformed federalism. In fact, as more recent research has shown, the basic lines were established as early as the mid-1520s.

For many other scholars, it appears that federalism of any sort, whether medieval or Protestant is necessarily in tension with Luther's doctrine of justification. For example, see A. E. McGrath, 'The Anti-Pelagian Structure of 'Nominalist' Doctrines of Justification', *Ephemerides Theologicae Louvainienses* 57 (1981), 117; idem, 'Mira et Nova', 59. C. Lindberg illustrates Luther's movement from medieval to Protestant theology by juxtaposing Luther's earlier 'covenantal theology' with his Protestant 'theology of testament' (idem, *The European Reformations* [Oxford, 1996], 70). Along similar lines, D. A. Weir argues that the prelapsarian covenant was a novelty to Protestantism and that it was non-existent in the early Reformation. He further claims that Ursinus was the first Reformed theologian to make substantial use of the *foedus*. See idem, *The Origins of the Federal Theology in Sixteenth Century Reformation Thought* (Oxford, 1990), 101. Weir's monograph was based on his 1984 Ph.D. Diss. however, and his claims have more recently been rather seriously undermined by the research of A. A. Woolsey. See idem, 'Unity and Continuity'. S. Strehle

of the covenant to express his doctrine of the twofold benefit (*duplex beneficium*), i.e. that God, in the gracious covenant (*foedus gratuitum*) had promised both to justify and sanctify his people. By casting the Protestant doctrine of justification in federal terms, he attempted to bring justification and sanctification into stable relations with each other.

Yet, despite the controversies over the exact relations of sanctification and justification, there had been, since the publication of the *Augsburg Confession* (1530), a consensus among the magisterial Protestant theologians and confessions on the essentials of the doctrine of justification: grace is God's unmerited favour (*favor Dei*), faith is assent (*assensus*) and trust (*fiducia*) which receives the imputed justice of Christ (*iustitia imputata Christi*).[5]

---

argues that the true impetus for federal theology was Swiss, humanist moralism verging on synergism ('*Fides aut foedus*', passim).

Such questions about Reformed federalism are not new and can be traced to the seventeenth-century debate over who were Calvin's proper heirs. Arminius, for example, argued that a *foedus operum* was latent Pelagianism. See idem, *Apologia sive Defensio*, Art. XV, *Iacobi Arminii Opera theologica* (London, 1629); *Apology or Defence, The Works of James Arminius*, trans. J. Nichols and W. Nichols, 3 vols (London, 1825–75; repr. Grand Rapids, 1996], 2.15). On the other side, the Princeton theologian B. B. Warfield argued that seventeenth-century Reformed theology used federalism as a bulwark against the Amyrauldian theology of J. de la Place to uphold the Protestant doctrine of imputation. See idem, 'Imputation', *Studies in Theology* [New York, 1932], 307). For a more extensive critique of Weir and Strehle see R. S. Clark and J. R. Beeke, 'Ursinus, Oxford and the Westminster Divines', *The Westminster Confession into the 21st Century: Essays in Remembrance of the 350th Anniversary of the Publication of the Westminster Confession of Faith*, 3 vols, ed. J. L. Duncan (Fearn, Ross-shire, 2003–), 2.1–32.

[5]   The forensic emphasis of the Reformed theologians, confessions, and catechisms agreed with that of *Augsburg Confession* Art. IV. For example, Calvin says, 'Nam Paulus acceptionis nomine certe justificationem designat, quum dicit ad Ephesios 1, 5…id enim ipsum vult quod alibi dicere solet, Deum nos gratuito iustificare (Rom 3, 24). Quarto autem, capite ad Romanos (v. 6) primum appellat justitiae imputationem; nec eam dubitat in peccatorum remissione collocare…. Illic sane non de justificationis parte, sed de ipsa tota disputat' (Joannis Calvini, *Institutio Christianae Religionis 1559*, 3.11.4; *Opera Selecta*, ed. P. Barth and W. Niesel, 3rd edn 5 vols [Munich, 1963–74], 4.184.32–185.5; [hereafter *OS*]). The same basic Protestant emphasis is evident in Beza's *Theses de iustificatione* (Geneva, 1582) and *Apologia de iustificatione per unius Christi vera fide apprehensi iustitiam gratis imputatam* (Geneva, 1584; both works are in H. Heppe, ed., *Theodor Beza: Leben und ausgewählte Schriften* (Elberfeld, 1861).

Notae in Romanos: A Gateway to Olevian's Soteriology

Through most of the last three centuries, Olevian has rarely been studied for the sake of gaining a clearer understanding of the development of Reformed theology. Rather, he has been more often used as a pawn in some ecclesiastical or theological struggle.[6] In such circumstances, scholars were bound to focus on his dogmatic works.[7] As a result, his biblical commentaries have been neglected, helping to create a misleading picture of the nature of Reformed orthodoxy in the late sixteenth century. Despite this neglect, his biblical commentaries actually provide a useful point of entry to his soteriology.

Relatively late in his career, Olevian published his largest volume (760 pages): *Commentary on the Epistle to the Romans* (*In epistolam ad Romanos notae*, 1579).[8] This was one of three New Testament commentaries which he published in 1578-9.[9]

Among Reformed symbols Q.60 of the Heidelberg Catechism (1563) is undistinguishable from any of the normative Lutheran statements on this aspect of justification. A strong forensic element is also apparent in the Second Helvetic Confession (1566), Art. 15, and the French Confession (1559), Art. 18. See also A. E. McGrath, 'Humanist Elements in the Early Reformed Doctrine of Justification', *Archiv für Reformationsgeschichte* 73 (1982), 14, 18; L. C. Green, 'The Influence', 199.

    6 In the nineteenth century Heppe used him to justify his antipathy to certain aspects of Reformed theology. In the twentieth century, Barth used him in support of his existentialist reading of Protestant theology.

    7 Heppe, in his *Dogmatik*, for example, cited only Olevian's 1585 commentary on the Apostles' Creed, *De substantia foederis gratuiti inter Deum et electos* (Geneva, 1585).

    8 Caspar Olevian, *In epistolam ad Romanos notae, ex Gasparis Oleviani concionibus excerptae* (Geneva, 1579), hereafter *Ad Romanos*. In his epistle dedicatory, Beza said of the later Reformation *epigones*: 'Sed ne hos quidem tamen omnia, sive quod ad sententiam ipsam, sive quod ad disputationis seriem attinet, perspexisse, ex aliorum aetatis nostrae doctissimorum Theologorum scriptis apparet' (*Epistola*, 6-7). Nevertheless, he considered Olevian's notes 'non inutilis' and 'eruditus non paucis' (ibid., 9). Comments which are best taken as muted, scholarly, approval of the commentary. One finds Beza making similar remarks in the preface to Olevian's commentary on Galatians: 'Etsi iustis aliorum doctissimorum vivorum commentariis inter Paulinas caeteras illustris Epistola sic est diligenter & accurate explicata, ut vix ulla in ea locus supersit cuius difficultas lectorem merito remoretur: tuas tamen in eam notas nactus, dignas putavi quae in publicum ederentur' (*Ad Galatas, epistola*).

    9 *Ad Galatas* (Geneva, 1578); *In Epistolem d. Pauli apostolici a d Philippenses & Colossenses notae* (Geneva, 1579); hereafter *Ad Philippenses &*

Having been expelled from Heidelberg and now in the midst of establishing a new school in Herborn and a new synod in the Wetterau Counties, he somehow found time to gather and edit his lectures for publication.[10] It is uncertain whether these lectures were delivered in Heidelberg or Herborn, but they certainly served to promote his new college. As the fame of the Heidelberg theologians spread via their catechism, academic publishing, and the events surrounding their expulsion from the University, the public appetite for their books grew sufficiently to warrant two editions of the *Notae in Romanos* in the first year.[11] It was clearly aimed at an international audience. As a selling point, the publisher included a Latin translation of the German sentences used within it.[12]

Like his commentaries on the Apostles' Creed, Olevian's commentary on Romans belonged to an established genre and substantial body of literature in the sixteenth century.[13] On the

---

Colossenses. His lectures on the Gospels (*Notae Gasparis Oleviani in Evangelia* [1587]) were published by his son in Herborn. His lectures on Ephesians (*In Epistolam d. Pauli apostolici ad Ephesios notae*) were published posthumously (1588) by his son-in-law, J. Piscator, in Herborn.

[10] I am grateful to David F. Wright for his suggestion that it may well have been Theodore Beza, who edited three of his commentaries, who made the publication of these works possible.

[11] Two editions of the *Notae* have been used for this research, both published by Vignon in 1579. One has the promotional notice: 'Editio secunda ab ipso Authore recognita' and the other does not. There are also typographic variants between the two editions, which suggest that it was re-typeset. This fact indicates brisk and early sales. References in this chapter follow the pagination of the first edition.

[12] 'Germanicas sententias, quae hisce Commentariis inspersae occurrunt, Latine expositas ad calcem operis reiecimus.'

[13] See D. Steinmetz' extensive list of Patristic, medieval, and sixteenth-century commentaries ('Calvin and Abraham: The Interpretation of Romans 4 in the Sixteenth Century', *Church History* 57 [1988], 443–55). This list has been developed independently of Steinmetz. For a detailed discussion of commentaries earlier in the sixteenth century see T. H. L. Parker, *Commentaries on the Epistle to the Romans 1532–1542* (Edinburgh, 1986).

Roman Catholic humanist scholars such as Lefèvre (1517), Erasmus (1523), Jacopo Sadoleto (1535), Cardinal Cajetan (1540) and Girolamo Seripando (1567) were commenting on the text to make their case for reform within the old Church. J. Sadoleto, *In Pauli epistolam ad Romanos commentariorum libri* (London, 1535); Seripando's commentary has been republished in a modern critical edition: *In d. Pauli epistolas ad Romanos et ad Galatas, commentaria* (Naples, 1971).

face of it, such a development makes sense.[14] Luther's own lectures (*glossae et scholia*) in Romans (1515–16) were an essential part of the development of his forensic doctrine of justification.[15] Yet, because they were not published in the sixteenth century, they were not well known among his contemporaries.[16] Nevertheless, like Luther, other sixteenth-

---

Radicals such as Karlstadt (Augsburg, 1524), Faustus Socinus, and Bernardino Ochino (1550) also used Romans to vindicate their break with the Church. Ochino is included among the Radicals because after his theological pilgrimage from Rome to Zürich he broke with Protestantism in 1563, in favour of anti-Trinitarianism. In this respect, it is significant that it was one of Calvin's chief critics, Sebastian Castellio, who translated Ochino's Italian commentary into Latin and published it. One suspects that Castellio had more than just a scholarly interest in Ochino's work and published it in support of his own intellectual trajectory toward scepticism and rationalism.

[14] J. Atkinson notes that it is 'universally assumed that the epistle to the Romans' was the 'textbook of the Reformation'. The volume of commentaries produced by Protestants in the sixteenth century justifies this assumption (idem, *The Great Light: Luther and the Reformation* [Grand Rapids, 1968], 30).

[15] There is some uncertainty about the exact dates of Luther's lectures. G. Rupp says that Luther lectured on Romans from 3 November 1515 to 7 September 1516 (idem, *The Righteousness of God: Luther Studies* [London, 1953], 159). W. Pauck and H. C. Oswald, however, following J. Ficker, argue that Luther began his lectures in the Summer term of 1515 and finished in the Summer term of 1516. See Pauck, ibid., xx; *LW*, 25.ix).

[16] According to W. Pauck, Luther's lecture notes were probably used by Philip Melanchthon (see below) and 'appear to have circulated also among others of Luther's friends, followers, and colleagues' (M. Luther, *Luther: Lectures on Romans*, trans. and ed. W. Pauck, [Philadelphia, 1961], xxi). Further, the substance of Luther's reading of Romans was available in his 1522 and 1546 prefaces to Romans. See *Luther's Works*, [hereafter, *LW*] 55 vols, trans. and ed. J. Pelikan and H. T. Lehmann et al. [Philadelphia and St Louis, 1955–], 35.365, n. 15. See also *De servo arbitrio* (1525) in which he relied heavily upon proof texts from Romans (J. K. F. Knaake, G. Kawerau et al., eds, *Luthers Werke Kritische Gesamtausgabe* (Weimar, 1883), 18 [hereafter *WA*]).

The MSS of Luther's *glossae et scholia* were preserved by his son Paul and probably sold to the Margrave of Brandenburg in 1594. A copy was made for Ulrich Fugger (†1584) and upon his death was deposited (ironically not far from Olevian) in the Church of the Holy Spirit in Heidelberg. After the Thirty Years War this copy was taken, with the *Bibliotheca Palatina*, to the Vatican Library and the lectures were largely forgotten. The Vatican MSS were recovered by Ficker in 1899.

Sometime before 1668, perhaps during the reign of Frederick William (1640–88), Luther's original MSS were probably transferred from the estate of the Margrave to what became the Royal Library of Berlin. The MSS were displayed in 1846 for the tercentennial of Luther's death, but were thereafter

century Protestants defended their theological, ecclesiastical, and moral Reformation of the Church by expositing the epistle.

One of the reasons Luther's lectures were never published may be that Philip Melanchthon replaced him in Wittenberg as lecturer on Romans in 1518.[17] In 1519, Philip tried to create a textbook, *Theological Instruction* (*Theologica institutio*) from his lectures on Romans, but abandoned that project in favour of his *Common Places* (*Loci communes*, 1521). Student notes from his lectures on Romans were first published as *Annotationes Philippen Melanchthons*, in German, in Nuremberg in 1522 and reprinted the next year with a preface by Luther. A second preliminary work was first published in 1529 and was published for at least seven years in Hanau, Brunswick, and Wittenberg.[18] The commentary proper appeared first in 1532 in Wittenberg, and was republished in 1533, 1535, 1536, and 1539 in Hanau, Marburg and Strasbourg. The 1540 revision of the commentary appeared first in Strasbourg. Melanchthon's commentary was among the most important theological works of the sixteenth century for two reasons: first because it combined mature theological and exegetical reflection with humanist eloquence; and second, because it was widely read.[19] Theodore Beza described Philip Melanchthon as, 'that most outstanding man of blessed memory' whose commentary 'first broke the ice' for Protestant exegesis in Romans.[20]

The Lutheran orthodox theologians also commented on Romans. Among the more notable of this class of commentators were Johannes Bugenhagen (1527), Andreas Hyperius (1548),

---

forgotten again not to be recovered until early in the twentieth century. They were published by J. Ficker provisionally in 1908 and definitively in 1938 as *Der Brief an die Römer*. See WA, 56; LW, 25.xii–xiii; Pauck, ibid., xxi–xxiv.

For a brief introduction to and bibliography of the Renaissance in Luther studies see, T. A. Brady, s.v. 'Luther Renaissance', in H. J. Hillerbrand, ed., *The Oxford Encyclopedia of the Reformation*, 4 vols (Oxford, 1996).

[17] *LW*, 25, xii.

[18] *Dispositio orationis in Epistola Pauli ad Romanos.*

[19] See R. Keen, *Sixteenth Century Bibliography: A Checklist of Melanchthon Imprints Through 1560* (St Louis, 1988), 135–7.

[20] '...praestantissimus ille vir beatae memoriae'; 'qui primus hanc glaciem perfregit' (*Epistola*, 6). Because of its selectivity, Beza's taxonomy of commentaries raises some interesting questions. One wonders if he ignored Vermigli, Musculus, Zwingli, and Bullinger, for example, because he had not read them or because he thought them relatively unimportant?

Georg Major (1556), Tilemann Hesshusius (1571), and Johannes Brenz (1564).[21]

Lectures on Romans were a commonplace among Reformed theologians as well. Zwingli, Oecolampadius (Basle, 1525), Heinrich Bullinger (1533) and Rudolf Gwalther (1552) each published commentaries.[22] Martin Bucer, 'that strongest of athletes' who taught 'with great copiousness' first published his *Paraphrases and Continuous Commentary on the Epistle to the Romans* (*Metaphrases et enarrationes perpetuae...in epistolam ad Romanos*) in 1536, in Strasbourg.[23] Peter Martyr Vermigli (1499–62) published his Oxford lectures on Romans in Basle in 1558.[24] Wolfgang Musculus (1497–1563) also published his in 1559.[25] 'Chief of them all' was Calvin, who wrote his first biblical commentary on Romans in 1540, the fruit of some of his earliest lectures in Geneva (1536–8).[26]

Olevian's commentary was a part of the broader Protestant use of Romans and specifically of the defence of Reformed theology through the exegesis of Romans. His lectures deserve attention since he alone among the Heidelberg theologians (i.e. Tossanus, Dathenus, Ursinus, Zanchi, Boquin, and Tremellius)

---

[21] Joannes Bugenhagen, *In epistolam Pauli ad Romanos interpretatio*...(Haganoae, 1527); Andreas Hyperius, *In d. Pauli ad Romanos epistolam exegema* (Marburg, 1548); Johannes Brenz, *In epistolam...ad Romanos...commentariorum libri tres* (Frankfurt 1564); Georg Major, *Series et dispositio orationis in epistola Pauli ad Romanos* (Wittenberg, 1556); Tilemann Hesshusius, *Explicatio epistolae Pauli ad Romanos* (Jena, 1571).

[22] *Annotationes in epistolam ad Romanos.* See M. Schuler and J. Schultess, eds, *Huldrici Zuinglii opera completa editio*, 8 vols (Zürich, 1828/9–42), 6.76–133. See also H. Bullinger, *In sanctissimam Pauli ad Romanos epistolam Heinrychi Bullingeri commentarius* (Zürich, 1533). For further bibliographic information see F. Büsser, ed., *Heinrich Bullinger Werke*, 3 vols (Zürich, 1972–7), 1.24–6.

[23] '...fortissima athleta'; 'maximis instructus copiis' (Beza, *Epistola*, 6–7).

[24] Peter Martyr Vermigli, *In epistolam S. Pauli ad Romanos D. Petri martyris Vermilii Florentini, Professoris divinarum literarum in schola Tigurina, commentarii doctissimi* (Basle, 1558). It was translated into English and published in London, 1568. For further bibliographic information on the editions of his commentary see J. P. Donnelly and R. M. Kingdon, *A Bibliography of the Works of Peter Martyr Vermigli* (Kirksville, MO, 1990), 18–31.

[25] W. Musculus, *In epistolam apostoli Pauli ad Romanos, commentarii* (Basle, 1559).

[26] '...omnium optimam' (Beza, *Epistola*, 7). For a summary of the literary history of Calvin's commentary see W. de Greef, *The Writings of John Calvin*, trans. L. D. Bierma (Grand Rapids, 1993), 94–5.

produced a commentary on Romans. Thus as a representative of the Heidelberg theology in the last quarter of the century Olevian's commentary had no peers, and might be considered as having come at the end of an era since many of the major Reformed theologians (e.g. Beza, Bucanus, Polanus, Wollebius) of the same period did not produce commentaries on Romans. Indeed, the Protestant production of them seems to have dipped markedly at the end of the century.[27]

Olevian's exegesis was primarily theological, interested mostly in harvesting doctrine from the epistle. His exposition was patient and usually brief at each stop, though he stopped often – explaining virtually every clause in the epistle – hence the extraordinary length of the book. If this commentary reflects accurately his class lectures, his course in Romans must have required more than one term to complete.[28]

He was influenced by his education in the Arts faculties in Orleans, Bourges, and Paris. He found himself, however, at odds with some of his extreme humanist contemporaries such as Sebastian Castellio (1515–63). Unlike Castellio, he refused to question the divine authority or the reliability of the Scriptures.[29] In fact, he simply assumed that the 'mind of Paul', in

---

[27] There were a few commentaries on Romans published after Olevian's. For example, the gnesio-Lutheran theologian and controversialist Johann Wigand (1523–87) published his in 1580. Olevian's son-in-law Piscator produced his *Analysis logica epistolae Pauli ad Romanos* in 1589. It would be worth conducting a comparison of Olevian's commentary with Piscator's to track the development of Palatinate theology after Olevian.

[28] Apart from the obvious (the title includes the phrase '*e concionibus*') there are indications throughout that these are revised lectures. For example, he moved frequently from the third person to the second person plural and from the indicative to the imperative mood.

[29] 'Habemus igitur caussas [sic], cur initio dicat Paulus, *servus Iesus Christi ex Dei vocatione Apostolus, separatus ad praedicandum Evangelium Dei*. Iam doctrina illa non est data ut evanesceret sed ut ad finem usque mundi esset efficax, auctoritatemque suam retineret (*Ad Romanos*, 2). Compare Castellio's considerably more liberal attitude toward Scripture displayed in the tract *De arte dubitandi et confidendi, ignorandi & sciendi* which is MS. No. 505, Bibliotheek der Remonstrantschgereformeerde Gemeente te Rotterdam and translated as 'Concerning Doubt and Belief Ignorance and Knowledge' and published in *Concerning Heretics*, R. H. Bainton trans. and ed. (New York, 1935), 287–305. H. R. Guggisberg concluded that Castellio had both 'obvious sympathy for the spiritualist tradition' and 'equally obvious rationalist leanings' of which this tract is evidence. See idem, 'Castellio: Problems of Writing a New

Romans, was also the 'mind of the Holy Spirit'.[30] 'The world,' he remarked, 'claims I have asserted a new doctrine, but the Gospel is not new'.[31] Yet, he did not concede superior rationality or information to his adversaries, instead he faulted their religion. Most people hold divine and Pauline doctrine in contempt '[b]ecause they do not realise that it is God who speaks in the Scriptures'. [32] Here one finds in Olevian hints of a certain consciousness of the rise of rationalism among his humanist peers. Though he considered 'most Christians' to be confused about the true nature of the gospel and salvation, it is significant that, relative to late humanism, he yet believed them to be Christians. This distinction is evident in his discrimination between 'Christians' (*Christiani*), 'the wisdom of God' (*sapientia Dei*) on the one hand, and the 'world' (*mundus*), or 'the wisdom of the flesh' (*sapientia carnis*) on the other.[33]

His debt to the traditional western theological method was also evident in the *Notae*. Throughout the commentary, he frequently reduced large portions of Romans to one or two theological propositions, which he would then set out to demonstrate. For example, he regarded the first three chapters as being composed of a minor and a major proposition.[34] The thoroughly dialectical approach used in the commentary testifies to its scholastic or academic origins. The classroom dialogues which he conducted with mythical opponents, for the benefit of

---

Biography', *The Emergence of Tolerance in the Dutch Republic*, ed. C. Berkvens-Stevelinck et al. (Leiden, 1997), 84.

[30] 'Hanc esse genuinam Pauli sive Spiritus sancti mentem' (*Ad Romanos*, 191).

[31] E.g. 'Mundus clamat doctrinam novam asseri. At Evangelium novum non est' (*Ad Romanos*, 2).

[32] 'Qui sit autem quod hodie apud plerosque tantus est contemptus doctrinae, & in viris etiam bonis, cum contemptum illum vident, tanta haesitatio? Quia non cogitant Deum esse qui loquitur in scripturis' (*Ad Romanos*, 2).

[33] When he said that most 'Christians' are confused about justification, he seems to have been thinking primarily of those still in the old Church (*Ad Romanos*, 108). See also ibid., 6.

[34] *Ad Romanos*, 189-90. 'Hactenus probavit minorem demonstrationis constitutae capite tertio, v. 21 & sequentibus. Maior haec fuerat: necesse est eam esse veram iustitiam quae coram Deo consistat...'(ibid., 189). On Olevian's 'regulae argumentandi' for distinguishing the major and minor propositions and his use of biblical examples see his *De inventione dilaecticae* (Geneva, 1585), 142-53.

[handwritten: Gospel of forensic justification]
[handwritten: O. defined as forgiveness of sins]

his students ('objectio...respondeo... summa est') were carried over into the commentary itself.[35]

[handwritten: was at the center of Christian religion]

Justification: The First Part of the Double Benefit

For Olevian, the gospel of forensic justification, which he defined as the 'forgiveness of sins' (*remissio peccatorum*), was at the centre of the Christian religion.[36] Published only 11 months before the appearance of his commentary on Romans, his *Notae in Galatians* (February 1578) made it clear that the question of justification was 'the greatest question in the entire world'.[37] 'That is, our righteousness before God, that Christ gave himself for our unrighteousness.... Why did he rescue us? Not because of our merit, but of his grace. This is our consolation, that the Gospel is an infallible testimony to us, that God is not only our creator, but also our Father...'.[38] The second benefit is the renewal (*renovatio*) wrought in the elect by God the Spirit through the means of grace.

Though distinct, the two chief benefits of the covenant were said to be unified in that both were said to be received only by faith, which is the subjective appropriation of Christ's work. One sees this same pattern in his comments on Romans 1:16 (the power of God unto salvation to all those who believe):

> We speak about the purpose for which God instituted the ministry of the gospel. The purpose is that the Lord might powerfully lead to salvation those who believe, sealing in their hearts the gracious remission of sins and renewing the heart unto his image and beginning in them eternal life.[39]

---

[35] For example, see *Ad Romanos*, 434–5.

[36] *Ad Romanos*, 140–51.

[37] 'Maxima fere quaestio est in toto mundo' (*Ad Galatas*, 1). N.B. The pagination of the first four leaves is incorrect. The first number 4 should actually be 2.

[38] 'Quae sit nostra iustitia coram Deo, nimirum, quod Christus dederit semetipsum pro nostra iniustitia.... Cur nos eripit? non quod meriti, sed ex gratia. Consolatio. Quod Evangelium nobis infallibile testimonium est, Deus non solum creatorem nostrum esse sed & patrem Ioan. 20' (*Ad Galatas*, 2).

[39] 'Dicamus de fine in quem Deus instituit ministerium Evangelii. Finis est, ut Dominus potenter ad salutem adducat credentes: obsignans eorum cordibus remissionem peccatorum gratuitam & renovans corda ad sui imaginem & incohans in eis vitam aeternam' (*Ad Romanos*, 23).

This benefit is restricted to those who believe, i.e. those 'predestined by God' (*destinata est à Deo*).[40]

Olevian's double-benefit soteriology can only be understood in the light of his fundamental commitment to the Protestant law-gospel dichotomy in justification.

> For the law teaches that sin is ἀνομίαν, i.e. whatever is contrary to the law of God...and is both original and actual. Original sin has two parts. The first is the defection from God in Adam's loins of all his natural heirs and the second is the corruption of our entire nature.[41]

Law and gospel perform radically different functions in the economy of justification. It is only from the law that one knows sin and only from the gospel that one knows justification. It was out of this very commitment that he argued that the gospel, not the law, is the 'principal doctrine' of the Scriptures. For the law does not teach 'how sin, the wrath of God, and eternal death, are removed, but rather the principal life-giving doctrine, by the outpouring of the Spirit of God was, is, and shall be, the promise of the Gospel'.[42]

Indeed, like Luther, Olevian interpreted the entire book of Galatians as being about nothing more than the distinction between law and gospel: 'The sum of the Epistle is to teach what is that righteousness by which we are able to stand before God, that is to say it is not from the law, but from the Gospel'.[43] Likewise, he also read the Epistle to the Romans through the lenses of his law-gospel dichotomy. At the beginning of the commentary, he made

---

[40] *Ad Romanos*, 23.

[41] 'Docet autem Lex peccatum esse ἀνομίαν id est, quicquid adversatur Legi Dei...Et est aut originale aut actuale. Originale duas habet partes: una est defectio à Deo in lumbis Adae omnium ipsius naturalium haeredum: altera est corruptio totius eorum naturae' (*De substantia*, 2.10).

[42] 'Lex igitur non fuit, neque hodie est principalis doctrina: ea enim natura insita est, ante & post lapsum, nec docet quomodo tollatur peccatum, ira Dei, & mors aeterna, sed principalis doctrina vivificans corda afflante Dei Spiritu fuit, est & erit promissio Evangelii' (*Ad Romanos*, 224).

[43] 'Summa Epistolae est, ut doceat, Quae sit illa iustitia qua consistere possumus coram Deo, scillicet non Legis Sed Evangelii' (*Ad Galatas*, 1). Olevian's rhetoric on this point was as strong as anything found in Luther's 1535 lectures on Galatians. For example, see Luther's introduction to his lectures on Galatians. *WA*, 50.41–51.

it clear that it was at the heart of his conception of the *evangelium*.

> Thus the Holy Spirit constantly affirms through Paul that the doctrine of the gospel about the forgiveness of sins and eternal life given freely for the sake of the Son to those who believe, is not in any way new. But from the beginning of the world Christ was promised with his gospel. In order that this might be understood the distinction between law and Gospel must be considered.[44]

He began his definition of law by turning to creation. The moral law (*lex moralis*) is written (*inscripta*) in the hearts of 'all men' in every time. The law has been known from the time of Adam. The Sinaitic law and the teaching of the patriarchs and prophets were only a re-publication and sealing of the same.[45] Its primary function is to prosecute sinners. Because of its universality, no one is excusable and because of our primeval corruption no one is 'able to be justified, i.e. able to obtain from God forgiveness of sins and eternal life, by their natural goodness and actions according to the law of nature'.[46] In our natural state, rather than making moral progress, we are more grossly contaminated by horrendous sin. 'At any event, the justice which can stand before God's most righteous judgement ought to be perfect in all respects.'[47] 'The law', however, 'does not give righteousness, but requires it'.[48]

---

[44] 'Etenim Spiritus Sanctus per Paulum constanter affirmat, doctrinam hanc Evangelii de remissione peccatorum & vita aeterna gratis donanda credentibus propter filium, nequaquam novam esse: Sed Christum cum suo Evangelio promissum fuisse ab exordio mundi. Hoc ut intelligatur cogitandum est discrimen legis & Evangelii' (*Ad Romanos*, 2).

[45] 'Una quidem fuit lex moralis omnium temporum cordibus hominum inscripta, & deinde literis consignata: hoc est, inde ab Adamo sciverunt homines quales esse, quae mala vitare, contra quae bona facere debuerint, et idem scient homines usque ad extremum iudicium…' (*Ad Romanos*, 2–3).

[46] '[P]robitate naturali & actionibus secundum legem naturae nequaquam iustificari, id est remissionem peccatorum & vitam aeternam obtinere à Deo' (*Ad Romanos*, 57).

[47] 'Atqui iustitia, quae coram Deo iustissimo iudice queat consistere, debet modis omnibus esse perfecta' (*Ad Romanos*, 57). 'Haec lex naturae vocatur, & est ius Dei seu divinum. Obser. 1. Est enim lux in mentibus nostris condita. 2. Obser. Ius Dei naturale & ius Dei scriptum sive decalogus, idem est' (ibid., 65). See also his comments on Romans 2:14, ibid., 97–100.

[48] 'Sicut enim lex non donat nobis iustitiam, sed requirit' (*Ad Philippenses & Colossenses*, 43).

Purpose of law not to justify but to drive sinners to Christ

The gospel promises, however, are equally ancient: the seed of the woman will crush the head of the serpent.[49] The key to keeping law and gospel in proper order is to remember their respective purposes. The purpose of the law was not to justify, but to drive sinners to Christ.[50] The purpose of the gospel was to justify and liberate sinners from sin and death.[51]

Because law and gospel have different purposes, they perform distinct functions. The law only condemns, and only the gospel justifies. Since it was God's will to redeem his people from all eternity, the gospel must have priority in Scripture. Thus, in his comments on Romans 1:5, 6 the forgiveness of sins (*remissio peccatorum*) is the first 'offered benefit' (*oblatum beneficium*) which is received by faith. 'The obedience of faith contains two parts, first, by denial of all fleshly wisdom, we might believe and trust, that our sins are forgiven for the sake of the sacrifice of the Son...the second part is sanctification, or inchoate obedience...'.[52] Because humans are naturally sinful, the first benefit must be objective. One is not forgiven or justified because of an increase in sanctification but 'for the sake of the sacrifice of the Son' (*propter sacrificium filii*).

Both Olevian's commentaries on Romans and Galatians give abundant evidence of his commitment to the forensic conception of justification, that justification is a matter of God's binding, legal declaration of the sinner's justification, as opposed to justification by infused grace (*gratia infusa*) or justification through sanctification. 'Justification' is 'the pronouncement that we are absolved of our sins in the body of Christ'.[53]

Since justification is accomplished 'for us' (*pro nobis*) and 'without the works of the law' (*sine operibus legis*), it is Christ's obedience to the law, not ours, which is the legal ground of our

---

[49] 'Quomodo igitur remissionem peccatorum & salutem aeternam acceperunt? Respondeo, Una est promissio remissionis peccatorum & vitae aeternae omnium temporum edita initio his verbis: Semen mullieris conculcabit caput serpentis' (*Ad Romanos*, 3).

[50] *Ad Romanos*, 488.

[51] *Ad Romanos*, 223–4.

[52] 'Obedientia fidei duas partes continet, Una, ut abnegata omni sapientia carnis, credamus & confidamus, remissa nobis esse peccata propter sacrificium filii.... Altera pars est sanctificatio, sive inchoata obedientia...' (*Ad Romanos*, 6–7).

[53] 'Iustificatio, id est, pronuntiatio nos esse solutos a peccatis in corpore Christi' (*Ad Romanos*, 374).

righteousness before God.[54] It was the 'obedience of Christ's bloody death' and the 'merit of the Son' (*meritum filii*) particularly which has been imputed for righteousness to all the elect, who receive it by faith.[55] He contrasted the Protestant trust in Christ's imputed merit with the 'Papists who glory in merit falsely named, since to the same degree they detract from the grace of Christ, (and they seek their own glory)'. Thus, for Olevian, it was not a matter of whether sinners are justified by merit, rather the question was whose merit and how the sinner receives that merit.[56]

Because Olevian understood divine justice to be necessarily and naturally alien to sinful creatures, he was virtually obligated to consider the Tridentine view as teaching justification by one's 'own righteousness' (*iustitia propria*), i.e. a righteousness from within. *Pace* Trent, he consistently regarded our justification as a legal declaration, the ground of which is Christ's righteousness which is imputed to the believer.[57] In fact, imputation is justification.[58] The 'justified', he taught, are those 'clothed with Christ's righteousness' (*induti iustitia Christi*).[59] By the imputation of Christ's righteousness, one's holiness is 'most perfect'.[60] Because 'neither guilt nor penalty is imputed to the true members of the Church' one can say that with respect to imputation 'believers are not sinners...but only holy and just'.[61] The Pauline doctrine of justification strips away 'all praise of the righteousness of men and extols only Christ's righteousness...only Christ's righteousness is true righteousness'.[62]

---

[54] *Ad Romanos*, 140.

[55] 'Quod res imputatur in iustitiam, seu qua nititur fides, est obedientia sanguinolentae mortis Christi' (*Ad Romanos*, 145, 7). See also idem, *Expositio symboli apostolici* (Frankfurt, 1584), 170.

[56] 'Contra Papistae qui in falso nominatis meritis gloriantur: tantum detrahunt gratiae Christi (& propriam gloriam quaerunt)' (*Ad Romanos*, 151).

[57] *Ad Romanos*, 145.

[58] *Expositio*, 132.

[59] *Ad Romanos*, 374.

[60] 'Imputatione vero sanctitas eius est perfectissma in Christo' (*Exposito*, 178).

[61] '...non imputari culpam aut poenam veris membris Ecclesiae. Quia credentes in Christum non sunt peccatores...sed simpliciter sancti & iusti' (*Expostitio*, 178).

[62] '...omnem laudem iustitiae detrahit homini, & solam Christi extollit...solam Christi iustitiam, veram iustitiam esse' (*Ad Galatas*), 13.

The forensic idea makes Christ's *iustitia* alien or external rather than internal, as the ground of our righteousness but it is credited to us as if it were internal. He made this same point in his lectures on the Gospels, commenting on Matthew 5:20–27.

> [T]he righteousness of Christ is ours, a gift to us, granted as if it were from us. Which also God promises us by the application of the sacramental signs to our bodies; and also that our righteousness is greater than that of the Pharisees, no even than that of all the angels.[63]

These comments are of interest as a way of highlighting his consistency in this teaching. It was not something he taught only in his lectures on Romans and Galatians. Rather, he found it throughout the Scriptures, even in the Sermon on the Mount, which is not an obvious place for a discourse on a forensic doctrine of justification, unless one is fully committed to a strong law-gospel hermeneutic whereby the Sermon becomes law.

According to Olevian, one benefits from the gospel 'through faith alone' (*per solam fidem*), which is the sole divinely ordained instrument by which the sinner should apprehend Christ's extrinsic righteousness.[64]

> Faith is to assent to God, as the only true and omnipotent God, his will known in his every word, and so to give glory to God and not to consider anything in ourselves or other creatures which seems to oppose him. And to regard this word as his special purpose, the promise of the gospel, that the Father reveals himself truly in Christ, and that he justifies freely and daily sanctifies those united to Christ through the Holy Spirit and preserves us through the same power by which Christ was raised from the dead by which he has subjected all things to himself so that, grounded in his power, the hope of everlasting life might be most certain.[65]

---

[63] '...iustitia Christi nostra est, nobis donata, ac si a nobis esset praestita: quod etiam nobis testatur Deus applicatione signorum sacramentalium ad nostra corpora; eaque abundat quam Pharisaeorum, imo superat omnem angelorum iustitiam' (*Notae in Evangelia*, 218). See also *Vester Grund* (Herborn, 1590) repr. in *Der Gnadenbund Gottes 1590*, ed., G. Franz, J. F. G. Goeters, W. Holtmann [Bonn, 1994], Q.123.

[64] '...per solam fidem gratis iustificari hominem cum qua iustitia salus coniuncta est' (*Ad Romanos*, 152).

[65] 'Fides est Deo in omni verbo suo, voluntate ipsius cognita, assentiri, ut

Moreover, this faith 'is not from ourselves, but a gracious gift of God, flowing from election' and wrought by God the Spirit working through the Word.[66]

Olevian versus Canisius

The Protestant character of Olevian's doctrine of faith appears clearly in contrast with that of the Jesuit apostle to the Germans, Peter Canisius (1521–97), as it appeared in his *Appendix* to his *Summary of Christian Doctrine* (*Summa doctrinae Christianae*, 1574).[67] Canisius, like Olevian, confessed justification through 'faith', but by faith he meant 'the sacrament of faith, without which no one approaches justification', i.e. baptism.[68] The contrast between what Canisius meant by *iustificatio* and what

---

veraci et omnipotenti, atque ita gloriam dare Deo: et non considerare quidquid in nobis vel aliis creaturis ei adversari videtur: et in hoc verbo, ut praecipuum scopum, intueri promissionem Evangelii, quod vere se nobis Patrem exhibeat in Christo, et quod per Spiritum sanctum Christo insitos gratis iustificet, et indies sanctificet, nosque conservet eadem virtute, qua Christus excitatus est a mortuis, quaque subiecta sibi habet omnia, ut spes vitae aeternae in veritate et potentia ipsius fundata, sit certissima (*Expositio*, 14).

[66] 'Quia fides illa non ex nobis est, sed gratuitum Dei, fluens ex electione' (*Ad Romanos*, 150; ibid., 428–9). Therefore, *resipiscentia* (repentance) is also a divine gift. See *De substantia*, 1.1.2.

[67] Peter Canisius, *Appendix de hominis lapsu et iustificiatione secundum sententiam & doctrinam concilii Tridentini* (1574) was appended to his *Summa doctrinae Christianae* (Antwerp, 1574). The *Summa* was first published in 1554. The Appendix used in this study is found in a later edition. NB. The pagination of the *Appendix* is continuous with the *Summa*, so questions from the Appendix will be designated by their number rather than by their page to preserve the distinction between the *Appendix* and the *Summa*.

Canisius provides a useful contrast to Olevian, since like the latter, he too was dedicated to bringing the gospel to the Germans. It is clear that Olevian had the Tridentine soteriology in view much of the time – he refers frequently to 'Papistae'. For example, in his defence of imputation he answers the 'obiectio Papistarum' (*Ad Romanos*, 151) – and given Canisius' fame and the widespread use of his Catechism in Germany, it is reasonable to imagine that Olevian was thinking of him when he wrote on justification. The comparison is also interesting since they use several terms in common but with distinctly different meanings. For a brief introduction to Canisius see J. P. Donnelly, 'Peter Canisius', *Shapers of Religious Traditions in Germany, Switzerland, and Poland 1560–1600*, ed. J. Raitt (New Haven, 1981).

[68] '...sacramentum fidei, sine qua nulli unquam contigit iustificatio' (Canisius, *Appendix*, Q.11).

Olevian meant by the same was quite pointed. Olevian denied categorically the Tridentine definition of faith. Saving faith he said is not a 'virtue or an infused quality'. Rather '*fiducia*' empties itself of 'proper justice and riches', calls upon God, and is enriched in Christ.[69]

'Further,' he argued, faith is something created in the elect through gospel preaching.[70] Because faith is the work of the Holy Spirit, certainty is an 'essential property' of faith.[71] It is confident in the promise of the gospel, which sees God's eternally benevolent will toward the elect in Christ, that God will never be angry with us. Certainty belongs to faith because faith has as its object the promises, which cannot be separated from Christ.[72] It is not the virtue of one's faith which is efficacious, but that faith is the fit instrument to lay hold of the promises by a 'certain testimony' (*indubitato testimonio*).[73]

It is not, however, as though Olevian envisioned that Christians would have a perfect faith in this life. There remains in every believer a part of the soul which remains unregenerate, or not dominated by the 'knowledge of God' (*cognitio Dei*).[74] In that portion of the soul, 'terrors of the conscience' (*terrores conscientiae*) will continue to afflict the faithful. Nevertheless, the believer ought to fight against such doubts and rest on the promise of God that he will never leave his people. For this reason, Christ has instituted the means of grace to strengthen the infirmity of our faith.[75]

For Olevian, the Protestant doctrine of faith as the instrument by which one apprehends Christ's alien righteousness (*iustitia aliena*) is irreconcilable with the idea of co-operating toward justification. Such synergism, even under the exciting, inspiring work of the Spirit was justification by works. Because of our

---

[69] 'Hinc videmus fidem non iustificare & salvare, quoad virtus est, vel qualitas infusa, sed quatenus fiducia est in Deum, quae vacua omni propria iustitia & divitiis, atque adeo egena, Deum invocat, ut in Christo ditetur' (*Ad Romanos*, 527).

[70] See *De substantia*, 2.16, 29. 'Nam ut per Evangelium creatur fides' (ibid., 2.26).

[71] '...quanta sit fidei certitudo, quae est velut essentalis proprietas' (*De substantia*, 2.18).

[72] *De substantia*, 2.47.

[73] *De substantia*, 2.18.

[74] '...a parte animae non regenita' (*De substantia*, 2.19).

[75] *De substantia*, 2.19.

natural state in Adam, one could never begin to co-operate with grace much less expect to satisfy the divine justice through obedience. Moreover, such ideas run contrary to the very intention of the divine law. Its purpose was to render the unjustified without excuse, not to justify.[76] The contrast between Olevian's conception of faith and Canisius' could hardly be sharper. What Olevian defined as faith, *fiducia*, Canisius rejected as the presumption of schismatics and heretics.[77]

For Canisius, like the medieval intellectualist tradition, justification is an ontological matter, an essential transformation of the soul from the state of sin to the state of grace.[78] Therefore, according to his doctrine of God, the beginning of justice (*exordium iustitiae*) was sufficient to satisfy God. The assumption behind the condign merit (*meritum de condigno*) scheme was that God holds his judgement in abeyance until final justification or sanctification is achieved.[79]

By contrast, Olevian, like Calvin, worked within a conceptual framework, which in its doctrine of God was partly voluntarist and partly intellectualist. On the one hand, his doctrine of God was marked by a strong voluntarism. Divine freedom was an important assumption behind his notion of grace and predestination. Since, considering absolute power (*de potentia absoluta*), God is free not to save any, salvation is contingent only upon the divine will. Salvation is truly gracious because it is entirely without coercion. Yet, Olevian was not unreservedly voluntarist. There was also a sort of intellectualism in his soteriology. Having decreed to save sinners, *de potentia ordinata*, he could do so in no other way than by the incarnation. In this he agreed with Anselm and never questioned the notion that God's *iustitia* is a wrath which must be satisfied.[80]

---

[76] *Ad Romanos*, 133.

[77] '...nemini tamen fiduciam & certitudinem remissionis peccatorum suorum iactanti & in ea sola quiescenti, peccata dimitti, vel dimissa esse dicendum est, cum apud haereticos & schismaticos possit esse...' (Canisius, *Appendix*, Q.13).

[78] Canisius' use of *pactum* in Q.20 of the *Appendix* suggests perhaps some influence by the *Via Moderna*.

[79] On the medieval merit schemes see McGrath, *Iustitia Dei*, 1.109–19.

[80] On the relations between Anselm and Reformed theology see R. B. Strimple, 'St. Anselm's *Cur Deus Homo* and John Calvin's Doctrine of the Atonement', *Anselm, Aosta, Bec and Canterbury*, ed. D. E. Luscombe and G. R. Evans (Sheffield, 1996). For example, Olevian said: 'Merito quidem, dum

Olevian also began with an eschatology which was considerably different from Canisius'. Because the latter conceived of salvation in ontological terms, he could envisage a mediating place between absolute righteousness and condemnation. Olevian, however, denied any middle place *coram Deo* principally because he thought that there was an absolute ontological distinction (though there are analogies) between the Creator and his creatures.

For Canisius, the justification of the impious, was a 'translation' and the result of the mediation of grace through the 'laver of renewal' (*lavacro regenerationis*).[81] It was also the result of the Christian's 'disposition or preparation' (*dispositionem seu praeparationem*) and 'not only the remission of sins' (*non est sola peccatorum remissio*).[82] The impious are justified as the 'merit of the passion of our Lord Jesus Christ is communicated' to them and not as something is accomplished legally or extrinsically. He was quite insistent about this distinction. 'We are renewed in the spirit of our mind and we are not only reputed, but are rightly called just and we are just, receiving justice in ourselves'.[83] Just as Adam's 'sin was transfused into all humanity', so also one's sanctification must be the very stuff of justification; it is the pouring forth of 'the love of God' (*charitas Dei*) into the hearts of those who are being justified'.[84] For Canisius to say that Christ has become our 'justice, sanctification and redemption' (*iustitia, sanctificatio, et redemptio*)' was to say he is being made that

---

Christus sacerdotio suo, hoc est intercessione sua & sacrificio fundamentum aeternum regno suo substernens, iustitiae Dei satisfacit, a peccato, & a maledictione legis, atque ita a potestate & regno diaboli nos liberat, & spiritum sanctificationis, per quem ipse in nobis regnet, impetrat' (*Expositio*, 4).

[81] Canisius, *Appendix*, Q.8.

[82] Canisius, *Appendix*, Q.11.

[83] '...renovamur spiritu mentis nostrae: & non modo reputamur, sed vere iusti nominamur, & sumus, iustitiam in nobis recipientes' (*Appendix*, Q.11).

[84] '...peccatum...in omne genus humanum transfudit' (Canisius, *Appendix*, Q.2); 'Quamquam enim nemo possit esse iustus, nisi cui merita passionis Domini nostri Iesu Christi communicantur, id tamen in hac impii iustificatione sit, dum eiusdem sanctissime passionis merito per Spiritum sanctum, charitas Dei diffunditur in cordibus eorum, qui iustificantur, atque ipsi inhaeret' (ibid., Q.11). C. P. Carlson argues that Trent's teaching on justification was a development and not a break with medieval tradition. See idem, *Justification*, 135.

within Christians, progressively, through the means of justifying grace.[85]

Thus, Christ's benefits are applied to one 'through the sacrament of baptism' (*per baptismi sacramentum*).[86] He juxtaposed quite sharply the infused grace of baptism with the Protestant notion of imputation.[87] For Canisius, the *beneficium* is not *duplex* as with Olevian, but, one might say, *complex*. That is, sanctification, through infused grace, *is* justification.[88] For Canisius, it is God's 'exciting and assisting grace' which inspires and enables the sinner to 'assent and co-operate' and by which he is justified before God.[89]

With Canisius, Olevian accepted universal descent from Adam as an article of faith, which has us all liable to Adam's corruption. Like the rest of his reformed brethren, he considered our connection to Adam to be realistic as well as forensic.[90] The human 'defection from God' affects 'all the sons of Adam' because he is also our father 'naturally' (*naturaliter*) and when he sinned we were 'in his loins' and because of this connection our 'whole nature is corrupt'.[91]

Nevertheless, he retained the parallel between justification and the Fall. If the latter was forensic, so is our justification. By

---

[85] Canisius, *Appendix*, Q.3. Olevian used a nearly identical expression, 'Christus factus est nobis à Deo, sapientia, iustitia, sanctificatio & redemptio, ut qui gloriatur in Domino glorietur' (*Ad Romanos*, 131).

[86] Canisius, *Appendix*, Q.3.

[87] 'Praeterea consitendum est, reatum originalis peccati per Iesu Christi, quae in baptismate confertur, remitti, & in baptizatis totum id quod veram & propriam peccati rationem habet, tolli, non radi tantum aut non imputari' (Canisius, *Appendix*, Q.4).

[88] Q.11 makes clear the identity of justification with sanctification: 'Hanc dispositionem seu praeparationem iustificatio ipsa consequitur, quae non est sola peccatorum remissio, sed & sanctificatio, & renovatio interioris homnis per voluntarium susceptionem gratiae...'. What Canisius, two questions later, described as the '*exordium iustificationis*' (Q.9), in Q.7 is the '*beneficium*' which the baptised receive.

[89] '...excitantem atque adiuvantem gratiam'; 'assentiendo & cooperando' (Canisius, *Appendix*, Q.9).

[90] According to the Belgic Confession Art. 15 sin is 'une vice héréditaire' (*Confessio Belgica*, in *The Creeds of Christendom*, ed. P. Schaff, 3 vols, 6th edn (Grand Rapids, [repr.] 1983), 3.400.

[91] '...sed est defectio à Deo omnium filiorum Adae ab ipso naturaliter progenitorum, facta in ipsius lumbis unde corruptio totius ipsorum naturae extitit' (*Ad Romanos*, 200).

the sin of the first Adam, all humanity was plunged into 'ruin' and by the righteousness of the second Adam, the elect have been redeemed.[92] Further, he agreed with Canisius that Christ has become our '*iustitia, sanctificatio, & redemptio*'.[93] The question was not *whether*, but *how*. Where, for Canisius Christ fulfils these offices in our sanctification, i.e. internally, for Olevian Christ has already fulfilled all righteousness and one benefits from it when one lays hold of Christ and his obedience 'through faith' (*per fidem*).

Thus it is not surprising to find that, for Olevian, 'not one part of justification can be ascribed to us, but all the glory is owed to God alone'.[94] This principle was explicitly intended to exclude co-operation with divine grace in justification. Further, given Olevian's forensic premises, it was almost impossible for him to have regarded the Tridentine doctrine of justification as anything other than a sort of works righteousness, so far as it entailed co-operation with divine grace as a prerequisite to justification. Having begun with the law-gospel dichotomy, he could not allow that the law or obedience should sanctify or contribute toward eventual justification. The voice of nature (*vox naturae*) or law of the covenant (*ius foederis*) requires that justice before God (*iustitia coram Deo*) must be either completely proper or alien to oneself. For this reason Scripture says that it was not for the pious, but the impious that Christ died, indicating that by nature divine righteousness is alien and that Christ did not die for those who were in the midst of becoming righteous.[95] For Olevian, the divine justice is totalitarian. Therefore, the objects of divine grace cannot be partly righteous and partly corrupt.[96] Hence the necessity, in Olevian's system, of the instrumental definition of faith. The alien justice is of God revealed efficaciously in the gospel 'through faith' (*per fidem*), which according to its nature looks to Christ and away from the believer.[97]

---

[92] *Ad Romanos*, 192.

[93] *Ad Romanos*, 131.

[94] '...nulla pars iustificationis nobis ascribenda est, sed omnis eius gloria debetur Deo in solidum' (*Ad Romanos*, 149).

[95] *Ad Romanos*, 187.

[96] 'Nullus peccator potest gloriari coram Deo de iustitia' (*Ad Romanos*, 141).

[97] 'Omnino opus est iustitiam coram Deo, aut propria, quam ipse voce creationis & iure foederis legalis à propriis nostris viribus requirit aut aliena hoc

In Olevian's scheme, left to inherent justice (*iustitia propria*) both Jews and Gentiles would remain in their natural condition 'under condemnation' (*sub condemnatione*). It is only in the gospel that one finds righteousness 'outside himself' (*extra se*), because righteousness is something which God gives to 'sinners placed under damnation' (*peccatores sub damnitio positos*).

> This is the true ground for justifying all, whether Jews or Gentiles, found under sin...that one shall transcribe to God all glory for salvation and tranquillity of [our] consciences shall be chiefly considered. The boasting of men, however, is not excluded by works righteousness, but by the righteousness of faith. And the promise is not sure for the consciences of all...if justification should be of the law or by works or by heredity, but only of faith, by grace. Therefore, this is the true ground for justifying: that God justifies the impious not by works but by faith through grace.[98]

As proof of the forensic nature of justification, Olevian appealed to the objective nature of Christ's propitiation of the divine wrath. Justification cannot be something accomplished within us, since Christ has already accomplished it externally, once for all in history.[99]

He also appealed to Abraham's experience. How could justification be something wrought internally when Abraham was said to have been justified before even the incarnation occurred in history? For Olevian, Romans teaches that it is Christ's finished work of obedience which is imputed, first to Abraham and now 'to all, without distinction, who believe'.[100] Further, only an extrinsic righteousness, which looks to Christ's satisfaction of the

---

est Dei, quam evangelio efficaciter revelat per fidem' (*Ad Romanos*, 133–4).

[98] 'Ea est vera ratio iustificandi omnes tam Iudaeos quam Gentes sub peccato constitutos...omnem gloriam salutis transcribit Deo, & tranquilitati conscientiarum maxime consulit. Atqui gloriatio hominum non excluditur iustitia operum, sed iustitia fidei, & promissio non est firma conscientiis universi seminis tam incircuncisi [sic], quam circumcisi, si ex lege sive operibus sit haereditas, sed si ex fide gratis. Ergo ea est vera iustificandi ratio, dum Deus non ex operibus sed ex fide gratis impium iustificat' (*Ad Romanos*, 134–5; see also 142,7).

[99] *Ad Romanos*, 143–7.

[100] 'Dum igitur Adam ut typum Christi, ipsiusque iustitiae omnibus sine distinctione credentibus communicandae proponit ex scriptis Propheticis, atque adeo Spiritu prophetico Prophetarum scripta de Adamo & miserabili generis humani ruina...' (*Ad Romanos*, 191–2; see also ibid., 144–5).

divine justice, is capable of producing peace of mind, i.e. certainty of election and of reception of the perpetual divine favour for believers.[101]

He made the same argument about faith in his commentary on Galatians.

> The sum of the Gospel Paul taught is: we are justified or receive the remission of sins by faith alone in Christ. It is the Pseudoapostles who confuse circumcision and the merit of works.... It is worth observing how often merit, whether from the sacraments or other works, is confused with faith. That is another gospel, not of Christ, but rather a perversion of the ground of the gospel itself.[102]

When Olevian said 'a perversion of the ground of the Gospel' he meant that one who attempts to use the sacraments as means of justification, has corrupted tokens of Christ's unmerited favour into levers by which one attempts to control God. Such abuse of the means of sanctifying grace constitutes an attack on the divine prerogative to impute Christ's finished work to believers.

Along with his doctrine of infused grace, Canisius taught the Tridentine doctrine of incremental justification.[103] The justified are those who are renovated from virtue to virtue, 'faith co-operating with good works'.[104] His conception of progressive justification was made possible by his assertion that God does not command anything which is impossible, therefore one must be able to co-operate with grace toward final justification.[105] Christ is infusing virtue into his people, producing good works, without which 'covenant' (*pactum*) works cannot be both 'gracious and meritorious' (*grata et meritoria*) to God simultaneously.[106] Hence,

---

[101] *Ad Romanos*, 190–91.

[102] 'Summa est, Paulus docverat, Evangelium, sola fide in Christum nos iustificari sive remissionem peccatorum accipere: pseudoapostali admiscebant circumcisionem & merita operum.... Observandum, quoties meritum sive ex sacramentis sive aliis operibus, fidei admiscetur, esse aliud Evangelium, non Christi, imo eversione, Evangelii ex ipsis fundamentis' (*Ad Galatas*, 3).

[103] Canisius, *Appendix*, Q.13.

[104] '...de virtute in virtute, renovantur...cooperante fide bonis operibus...' (Canisius, *Appendix*, Q.14).

[105] Canisius, *Appendix*, Q.15.

[106] '...in ipsos iustificatos iugiter virtutem influat: quae virtus bona eorum opera semper antecedit, comitatur & subsequitur, & sine qua nulla pacto Deo gratia & meritoria esse possent' (Canisius, *Appendix*, Q.20).

for Canisius merit and grace (or law and gospel) are complementary, not antithetical means of justification.

Canisius also denied that he taught that Christians are justified by inherent justice (*iustitia propria*), at least not strictly considered, since that would be Pelagian. Rather, he said, one is justified through Christ's infused merits, which produce inhering justice.[107] Nevertheless, for Canisius and Trent, co-operation with divine grace is of the essence of justification. One is becoming just because God has actually distributed his justice to us and one has co-operated with that gift.

Federalism and Justification

In his exegesis of Romans, Olevian tied his Protestant-forensic teaching of justification to his doctrine of God's federal administration of salvation. There were two aspects to Olevian's federalism: (1) the covenant relations between God and his people; (2) the relations of Adam and Christ as the respective representative heads of humanity ruined and humanity redeemed.

The contrast between Canisius and Olevian on justification existed because they represented competing federal theologies. Canisius was defending a notion of the *pactum* in which God has agreed to reward those who co-operate with divine grace with eventual justification. Olevian, on the other hand, was defending a conception of the covenant (*foedus*) in which God willed from all eternity to justify his elect by imputing to them Christ's righteousness with the result that one can and should be certain of one's justification in this life.[108] Considering the covenant in this absolute sense Olevian declared that one is justified 'without condition or stipulation' ('*citra conditionem aut stipulationem*') on our part, so that grace might be grace.[109]

Nevertheless, for Olevian, there was certain mutuality to the covenant, considered experientially. By means of the covenant, Olevian sought to reconcile God's justice to his grace. He sought

---

[107] 'Quae enim iustitia nostra dicitur, quia per eam nobis inhaerentem iustificamur, illa eadem Dei est, quia à Deo nobis infunditur per Christi meritum' (Canisius, *Appendix*, Q.20).

[108] Olevian says 'suo tempore' (*Ad Romanos*, 140).

[109] *De substantia*, 1.1.2.

to address those places in Scripture which require a believing response, arguing that God has ordained to use means to accomplish his decrees in history. For example, commenting on Romans 2:28 Olevian rejected the notion that the sacraments work justice 'from the working it works and without the conversion of the heart' (*ex opere operato sine fide et conversione cordis*).[110] He reminded the reader that just as the Jews also thought that circumcision, without faith in the mediator, worked justification, so in his day 'most Christians' hold the same error about baptism.[111] It is true, he conceded, that circumcision was the 'sign' (*signum*) of the covenant, but the sign is only half the covenant. There are conditions attached to the covenant, chiefly faith in God the Son. When God instituted the covenant with Abraham, he promised and confirmed it by a sign, but he promised on the condition that God's people should respond with obedience.[112] Though God's promise would have been sufficient, out of his goodness God bound himself by oath to a covenant (*foedus*).[113] There are, therefore, two parts to the covenant: 'promise' (*promissionem*) and '*repromissionem*' or believing response.[114] So closely connected is the sign to the thing signified that the 'sign is called the covenant...therefore to the same degree the verbal or audible covenant is promised only under condition...and by receiving the covenant through the sign we obligate ourselves to the condition of the covenant'.[115]

---

[110] *Ad Romanos*, 108.

[111] 'Ita etiam Iudaei Circuncisioni inesse vim putabant iustificandi & efficiendi eos filios Dei etiam sine conversione cordis & absque fide in mediatorem. Et plerique Christiani hodie, quoad Baptismum in eodem errore versantur' (*Ad Romanos*, 108).

[112] '...quam Deus promiserit & signo confirmarit: sed addite etiam alteram qua conditione promiserit, sive quid vos promiseritis, nempe vos fore integros & ambulaturos coram ipsius facie' (*Ad Romanos*, 108). He was paraphrasing Genesis 17:1.

[113] 'Cur Deus voluit foedere se obstringere? Respondeo: satis quidem fuisset promittere: at quia bonus est, nostrae imbecillitati succurrit, adeo ut se obliget iuramento & foedere' (*Ad Romanos*, 109).

[114] *Ad Romanos*, 109.

[115] 'Signum autem vocatur foedus, nempe testimonium & signum visibile. Ergo quemadmodum in verbo sive foedere audibili, non promittit nisi sub conditione.... Et recipiendo foedus per signum, obligamus nos ad conditionem foederis' (*Ad Romanos*, 109).

In Olevian's soteriological federalism, his doctrine of the conditionality of the covenant of grace was controlled by several other factors: (1) his definition of faith as a divine gift; (2) his prior commitment to a forensic doctrine of justification; (3) his doctrine of predestination.

Further, God's promise to Abraham did not imply that there would be law-keepers who would earn justification, but that God has always had 'sons of the promise or election'.[116] There is a condition to receiving the double benefit (*duplex beneficium*) of the covenant and that condition is faith in the mediator. Olevian did not consider, however, that faith is something which the Christian contributes to justification. Rather faith was said to be a divine gift and the sole instrument by which one apprehends Christ's righteousness, which is the ground of justification. Further, only those in whom faith has been produced by the Word and Spirit are 'Spiritual sons, that is, the elect' (*Spirituales filios, id est, electos*).[117]

After discussing mutuality, he returned immediately to the question of justification proper. The fault lay not with the divine covenant *per se*, rather the 'Jews did not keep the law, neither legally, i.e. by works, nor by faith. Therefore Paul concluded that no one justifies himself by the law'.[118] Why then the sign of circumcision? 'It was not for justification through the law...but for a seal of righteousness by faith'.[119] God has willed to become our God and placed his sign upon us, therefore we ought to respond with repentance and faith, laying hold of the 'fellowship with Christ' (κοινωνίας *cum Christo*).[120]

To vindicate this doctrine, he argued that Romans chapter 5 was organised into three parts, a protasis (v.12) and apodosis (v.18), separated by a parenthesis (vv.13–17).[121] This was a relatively sophisticated analysis of the passage (which neither Melanchthon nor Calvin achieved) as it had the effect of

---

[116] '...filios promissionis et electionis' (*Ad Romanos*, 422).

[117] *Ad Romanos*, 422. See also idem, 191.

[118] 'Atque Iudaei non servarunt legem, neque legaliter, id est operibus, neque fide. Ergo concludit Paulus, non solum non iustificari eos opere Circumcisionis...' (*Ad Romanos*, 109).

[119] 'Ad quid profuit Circumcisio? Respondeo, Non ad iustificationem per legem...sed ad obsignandum fidei iustitiam' (*Ad Romanos*, 109).

[120] *Ad Romanos*, 110.

[121] *Ad Romanos*, 193–4.

emphasising his teaching on the federal headship of Adam and Christ by reading most of the passage (vv.13–17) as merely illustrative of the great propositions at the beginning and end. This explains his motivation, in good Augustinian fashion, for reading the 'in whom' (*in quo*) of 5:12 as proof of Adam's representative position for all humanity.[122] When Adam sinned, all humans 'in Adam's loins' (*in lumbis Adami*) sinned with him and through his sin, God's just judgement passed to all humanity.[123]

If this analysis is correct, then those scholars are partly correct who have identified a connection between the Reformed federalism represented by Olevian and the Franciscan *pactum* theology, which taught 'to him who does what is in himself, God does not deny grace' (*facere quod in se est, Deus non denegat gratiam*, i.e. considering his ordained power (*de potentia ordinata*) God has pledged to honour one's co-operation with divine grace toward justification.[124] They have misidentified however, the nature of the connection.

It has yet to be shown that any of the Reformed federal theologians, including Olevian, taught anything like Biel's '*facere quod in se est*'. In this programme God was said to be able and willing (in view of the *pactum*) to reward those meritorious acts which, having met the necessary conditions, were said to be inherently worthy (*meritum de condigno*). He was also free to reward those works which did not meet the necessary conditions (*meritum de congruo*). Every aspect of Olevian's soteriology was a conscious rejection of that very same notion. Further, there is no evidence that the Reformed federal theologians unwittingly returned to a pre-Protestant construct – thus implicitly destroying the entire Protestant soteriological project.

There is, however, every indication that Reformed theology, having rejected Franciscan semi-Pelagian synergism for a consistent divine monergism (predestination), reconstituted the idea of a divine pledge by placing it within the context of their

---

[122] Translating the ἐφ᾽ ᾧ of Romans 5:12 as 'in quo' and interpreting it as a locative phrase was as ancient and traditional as Augustine's anti-Pelagian writings, e.g. *De peccatorum meritis et remissione*, 1.9–20.

[123] 'Dum inquit *In quo*, Ostendit mortem merito & iusto Dei iudicio in omnes homines transisse: quia causa mortis in omnibus fuerit, sive omnes in Adamo peccarint' (*Ad Romanos*, 194).

[124] E.g. S. Strehle.

forensic scheme. Implicit in his analysis of Christ and Adam as federal heads was his belief in a prelapsarian covenant of works (*foedus operum*).[125] Far from being only a postlapsarian arrangement, the *foedus* was of the essence of God's relations to Adam. That old serpent ('*serpens ille antiquus*') intended only to lead man away from the 'word of the law' or the 'covenant of creation' ('*a creationis foedere*') in order to offer a competing confederation with himself.[126] Because it was a prelapsarian covenant of works, 'there was no need of the Gospel'.[127]

For Olevian, the very meaning of the verb 'to justify' and the issue of the law (and its difference from the gospel) entailed a federal or covenantal arrangement.

> For this reason the distinction between law and Gospel is retained. The law does not promise freely, but under the condition that you keep it completely. And if someone should transgress it once, the law or legal covenant does not have the promise of the remission of sins. On the other hand, the Gospel promises freely the remission of sins and life, not if we keep the law, but for the sake of the Son of God, through faith.[128]

All were accounted sinners before the promulgation of the Sinaitic law. How could this have been? Because the substance of the law was already in force, in the law of nature, in a '*pactum*'. Unless 'in Adam they had the law or mandate', Paul could not have said that all sinned before the law.[129] Thus, we are 'constituted sinners in Adam'.[130] The twofold federal-forensic scheme was Olevian's bulwark against the notion held by Pelagius, the Anabaptists and other ignorant folk, that sin

---

[125] See W. J. van Asselt, *The Federal Theology of Johannes Cocceius (1603–1669)*, trans. R. A. Blacketer (Leiden, 2001), 254–6.

[126] *De substantia*, 2.27.

[127] '...neque enim ante lapsum opus habeat Evangelio' (*De substantia*, 2.27).

[128] 'Causa. Ut retineatur legis & Evangelii. Lex non promittit gratis, sed sub conditione, si omnia feceris. Et si quis eam semel sit transgressus, non habet lex seu foedus legale promissionem remissionis peccatorum: evangelium vero gratis promittit remissione peccatorum, & vitam si non praestiterimus legem, propter Filium Dei, per fidem' (*Ad Romanos*, 148).

[129] 'Ergo in Adamo habverunt legem seu mandatum quod transgressi in ipsius lumbis...' (*Ad Romanos*, 195).

[130] '...sumus constituti peccatores in Adamo' (*Ad Romanos*, 196).

consists in the imitation of one's parents.[131] It cannot have been a matter of imitation since the law of death was in force before the law. 'Therefore before the law, sin was in all who are dead.'[132]

Olevian's consistent teaching was that the natural law, in force before the Sinaitic law, was substantially identical to the decalogue and performed the same function: convicting sinners and driving them to Christ.[133] As with the Decalogue the condition of the primeval covenant was: do this and live. Adam, and we in him, failed to obey thereby inheriting his sin, death, and condemnation.[134] Such is the nature of the divine law. It requires perfection, both before and after the Fall.[135]

Olevian's conception of the natural law (*lex naturae*) was completely intertwined with his understanding of Adam's federal headship of all humanity. For him to speak of the *lex naturae* was to speak of the ante-lapsarian covenant between God and Adam, the latter as representative of all humanity. He regarded this law as the 'first covenant' (*primum foedus*), the 'creational covenant' (*foedus creationis*) 'natural covenant' (*foedus naturale*), 'the law of creation' (*ius creationis*) or the 'legal covenant' (*foedus legale*).[136] It was transgression of the 'creational law' which corrupted the image of God in humanity and plunged all of humanity into spiritual death.[137] Violation of this covenant was

---

[131] 'Non est tantum propensio ad peccandum, ut Pelagius & Anabaptistae affirmant: neque etiam imitatione dumtaxat parentum simus mali, ut multi putatant quam simus miseri' (*Ad Romanos*, 199–200).

[132] '...etiam ante legem mortui sunt. Ergo ante legem peccatum fuit in omnibus qui mortui sunt' (*Ad Romanos*, 200).

[133] See *Ad Romanos*, 27, 57, 58, 97, 272, 288, Ad *Galatas*, 68; *Ad Philippenses & Colossenses*, 42; *De substantia*, 1.1.2, 9. See also L. D. Bierma, 'Covenant or Covenants in the Theology of Olevianus?' *Calvin Theological Journal* 22 (1987), 244.

[134] *De substantia*, 1.1.8.

[135] That the *lex naturalis* was substantially identical to the decalogue was virtually the universal conception of natural law among the magisterial Protestant theologians. See *WA*, 2.580; 56.197,9; Philip Melanchthon, *Corpus Reformatorum*, ed. C. G. Bretschneider, 101 vols (Halle, 1834-1959), 21.711–16 (hereafter *CR*); John Calvin, *CR*, 54.392, ibid., 77.37–8; idem, *Institutio*, 1.15.1; 2.8.1; 2.2.22; 4.20.16; *OS*, 3.173–4; 3.343–4; 3.264–5; 5.487–9). See also R. S. Clark, 'Calvin and the *Lex Naturalis*', *Stulos Theological Journal* 6 (1998), 1–22.

[136] See *De substantia*, 1.1.7, 8, 1.2.1; 1.5.31; 2.5, 8; 2.41, and passim in ibid., pars altera.

[137] 'Quoniam iure creationis excideramus per peccatum, quo et maiestati divinae inobedientes fueramus, et imaginem Dei in nobis corruperamus, non

blindness, perversity and entailed even a rejection of the Trinity and the eternal intra-trinitarian covenant.[138]

In his *Notae* in Romans, he also made clear the connection in his theology between the doctrine of the covenant of works and his doctrine of imputation. Beginning with the gospel fact of our righteousness by imputation, he reasoned back to the prelapsarian situation. 'Where there is no law and transgression of law, it is not possible to impute sin'. For Olevian, Scripture teaches plainly the imputation of Adam's sin to the entire human race. Therefore, there must have been a prelapsarian, natural law, which Adam transgressed. Because of his federal headship of humanity, violation of the law brought the death penalty, even to infants.[139]

As a corollary to his understanding of Adam's federal headship, he believed that the righteousness which is imputed to believers was not only Christ's *obedientia passiva*, i.e. his suffering and crucifixion, but also his active obedience (*obedientia activa*), to the divine law. 'We speak about Adam's sin and, in turn, about Christ's obedience'. Just as Adam's sin was imputed to us, our sin and penalty was imputed and imposed upon Christ.[140] In his comments on Galatians 3:13–14, he made this view even more explicit.

> This obedience of the Son was superior to all the justice of the law. For Adam also, if he willed, could have remained in the righteousness of the law. And to the degree that the curse was owed for every sin of the elect, to the same degree he had to fulfil all righteousness without any complaint; not even all the Angels were able to do this. Therefore, this obedience of the Son was not only

---

ferebat Dei iustitia, ut peccatoribus se in Patrem exhiberet, qui & peccata condonaret et peccatores instauraret sine Mediatore' (*De substantia*, 1.2.1).

[138] 'Haec ideo tantum ut appareat eorum imprudentia et excæcatio, qui iam negatione illius veritatis a vero Deo, redemptionisque fœdere se abduci patiuntur, cuius affirmatione, Dei ore comprobata, in perversum tamen finem detorta Sathan initio hominem à Deo et creationis foedere abduxit' (*De substantia*, 1.1.7). See Bierma, 'Covenant or Covenants', 235–6, n. 46.

[139] 'Si quis hoc pacto velit resolvere non repugno: ubi nulla est lex legisque transgressio, ibi peccatum non potest imputari ideoque nec poena. At peccatum etiam usque ad legem per Mosen datam fuit in mundo, & quidem imputatum omnibus ad poenam, etiam infantibus' (*Ad Romanos*, 195). See also ibid., 224.

[140] 'De Adae peccato diximus & vicissim de obedientia Christi' (*Ad Romanos*, 205).

regarding the righteousness of the law, such as Adam received in creation, and such as the law required of him, but also it exceeded the righteousness of all the Angels.[141]

In making Christ's obedience parallel to Adam's disobedience, Olevian was placing all of Christ's life and not just his sufferings in a probationary, legal framework.[142] In obeying the law, Christ was acting in his capacity as representative of the Church, as the Second Adam. Given his Reformed Christology and the distinction between the two natures, Olevian assumed that, as fully human, Christ must fulfil all righteousness. He did not conclude (in contrast to Piscator) that Christ's *obedientia activa* was sufficient only for himself.[143] Rather he assumed that, given

---

[141] 'Haec obedientia Filii omni Legis iustitia est superior. Nam & Adamus in Legis iustitia permanere potuisset, si voluisset. At tantam maledictionem singulis electorum peccatis debitam, tanta obedientia sine indignatione ulla perferre, ne omnes quidem Angeli potuissent. Itaque haec obedientia Filii non modo Legis iustitiam, qualem Adamus in creatione acceperat, qualemque Lex iure suo requirit, superat, sed omnium etiam Angelorum iustitiam' (*Ad Galatas*, 57).

[142] *Ad Romanos*, 143.

[143] J. Piscator (1546-1625) affirmed only the imputation of Christ's *obedientia passiva* and denied the imputation of Christ's *obedientia activa*. He was following the Lutheran theologian (Georg Karg or *Cargius* or *Parsimonius*) who argued, in 1563, that if Christian obedience is necessary, then Christ's active obedience could have no substitutionary value since he owed it to God himself. Karg, however, renounced this view in 1570 (See K. R. Hagenbach, *A History of Christian Doctrines*, trans. C. W. Buch et al., 3 vols [Edinburgh, 1883-95], 3.218-9; McGrath, *Iustitia*, 2.45-7; A. Ritschl, *A Critical History of the Christian Doctrine of Justification and Reconciliation*, trans. J. S. Black [Edinburgh, 1872], 248-55).

According to E. F. K. Müller, J. Buchanan and A. C. Clifford, however, Piscator argued this view for the same reasons as the Amyrauldians and Arminians, because the imputation of Christ's active obedience diminishes the Christian's need for obedience. Clifford attempts to link Piscator, Calvin, Arminius, and Wesley in support of his own rejection of the doctrine of double imputation (idem, *Atonement and Justification* [Oxford, 1990], 190-91). On its face, this association seems quite unlikely. See *Institutio* 2.16.5 (*OS*, 3.485), where Calvin explicitly affirmed justification on the basis of the imputation of both Christ's active and passive obedience. Not only did Calvin teach this but also Wollebius and Alsted (see Müller, s.v. Piscator, *The Schaff-Herzog Encyclopedia of Religious Knowledge*, 12 vols, ed. S. M. Jackson [London, 1912]; J. Buchanan, *The Doctrine of Justification* [Edinburgh, 1867], 174-5; Heppe, *Dogmatik*, 336).

Neither Piscator's *Thesum theologicorum* (1596-1618) nor his *Apologia disputationis de causa meritoria justificationis hominis coram Deo* (Herborn,

Christ's deity, his active obedience vicariously satisfied the divine wrath and was imputed to all the elect.[144] 'Hence it is only to those who believe, i.e. the elect, that the formula of the covenant: 'I will be a God to you and to your seed' (*formula foederis: 'Ero Deus tuus & seminis tuî'*) and the 'promise of Christ: "*Horum est regnum caelorum*"' is given.[145] For Olevian, one is reprobate or justified because one is reckoned such by God, on the basis of one's legal connection to Adam or faith in Christ as federal head.

Predestination and Justification

Olevian's doctrine of predestination was in the background of and inseparable from his entire doctrine of justification. This is because grace, by definition, must be free and sovereign and those qualities necessarily imply predestination. Not surprisingly, he found the epistle to the Romans teaching a strong doctrine of predestination.

Of course, at least from Augustine's anti-Pelagian writings, some form of the doctrine of predestination was a commonplace in the western theological tradition. As a western, anti-Pelagian theologian, Olevian shared that predestinarian tradition.[146] This is

---

1618) is available to me. The 1599 English translation of his *Libri duo de iustificatione hominis coram Deo oppositi sophismatis Roberti Bellarmini* (Herborn, 1590) was consulted. In it he nowhere taught the imputation of Christ's active obedience (see J. Piscator, *A Learned and Profitable Treatise of Man's Justification. Two Books. Opposed to the Sophismes of Robert Bellarmine, Iesuite* [London, 1599]).

Following the publication of the first part of the *Thesum theologicorum*, questions were raised, in 1603, at the 17th National Synod of the French Reformed Church, regarding Piscator's rejection of double imputation. Piscator's answer to Synod's questions and his views were rejected by the 18th Synod convened at La Rochelle in 1607 (See J. Quick, *Synodicon in Gallia Reformata: or the Acts, Decisions, Decrees, and Canons of those Famous National Councils of the Reformed Churches in France*, 2 vols [London, 1692]. For a full bibliography of Piscator's works see F. W. Bautz, ed., *Biographisch-Bibliographisches Kirchenlexikon*, 11 vols (Hamm, Westf. 1970–), s.v. 'Piscator, Johannes'.

[144] '...imputat iis obedientiam suae mortis...'(*Ad Romanos*, 97). See also ibid., 510.

[145] *Ad Romanos*, 220.

[146] D. Steinmetz sees substantial continuity between Augustine's doctrine of predestination and Luther's (idem, 'Luther and Augustine on Romans 9', *Luther*

not to say, however, that the Protestants were uniform in their predestinarian theology, but only that there was a general consensus that those who are saved are the elect and that the elect are those whom God has predestined.

Luther considered the biblical doctrine of predestination to be the first part of the remedy for moralism which had long controlled the soteriology of the western church. It was not that the entire medieval Church had rejected formally Augustine's doctrine of predestination (e.g. Scotus and Ockham), rather she often simply ignored it. This neglect co-operated in the rise of what Richard Hooker called 'demi-Pelagianism'.[147]

Luther had been thoroughly trained in Biel's *pactum* theology.[148] He, however, rejected Biel's teaching on co-operation with divine grace for justification by rejecting the doctrine of the freedom of the will and by embracing the doctrine of predestination.[149] His movement away from Biel toward Augustine, at least regarding the effects of original sin, was evident in his lecture on Psalm 51.[150] Certainly five years later, in

---

in Context [Bloomington, IN, 1986]). For the opposite view see McGrath, *Iustitia*, 2.18.

[147] Richard Hooker, *The Works of Mr. Richard Hooker*, ed. J. Keble, 6th edn, 3 vols (Oxford, 1874), *Ecclesiastical Polity*, appendix 1.12. The *Epitome of the Formula of Concord* Art. 2, Negative thesis 3, rejected the doctrine of the 'semipelagianorum' that man, 'propriis viribus' is able to begin his conversion, but unable 'to complete' (absolvere) it 'without the grace of the Holy Spirit'. F. Bente, ed., *Concordia triglotta libri symbolici ecclesiae Lutheranae* (St Louis, 1921), 788.

[148] See H. A. Oberman, *Luther: Man Between God and the Devil* (London [repr.], 1993), 138; B. Hägglund, *The Background*, 18–33. A. E. McGrath, J. Farthing and C. P. Carlson agree that Biel was Luther's primary contact with medieval theology (see McGrath, *Iustitia Dei*, 1.19; Farthing, *Thomas Aquinas*; Carlson, *Justification*, 130–31).

[149] His 1513–14 *Dictata super Psalterium* reveal his theological development toward Protestantism. For example, his lecture on Psalm 1 demonstrated a rather more generous conception of the freedom of the will than appeared in later lectures. This denial of free-will was an essential component in his move toward his later positions reflected in *De servo arbitrio*. See *WA*, 3.25–6.

[150] *WA*, 3.288ff. On Luther's relations to Staupitz' relative to the doctrine of predestination see D. Steinmetz, *Luther and Staupitz: An Essay in the Intellectual Origins of the Protestant Reformation* (Durham, NC, 1980). For a slightly different view of Luther and Staupitz see L. Graf zu Dohna 'Staupitz and Luther: Continuity and Breakthrough at the Beginning of the Reformation', *Via Augustini: Augustine in the Later Middle Ages, Renaissance and Reformation* (Leiden, 1991).

thesis 13 of the Heidelberg Disputation (1518), Luther expressed one of the central arguments of the later *De servo arbitrio* (1525), 'Free will, after the fall, exists in name only...'.[151] His radically predestinarian soteriology was, of course, on full display in *On the Bondage of the Will* (*De servo arbitrio*, 1525).[152] Whatever one thinks of the doctrine of predestination, the fact is that it was an early and important part of the development of Protestantism, so much so that it was among Luther's earliest steps toward what became the Protestant soteriology.

In the early 1520s, Melanchthon was as fundamentally committed to as radical a predestinarian scheme as was Luther. In his earliest attempt to write a dogmatic theology, *Theological Instruction in the Epistle of Paul to the* Romans (*Theologica institutio in epistolam Pauli ad Romanos*, 1520), he was decidedly predestinarian.[153] In the first edition of the *Common Places* (*Loci communes*, 1521) he declared to be 'impious dogma' and 'profane' any teaching which 'obscures the benefits of Christ', i.e. any notion that humans have free will (*liberum arbitrium*) relative to the divine decree.[154] He was unequivocal that whatever occurs in this life is the direct result of 'divine predestination and not the freedom of our will'.[155] He was so thoroughly predestinarian that he did not even offer a specific locus on predestination because he said that it was virtually the first and last of his theology.[156]

By the 1543 edition of his *Loci communes*, however, his views had changed. He called the teaching that God predestined all things, 'stoic'.[157] This was certainly a marked reversal of his

---

[151] '13. Liberum arbitrium post peccatum res est de solo titulo...' (*WA*, 1.354).

[152] See especially *WA*, 17.756ff.

[153] See *CR*, 21.49ff.

[154] '...impium de libero arbitrio dogma, et obscurata Christi beneficia per prophanam illam et animalem rationis nostrae sapientiam' (*CR*, 21.86).

[155] 'Si ad praedestinationem referas humanam voluntatem nec in externis nec in internis operibus ulla est libertas, sed eveniunt omnia iuxta destinationem divinam' (*CR*, 21.93); 'Quandoquidem omnia quae eveniunt necessario iuxta divinam praedestinationem eveniunt, nulla est voluntatis nostrae libertas' (*CR*, 21.87–8).

[156] He defended discussing predestination early and often. 'Quanquam quid attinet in Compendio primo, an postremo loco id agam, quod in omnes disputationis nostrae partes incidet' (idem, *CR*, 21.89).

[157] See *CR*, 21.919.

rhetoric. Yet, he did not abandon predestination entirely. 'God,' he said, 'always, for the sake of his Son, through his mercy, calls, gathers, assembles, the Church and receives believers.'[158] It is important to note that beyond rhetorical revisions, Melanchthon also reorganised the *Loci* in the second and third editions. In so doing, he relocated his discussion of predestination away from soteriology proper. From 1533, he had placed a locus on predestination after his ecclesiology and sacramental theology so that it functioned more as a subset of his ecclesiology than of his soteriology. For Melanchthon, after 1533, the function of predestination was to encourage those in the visible Church. Whatever one makes exactly of his revision of his doctrine of predestination it is certain that he remained predestinarian in some sense, in every edition of the *Loci communes*.

Here too, Canisius provides a clear Tridentine counter-point to Olevian's theology. In line with the general western tradition, he affirmed the 'arcane mystery of divine predestination'. Yet, his doctrine of predestination functioned quite differently from the Protestant doctrine. Luther, Melanchthon, and Calvin agreed that predestination ought to bring comfort and assurance to the Church. They had little difficulty imagining that one could be certain that he was elect.

To Canisius, however, on analogy with his doctrines of faith and justification, it was inconceivable that one should 'presume to be among the number of the predestined...or that he is justified'. The only way one could possibly know such things is by special revelation, which Canisius assumed to be unlikely in the normal course of things.[159] Hence, predestination remained

---

[158] '...semper propter filium per misercordiam vocare, trahere et colligere Ecclesiam et recipere assentientes...' (*CR*, 21.920). How he could have moved away from Luther, in this aspect of his soteriology, so sharply without incurring his wrath is a very interesting question and one worthy of further research. Perhaps it was that the earlier doctrine was considered to have focused on what he called 'internal freedom' and in the later editions he paid more attention to 'external freedom'. For example he said, 'Si ad opera externa referas voluntatem, quaedam videtur esse iudicio naturae libertas. Si adfectas referas voluntatem, nulla plane libertas est etiam naturae iudicio. Iam ubi adfectus coeperit furere et aestuare, cohiberi non potest quin erumpat' (*CR*, 21.93). One wonders whether Luther ever read the 1533 or 1543 editions of the *Loci*. It is quite possible that he did not, preferring instead to use the more familiar first edition.

[159] 'Nemo quoque, quandiu in hac mortalitate vivitur, de arcano divinae praedestinationis mysterio usque adeo praesumere debet, ut certo statuat, se

primarily a divine mystery to be affirmed but not explored or used in spiritual counsel.

Against Canisius, Olevian taught that one could not only know that one is justified, but also that one is predestined. In fact, the primary purpose of the doctrine of election is to fuel one's assurance that one has been redeemed.

> The first benefit of the doctrine of election is that our faith might have a more firm foundation than the entire structure of heaven and earth, namely God's indisputably immutable decree and not the condition of works.[160]

Indeed, because the divine decree is immutable, 'the salvation of the elect is most certain'.[161] Its second purpose is 'that all glory should go to God alone' for he called those in whom there was no merit at all.[162] This doctrine was particularly clear in his exposition of chapters 8 and 9, but throughout the *Notae* he juxtaposed merit and election as mutually exclusive categories. Election was so comprehensive of his soteriology that it served as a synecdoche for his entire scheme of gracious salvation, including imputation, the gift of faith, and justification, since these latter benefits presuppose God's free, eternal decree.[163] 'The sources of our salvation...flow from God to us, not from our merits to God.'[164]

Olevian based his argument here in his doctrine of God, beginning with the very word 'God' ('who is the *summum*

---

omnino esse in numero praedestinatorum: quasi verum esset, quod iustificatus aut amplius peccare non possit, aut si peccaverit, certam sibi resipiscentiam promittere debeat. Nam nisi ex speciali revelatione sciri non potest, quos Deus sibi elegerit' (Canisius, *Appendix*, Q.16).

[160] 'Utilitas prima doctrinae de electione est, ut fides nostra fundamentum habeat firmius tota machina coeli & terrae, nimirum immutabile Dei decretum & nullam prorsus conditionem operum' (*Ad Romanos*, 379; see also ibid., 141).

[161] '...salutem electorum esse certissimam' (*Ad Romanos*, 425). He cited Malachi 3:6 as his proof text: 'Ego Dominus, & non mutor'.

[162] 'Utilitas doctrinae de electione, ut omnis gloria soli Deo datur.... Quemadmodem nullum est meritum in vocatione, ut nos vocavit' (*Ad Romanos*, 381).

[163] 'Electio secundum propositum, primus fons est, non ex meritis nostris' (*Ad Romanos*, 379).

[164] 'Fontes nostrae salutis...qui à Deo ad nos fluunt, non a nostris meritis ad Deum' (*Ad Romanos*, 379).

bonum') itself.[165] God is by his nature eternal, immutable, and sovereign.[166] Therefore, there can be 'no counsel against the Lord'.[167] Because it is eternal and therefore unconditioned by any creature, the divine purpose (*propositum*) was the 'reason' (*ratio*) or 'foundation' (*fundamentum*) of his argument. Predestination is purely the product of the immutable divine will.[168]

This will, however, was twofold. From all eternity, God decreed freely to preserve some 'in the Son' (*in filio*), to communicate efficaciously the offered salvation to them but 'he willed to hate the rest'.[169] He accepted as a matter of fact that there is a class of humans who have been, from all eternity, reprobated by God. Jacob and Esau are types of the elect and the reprobate. Some are predestined to eternal life because they are predestined. The predestinate accept the gift of faith, but there are also those who reject the same gift because they are not elect.[170] He was so convinced of the efficacy of the biblical teaching, and apparently so little worried about offending his readers, that he put his doctrine of double predestination quite plainly: some he clothes (with Christ's *iustitia*), others he blinds.[171]

---

[165] 'In voce *Deus*, qui summum bonum est, latet argumentum' (*Ad Romanos*, 375).

[166] 'Prima ex caussa [sic], quia Deus id sibi immutabiliter proposuit, & quomodo proposuerit'...(*Ad Romanos*, 378). See also ibid., 425.

[167] 'Non est consilium contra Dominum' (*Ad Romanos*, 375).

[168] 'Ratio sive fundamentum huius propositionis est in his verbis: *Qui iuxta propositum vocati sunt*. Propositum Dei est aeternum illud Dei consilium & immutabilis voluntas, qua ante ullam rem creatorem'...(*Ad Romanos*, 377). See also ibid., 424–5.

[169] '...decrevit, gratis in filio servare, quorum voluit misereri, & ita servare ut iis partam & oblatam salutem efficaciter communicet' (*Ad Romanos*, 377).

[170] '...diximus in definitione: certos homines Electos esse ad vitam: id manifestatum est, ex hoc loco Pauli: nominatim assumitur Iacob & Esau reiicitur: Et hi ponuntur hic ut exempla Electorum et reproborum omnium, Iohan. 13. Ego scio quos elegerim. ...Nomina vestra scripta sunt in coelis. Ergo certi homines sunt Electi. Falsum igitur est, quod multi putant omnes esse promiscue electos, sed ea conditione si credant. Contra se res habet. Quidam enim sunt ad vitam aeternam praedestinati, ut, quia praedestinati sunt. Sint etiam donorum fidei accepturi à Deo. Contra, quidam non electi ad vitam: et quia non electi sunt, donum fidei non sunt accepturi, sed oblatam gratiam propria contumacia reiecturi' (*Ad Romanos*, 426–7).

[171] '...Deus ipse aliquos induret, excaecet' (*Ad Romanos*, 441).

He distinguished between the external and internal call of God. The latter is always efficacious. The former he associated mostly with the preached Word and the administration of the sacraments.[172] The internal call, however, always comes via the external. To those whom God calls internally, he gives faith and implants into Christ. It is by this faith that one can be certain that one is elect since only the elect believe. Why is this? 'Because faith comes not from free will...but from heaven out of election'. [173] The 'internal call' (*vocatio interna*) is a corollary to election and just as efficacious. Against the 'Pelagians' he argued that election is not grounded in 'foreseen merit (*meritum praevisum*) so that God alone should have the glory'.[174] Rather, 'faith is given to no one but the elect'.[175] Implied in this argument is the syllogism: Only the elect believe. I believe, therefore I am elect. This was not the only subjective turn in his doctrine of assurance. He also appealed to the presence of Christ's sanctifying work in the Christian's life as evidence of one's election, which he connected to Christ's perpetual intercessory work.[176]

Election, however, was not considered a divine operation wrought in abstraction from the appointed means. Because our faith is weak, God uses certain instruments to accomplish his purposes. He works his effectual call in his elect through the preached Word and the administration of the Sacraments. Thus, the external gospel call to faith comes with the Holy Spirit himself.[177]

---

[172] For example, expressions such as 'oblatam salutem' and 'oblatam iustitiam' are relatively frequent in Olevian and suggest a strong consciousness of the preached offer of the gospel. His doctrine of the church and sacraments will be discussed in the next chapter.

[173] 'Vocatio efficax & externa & interna alterum est. Nam alioqui externe multi vocati, pauci electi. Haec est donatio fidei per quam inserimur Christo. Inde cognoscimus nos electos esse, quia fides non ex libero arbitrio venit...sed e coelo in nos plantatur ex electione. Fides enim nemini datur nisi electis' (*Ad Romanos*, 373).

[174] '...sicut in electione, ita & in vocatione nullum meritum praevisum, ut solus Deus gloriam habeat' (*Ad Romanos*, 373).

[175] 'Fides enim nemini datur nisi electis' (*Ad Romanos*, 373). In his *Notae* on Romans 9:11, he adduced the 'fructum sive effectum electionis' and that 'Deus nos gratis insitos Christo, & gratis iustificatos renovare quoque gratis ad sancte vivendum' as proofs of his doctrine of election' (*Ad Romanos*, 431; he made the same argument also in ibid., 140).

[176] *Ad Romanos*, 145–6.

[177] 'Haec vocatio in nobis facta est, & quia fides infirma, pergit nos vocare in Verbo & Sacramentis. Et cum externa vocatio per Spiritum sanctum dat echo

Only those who are called internally, however, are believers; but all those who are called do believe.[178] Therefore, the *locus* of God's calling activity is the visible Church.[179] It is in the assembly that parents apply the '*signum foederis*' to their children according to the unqualified divine promise (since God alone knows who is elect), just as God commanded Abraham. Christian parents apply the sign to their children trusting in God's election.[180]

God, the Trinity and the *Pactum Salutis*

In light of the way Olevian has been often characterised, as a type of Christocentric anti-scholastic and as a sort of covenantal anti-Calvinist, it is important to recognise that his conception of the gospel and his conception of predestination were, in his mind, inseparable. In fact, his idea of justification was logically dependent upon his doctrine of election and his doctrine of election was rooted in his belief in the pre-temporal intra-trinitarian covenant of redemption (*pactum salutis*) or 'the covenant of peace and of sworn eternal mercy' (*foedus pacis & misericordiae aeternae iuratae*).[181]

It is also important to realise not only how thoroughly predestinarian Olevian was, but also how traditional he was. It is true that the incarnation was pivotal to his theology – indeed the incarnation of the Son, his obedience and death and the resulting justification and subsequent sanctification of his people is at the heart of the substance of the covenant considered objectively – but it is also true that he began with a received doctrine of God which he assumed to be true and biblical. Hence, his doctrine of election was closely connected to his doctrine of God. He only taught election because he believed that God is free and sovereign. Because his definition of grace flowed from his doctrine of God, it was logically prior to his doctrine of

---

in corde Davidis...' (*Ad Romanos*, 374).

[178] 'Observatio, Omnes vocati sunt credentes' (*Ad Romanos*, 374).

[179] 'Qui igitur plantatur? Electi. Ubi? In Ecclesia' (*Ad Romanos*, 426).

[180] 'Quemadmodum Abraham omnibus suis dat signum foederis, iuxta promissionem indefinitam, quia ignota ei est electio (Eam enim Deus reservavit) ita & nos liberis nostris signum foederis damus, Deo libera relicta sua electione' (*Ad Romanos*, 423–4).

[181] *De substantia*, 2.28. See also van Asselt, *The Federal Theology of Johannes Cocceius*, 227–9.

justification. This is why he said that the foundation (*fundamentum*) of the decree itself is the immutable will of God.[182] Believers can be entirely confident of their election and salvation precisely because it is quite impossible to frustrate the divine intention and the divine intention has always been to save his people.[183] Hence, he explained his doctrine of predestination by framing it in terms of God's 'eternal covenant for us'.[184]

Though he did not discuss intra-trinitarian operations in great detail, he did teach the *pactum salutis*.[185]

> [T]he Son of God, having been constituted by the Father as Mediator of the covenant, becomes the guarantor on two counts: 1) He shall satisfy for the sins of all those whom the Father has given him (John 17) and he decreed from eternity to adopt them into sonship through Christ (Ephesians 1); 2) He shall also bring it to pass that they, being planted in him, shall enjoy peace of conscience and be renewed daily in the image of God.[186]

In this pre-temporal, eternal covenant, the Son assumed an economically subordinate role to the Father, hence Olevian says the Son was 'constituted' Mediator of the covenant. His chief work is to redeem the elect, to secure their adoption. Here again, one sees the penetration of the double benefit (*duplex beneficium*) into his soteriology. The first part of the *pactum* is also first part of the double benefit, the objective work of the Son *for* sinners.

---

[182] *Ad Romanos*, 372. Divine immutability was essential to other *loci* in his theology. For example, he also considered Christ's ascension and accession to be grounded in the immutable divine promise. See *De substantia*, 1.6.14–7. The *foedus* itself was efficacious only because of God's immutability. See *De substantia*, 2.12–5.

[183] 'Quia propositum Dei immutabile, sive impossibile Deum frustrari sua intentione…' (*Ad Romanos*, 372). See also ibid., 425–6.

[184] 'Insiste meditationi, Deus est foedere aeterno pro nobis' (*Ad Romanos*, 375).

[185] Calvin taught substantially the same doctrine. See *Institutio*, 2.11.4 (*OS*, 2.427.19–23), 3.22.6 (*OS*, 4.386.9–12).

[186] '…Filius Dei mediator foederis a Patre constitutus spondet pro duabus rebus, primo se satisfacturum pro peccatis omnium quos Pater ei dedit Ioan. 17: & ab aeterno per Christum in filios adoptare decrevit Ephes. 1. Secundo se etiam effecturum ut sibi insiti pace conscientiae fruantur atque indice renoventur ad Dei imaginem (*De substantia*, 1.2.1).

iustitia aliena inputata
dichotomy of law and gospel

The *pactum salutis* also entails the second benefit, the subjective application of Christ's work *to* sinners, which is their daily renewal in the image of God. As a consubstantial trinitarian person, the Son entered into this covenant voluntarily and is not only the Mediator but was also the 'foundation' in whom the Father accepted the elect beforehand.[187] In fulfilment of this covenant between the Father and the Son, the latter accomplished redemption, and the Spirit applied redemption to the elect by uniting them to the Son and through him to the Father. This was Olevian's doctrine throughout his teaching career. It is the opening theme of *Vester Grund* (1567) and was repeated in *De substantia*, his last major commentary on the Creed published in 1585.[188]

Hence, the salvation of God's elect was the product of an eternal promise (*sponsio*) between the Father and the Son. The Son promised from all eternity to accomplish priestly obedience on behalf of God's people and the Father agreed to accept such obedience as satisfaction for the sins of the elect.[189] This 'surety' (*fideiussio*) was said to have been borne of divine love, and the proper cause of redemption.[190] Those for whom the Son accomplished redemption are given the Holy Spirit who effects a mystical union between Christ and the believer, regeneration and moral renewal unto glorification.[191]

Caspar Olevian taught a Protestant, federalist, predestinarian soteriology. That is, at the core of his soteriology was the dichotomy of law and gospel; the doctrine of *iustitia aliena imputata*; and a definition of faith as the sole, receptive, instrument by which one apprehends Christ's active and passive obedience. Behind these doctrines lay his commitment to absolute divine sovereignty, immutability and freedom from which issued his doctrine of predestination.

---

[187] '...ideo Filium incarnatum summi huius et æterni foedus voluit esse fundamentum' (*De substantia*, 1.2.5); 'Ad utramque foederis partem sponsionis Christi...' (idem, 1.6.1).

[188] See also Vester Grund, Questions 1–4.

[189] *De substantia*, 1.2.2.

[190] *De substantia*, 1.2.4.

[191] '...quodque per hanc personam dare velit Spiritum, quo ipsi fide coniuncti innovemur regeneremur a peccatis ad gloriam filiorum Dei' (*De substantia*, 1.2.2).

Olevian's elaboration of the Reformed, federal approach to justification was his attempt to establish a safe-house, as it were, for the Protestant doctrine of sanctification so it should not intrude on the doctrine of justification (thus confusing law and gospel) but also so that it should give proper expression to the double benefit of Christ (*duplex beneficium Christi*).

CHAPTER 7

SANCTIFICATION:

The Second Benefit of the Covenant of Grace

On his deathbed, Olevian continued his ministry by receiving visitors and providing leadership to the churches of the Wetterau counties. He spent the morning of 11 March 1587 sorting out various ecclesiastical difficulties – indeed he seems to have functioned as a bishop among presbyters – and about noon he dictated his last will and testament in which he commended his soul to his 'beloved God, Father, Son and Holy Ghost' and declared that he was relying on the gracious covenant promises and concluded with a postscript declaring that he stood by everything he had taught and preached.[1]

The next day he wrote a touching farewell letter to his son Paul, who was himself ill and living with the Olevian family in Trier. 'My dear son, Paul! With the Patriarch Jacob, I say: "I wait for thy salvation O, Lord;" for I have arrived at that point where I exclaim with the apostle: "I have a desire to depart and to be with Christ."'[2] A few lines later he repeated his expectation that he was

---

[1] '...meinem lieben Gotte, Vater, Sohn und hl. Geist' (in K. Sudhoff, *C. Olevianus und Z. Ursinus: Leben und ausgewählte Schriften der Vater und Begründer der reformierten Kirche*, [Elberfield, 1857], 467). See also ibid., 465–75; M. Göbel, 'Dr. Caspar Olevianus', trans. H. Harbaugh, *Mercersburg Quarterly Review* 7 (1855), 305; K. Müller, 'Caspar Olevian – Reformator aus Leidenschaft Zum 400. Todestag am 15. März 1987', *Monatshefte für Evangelische Kirchengeschichte des Rheinlandes*, 37/38 (1988–89), 81; T. C. Porter, 'The Authors of the Heidelberg Catechism', *Tercentenary Monument in Commemoration of the Three Hundredth Anniversary of the Heidelberg Catechism* (Chambersburg, PA, 1863), 228.

[2] 'Junig geliebter Sohn Paulus! Ich sage mit dem Vater Jakob: Herr ich warte auf dein Heil. Denn meine Sachen stehen also, daß ich mit dem Apostel spreche: "Ich habe Lust abzuscheiden und bei Christo..." (Sudhoff, *C. Olevianus*

'about to depart to the Lord' and again 'I expect hourly to make my pilgrimage to the Lord'.[3] He commended his son to Christ, 'as I did in holy baptism', and lamented that he would not likely see him again in this life.[4] He also urged his eldest son to make all the necessary arrangements to care for the family Caspar was about to leave behind.

In his signature he provided his own epitaph, 'Your Father, Caspar Olevianus, of Trier, minister of the Word of God. Lord Jesus receive my spirit.'[5] On the morning of the 15th, Jacob Alsted the deacon and Piscator paid him a final pastoral call with the latter reading to him from various portions of Scripture. Bernhard Textor spoke a few words of comfort and they sang a hymn together. Finally, Alsted is said to have asked Caspar if he was confident of his salvation. Olevian's reply was said to have been: 'Most certain.' (*Certissimus*).[6]

His final will and letter to his son are of interest for theological as well as historical reasons. They give one not only a clearer understanding of Olevian the father and family man and therefore a holistic understanding of Olevian through his personal experiences, but also a better conception of how his theology actually functioned in his life and death. Particularly these documents also reflect the twofold benefit (*duplex beneficium*) structure of his soteriology. In both his will and the letter he confessed the objective grounds of his faith and its subjective benefit, the assurance of salvation and progress in sanctification.

Although, in Olevian's theology, sanctification was made a parallel benefit to justification, his doctrine of sanctification has received scant attention in the scholarly literature. Given the *duplex beneficium* organisation of his theology, a consideration

---

und Z. Ursinus, 468). The English translation is taken from Göbel, 'Dr. Caspar Olevianus', 305–6.

[3] 'Heimfahrt zum Herrn.... Ich erwarte stündlich meinen Heimgang zum Herrn' (Sudhoff, 468).

[4] '...zu sein, dem ich auch Dich ganz und gar, gleichwie in der hl. Taufe...' (Sudhoff, 468).

[5] 'Gegeben zu Herborn am 12. März zwischen 4 und 5 Uhr und auf dem Bette dictirt 1587. Die eigenhändige Unterschrift lautet. Ich, Dein Vater Caspar Olevianus von Trier, Diener des Wortes Gottes habe mit eigener Hand unterschrieben. "O Herr Jesu! nimm meinen Geist auf"' (Sudhoff, 468).

[6] Good, *Origins*, 265.

of Olevian's theology would be incomplete without touching on his view of the Christian life. According to Olevian, sinners are redeemed not just to be redeemed, but to be sanctified as a result. Christ died so that 'sin should be extirpated daily from our nature'.[7]

Since the middle of the nineteenth century, Olevian has been portrayed in the scholarly literature as an anti-Puritan and anti-federalist. According to this theory, those federal theologians who made use of sanctification (e.g. the *syllogismus practicus*) in their doctrine of assurance should be considered legalists.[8] For example, R. W. A. Letham juxtaposed Olevian and Ursinus; the latter as a federal-legalist and the former as gracious-covenantal theologian. He says that for Olevian, in contrast to Ursinus, 'in no sense is there mention of sanctification as a basis for assurance'. Further, Olevian was said not even to allow sanctification a subordinate function in relation to assurance.[9]

---

[7] '...ut peccatum in dies e natura nostra extirpatur...' (idem, *In epistolam ad Romanos notae* [Geneva, 1579], 206).

[8] E. F. Rogers, Jr is even more pointed in his critique of what he calls the 'Calvinist mistake' (idem, 'Good Works and Assurance of Salvation in Three Traditions: *Fides Praevisa, the Practical Syllogism, and Merit*', Scottish Journal of Theology 50 [1997], 131–56). The practical syllogism is thus: only believers are sanctified, I am sanctified, therefore I am a believer. This syllogism was implied, e.g. in the Heidelberg Catechism, Q.86, 'dass wir bei uns selbst unsers Glaubens aus seinen Früchten gewiss seien' (P. Schaff, ed., *The Creeds of Christendom*, 3 vols, 6th edn. [Grand Rapids, 1983], 3.338). On the practical syllogism, see R. A. Muller, *Dictionary of Latin and Greek Theological Terms* (Grand Rapids, 1985), s.v. 'syllogismus practicus'. The historical issue in this chapter is not whether the practical syllogism was good or bad or even whether Calvin used it, but that Olevian, whom Barth (among others) regarded as a faithful student of Calvin, did use it (see below).

[9] R. W. A. Letham, 'Saving Faith and Assurance in Reformed Theology: Zwingli to the Synod of Dort', 2 vols (Ph.D. Thesis, Aberdeen, 1979), 1.203. On the other hand, McCoy and Baker claim that Olevian belonged to Bullinger's conditional, mutual, contractual strain of covenant theology and that he took 'federalism nearer to its fully articulated form' (C. S. McCoy and J. W. Baker, *Fountainhead of Federalism: Heinrich Bullinger and the Covenantal Tradition with a Translation of De Testamento seu Foedere Dei Unico et Aeterno* [1534] [Louisville, 1991], 37; See also C. S. McCoy, 'The Covenant Theology of Johannes Coccceius', Ph.D. Diss. [Yale University, 1956], 73–6). Though McCoy and Baker are opposed to Letham's interpretation, they agree with him that there is a federal type of reformed theology as distinct from a covenantal type. Cornelis P. Venema, *Heinrich Bullinger and the Doctrine of Predestination* (Grand Rapids, 2002) offers

Yet, the very framework of Olevian's theology contradicts the claim that he was an anti-federalist theologian. It is my contention that this sort of reading of Olevian is exactly wrong because it overlooks his doctrine of the double benefit and therefore misconstrues the role of Olevian's doctrine of sanctification in his theology. Further, Letham's interpretation rests on an assumption which has been shown to be false: that Reformed federal theology was inherently sub-Protestant. On the contrary, just as Olevian synthesised his federalism with a Protestant doctrine of justification so also he synthesised his federalism with a Protestant doctrine of sanctification. In fact, through his use of the motif of the covenant, Olevian recast and developed the received Protestant doctrine of sanctification, giving the doctrine a more distinctively Reformed appearance.

Sanctification: The Second Part of the Double Benefit

For Olevian, justification by the imputation of Christ's active and passive obedience is the first part of the twofold benefit of being in Christ. Though justification is forensic, justification does not exhaust his soteriology. There are two 'special' benefits to the covenant: justification (gracious remission of sins and the imputation of Christ's justice) and sanctification (renovation in the image of God), or inward moral renewal.[10] Like Calvin,

---

a quite different and rather more cogent interpretation of Bullinger's soteriology and its relations to Calvin and Calvinism.

[10] E.g. Caspar Olevian, *De substantia foederis gratuiti inter Deum et electos* (Geneva, 1585), 2.69. See also ibid., 1.1.2. In *De substantia* 2.65 he did not use the expression *duplex beneficium*, but the notion was present: 'Cum enim tota substantia foederis gratuiti ad duo capita à Deo ipso referatur...remissionem peccatorum, & renovationem ad vitam aeternam'.

He also used the expression twice in his exegesis of Romans 3:10–18: 'Observatio. Duo status hominis considerandi, antequam sit fidelis, & postquam est fidelis. Antequam esset fidelis omnia quoque haec de ipso Paulo dicta erant, sicut 7, cap. ostenditur. At postquam fidelis factus est, duplex beneficium accepit: ita & nos. Fructus ne propter haec iniusticiae nostrae testimonia, iustitiae fidei obliviscamur. 2. Aut Spiritum regenerationis in nobis locum habere non putemus.... Paulus antequam crederet in Christum, non poterat se eximere ex hoc catalogo. At postquam credidit, duplex beneficium accepit. 1. Ne imputetur illi ista corruptio. 2. Renovationem per Spiritum sanctum, ut resistat illis peccatis, & quotidie magis magisque ad Dei imaginem renovetur' (*Ad Romanos*, 128).

Olevian often used terms such as renewal (*renovatio*), conversion (*conversio*) and regeneration (*regeneratio*) for moral renewal or sanctification.[11]

Together justification and sanctification comprise the *duplex beneficium*.[12] This theme in his soteriology corresponded to his definition of sin. 'Sin is twofold, original and actual.'[13] The twofold benefits of Christ address both. By his merit, Christ delivers the elect from the penalty induced by sin. After justification, by the efficacious work of his Spirit, the elect become, through faith, 'partakers in his mind' by which process sin is daily 'extirpated' from their nature.[14]

He moved to the renewal in the image of God – itself the work of the 'Spirit of regeneration' – only after establishing his doctrine of justification. Further, the *renovatio* was also premised on prevenient, unmerited divine mercy. That one should actually trust that one's sins have been forgiven was itself said to be the 'gift of the Holy Spirit'.

Moreover, Olevian had a quite realistic notion of sanctification. In this life one only achieves 'the beginning of

---

[11] Calvin did use *regeneratio* also to describe the moment of initial spiritual awakening. Among the Reformed, after the Arminian crisis, the word came to be used less to describe the process of sanctification and more to denote 'de primo momento, quo primum convertitur, et novam vitam per regenerationem accipit' (F. Turretini, *Institutio theologiae elencticae*, in *Francisci Turretini opera*, 4 vols [Edinburgh, 1847], 15.5.2). See also P. van Mastricht, *Theoretico-practica theologia*. Editio nova (Utrecht, 1699), 657–64; Muller, *Dictionary*, s.v. 'renovatio'. For an example of the earlier use of the term outside Olevian see Joannis Calvini, *Institutio Christianae Religionis 1559*, 1.15.4; *Opera Selecta*, ed. P. Barth and W. Niesel, 3rd edn, 5 vols [Munich, 1963–74], 3.179.27–30 (hereafter, *OS*).

[12] '...duplici beneficio, nempe gratuita iustitia in remissione peccatorum lucente in ipsius sanguine, et renovatione ad Dei imaginem' (*De substantia*, 1.1.2). '...peccatorum remissionem in Christo amplectatur, & hominis quoque instaurationem, sive renovationem ad Dei imaginem' (Caspar Olevian, *Expositio symboli apostolici* [Geneva, 1583], 12).

[13] 'Duplex autem est peccatum, Originale & Actuale' (*Ad Romanos*, 199).

[14] 'Dupliciter Christus liberat, merito & efficacia. 1. Meretur ne imputentur nobis peccata, vel quod idem est, sua obedientia tegit nostram inobedientiam. 2. Efficacia sui Spiritus in nobis operatur, ut ei per fidem insiti meriti huius participes fiamus: & ut peccatum in dies e natura nostra extirpatur...' (*Ad Romanos*, 206–7). Calvin made the exact same argument even connecting it with Christ's federal role as the second Adam. See *Institutio*, 1.15.4; *OS*, 3.179.11–19.

obedience' (*inchoata obedientia*).[15] Though a divine gift and the instrument of justification, he consistently described faith as 'weak' (*infirma*).[16] We are 'miserable sinners, condemned in ourselves and wholly corrupt'.[17] This profound awareness of human frailty and sinfulness was a significant motivation for his reflection on the sacraments as the divinely appointed means of grace for his people.

Olevian's fellowship in the churches under the cross and his conflicts in the Palatinate also shaped his Christian consciousness and theology. His doctrine of the Christian life was not a triumphalist theology of glory (*theologia gloriae*), but rather a theology of the cross (*theologia crucis*). Christ is reigning 'at the right hand of God' (*ad dextram Dei*) defending his 'allies' (*federatos*) but he is also subjecting them 'under the cross (*sub cruce*) to injury at the hands of their enemies 'in order to mortify sin' (*ad mortificandum peccatum*). The more the elect suffer, the more they shall 'lift up their heads expecting his advent'. [18] The greater their suffering, the more certain they should be of their 'triumph' and the 'righteous ruin of all the impious enemies of God'.[19]

'Sanctification or the beginning of obedience' must be the second part of the *duplex beneficium* because the epistle to the Romans says 'unto the obedience of faith' (*ad obedientiam fidei*) and not simply 'to faith' (*ad fidem*), teaching that one is 'obligated by right', i.e. one owes 'obedience to God', the first part of which is to 'embrace the promise of the gracious remission of sins and the gift of the Holy Spirit'.[20] Christian obedience is the natural product of saving faith, not a second blessing.

---

[15] *Ad Romanos*, 6.

[16] For example see *Ad Romanos*, 374.

[17] '...nobis miseris peccatoribus, in nobis ipsis damnatis, & prorsus corruptis' (*De substantia*, 2.64).

[18] '...elevare capita nostra ad expectandum eius adventum' (*Expositio*, 166).

[19] '...ut quo maiores erunt miseriae, eo simus certiores, instare diem nostri triumphi, & iusti exitii omnium impiorum Dei hostium' (*Expositio*, 167).

[20] 'Altera pars est sanctificatio, sive inchoata obedientia, quam pauci considerant.... Postremo, Cur ait *ad obedientiam fidei*, non simpliciter ad fidem? Docet non esse relictum nobis liberum, ut credamus, vel non credamus, sed iure, quo obedientiam Deo debes, obligatus es, ut promissionem gratuitae remissionis peccatorum, & donationis Spiritus Sancti, amplectaris. Mar. 1. Act. 17' (*Ad Romanos*, 6-7; See also ibid., 150). Theodore Beza's *Iesu Christi D. n.*

Olevian's arrangement of sanctification as a parallel benefit should be seen as a development of, not deviation from, the established Protestant soteriology. From the early 1530s the Protestants were forced to develop their trinitarian theology and hence their doctrine of the knowledge of God. In a similar way, Olevian contributed to the development of Protestant theology through his *duplex* soteriology. It was his trinitarianism and specifically his focus on God the Spirit, combined with use of the covenant which had the effect of creating a *locus* in his theology for a doctrine of evangelical obedience without internally threatening his doctrine of justification by imputation.

In the twofold benefit scheme the objective fact of justification and the subjective appropriation of that justification were distinct but not separated. Hence Olevian described the redeemed not only as 'elect' but also as 'confederates' (*confoederati*), i.e. those with whom Christ has made covenant.[21] 'One ought to have a twofold purpose in view in justification: 1. that all glory should be given to God; 2. that our consciences should have peace.'[22] Justification, the objective aspect of salvation, is directed toward the divine glory. The subjective aspect of justification also glorifies God, but its direct object is our rest.[23] The order of his soteriology was unmistakably Protestant: justification is distinct from, precedes and produces sanctification.

This twofold benefit was of the essence of Olevian's definition of the covenant and therefore his doctrine of sanctification was a constituent of his definition of the covenant. He had sanctification in view in everything he taught. For Olevian, 'Christ has been made not only our righteousness, but also our sanctification', he died not only to justify, but also to renew inwardly his people.[24]

---

novum testamentum sive novum foedus (Geneva, 1565) uses 'obedientiam fidei' in Romans 1:15, 16:26.

[21] *Expositio*, 46, 57, 81.

[22] 'Duplicem scopum oportet habere in conspectu in iustificatione. 1. ut Deo detur omnis gloria. 2. Ut quietem habeant nostrae conscientiae' (*Ad Romanos*, 130). See ibid., 131–2; 180–81.

[23] The verbal parallel to Q.1 of the Westminster Shorter Catechism (1647) is unmistakable: 'What is the chief end of man? To glorify God and enjoy him forever.' There is probably no direct link between Olevian and the divines except their Calvinism, which had the same basic theological impulses.

[24] 'Christus non solum factus est nobis iustitia, sed etiam sanctificatio' (*Ad Romanos*, 207).

Under his exposition of the article, 'I believe the holy catholic Church' (*credo sanctam Ecclesiam catholicam*), he asked, 'why is the church called "holy"?'

> The Church is holy on two accounts, by renewal and imputation (John 13). That same holiness is only begun in renewal (Romans 7)...[b]ut by imputation her holiness is most perfect in Christ.[25]

The difference of course was that according to Olevian's *duplex beneficium* scheme, justification was said to be entirely forensic, but sanctification was not. The latter is progressive and the result of the infusion of sanctifying grace which is never complete in this life.

In his 1583 handbook on logic, he deduced a 'use' (*usus*) under each head which was directed toward improving Christian morality and intellectual rigor.[26] This prevailing concern for conformity to Christ explains why, even in the midst of his decidedly forensic exposition of justification in Romans 5, he spent much of his commentary on Romans 5:17–20 dealing with spiritual renewal (*'vivificatio'*).[27] For the same reason in his *Expositio symboli apostolici* (1576), he included a meditation on the fruit (*fructus*) or *beneficium* of each doctrine so that his doctrine of sanctification was integrated into his theology.

The same *duplex beneficium* scheme controlled *De substantia* (1585). In *pars prima* he addressed the substance of the covenant, i.e. the doctrines of God, man, Christ, and salvation, all of which is comprehended in the articles of the Creed.[28] *Pars altera* concerned the 'means by which this same *substantia* is communicated to us', i.e. its visible and audible administration to the visible covenant community and its mystical application to

---

[25] 'Dupliciter autem Ecclesia sancta est: Renovatione & imputatione, Iohan.13. Renovatione in semet ipsa sanctitas illa tantum est inchoata, ad Rom.7...Imputatione vero sanctitas eius est perfectissma in Christo' (*Exposito*, 178).

[26] For example after his discussion of causalities, he concluded that with a right dividing of causalities one should be able to understand how the Holy Spirit works through the ministry of the Word and sacraments (Caspar Olevian, *De inventione dialecticae* [Geneva, 1583], 36–7).

[27] See *Ad Romanos*, 220–23.

[28] 'Quis sit Deus foederis author: secundo quis homo sit cui foedus hoc promittit: tertio quale foedus velit ferire: quarto in quem finem' (*De substantia*, 1.1.3). See also ibid., 2.1; 2.80–82.

the elect within the assembly.[29] Thus, Olevian's doctrine of sanctification includes both the mystical union (*unio mystica*) between Christ and his people, and the external means by which he administers his grace.[30]

The Trinitarian Structure of the Christian Life

Olevian's trinitarian doctrine of God penetrated his doctrine of the Christian life in that the administration of the covenant requires three consubstantial triune subsistences.[31] 'It does not say God sent the flesh of his Son into your hearts but...he sent the Spirit of his Son into your hearts.'[32] We are body and soul 'members of Christ our head' by virtue of the Spirit.[33] This mystical union through the Spirit is of the essence of salvation since he alone is the means by which one receives Christ's benefits.[34] For Olevian, one of the great blessings of the new covenant (*foedus novum*) is that God promised to be our God and to write his law on our hearts which is principally the work of God the Spirit.[35] Because of our union with Christ through the Spirit, there is in the new covenant an intimacy with God not possible under the old.

Thus, the 'second fruit' of Christ's death was said to be 'the mortification of sin'.[36] Just as the Spirit was given to the Church following the resurrection, so also by union with Christ 'renewal'

---

[29] 'De foederis substantia in priore huius tractationis parte agemus: secundo loco de testimoniis quibus tanquam externis mediis, ea ipsa foederis substantia nobis administratur' (*De substantia*, 1.1.2). The title page of *De substantia* reads: *De substantia foederis gratuiti inter Deum et electos, itemque de mediis, quibus ea ipsa substantia nobis communicatur.*

[30] This structure is virtually identical to that of books 3 and 4 of Calvin's *Institutio*. The latter is 'de externis mediis'.

[31] '...plurimum foedus gratuitum sic administrat Deus Pater, Filius & Spiritus sanctus' (*De substantia*, 2.5).

[32] 'Quod non ait, misit Deus è caelo carnem Filii sui in corda vestra sed...misit Spiritum Filii sui in corda vestra' (Caspar Olevian, *In epistolam d. Pauli apostoli Ad Galatas notae* [Geneva, 1578], 90).

[33] 'Cum non solum animae nostrae, sed & corpora membra sint capitis nostri Christi, per vinculum spiritus fidei' (*Expositio*, 139).

[34] *De substantia*, 1.2.2.

[35] '...corda quoque nostra innovaturus sit, quod vocat inscribere leges cordibus' (*Expositio*, 12).

[36] 'Secundus fructus est mortificatio peccati' (*Expositio*, 112).

(*vivificatio*) flows from mortification, so that whoever believes in Christ is both 'justified' (*iustificatus*) and 'made alive' (*vivificatus*).[37] The second fruit of Christ's resurrection is that by it the Father 'through and because of this Christ' (*per et propter hunc Christum*) 'vivifies' (*vivificat*) believers.[38]

Olevian's Federalist Doctrine of Sanctification

Olevian's theology of the Christian life was federal in both a formal and substantial sense. His doctrine of sanctification was formally federal in that for him to discuss divine-human relations was to discuss the covenant (*foedus*), by which he meant an arrangement between the triune God and sinners whereby God graciously and freely promised to redeem sinners, who in turn accept the offered redemption by faith in Christ, and who in response pledge their lives in gratitude to their Lord and Redeemer. His doctrine of sanctification was federal in a second sense as well. Because of his commitment to the *duplex beneficium* he taught a divine monergism in the doctrine of justification (i.e. *foedus monopleuron*) and he also taught that the covenant of grace entails mutuality in its administration, i.e. he also taught a *foedus dipleuron*.[39]

By definition, the covenant entailed a *duplex beneficium*, free justification and divinely wrought sanctification through the means of grace (*media gratiae*), i.e. renovation in the image of God.[40] Though Christ's merits are 'given freely to us' and imputed to us, this graciousness is not without expectations.[41] In the same

---

[37] *Expositio*, 136.

[38] Olevian, *Exposition*, 191, 2; *Expositio*, 162.

[39] For a discussion of the usage of these terms in Reformed scholasticism, see Muller, *A Dictionary*, s.v. 'foedus monopleuron'.

[40] 'Deus promiserat per Ieremiam Prophetam se percussurum nobiscum foedus novum, non secundum foedus illud, quod pepigerat cum Patribus, cum educeret eos e terra Aegypti: quia irritum fecerant pactum illud: sed hoc fore foedus: Daturum se Legem suam in medio nostri, & in corde nostro inscripturum eam: et futurum nobis in Deum, nosque ipsi in populum: quia propitiandus sit iniquitati nostrae et peccatorum nostrum nolit recordari amplius Ierem. 31. Hebr.8. Hoc foedus huiusmodi veri Dei cognitionem nobis promittit, quae et gratuitam remissionem peccatorum in Christo amplectatur, et hominis quoque renovationem ad Dei imaginem ex se generet' (*De substantia*, 1.1.1).

[41] 'Foedus hoc inter Deum & nos gratuitum esse, nullaque conditione nostrae dignitatis aut meritorum niti, sed sola fide constare, hinc perspici

paragraph in which he said, 'this whole covenant is purely free' (*totum hoc foedus mere est gratuitum*) he also said that grace which regenerates, connects us to Christ and produces faith and 'embraces the free remission of sins in Christ' (*gratuitum peccatorum remissionem in Christo*) also 'begets from itself the renewal or renovation of man to the image of God'.[42] According to his *duplex beneficium* scheme, the Christian life was essential to his doctrine of the covenant as his doctrine of the covenant was essential to the Christian life.

The Means of Grace

One of the differences between Olevian and the Anabaptists to his theological, ecclesiastical, and political left was his emphasis on the church as the visible covenant people of God and upon the means of grace (*media gratiae*): Word and sacraments. Together these means comprised what he called 'ordinary divine testimonies' which themselves testify to the 'substance of the covenant of grace' (*substantia foederis gratuiti*).[43] For Olevian, the Spirit is given 'through the ministry of the Gospel' (*per ministerium Evangelii*) as the 'ordinary means' (*medium ordinarium*) or the 'means and instrument' (*medium et instrumentum*), 'partly audible and partly visible', through which 'God works salvation' in his elect.[44] They are the 'external voice and visible seals' by which the substance of the covenant is administered to the elect in the visible church.[45]

---

potest. Etenim quoad Deum, is proprie foedus nobiscum percutit, cum promissionem reconciliationis gratuitae in Evangelio oblatam per spiritum suum cordibus nostris obsignat.... Quo ad nos, a nobis recipitur sola fide, dum nobis gratis donatur spiritus sanctus, qui efficit, ut velimus, & possimus credere gratuitae promissioni de reconciliatione per Christum.... Quod Mediatorem spectes, accepit quidem ab eo pretium reconciliationis coelestis' (*Expositio*, 11).

[42] '...hominis quoque instaurationem, sive renovationem ad Dei imaginem, ex se generet' (*Expositio*, 11–12).

[43] *De substantia*, 2.1, 5.

[44] *Expositio*, 175. *De substantia*, 2.5. 'Deum autem velle salutem in nobis operari per Evangelium, id est, fidem qua servemur...Magnum est que servantur homines per ministerium, nempe quatenus medium & instrumentum est, quo Deus fidem dat electis' (*Ad Romanos*, 23).

[45] '...externe voce, et visibilibus sigillis' (*De substantia*, 1.1.2); 'pro eius administratione in visibili Ecclesia' (ibid., 1.1.1).

The first of these testimonies is the preaching of the Word, or the 'administration of the covenant of grace through the Word'.[46] Even the Apostle Paul received a 'double call' (*duplex vocatio*). The first was immediate, from heaven. The second was 'mediate, since the Lord calls his ministers to the ministry through the Church'.[47] Though it is a very personal matter, salvation was not to be found privately, apart from the visible church. For Christ has given his name and authority to the visible church.[48] To her he has given the 'power of the keys' (*potestas clavium*) by which he 'preserves the discipline or regimen of the Church'.[49] Holding the power of the keys, the minister, who is the 'legate of Christ and organ of the Holy Spirit', pronounces reconciliation with God and remits sins. By this ministry 'men are drawn to penitence'.[50]

Given the importance of preaching in Olevian's own ministry, the prominence of preaching in Olevian's theology of the means of grace is not altogether surprising. It is through preaching that the Spirit is given and by which sinners receive him.[51] 'The preaching of the gospel is the testimony to Christ'.[52] It is the first call of the royal word to those in darkness under the conviction of the natural and written law.[53]

Proclamation had this central importance because it is through the Christ offered in the preached word (*in verbo oblatum*) that the Spirit begets faith, which is the greatest benefit mediated by preaching: 'reconciliation with God through Jesus

---

[46] '...administratio gratuiti foederis per verbum' (*De substantia*, 2.5).

[47] 'Altera est mediata, cum per Ecclesiam, eiusque ministros Dominus vocat ad ministerium' (idem, *Ad Galatas*, 2). N.B. The first four leaves of this edition were mispaginated.

[48] '...nomine et authoritate' (*De substantia*, 2.38–9).

[49] '...qua munivit disciplinam seu regimen Ecclesiae' (*De substantia*, 2.32).

[50] '...legatus Christi & Spiritus Sancti organum quo homines adducuntur ad poenitentiam' (*De substantia*, 2.33). See also ibid., 2.34–7.

[51] 'Testimonia autem divina ordinaria in Ecclesia (nemo enim de Deo eiusque gratuita benovolentia aeterna idoneus est testis quam Deus ipse) sunt partim audibilia, partim etiam visibilia' (*De substantia*, 2.5). See also ibid., 2.16.

[52] 'Paulus vocat praedicationem Evangelii testimonium de Christo' (*De substantia*, 2.1).

[53] 'Administratio autem foederis gratuiti per testimonium seu sceptrum verbi est vocatio e tenebris (quarum convincuntur e lege partim naturae partim scripta) hoc est a peccato et poena peccati ad lucem' (*De substantia*, 1.1.2)

Christ'.[54] He distinguished this role of preaching from that of the sacraments which were intended to confirm and strengthen faith, not to create it.[55]

The preaching of the gospel was said to be the 'chief testimony and principal organ of the Holy Spirit by which the substance of the covenant is offered to us'.[56] Thus, the preached gospel offer must have priority over the seals (*sigilla*). If receiving the sign and seal of entrance into the visible covenant people were sufficient, all the Israelites should have been regenerate. Of course, such was not the case. Why? Because there were parents who rejected the 'offered covenant' (*foedus oblatum*).[57] Even if the Jews should have received holy baptism it would have been to no effect unless the Holy Spirit had wrought faith in their hearts through gospel preaching. For this reason the visible assembly is a mixed body. The elect are those who receive the promises with faith, for whom the covenant seals are efficacious. They form an 'assembly' (*coetus*) within the visible assembly. The promises do not pertain to unbelievers (*infideles*) or their children even if they have received the seal of baptism.[58]

Preaching however not only creates faith, but it is the chief means by which God 'conserves and strengthens' it and 'through it not only communicates that substance of the covenant (*substantia foederis*) to all the elect', but also 'daily promotes by degrees' the beginning of the mystical fellowship between Christ and his people.[59] The proclamation of the gospel (*praedicatio evangelii*) strengthens and confirms faith in the elect by the pronouncement of repentance (*poenitentiae*) and forgiveness of sins in the name of Christ.[60] Through gospel teaching, Christ is

---

[54] '...reconciliationem cum Deo per Iesum Christum' (*De substantia*, 2.29). See ibid., 2.30–31.

[55] '...fidem virtute Spiritus sui in electis generat atque indies confirmat' (*De substantia*, 2.1).

[56] 'Evangelii praedicatio sit praecipuum testimonium & principale Spiritus sancti organum quo foederis substantiam nobis offert' (*De substantia*, 2.51).

[57] *De substantia*, 2.48.

[58] *De substantia*, 2.48.

[59] 'Placet enim Deo testificatione verbi velut medio, non modo fidem semel creare, sed etiam conservare & augere, ac per eam foederis quoque illam substantiam electis universis non tantum semel communicare, sed etiam quotidie & in finem usque semel inchoatam κοινωνίαν suis velut gradibus promovere' (*De substantia*, 2.1).

[60] *De substantia*, 2.1.

offered to us daily, clothed in the covenant of grace or the promise of the forgiveness of sins and the gift of the Holy Spirit.[61]

Such has been the divine pattern since the beginning. Even before the ministry was instituted God has always revealed himself with the testimony of his Word. As the divine self-disclosure has always been mediated through the Word, likewise the latter is never separated from the Spirit.[62] Though for pedagogical purposes they may be distinguished, the substance of the covenant (*substantia foederis*) is never to be separated from the testimony of the Word.[63] The Word sets forth Christ as the Saviour of sinners and so he is to be offered to the church. Faith is able to apprehend Christ only when he is clothed in the covenant of grace, i.e. as the fulfilment of the covenant of grace.[64]

Preaching is not only the sweet gospel offer however. According to Olevian, the administration of the audible word contains two parts. 'The first is the preparation for faith, the second is the preaching of grace in the name and authority of God in which Christ with the adjoining command is offered to the audience.'[65] Here it becomes evident how Olevian's trinitarian doctrine of God controlled his theology of preaching. Just as the trinitarian persons operate in the economy of redemption, they also operate in the steps of the ratification and administration of the covenant.

The first step in the administration of the covenant was God's promulgation of the law both in the 'natural covenant' (*foedus naturale*) and on the two tables. The Lord not only 'leads his elect to faith through the word' but he does so specifically through the preaching of the law in order that God the Father, Son and Holy Spirit 'might prepare the hearts of the elect to perceive his eternal

---

[61] '...quotidiana vocatione per doctrinam Evangelii, qua nobis offertur Christus vestitus foedere gratiae seu promissione remissionis peccatorum & donationis Spiritus sancti' (*De substantia*, 2.1).

[62] *De substantia*, 2.2.

[63] 'Quoniam igitur Deus substantiam illam foederis a testimonio verbi...non vult esse separatam, licet sit distincta'(*De substantia*, 2.3).

[64] *De substantia*, 2.3.

[65] '...continet duas partes: una est praeparatio ad fidem, altera est praedicatio gratiae qua nomine & authoritate Dei offertur Christus quibus suis audientibus cum annexo mandato, ut eum recipiant, quod naturae omnes debent: in electis autem simul vi Spiritus creatur fides, qua oblatum cum suo officio recipiant' (*De substantia*, 2.5).

wisdom'.[66] All humans exist in a natural covenant or obligation to God, since he is their creator and they were made in his image. The function of the natural covenant was to remove excuse before God, not to save.[67] The divine law is one of the ordained testimonies (*testimonia*).

Unlike the gospel which produces peace, the law was designed to inflict 'horrors of conscience' (*horrores conscientiae*) in the elect as a preparation for faith.[68] These horrors, however, are themselves evidence of the work of the Spirit who is 'kindling the desire to reconcile oneself to God'.[69] In contrast to the reprobate who refuse to feel that they merit the divine wrath, only the elect experience this dread of God's justice.[70] The reprobate remain in the old covenant, under certain condemnation, 'until they should pass over into the new covenant'.[71] Those thus living in sin and death are prepared solemnly for this transition by preaching the law.[72] The Holy Spirit uses the preaching of the law to prepare the hearts of sinners for the gospel offer of Christ since it 'belongs to the office of the law to call consciences to God's judgement'.[73] He did not consider that a sinner could prepare himself for faith. Indeed, 'men do not naturally believe in Christ'.[74] Moreover, for Olevian, the 'preparation for faith' (*praeparatio ad fidem*) by the Spirit 'is only the beginning of the

---

[66] 'Dominus non uno modo per verbum electos suos ad fidem adducat, tamen ut plurimum foedus gratuitum sic administrat Deus Pater, Filius & Spiritus Sanctus, ut pro aeterna sua sapientia corda electorum ad id percipiendum praeparet' (*De substantia*, 2.5).

[67] '...omnem excusationem adimat ostendendo quem fuerit naturale foedus, seu naturalis obligatio inter Deum, quatenus est creator, & homines ad ipsius imaginem conditos'; 'Huius naturalis obligationis testimonium Deus extare voluit partim in lege naturae inscripta mentibus, partim in lege scriptura in duabus tabulis' (*De substantia*, 2.5).

[68] 'Hinc horrores conscientiae, qui electis quaedam sunt ad fidem praeparatio' (*De substantia*, 2.7).

[69] 'Spiritus Sanctus in iis accendit desiderium reconciliandi se Deo' (*De substantia*, 2.7).

[70] '...velint nolint coguntur sentire quam meriti sunt Dei iram' (*De substantia*, 2.7).

[71] '...sub certa damnatione sint, donec transeant ad foedus novum' (*De substantia*, 2.7).

[72] *De substantia*, 2.9.

[73] 'Propriam quidem est legis munus conscientias vocare ad Dei iudicium' (*De substantia*, 2.12).

[74] '...homines natura non credere in Christum' (*De substantia*, 2.11).

administration of the covenant of grace'.[75] By its own nature the law shows that it is not the gospel, for it is powerless to deliver men from sin and 'neither do we have it in ourselves to obey God. Therefore, the Gospel offers us Christ'.[76]

The gospel offer is the second part of the preaching of the Word. Though not all receive him, Christ is to be offered to all, since it is through the preaching of the gospel that God creates faith in the elect.[77] Indeed, because he is the only way of salvation for sinners, 'the Son of God is to be offered through the Gospel as the sun of righteousness to all the world'.[78] Through the gospel the Holy Spirit efficaciously creates faith, 'by which we receive Christ offered with the eternal righteousness which he imputes to us'.[79] As one receives Christ and his imputed righteousness, one also receives the 'Spirit of sanctification whom it is impossible to separate from Christ, who renews us to repentance which consists of the mortification of the old and the vivification of the new man'.[80] As Christ is not divided, neither can the two benefits be divided, though they may be distinguished for pedagogical purposes.[81] The preacher must preach not only justification, but also sanctification: 'a Gospel sermon consists of two parts: embracing the gracious remission of sins by faith and repentance'.[82]

Olevian interpreted the 'spirit-flesh' dichotomy of Romans 7 to mean that the 'flesh' (*caro*) is that part of the soul which remains 'unregenerate' (*non regenita*) in which resides 'unbelief'

---

[75] 'Hoc administrandi foederis gratuiti exordium est' (*De substantia*, 2.11).

[76] '...nec vires a nobis ipsis habere possimus ad obediendum Deo: ita Evangelium offert Christum' (*De substantia*, 2.13).

[77] *De substantia*, 2.14–5.

[78] 'Sic Filius Dei per Evangelium ut sol iustitiae offertur toti mundo' (*De substantia*, 2.15).

[79] 'Per evangelium enim in nobis efficax est Spiritus Sanctus, qui in Christo nos inserit creando in nobis fidem, qua Christum oblatum recipimus cum iustitia aeterna, quam nobis imputat' (*De substantia*, 2.16).

[80] '...cum Spiritu sanctificationis, qui nunquam a Christo separari potest, quo nos renovat ad resipiscentiam, quae constat mortificatione veteris & vivificatione novi hominis' (*De substantia*, 2.16).

[81] 'Et ut Christus non dividitur, ita nec haec duo sunt divellenda, licet, ut demonstratum est, sint distincta' (*De substantia*, 2.17).

[82] 'Ideo etiam Evangelii concio duabus partibus constat: fide gratuitam remissionem amplectente & resipiscentia' (*De substantia*, 2.17).

(*diffidentia*) and in which 'there is an awareness of sin'.[83] Sanctification therefore – in this case confidence in the gospel – is advanced through preaching. Through it the Spirit not only works faith, but also certainty which is to some degree of the essence of faith and the antidote for doubts and fears. As one hears the gospel promises, the Holy Spirit illumines the believer's heart, 'that part of the soul illuminated by faith and regenerated' and confirms to him that God has not withdrawn from him.[84] Olevian called this 'persuasion'.[85] The Spirit reminds one of God's eternal oaths ('*de iurata aeterna*') and of his gracious mercy in Christ, that he is never angry with us.[86] Through the preaching of the Word the part of the soul illuminated by faith is freed from the sense of any guilt.[87]

In contrast to the 'anti-Christ rabble', those 'dreamers' who deny the certainty of faith, Olevian proposed gospel preaching as the means by which one may not only have assurance but also fellowship (κοινωνία) with the triune God.[88] One's faith may be certain because it is impossible to rend what God has joined together. In this case the Spirit has effected a 'spiritual union' (*spirituali coniugio*) between Christ and the elect which is indestructible. Hence faith is not 'uncertain and mere expectation' (*incerta et nuda expectatio*) but grounded in the divine Word.[89]

The double benefit also directed Olevian's doctrine of faith. He distinguished faith from repentance (*resipiscentia*) and assigned the latter to sanctification and the former to justification. He called repentance 'the second part of the Gospel' because it is 'born of faith'.[90] Repentance is the 'change of mind' (*mentis mutatio*) proceeding from the Holy Spirit which results in transformation of the sinner from 'natural depravity' to a serious

---

[83] *De substantia*, 2.19. 'In parte non regenita est conscientia peccati' (*De substantia*, 2.20).

[84] 'Pars fide illuminata & regenita' (*De substantia*, 2.20).

[85] *De substantia*, 2.19.

[86] *De substantia*, 2.19.

[87] *De substantia*, 2.20.

[88] 'Antichristi rabulae...somniantes' (*De substantia*, 2.21).

[89] *De substantia*, 2.22. He appealed to Hebrews 11 in defence of his claim that assurance is of the essence of faith.

[90] 'Resipiscentia, quam alteram partem Evangelii...sic ex fide nascitur' (*De substantia*, 2.24).

and filial fear of God arising from a 'sense of just divine judgement and partly from the experience of sworn eternal mercy in Christ'.[91] Repentance is not only a mental transformation, rather it is a synonym for the whole complex of events which make up the progressive sanctification of the Christian.[92] Because repentance is sanctification, it cannot be a condition of the 'remission of sins' (*remissio peccatorum*) or justification, but repentance is to be preached according to the 'purpose of God' (*scopus Dei*) which is that God's goodness should shine through us.[93]

Hence repentance is a parallel benefit along with assurance, flowing from the preaching of the gospel. Repentance, as all other aspects of sanctification, is a 'gift of God' (*donum Dei*) flowing primarily from Christ though, 'as they say in the schools', it is received instrumentally through faith.[94] Thus through the justice of God the Father preached to sinners ('that one is unable to sustain the rigours of the law'), one is made aware of his need.[95] The faith which apprehends Christ is created through the preaching of the gospel. In this testimony God the Spirit is at work convicting sinners, drawing and uniting them to Christ for justification only by the imputed righteousness of Christ (*sola imputata obedientia Christi*) and working sanctification in them.[96]

Signs, Seals and Sanctity

The promises of the gospel are for Christian parents and their children who are holy because of the covenant of grace and heirs of the promises.[97] The substance of the covenant of grace is not only offered to them but it is confirmed to them through the use

---

[91] '...profecta a Spiritu Sancto a naturali pravitate ad serium & filialem timorem Dei, quae oritur partim ex agnitione & sensu iusti iudicii divini adversus peccata, eiusque sanctitatis, partim ex gustu iuratae aeternae misericordiae in Christo' (*De substantia*, 2.24).

[92] *De substantia*, 2.25.

[93] *De substantia*, 2.25.

[94] '...instrumentaliter accipienda, ut loquuntur in scholis, quia fides Christum amplectitur' (*De substantia*, 2.24).

[95] '...rigorem Legis non sustineat' (*De substantia*, 2.16).

[96] *De substantia*, 2.16.

[97] *De substantia*, 2.48.

of 'appendices' to the preached word. These 'seals' (sigilla) are a measure of divine condescension, annexed to the testimony of the Word, because 'our infirmities require it'.[98] The promises are offered to covenant children first in the preaching of the gospel, and are sealed or confirmed visibly in baptism.[99] One of the marks of the elect is that they respond in faith to Christ offered and make use of the testimonies of the covenant, while the reprobate 'contumaciously reject' him.[100]

Though the sacraments are called σφραγίδες or appendices to the promises, they are not on that account to be belittled. Quite the opposite.

> The testimony of the covenant, which sounded in our ears through the preaching of the Gospel, leads us to the death of Christ...so also do the visible seals of the testimony lead us as if by hand to that same death of the Son.[101]

These appendices are testimonies of the divine goodness toward his people. They are public, visible, palpable examples of his love for his people.[102]

If they are not to be neglected, neither are the sacraments to be considered a condition of election. 'It is not right to bind men to the sacraments as a condition of election for [in such a case] they leave the sacraments more uncertain than when they came.' After all both the elect and the reprobate share the sacraments.[103] Rather the purpose of the sacraments is to call one to Christ and seal to him the covenant promises.

According to the twofold benefit (duplex beneficium), however, the gospel offer was only the first degree of the administration of the covenant of grace. The second is the

---

[98] '...infirmitas nostra id requirat' (*De substantia*, 2.3). See also ibid., 2.107.

[99] *De substantia*, 2.48.

[100] '...contumaciter respuunt' (*De substantia*, 2.1). See also ibid., 2.23 and 2.109.

[101] 'Sicut autem testimonium foederis per praedicationem Evangelii auribus insonat, ad mortem Christi nos...ita etiam testimonii illius visibilia sigilla ad eandem mortem Filii velut prehensa manu nos ducunt' (*De substantia*, 2.50).

[102] '...sed ipsis veluti oculis conspici, palpari, gustari' (*De substantia*, 2.57).

[103] 'Nec vero a Sacramentis ad conditionem electionis fas est homines religare. Sic enim a Sacramentis incertiores abirent quam venissent' (*De substantia*, 2.61).

response to the preached and sacramental gospel. He called the Word and sacraments the 'obligation of the conscience' (*obligatio conscientiae*) which assents to the covenant stipulations. The third is the obligation 'on God's part' (*ex parte Dei*) toward our consciences, through his sworn covenant, that he will never change his mind about people.[104]

Because the sign and the thing signified are joined so closely in the sacraments, the sign can stand in place of the thing signified. Therefore, baptism can be said to be the 'effusion of blood' even though it has reference to Christ's death for sinners.[105] So also in the administration of the sacred eucharist it is as the minister says 'the body of the Lord given for us' that the supper thus becomes 'food for our souls'.[106]

Further this mystic, organic relationship between the sign and its substance meant for Olevian that the signs themselves entail covenant '*stipulationes*', i.e. assent or faith in the grace offered and a solemn assumption of one's obligation toward the covenant sworn by participation in the supper.[107] This oath-swearing, covenant-making aspect of Olevian's theology of sacraments is most significant. He considered that God had sworn an eternal oath of redemption which he had fulfilled in Christ. He viewed baptism and the eucharist as the instruments and the 'stipulation' (*stipulatio*) by which one formally takes up or renews his participation in that same covenant of grace which he described as visibly contracting the covenant.[108] Since the seals are joined to the gospel by divine command, they are therefore not mere human inventions. By rejecting them, one is rejecting the covenant itself.[109] Such a covenant breaker has not 'concluded the negotiation of the covenant or the promise and consequently of the thing promised'.[110] So profound was his commitment to the

---

[104] *De substantia*, 2.63.

[105] '...effusionis sanguinis mentio diserte in verbis promissionis exprimitur' (*De substantia*, 2.50).

[106] 'In sacra Eucharistia diserte annunciatur atque prommititur corpus Domini pro nobis esse traditum, atque ita esse cibum nostrarum animarum' (*De substantia*, 2.50).

[107] *De substantia*, 2.59. See also ibid., 2.60.

[108] *De substantia*, 2.53. '...visibili contractu' (ibid., 2.54). Calvin also described the Christian baptismal vow as a 'stipulatio in foedere gratiae'. See *Institutio*, 4.13.6; *OS* 5.243.16–32.

[109] *De substantia*, 2.49.

[110] 'At privatio signi adiuncti sine contemtu non infert seu concludit

use of what he believed to be divinely established means of grace for administering the covenant in the visible assembly that despite his strong predestinarian soteriology he even described the sacraments as a 'voluntary contract' (*voluntarium contractum*) between God and his people along the lines of a marriage.[111] Taken out of context, such language could be easily misunderstood. Yet for Olevian, the substance of the covenant cannot be separated from its 'form of administration'.[112]

'Voluntary contract' and 'stipulation' are of course terms which suggest mutuality in Olevian's theology. If those scholars are correct who see mutuality as the essence of federal theology, then certainly it is correct to describe Olevian as a 'federal theologian'. When he had the means of grace or the administration of the covenant in view he used plainly mutual language. He even described the process of covenant making as 'contracting the covenant' and the agreement itself as the 'solemn contract of the covenant'.[113] Nevertheless it is clear that Olevian was a Protestant theologian and it is unsatisfactory to suggest that the moment Olevian used such language he somehow become another sort of theologian. Rather, this contractual language is but another example of the effect of the *duplex beneficium* notion upon his theology.

In fact, Olevian is a good example of the weakness of the distinction between federal and covenantal theology.[114] Under the doctrine of justification, Olevian was a divine monergist, i.e. a predestinarian Protestant. He was no less Protestant and predestinarian in his doctrine of the Christian life, yet he spoke about conditions in the covenant. Either he was contradicting himself or he was speaking about conditions in some other way, which did not affect his doctrine of justification. The latter is clearly the better interpretation of Olevian's theology.

---

negotiationem foederis sive promissionis, & per consequens rei promissae' (*De substantia*, 2.49).

[111] *De substantia*, 2.52. '...in solemni contractu ceu sponsalibus' (ibid., 2.54).

[112] 'Forma itaque administrandi foedus gratiae' (*De substantia*, 2.53).

[113] '...contrahendi foedus...solemni foederis contractu' (*De substantia*, 2.54). See also ibid., 2.56, 7.

[114] In fact he made no distinction between the terms 'testamentum', 'foedus', or 'pactum'. The expression 'novum testamentum seu foedus' is not unusual in Olevian (e.g. *De substantia*, 2.79).

The reason he adopted conditional language in his doctrine of sanctification was that under the double benefit (*duplex beneficium*) scheme, he had to use two different kinds of language to describe the two aspects of Christ's benefit. The forensic language was inherent to his forensic doctrine of justification and the experiential language was inherent to his doctrine of sanctification. When he spoke of 'contracting the covenant' he was not writing of his doctrine of justification, but explaining the means by which the covenant is administered among those whom Christ has justified. He was speaking from the point of view of those in the subjective experience of entering into formal relations with the covenant making God and his people. He was also speaking about and to visible assemblies consisting of believers and unbelievers.

Thus he argued that just as the Israelites offered their circumcised children to Moloch and as externally righteous Pharisees rejected Christ, so also there are 'hypocrites or reprobates' (*hypocritae seu reprobi*) who participate in the 'external worship' (*externum cultum*) without actually entering into fellowship with Christ, i.e. there are those in the visible church who have not received the substance of the covenant (*substantia foederis*).[115] For Olevian, it was not that Christ's presence in worship or the means of grace was strictly contingent upon the worshipper or communicant being regenerate, but that in the administration of the covenant, though he offers himself freely in the gospel, Christ will not communicate himself to the reprobate.[116] Christ is present and offered, but one only receives the benefits of the covenant when one embraces its substance by faith alone. The second explanation for Olevian's dipleuric language lies in his complete trust in the divinely appointed instruments of the covenant. Because he believed that the signs and seals testify clearly to the gospel, he was willing to make use of the full range of language regarding covenant keeping and breaking.

Though there is a certain jeopardy attached to abuse or neglect of the sacraments, they are fundamentally an 'offer of grace' (*oblatio gratiae*) annexed to the promises.[117] That is to say

---

[115] *De substantia*, 2.53. See also ibid., 2.103.
[116] *De substantia*, 2.56.
[117] *De substantia*, 2.52.

that they are gospel, not law. They are not primarily intended by God to be a means of condemnation, but rather they are intended as a means of confirming the grace of justification. He did after all consider them to be testimonies to and means of God's grace and not vehicles by which one is able to commend oneself to God.

As he detailed the administration of the covenant he further distinguished between baptism and the eucharist according to the function they perform although not according to the grace they mediate. His doctrine of baptism was a subset of his broader federal theology of the sacraments and thus his exposition of baptism itself was quite brief.[118] He distinguished three aspects of baptism. The first was its testimony to the *duplex beneficium*. Baptism is part of the Father's offer of grace in Christ to corrupt, damnable sinners. Annexed to the word preached, baptism testifies to Christ's 'merit...and efficacy' (*meritum...et efficacia*). Like the preached word, jeopardy (*mors aeterna*) is also attached to baptism for those who repudiate the faith by infidelity.[119] Second, baptism was commanded by God as a testimony of the 'assent of faith in the offered grace'.[120] Third, 'it seals to those thus affected the κοινωνία with Christ'.[121] In baptism 'we bear the divine testimony of our adoption or union with Christ the Son of God...'.[122]

Baptism is a visible summary of the Christian faith since it has reference to the 'whole substance of the covenant' to which God himself refers 'in two heads...the remission of sins and the renovation to life eternal'.[123] For this reason we are said to be baptised 'in Christ and in his death and resurrection' (*in*

---

[118] Olevian did not distinguish between Christian baptism and John's baptism, perhaps for the same reasons as Zwingli, i.e. polemic against the Anabaptists. On Zwingli see W. P. Stephens, *The Theology of Huldrych Zwingli* (Oxford, 1986), 198.

[119] *De substantia*, 2.64.

[120] 'Mandat ut in testimonium assensus fidei in oblatam gratiam' (*De substantia*, 2.64).

[121] 'Obsignat iis, qui ita affecti sunt, κοινωνίαν cum Christi' (*De substantia*, 2.64).

[122] 'Ita gestamus testimonium divinum adoptionis nostrae seu unionis cum Christo Dei Filio...' (*De substantia*, 2.65).

[123] 'Cum enim tota substantia foederis gratuiti ad duo capita à Deo ipso referatur...remissionem peccatorum, & renovationem ad vitam aeternam' (*De substantia*, 2.65).

Christum eiusque mortem et resurrectionem).[124] It is a constant gospel call to us that 'God requires of us nothing but faith and repentance all the days of our life' and even these come 'from the gift of Christ' (*ex donatione Christi*).[125] It testifies to and seals the 'engrafting' (*insitio*) in the covenant of grace, into its mediator (Christ) and into his imputed righteousness and the 'beginning of regeneration' as well.[126] Because it is the 'sacrament of adoption and regeneration' which occur 'once for all' (*semel tantum*), it is unrepeatable.[127]

Olevian used interchangeably two expressions to refer to the second sacrament: 'Lord's Supper (*coena Domini*) and 'holy eucharist' (*sacra eucharistia*) and distinguished it from baptism in several ways. First, it differs according to the outward form of the testimony. The Lord gave us two different signs to perform two different functions as an accommodation to 'our rudeness'.[128] They also differ as to the 'internal degrees of fellowship' (*internis gradibus* κοινωνίας). Put sharply, baptism is about our union with Christ as 'bloody victim' (*cruenta victima*). The supper is a 'joyful celebration' (*laeta celebratio*) and strengthening of our Spiritual union with the resurrected Christ who 'intercedes for us' (*pro nobis intercedente*).[129] Baptism was said to be distinct from the holy supper, in that the latter is a means of covenant renewal whereas the 'covenant and its eternal substance are begun in baptism'.[130]

Second, baptism also differs from the supper in mode of administration. Where baptism like circumcision was intended to be observed once, the supper was meant to be celebrated repeatedly and frequently since it was intended for those who

---

[124] *De substantia*, 2.65.

[125] 'Requirat igitur Deus non ex nobis, sed a nobis fidem, & resipiscentiam omnibus diebus vitae nostrae' (*De substantia*, 2.66).

[126] 'Baptismus enim insitionem nostram in foedus gratuitum, eiusque Mediatorem Christum testificatur & obsignat, atque ita imputatam iustitiam & regenerationis initium' (*De substantia*, 2.68).

[127] 'Baptismus repetisas [sic] non est. Qua, cum Baptismus sit Sacramentum adoptionis & regenerationis, ut semel tantum adoptamur atque renascimur, non saepius: ita testimonium non iteratur' (*De substantia*, 2.67).

[128] '...nostrae ruditati' (*De substantia*, 2.83).

[129] *De substantia*, 2.83. See also ibid., 2.85.

[130] '...foedus in Baptismo initum eiusque substantia aeterna sunt' (*De substantia*, 2.65).

have been already renewed.[131] For Olevian, there was another difference between baptism and the supper. He considered that baptism, as the sign of the beginning of the Christian life, as the beginning of the covenant, ought to be available to the children of all Christian parents. The eucharist, however, ought not to be celebrated by any but those who are 'in covenant' (*in foedere*), that is, those who have consciously entered into covenant relations with God. He was not saying that Christian children are not in the covenant, but that as infants they are not eligible for the feast of covenant renewal. Therefore, in Olevian's doctrine of the covenant, the circle of those eligible for baptism was wider than the circle of those eligible for the eucharist.[132] He made this distinction because baptism testifies to the divine promises, but the eucharist to 'the action of grace' and infants cannot testify to the work of grace within them.[133] According to Olevian, this is precisely why the supper is called 'the eucharist' because it is an act of thanksgiving by Christians.[134] Baptism is observed in expectation of the covenant blessings of justification and regeneration but the eucharist is to be celebrated in confirmation and application of the same by the Holy Spirit.[135]

Like baptism, the supper also testifies to the 'special benefit of redemption' and there is both the 'testimony' (*testimonium*) and the 'thing testified' (*res testata*).[136] In accordance with his reformed and Calvinist Christology (two distinct natures in one hypostatic union) he argued strenuously against either confusing or separating the *res* and the *testimonium*.[137] Those who are truly united to the ascended Christ by the Holy Spirit receive the 'substance of the holy eucharist' (*substantia sacrae eucharisticae*) or the *res testata*, who is Christ himself.[138] The very words of

---

[131] *De substantia*, 2.94. See also ibid., 2.67–8.

[132] *De substantia*, 2.68.

[133] '...testificandi gratiarum actioni' (*De substantia*, 2.68).

[134] '...unde & nomen Eucharistiae habet' (*De substantia*, 2.68).

[135] *De substantia*, 2.91 and 2.93. See also, ibid., 2.68, 2.83, 2.87–8.

[136] '...pro speciali redemtionis beneficio' (*De substantia*, 2.69). See also ibid., 2.70 and 2.86.

[137] *De substantia*, 2.75.

[138] See *De substantia*, 2.76 and 2.79. To confuse the *res* with the *testimonium* makes the supper into the *tabulae Antichristi* (ibid., 2.76) or the 'Papistarum mendaci[um]' of transubstantiation (ibid., 2.77). See also ibid., 2.89–90.

institution testify to our 'union with Christ himself, God and Man offered for us'.[139]

Thus he said the Lord's Supper (*coena Domini*) was designed to teach both justification and sanctification; justification in that Christ died 'for all and only the elect' (*pro omnibus et solis electis*) and sanctification in that in the supper Christ begins to work in his elect the renewal to the image of Christ (*renovatio ad imaginem Christi*).[140] In the words of the institution, Christ made two promises, 'the once for all bloody offering of his body on the cross and its once for all application through the Holy Spirit and the daily strengthening of faith'.[141]

In order that the eucharistic rite might best demonstrate what Christ accomplished in ratifying the covenant for the elect, Olevian prescribed six parts to the celebration, four of which concerned the administration of the bread: the breaking of the bread (*fractio panis*), the distribution (*traditio*), the reception (*acceptio*) and the 'consumption'. He mentioned only two parts to the administration of the cup, the 'distribution and the drinking of the cup'. According to Olevian, such a rite represents both the promised suffering of Christ and our perpetual union with him.[142] He admitted a notion of consecration of the elements since they are separated for sacred use, but he insisted that even after consecration, the elements remain what they were before consecration.[143] In these prescriptions of course, he was attempting to establish a dignified Reformed eucharistic rite but one which did not lapse into what he regarded as the Roman error of transubstantiation.

Olevian's exposition of the theology, use and benefit of the supper was much more detailed and lengthy than his teaching on baptism. This relative imbalance of course reflected the Christological and ecclesiastical controversies surrounding the theology and celebration of the eucharist in the sixteenth century.

---

[139] '...de coniunctione nostri cum ipso Christo, Deo & homine pro nobis oblato' (*De substantia*, 2.80).

[140] *De substantia*, 2.73.

[141] '...unicam corporis sui cruentam oblationem in cruce & unicam eius applicationem per Spiritum Sanctum & fidem indies augescentem' (*De substantia*, 2.71).

[142] '...fractio panis, traditio, acceptio, comestio, itidem & poculi distributio & bibitio' (*De substantia*, 2.91).

[143] *De substantia*, 2.102.

His more extensive treatment of the supper also reflected, however, his view that the supper is a more dominant experience of the Christian life. Where baptism is the sign and seal of initiation, the eucharist is the sign of nourishment. One can begin formal covenant relations once, but one should continue growing in grace throughout the Christian life.

Olevian believed that the regular use of the means of grace will produce increased sanctification among the elect. He so expected the substance (*res*) to be connected to the sign (*signum*) that he believed that one could perceive the inward work of the Spirit. 'For out of the [Spirit's] work you shall know that you are a partaker of the Holy Spirit'.[144] One knows the Spirit to be at work because one sees the results.[145] Among these effects in the Christian life is one's 'hatred of sin or war against' sin. [146] In Olevian's version of the practical syllogism (*syllogismus practicus*), the Christian's struggle with sin serves as a 'certain proof' that one has the Holy Spirit and that he is engrafted into Christ.[147]

Olevian taught that the right use of the means of grace and sound doctrine ought to have good results for the Christian life. His three moral deductions (*fructus sive usus*) from the doctrine of providence were typical of his application of doctrine to life. The first use of the doctrine of providence is that God ought to receive all glory. For Olevian, the act of glorifying God was not an abstraction but rather the Christian duty of the faithful. He taught that the God who created us is the same God who also preserves us by exercising no less power in the 'preservation and governance of all things' than in the first creation.[148] God the Creator also continues to 'gather daily the Church by the sound of the Gospel' and by the 'internal voice of the Son'.[149] Therefore this

---

[144] 'Ex operatione autem cognosces, te Spiritus sancti esse participem' (*Expositio*, 175).

[145] '...ita & Spiritus sanctus ex operatione cognoscitur' (*Expositio*, 175).

[146] '...odium peccati seu pugna adversus peccatum' (*Expositio*, 176).

[147] '...certum est documentum, nos Spiritum sanctum habere & Christo esse insitos' (*Expositio*, 176).

[148] '...non minorem potentiam in conservatione & gubernatione rerum omnium Deum exerere, quam in prima creatione' (*Expositio*, 59).

[149] '...quotidie colligere Ecclesiam voce Evangelii & interna voce filii' (*Expositio*, 59).

'doctrine of the providence of God ought to animate us to true thankfulness of mind'.[150]

Since it is therefore impossible that the Herods or Pilates of this world should afflict Christ's members any more than God's hand and counsel have decreed and since holding to the true gospel entails sufferings and persecutions, the doctrine of providence ought also to produce patience among the elect.[151] The cultivation of patience allows one to realise that one's enemies are but 'instruments' (*instrumenta*) in God's hands, who is at work (*operatur*) for his own purposes.[152] Trials in the Christian life should be regarded as 'benefits, and indeed benefits of God necessary to salvation'.[153] Armed with such knowledge, the faithful concentrate upon the fatherly wisdom of God's hand, not upon the creatures through whom they are afflicted.[154] The third fruit of this teaching is that one has 'that unbelievable security' (*incredibilis illa securitas*) that having been received by God as his confederate, one is under the care of God and his angels so that one is 'free from injury and all danger from creatures' except as they serve God's will toward our good.[155]

As with the rest of his theology, Olevian's doctrine of the Christian life was trinitarian and federal in character. As such, it was organised by the double benefit: justification and sanctification. The latter is subjective application by the Holy Spirit of the former. His doctrine of the Christian life was trinitarian in that it was driven by his trinitarian doctrine of God. Only the triune God could accomplish our sanctification through redemption by the Son, God's fatherly providence, and the internal work of God the Spirit.

Sanctification, to the extent it can be accomplished in this life, is wrought through the regular and right use of the divinely ordained means of grace, the preaching of the Word and the administration of the sacraments. He rejected what he regarded

---

[150] '...ad veram animi gratitudinem animare nos debet doctrina haec de Dei providentia' (*Expositio*, 60).

[151] '...omni vita, quae miseriarum est plena, tum in persequutionibus perferendis ob veritatem Evangelii' (*Expositio*, 60). See also ibid., 62.

[152] *Expositio*, 61.

[153] '...beneficia & quidem Dei beneficia, quaeque certo saluti sint, habeat oportet' (*Expositio*, 61).

[154] *Expositio*, 61.

[155] '...ab omni creaturarum periculo & noxa liberum esse' (*Expositio*, 62).

as the fanaticism of the Anabaptists who separated Word and Spirit. He also rejected what he attacked as Rome's confusion of the visible and audible witnesses of the covenant (*testimonia foederis*) for the substance about which they testified (*res testata*).

His doctrine of sanctification was federal in both the formal and substantial senses of the word. It was formally federal in that it was organised by his doctrine of the covenant. Christ the federal head obeyed the divine law and secured our justification. His death ratified the covenant.

Olevian's doctrine of sanctification was federal in the substantial sense of the word as well. He taught that there are stipulations to receiving the benefit of the covenant. The primary stipulation was said to be faith, itself a divine gift, which is the instrument by which one apprehends the benefit of the covenant, union with Christ. Through that union Christ communicates himself to his elect, who have received the substance of the covenant, and works moral renewal in and through them.

The right and regular use of the means of grace (*media gratiae*) were also said to be stipulations of the covenant. Considered experientially, Olevian said the covenant can be said to have been contracted at baptism, received in faith and augmented in the eucharist. Certainly there was no merit attached to the co-operation by sinners with sanctifying grace since his law-gospel dichotomy in justification and his doctrines of the *pactum salutis* and predestination formed the background to his doctrine of sanctification.

BIBLIOGRAPHY

I. Primary Sources

Adam, M. *Vitae Germanorum Theologorum*. Heidelberg, 1620.

Althusius, J. *Politica Methodice Digesta*. Herborn, 1603.

—. *The Politics of Johannes Althusius*. Trans. and ed. F. S. Carney. London, 1964.

Alting, H. *Historia de ecclesiis Palatiniis*. Amsterdam, 1644. Repr. *Monumenta pietatis et literaria virorum in republica et literaria illustrium, selecta quorum pars prior*. Ed. L. C. Mieg. Frankfurt, 1701.

Aquinas, T. *Summa Theologiae*. Blackfriars edition. Trans. T. Gilby. 61 vols. London, 1964–81.

—. *Opera Omnia*, Leonine edition. Vol 1–. Rome, 1882–.

—. *The Sermon Conferences of St. Thomas Aquinas on the Apostles' Creed*. Trans. and ed. N. Ayo. Notre Dame, IN, 1988.

Aristotle, *Aristotelis Opera*. 6 vols. Ed. I. Bekker. Second edition. Berlin, 1960.

—. *The Metaphysics*. Trans. H. Tredennick. Loeb Classical Library. London, 1933.

—. *De Partibus Animalium*. Loeb Classical Library. London, 1956.

Arminius, J. *Iacobi Arminii Opera Theologica*. London, 1629.

—. *The Works of James Arminius*. Trans. J. Nichols and W. Nichols. 3 vols. London, 1825–75. Repr. Grand Rapids, 1996.

Die Bekenntnisschriften der evangelisch-lutherischen Kirche. 2 vols. Göttingen, 1956–9.

Bellarmine, R. *Explicatio Symboli Apostolici*. Cologne, 1617.

Bente, F., ed. *Concordia triglotta libri symbolici ecclesiae Lutheranae*. St Louis, 1921.

Beza, T. *Correspondance de Théodore de Bèze*. Ed. H. Aubert. 16 vols. Geneva, 1960–93.

—. *A Briefe and Piththie* [sic] *Summe of the Christian Faith*. Trans. R. Filles. London, 1563.

—. *Confession de La Foy Chrestienne*. Geneva, 1561.

—. *Confessio Christianae fidei*. London, 1575.

— and A. de La Faye, eds. *Propositions and Principles of Divinitie propounded and disputed in the universitie of Geneva, by certaine students of Divinitie there, vnder M. Theod. Beza, and M. Anthonie Faius, professors of Divinitie*. Trans. J. Penry. Edinburgh, 1591.

— and A. de La Faye, eds. *Theses theologicae in schola Genevensi ab aliquot sacrarum literarum studiosis....* Geneva, 1586.

—, trans. *Iesu Christi D. n. novum testamentum sive novum foedus*. Geneva, 1565. Repr. 1582.

—. *The Christian Faith*. Trans. J. Clark. East Sussex, 1992.

—. *De iure magistratuum in subditos et officio subditorum erga magistratus*. Geneva, 1576.

——. *Concerning the Right of Rulers over their Subjects and the Duty of Subjects toward their Rulers*. Trans. and ed. H.-L. Gonin. Capetown, 1956.

——. *Tractatus pius et moderatus de vera excommunicatione, & christiano presbyterio*. Geneva, 1590.

Biblia Sacra iuxta Vulgatam versionem. Stuttgart, 1969.

Biel, G. *Quaestiones de justificatione*. Ed. C. Feckes. Münster, 1929.

Bodleian Library, *The first printed catalogue of the Bodleian Library 1605, a facsimile: Catalogus librorum bibliothecae publicae quam...Thomas Bodleius eques auratus in academia Oxoniensi nuper instituit*. Oxford, 1986.

Boquin, P. *Assertio veteris a c veri christianismi, adversus novum e t fictum iesuitismum seu societatem Iesu*. London, 1576.

——. *A Defence of the Olde, and True Profession of Christianitie, Against the New, and Counterfaite Secte of Jesuites*. Trans. T. G. London, 1581.

——. *Examen libri q u e m d. Tilemannus Heshusius nuper scripsit, a t q u e inscripsit de praesentia corporis Christi in coena Domini*. Basle, 1561.

Brenz, J. *Epitome colloquii inter illustrissimorum* [sic] *principum D. Frederici Palatini electoris, & D. Christophori Ducis Wirtenbergis theologis, de maiestate hominis Christi, deque vera eius in Eucharistia praesentia, Maulbrunniae instituti*. Württemberg, 1564.

——. *De personali unione duarum naturarum in Christo, de reali idiomatum communicatione, de ascensu Christi in coelum, & seßione eius ad dexteram Dei patris*. Tübingen, 1571.

——. *In epistolam...ad Romanos...commentariorum libri tres*. Frankfurt, 1564.

Bretschneider, C. G., ed. *Corpus Reformatorum*. 101 vols. Halle, 1834–1959.

Brutus, S. J. [pseud.], *Vindiciae Contra Tyrannos: or concerning the legitimate power of a prince over the people, and of the people over a prince*. Ed. and trans. G. Garnett. Cambridge, 1994.

Bucanus, W. *Institutiones Theologicae, seu Locorum Communionium Christianae Religionis, ex Dei Verbo, et Praestantissimorum theologicorum...expositorum, analysis*. Rev. edition. Geneva, 1604.

——. *Institutions of the Christian Religion*. Trans. R. Hill. London, 1606.

Bugenhagen, J. *In epistolam Pauli ad Romanos interpretatio....* Haganoae, 1527.

Bullinger, H. *Decades*. Trans. Parker Society. 5 vols. Cambridge, 1849.

——. *De testamento seu foedere Dei unico & aeterno expositio*. Zürich, 1534.

——. *Zwingli and Bullinger*. Ed. G. W. Bromiley. Philadelphia, 1953.

——. *A Brief Exposition of the One and Eternal Testament or Covenant of God*. Trans. C. S. McCoy and J. W. Baker. Philadelphia, 1991.

——. *Antiquissima fides et vera religio christianam fidem*. Zürich, 1544.

——. *The Old Fayth*. Trans. M. Coverdale. London (?), 1547.

——. *In sanctissimam Pauli ad Romanos epistolam Heinrychi Bullingeri commentarius*. Zürich, 1533.

Calvin, J. *The Bondage and Liberation of the Will. A Defence of the Orthodox Doctrine of Human Choice Against Pighius*. Trans. G. I. Davies, ed. A. N. S. Lane. Grand Rapids and Carlisle, 1996.

——. *Calvin's Commentary on Seneca's De Clementia*. Ed. and trans. F. L. Battles. Leiden, 1969.

——. *Commentary on Romans*. Trans. R. McKenzie. Ed. D. W. Torrance and T. F. Torrance. Grand Rapids, 1960.

——. *Dilucida explicatio sanae doctrinae de vera participatione carnis et sanguinis Christi in sacra coena ad discutiendas Heshuii nebulas. Corpus Reformatorum.* Ed. C. G. Bretschneider. 101 vols. Halle, 1834–1959.

——. *Institutes of the Christian Religion.* Trans. F. L. Battles. Ed. J. T. McNeill. Philadelphia, 1960.

——. *Joannis Calvini Opera Selecta.* Ed. P. Barth and W. Niesel. Third edition. 5 vols. Munich, 1963–74.

——. *Secunda defensio piae et orthodoxae de sacramentis fidei.* Geneva, 1556.

——. *Treatises Against the Anabaptists and Against the Libertines.* Trans. and ed. B. W. Farley. Grand Rapids, 1980.

Canisius, P. *Summa doctrinae Christianae.* Antwerp, 1574.

——. *A Summe of Christian Doctrine.* Trans. H. Garnet. London, 1596.

Canones et decreta...concilii Tridentini. Leipzig, 1860.

Catechesis sive brevis institutio christianae doctrinae quo modo illa in ecclesiis et scholis Palatinatus tum electoralis tum ducalis traditur. Trans. Pithopeus. Heidelberg, 1563. *Collectio confessionum in Ecclesiis reformatis publicatorum.* Ed. H. A. Niemeyer. Leipzig, 1840.

The Catechisme, or manner to teach children and others the Christian fayth: used in all the landes and dominions that are under the mighty Prince Fredericke, the Palsgrave of the Rhene. Trans. W. Turner. London, 1572.

Catechismus ex decreto concilii Tridentini. Leipzig, 1862.

Chemnitz, M. *De duabus naturis in Christo de hypostatica earum unione, de communicatione idiomatum et aliis quaestionibus inde dependentibus etc.* Leipzig, 1580.

Cicero, M. T. *De Finibus Bonorum et Malorum.* Trans. H. A. Rackham. Loeb Classical Library. London, 1961.

Cocceius, J. *Opera theologica.* 8 vols. Amsterdam, 1673.

Daneau, L. *Symboli Apostoli Explicatio.* Second edition. Geneva, 1592.

Ebrard, A. *Reformirtes Kirchenbuch.* Zürich, 1847.

Erasmus, D. *Dilucida et pia explanatio symboli quod Apostolorum dicitur, & decalogi praeceptorum.* Paris, 1533.

——. *Erasmus: Inquisitio de fide.* Ed. C. R. Thompson. New Haven, 1950.

——. *A Playne and Godly Exposition or Declaration of the Commune Crede.* London, c.1533.

Frederick III, *A Christian Confession of the late most noble and mightie Prince, Friderich of that name the third, Count Palatine by Rhein.* London, 1577.

Garnier, J. *A Briefe and Plane Confession of the Christian Faithe, Conteinyng 100 Articles after the Order of the Simbole or Crede of the Apostlelles.* Trans. N. Malbie. London, 1562.

The Heidelberg Catechism in German, Latin and English with an Historical Introduction. New York, 1863.

Der Heidelberger Katechismus in seiner ursprünglichen Gestalt, herausgegeben nebst der Geshichte seines Textes im Jahre 1563. Ed. A. Wolters. Bonn, 1864.

Heppe, H., ed. *Die Dogmatik der evangelisch-reformierten Kirche.* Elberfeld, 1861.

Hessels, J. *Brevis et Catholica Symboli Apostolici Explicatio.* Louvain, 1562.

Hesshusius, T. *Explicatio epistolae Pauli ad Romanos.* Jena, 1571.

Hooker, R. *The Works of Mr. Richard Hooker.* Ed. J. Keble. 6th edition. 3 vols. Oxford, 1874.

Hyperius, A. *In d. Pauli ad Romanos epistolam exegema.* Marburg, 1548.

Kluckhorn, A. *Briefe Fredrich des Frommen.* 2 vols. Brunswick, 1868.

Kolb, R. and T. J. Wengert, *The Book of Concord. The Confessions of the Evangelical Lutheran Church.* Minneapolis, 2000.

La Faye, A. *Disputatio de verbo Dei.* Geneva, 1591.

——. *Disputatio de traditionibus adversus earum defensores pontificios.* Geneva, 1592.

——. *Disputatio de Christo Mediatore.* Geneva, 1597.

——. *De legitima et falsa sanctorum spirituum adoratione.* Geneva, 1601.

——. *Disputatio de bonis operibus.* Geneva, 1601.

——. *Geneva liberata.* Geneva, 1603.

——. *De vera Christi ecclesia.* Geneva, 1606.

——. *De vita et obitu clarissimi viri D. Theodori Bezae* ὑπομνημάτιον. Geneva, 1606.

——. *Emblemata et epigrammata miscellanea selecta ex stromatis peripateticis* Geneva, 1610.

——. *Enchiridion theologicum aphoristica methodo compositum ex disputationibus.* Geneva, 1605.

——. *In librum Salomonis qui inscribitur Ecclesiastes, commentarius Antonii Fayii. Accessit commentarius in Psalmum xlix.* Geneva, 1610.

——. *In d. Pauli Apostoli epistolam ad Romanos commentarius.* Geneva, 1608.

——. *In d. Pauli Apostoli epistolam priorem ad Timotheum. Accessit commentarius in Psalmum 87.* Geneva, 1609.

Lang, A., ed. *Der Heidelberger Katechismus und vier verwandte Katechismen (Leo Jud's und Micron's kleine Katechismen, sowie die zwei vorarbeiten Ursins).* Leipzig, 1907.

Lombard, P. *Sententiae in IV Libris Distinctae.* 3rd edition. Rome, 1971.

Luther, M. *Luthers Werke Kritische Gesamtausgabe.* Ed. J. K. F. Knaake, G. Kawerau et al. Weimar, 1883–.

——. *Luther's Works.* 55 vols. Trans. and ed. J. Pelikan and H. T. Lehmann. Philadelphia and St Louis, 1955–.

——. *Luther: Lectures on Romans.* Trans and ed. W. Pauck. Philadelphia, 1961.

Major, G. *Series et dispositio orationis in epistola Pauli ad Romanos.* Wittenberg, 1556.

Melanchthon, P. *Loci Communes. Corpus Reformatorum.* Ed. C. G. Bretschneider. Vol. 21. Brunswick, 1854.

——. *Loci Communes 1543.* Trans. J. A. O. Preus. St Louis, 1992.

——. *Melanchthon on Christian Doctrine: Loci Communes 1555.* Trans. and ed. C. L. Manschreck. Oxford, 1965.

——. *Common Places.* Trans. and ed. W. Pauck. *Melanchthon and Bucer.* London, 1969.

——. *Commentary on Romans.* Trans. F. Kramer. St Louis, 1992.

Migne, J. P., ed. *Patrologia Latina.* 221 vols. Paris, 1844–66.

——, ed. *Patrologia Graeca.* 161 vols. Paris, 1857–66.

Musculus, W. *In epistolam apostoli Pauli ad Romanos, commentarii.* Basle, 1559.

Nicolas of Cusa, *Opera Omnia*. Ed. E. Hoffmann and R. Klibansky. Vol. 1-? Heidelberg, 1932-.

Niemeyer, H. A., ed. *Collectio Confessionum in Ecclesiis Reformatis Publicatarum*. Leipzig, 1840.

Niesel, W., ed. *Bekentnisschriften und Kirchenordnung der nach Gottes Wort reformierten Kirche*. Munich, 1937.

Olevian, Caspar. *A Firm Foundation*. Trans. L. D. Bierma. Grand Rapids, 1995.

——. *An Exposition of the Symbole of the Apostles or Rather the Articles of Faith*. Trans. J. Fielde. London, 1581.

——. *Brevis admonitio de re eucharistica*. Herborn, 1587.

——. *De inventione dialecticae liber, e praelectionibus Gasp. Oleviani excerptus*. Geneva, 1583.

——. *De substantia foederis gratuiti Inter Deum et electos*. Geneva, 1585.

——. *Der Gnadenbund Gottes*. Herborn, 1590. Repr. Bonn, 1994.

——. *Expositio symboli apostolici, sive articulorum fidei, desumpta ex concionibus catecheticis G. Oleviani*. Frankfurt, 1576 and 1584.

——. *Fundamenta dialecticae breviter consignate e praelectionibus*. Frankfurt, 1581.

——. *Fürschlag, Wie Doctor Luthers Lehr von den Heiligen Sacramenten (so in seinem kleinen Catechismo begrissen) auß Gottes Wort mit den reformirten Kirchen zu vereinigen seye*. np. nd. *Gnadenbund Gottes*. Herborn, 1590.

——. *In Epistolam d. Pauli apostoli ad Galatas notae, ex concionibus G. Oleviani excerptae*. Ed. T. Beza. Geneva, 1578.

——. *In Epistolam d. Pauli apostoli ad Romanos notae, ex concionibus G. Oleviani excerptae*. Ed. T. Beza. Geneva, 1579.

——. *In Epistolam d. Pauli apostolici ad Ephesios notae*. Ed. Johannes Piscator. Herborn, 1588.

——. *In Epistolas d. Pauli apostoli ad Philippenses & Colossenses notae, ex concionibus Gasparis Oleviani excerptae*. Ed. T. Beza. Geneva, 1579.

——. *Institutionis Christianae Religionis Epitome. Ex institutione Johannis Calvini excerpta, authoris methodo et verbis rententis*. Herborn, 1586.

——. *Notae Gasparis Oleviani in Evangelia*. Herborn, 1587.

——. *Predigt Von der ersten hauptursache alles Irrthum in den heiligen Sakramenten*. Heidelberg, 1565.

——. *Vester Grund Christlicher Lehre*. Ed. K. Sudhoff. Frankfurt, 1854.

Pearson, G., ed. *Writings and Translations of Miles Coverdale*. Cambridge, 1844.

Perkins, W. *An Exposition of the Symbole or Creed of the Apostles*. Cambridge, 1595.

——. *The Work of William Perkins*. Appleford, 1970.

Piscator, J. *Animadversiones argumentum in dialecticam P. Rami*. Second edition. London, 1583.

——. *Aphorismi Doctrinae Christianae maximam partem ex Institutione Calvini excerpti sive Loci Communes Theologici, brevibus sententiis expositi*. Herborn, 1594.

——. *Aphorismes of the Christian Religion*. Trans. J. Field. London, 1596. (Facsimile edition. Amsterdam, 1973).

—. *A Learned and Profitable Treatise of Man's Justification. Two Books. Opposed to the Sophismes of Robert Bellarmine, Iesuite.* London, 1599.

Polanus, A. *Partitiones Theologicae iuxta Naturalis Methodi Leges Conformatae duobus libris.* Basel, 1602.

—. *The Substance of the Christian Religion.* Trans. E. W. London, 1595.

—. *Syntagma Theologiae Christianae.* 1609.

—. *Syntagma Logicorum Aristotelico-Ramaeum.* Basil, 1605.

Quick, J. *Synodicon in Gallia Reformata: or the Acts, Decisions, Decrees, and Canons of those Famous National Councils of the Reformed Churches in France.* 2 vols. London, 1692.

Ramus, P. *Commentarium de Religione Christiana.* Frankfurt, 1576.

Reuter, Q., ed. *Catechesis religionis christianae, quae traditur in ecclesiis et scholis Palatinatus.* Heidelberg, 1585.

Rhegius, U. *A Declararation* [sic] *of the Twelve Articles of the Christen Faythe.* London, 1548.

Robinson, H. Trans. and ed. *The Zürich Letters (second series).* Cambridge, 1845.

Rollock, R. *Select Works of Robert Rollock.* 2 vols. Ed. W. M. Gunn. Edinburgh, 1849.

—. *Tractatus de vocatione efficaci.* Edinburgh, 1597.

—. *A Treatise of God's Effectual Calling.* Trans. H. Holland. London, 1604.

Rufinus, *A Commentary on the Apostles' Creed by Rufinus.* Trans. and ed. J. N. D. Kelly. London, 1955.

Schaff, P. *Nicene and Post-Nicene Fathers.* First Series. 13 vols. Grand Rapids, 1983.

Seneca, L. A. *Epistulae Morales.* Trans. R. M. Gummere. 3 vols. Loeb Classical Library. London, 1943.

—. *Moral Essays.* Trans. J. W. Basore. 3 vols. Loeb Classical Library. London, 1943.

Tremellius, I. and F. Junius, trans. and ed. *Testamenti Veteris Biblia Sacra sive libri canonici priscae iudaeorum ecclesiae a Deo traditi, Latini recens ex Hebraeo facti, brevibusque scholiis illustrati etc.* 2 vols. Frankfurt, 1579.

Turretini, F. *Institutio theologiae elencticae.* 3 vols. Geneva, 1688–9.

—. *Institutes of Elenctic Theology.* 3 vols. Trans. G. M. Giger. Ed. J. T. Dennison Jr. Phillipsburg, 1992–7.

—. *Francisci Turretini opera.* 4 vols. Edinburgh, 1847.

Ursinus, Z. *Opera Theologica.* 3 vols. Ed. Q. Reuter. Heidelberg, 1612.

—. *Tractationum theologicarum.* 2 vols. Neustadt, 1587–9.

—. *Doctrinae Christianae Compendium, seu Commentarii Catechetici.* Geneva, 1584.

—. *Commentary on the Heidelberg Catechism.* Trans. and ed. G. W. Willard. Phillipsburg, 1985.

—. *The Summe of Christian Doctrine.* Trans. H. Parrie. Oxford, 1587.

Ussher, J. *A Body of Divinity.* London, 1653.

Van Mastricht, P. *Theoretico-practica theologia.* Editio nova. Utrecht, 1699.

Vermigli, P. M. *Defensio doctrinae veteris & apostolicae de sacrosancto eucharistiae.* Oxford, 1572.

—. *Loci Communes ex variis libris collecti.* Ed. R. Massonius. London, 1576 and 1583.

—. *A Brief and Most Excellent Exposition, of the xii Articles of Our Faith commonly called the Apostles' Creed*. Trans. T. E. London, 1578.

—. *In epistolam S. Pauli ad Romanos D. Petri martyris Vermilii....* Basle, 1558.

Viret, P. *A Verie Familiare and Fruitful Exposition of the xii Articles of the Christian Faieth Conteined in the Commune Crede, called the Apostles Crede, made in dialoges*. London, c.1548.

—. *Instruction Chrestienne*. Geneva, 1563.

Wollebius, J. *Compendium theologiae Christianae*. Oxford. 1655.

Zanchi, G. *Operum Theologicorum*. 8 vols. Geneva, 1605.

—. *De Religione Christiana Fides*. Neustadt, c.1585.

—. *H. Zanchius. His Confession of the Christian Religion* Englished. Cambridge, 1599.

Zwingli, H. *Huldrici Zuinglii opera completa editio*. 8 vols. Ed. M. Schuler and J. Schultess. Zürich, 1828/9–42.

—. *Fidei Ratio. Collectio confessionum in Ecclesiis reformatis publicatorum*. Ed. H. A. Niemeyer. Leipzig, 1840.

—. *Zwingli and Bullinger*. Ed. G. W. Bromiley. Philadelphia, 1953.

—. *On Providence and Other Essays*. Ed. S. M. Jackson. Durham, NC, 1983.

2. Secondary Literature

Ackroyd, P. R. and C. F. Evans. *The Cambridge History of the Bible*. 3 vols. Cambridge, 1970.

Adams, H. M. *Catalogue of Books Printed on the Continent of Europe 1501–1600 in Cambridge Libraries*. Cambridge, 1967.

Agnew, D. *The Theology of Consolation*. Edinburgh, 1880.

Alexander, J. D. 'The Genevan Version of the Bible: Its Origin, Translation, and Influence', D.Phil. Thesis. Oxford University, 1957.

Althaus, P. *Die Prinzipien der deutschen reformierten Dogmatik im Zeitalter der aristotelischen Scholastik*. Leipzig, 1914.

—. *The Theology of Martin Luther*. Trans. R. C. Schultz. Philadelphia, 1966.

Anderson, M. W. 'Peter Martyr, Reformed Theologian (1542–1562): His Letters to Heinrich Bullinger and John Calvin', *Sixteenth Century Journal* 4 (1973), 41–64.

Armstrong, B. G. '*Duplex Cognitio Dei*, Or the Problem and Relation of Structure, Form and Purpose in Calvin's Theology', *Probing the Reformed Tradition: Historical Studies in Honor of Edward A. Dowey, Jr*. Louisville, 1989.

—. *Calvinism and the Amyraut Heresy: Protestant Scholasticism and Humanism in Seventeenth-Century France*. Madison, 1969.

—. 'Calvin and Calvinism', *Reformation Europe: A Guide to Research II*. Ed. W. S. Maltby. St Louis, 1992.

Atkinson, J. *The Great Light: Luther and the Reformation*. Grand Rapids, 1968.

Audi, R., ed. *The Cambridge Dictionary of Philosophy*. Cambridge, 1995.

Avis, P. D. L. *The Church in the Theology of the Reformers*. Basingstoke, 1981.

—, ed. *The History of Christian Theology. Vol. 1: the Science of Theology*. Basingstoke, 1986.

Backus, I. 'The Teaching of Logic in Two Protestant Academies at the End of the Sixteenth Century. The Reception of Zarabella in Strasbourg and Geneva', *Archiv für Reformationsgeschichte* 80 (1989), 240–51.

Bainton, R. H. *The Reformation of the Sixteenth Century.* Boston, 1952.

—, trans. and ed. *Concerning Heretics.* New York, 1935.

Baird, C. W. *A Chapter on Liturgies.* London, 1856.

Baird, H. M. *Theodore Beza. The Counsellor of the French Reformation.* New York, 1899.

Baker, D., ed. *Reform and Reformation: England and the Continent c.1500–c.1750.* Oxford, 1979.

Baker, J. W. 'Church, State and Dissent: The Crisis of the Swiss Reformation, 1531–1536', *Church History* 57 (1988), 135–52.

—. 'In Defense of Magisterial Discipline: Bullinger's *Tractatus de Excommunicatione* of 1568', *Heinrich Bullinger, 1505–1575: Gesammelte Aufsätze zum 400sten Todestag.* Ed. U. Gäbler and E. Herkenrath. Zürich, 1975.

—. *Covenant and Community in the Thought of Heinrich Bullinger.* Philadelphia, 1980.

—. *Heinrich Bullinger and the Covenant: The Other Reformed Tradition.* Athens, OH, 1980.

—. 'Church, State, and Dissent: The Crisis of the Swiss Reformation: 1531–1536', *Church History* 57 (1988), 135–52.

Bammel, C. P. 'Justification By Faith in Augustine and Origen', *Journal of Ecclesiastical History* 47 (1996), 223–35.

Barnes, J., ed. *The Cambridge Companion to Aristotle.* Cambridge, 1995.

Baron, H. 'Calvinist Republicanism and its Historical Roots', *Church History* 8 (1939), 30–42.

Barr, J. *Biblical Faith and Natural Theology.* Oxford, 1993.

Barraclough, G. *The Origins of Modern Germany.* Oxford, 1947.

Barth, K. *Church Dogmatics.* Trans. G. W. Bromiley. 13 vols. Edinburgh, 1936–1969.

—. *The Heidelberg Catechism for Today.* London, 1964.

—. *Theology and the Church. The Shorter Writings, 1920–1928.* London, 1962.

—. *The Göttingen Dogmatics: Instruction in the Christian Faith.* Vol. 1. Trans. G. W. Bromiley. Grand Rapids, 1991.

Barth, K. and E. Brunner. *Natural Theology.* Trans. P. Fraenkel. London, 1946.

Barth, P. *Das Problem der naturlichen Theologie bei Calvin.* Munich, 1935.

Battenhouse, R. W. 'The Doctrine of Man in Renaissance Humanism', *The Journal of the History of Ideas* 9 (1948), 447–71.

Battles, F. L. 'God Was Accommodating Himself to Human Capacity', *Interpretation* 31 (1977), 19–38.

—. 'Calculus Fidei', *Calvinus Ecclesiae Doctor.* Ed. W. Neuser. Kampen, 1978.

Bavinck, H. 'Calvin and Common Grace'. Trans. G. Vos. *Calvin and the Reformation.* London, 1909.

—. *Gerefomeerde Dogmatiek.* 4 vols. Kampen, 1895.

—. *Our Reasonable Faith: A Survey of Christian Doctrine.* Trans. H. Zylstra. Grand Rapids, 1956.

Bautz, F. W. et al., Ed. *Biographisch-Bibliographisches Kirchenlexikon*. 11 vols. Hamm, Westf. 1970-.

Beardsley III, J. W. *Reformed Dogmatics: J. Wollebius, G. Voetius, F. Turretin*. New York, 1965.

Beeke, J. R. *Assurance of Faith: Calvin, English Puritanism and the Dutch Second Reformation*. New York, 1991.

—. 'Faith and Assurance in the Heidelberg Catechism and its Primary Composers: A Fresh Look at the Kendall Thesis', *Calvin Theological Journal* 27 (1992), 39-67.

Bell, M. C. 'Calvin and the Extent of the Atonement', *Evangelical Quarterly* 55 (1983), 115-23.

—. 'Calvin and Scottish Theology: The Doctrine of Assurance', Ph.D. Thesis, University of Edinburgh, 1985.

Benoît, Jean-Daniel. 'The History and Development of the *Institutio*: How Calvin Worked', *John Calvin*. Ed. G. Duffield. Grand Rapids, 1966.

Benton, W. W. Jr. 'Federal Theology: Review for Revision', *Through Christ's Word: A Festschrift for Dr. Philip E. Hughes*. Ed. W. R. Godfrey and J. L. Boyd III. Phillipsburg, 1985.

Berkouwer, G. C. *The Triumph of Grace in the Theology of Karl Barth*. London, 1956.

—. *Studies in Dogmatics*. 18 vols. Trans. L. B. Smedes and R. D. Knudson. Grand Rapids, 1952-75.

Biel, P. 'Colloquy or Cul de Sac at Maulbronn in 1564', Presented to the American Society of Church History Conference, 28-30 December, 1991, Chicago. Portland, 1992.

Bierma, L. D. 'The Covenant Theology of Caspar Olevian', Ph.D. Diss., Duke University, 1980.

—. 'Covenant or Covenants in the Theology of Olevianus?', *Calvin Theological Journal* 22 (1987), 228-50.

—. 'Federal Theology in the Sixteenth Century: Two Traditions?' *Westminster Theological Journal* 45 (1983), 304-21.

—. 'Lutheran-Reformed Polemics in the Late Reformation: Olevianus' Conciliatory Proposal', *Controversy and Conciliation: The Palatinate Reformation, 1559-1618*. Ed. D. Visser. Pittsburgh, 1986.

—. 'Olevianus and the Authorship of the Heidelberg Catechism: Another Look', *Sixteenth Century Journal* 13 (1982), 17-27.

—. 'Philip Melanchthon and the Heidelberg Catechism', *Melanchthon in Europe: His Word and Influence Beyond Wittenberg*. Ed. K. Maag. Grand Rapids, 1999.

—. 'The Role of Covenant Theology in Early Reformed Orthodoxy', *The Sixteenth Century Journal* 21 (1990), 453-62.

—. 'Vester Grundt and the Origins of the Heidelberg Catechism', *Later Calvinism: International Perspectives*. Sixteenth Century Essays and Studies. Vol. 22. Ed. W. F. Graham. Kirksville, MO, 1994.

—. *German Calvinism in the Confessional Age: The Covenant Theology of Caspar Olevianus*. Grand Rapids, 1997.

—. s.v. 'Olevianus, Caspar', *Encyclopedia of the Reformed Faith*. Ed. D. K. McKim. London, 1992.

—. The Doctrine of the Sacraments in the Heidelberg Catechism: Melanchthonian, Calvinist or Zwinglian? Studies in Reformed Theology and History. Ed. D. Willis. Princeton Theological Seminary, 1999.

Black, J. B. *The Reign of Elizabeth 1558-1603*. Second edition. Oxford, 1959.

Boersma, H. 'Calvin and the Extent of the Atonement', *The Evangelical Quarterly* 64 (1992), 333-55.

Bohatec, J. *Budé und Calvin*. Graz, 1950.

Bolgar, R. R. *The Classical Heritage and its Beneficiaries*. Cambridge, 1954.

Bouwsma, W. J. *A Usable Past: Essays in European Cultural History*. Berkeley, 1990.

—. 'Calvin as Renaissance Artifact', *John Calvin and the Church: A Prism of Reform*. Ed. T. George. Louisville, 1990.

—. 'Calvin and the Renaissance Crisis of Knowing', *Calvin Theological Journal* 17 (1982), 190-211.

—. *John Calvin: A Sixteenth Century Portrait*. Oxford, 1988.

—. 'Renaissance and Reformation: An Essay in Their Affinities and Connections', *Luther and the Dawn of the Modern Era*. Ed. H. A. Oberman. Leiden, 1974.

—. 'The Two Faces of Humanism: Stoicism and Augustinianism in Renaissance Thought', *Itinerarium Italicum: The Profile of the Italian Renaissance in the Mirror of its European Transformations*. Ed. H. A. Oberman and T. A. Brady Jr. Leiden, 1975.

Bozeman, T. D. 'Federal Theology and the 'National Covenant': An Elizabethan Presbyterian Case Study', *Church History* 61 (1992), 394-407.

Brady, T. A. *Ruling Class, Regime*. Leiden, 1978.

—. et al. *Handbook of European History 1400-1600*. 2 vols. Grand Rapids, 1996.

—. s.v. 'Luther Renaissance', *The Oxford Encyclopedia of the Reformation*, 4 vols. Ed. H. J. Hillerbrand. Oxford, 1996.

Bray, J. S. 'The Value of Works in the Theology of Calvin and Beza', *Sixteenth Century Journal* 4 (1973), 77-86.

—. *Theodore Beza's Doctrine of Predestination*. Nieuwkoop, 1975.

Breen, Q. *Christianity and Humanism*. Grand Rapids, 1968.

—. *John Calvin: A Study in French Humanism*. Grand Rapids, 1931.

Broughton, L. C. 'Supralapsarianism and the Role of Metaphysics in Sixteenth Century Reformed Theology', *Westminster Theological Journal* 48 (1986), 63-96.

Brown, W. A. s.v. 'Covenant Theology', *The Encyclopaedia of Religion and Ethics*. 12 vols. Ed. J. Hastings et al. Edinburgh, 1911.

Bruggink, D. J. 'Calvin and Federal Theology', *Reformed Review* 13 (1959), 15-22.

Buchanan, J. *The Doctrine of Justification*. Edinburgh, 1867.

Burchill, C. J. 'The Urban Reformation and its Fate: Problems and Perspectives in the Consolidation of the German Protestant Movement', *The Historical Journal* 27 (1984), 997-1010.

—. 'Aristotle and the Trinity: the Case of Johann Hasler in Strasbourg, 1574-1575', *Archiv für Reformationsgeschichte* 79 (1988), 324-52.

—. *Bibliographica Aureliana: Bibliotheca Dissidentium: Répertoire des Non-Conformistes Religieux de Seizième et Dix-Septième Siècles.* Ed. A. Seguenny, I. Backus, J. Rott. Vol. 1, *The Heidelberg Antitrinitarians: Johann Sylvan, Adam Neuser, Matthias Vehe, Jacob Suter, Johann Hasler.* Baden-Baden, 1989.

—. 'Girolamo Zanchi: Portrait of a Reformed Theologian and His Work', *Sixteenth Century Journal* 15 (1984), 185–207.

—. 'On the Consolation of a Christian Scholar: Zacharias Ursinus (1534–1583) and the Reformation in Heidelberg', *Journal of Ecclesiastical History* 37 (1986), 565–83.

Burn, A. E. *An Introduction to the Creeds.* London, 1899.

—. *The Apostles' Creed.* London, 1906.

Büsser, F. 'Bullinger and 1566', *Conflict and Conciliation: The Palatinate Reformation, 1559–1618.* Ed. D. Visser. Pittsburgh, 1986.

—. 'Zwingli the Exegete: A Contribution to the 450th Anniversary of the Death of Erasmus', *Probing the Reformed Tradition.* Ed. E. A. McKee and B. G. Armstrong. Louisville, 1989.

Butin, P. W. 'John Calvin's Humanist Image of Popular Late-Medieval Piety and its Contribution to Reformed Worship', *Calvin Theological Journal* 29 (1994), 419–31.

—. *Revelation, Redemption and Response. Calvin's Trinitarian Understanding of the Divine-Human Relationship.* New York, 1995.

Cameron, E. *The European Reformation.* Oxford, 1991.

—. 'The Late Renaissance and the Unfolding Reformation in Europe', *Reform and Reformation: England and the Continent c.1500– c.1750.* Ed. D. Baker. Oxford, 1979.

—. Review of D. A. Weir, *The Origins of the Federal Theology in Sixteenth Century Reformation Thought. Religion* 22 (1992), 195–6.

Cameron, J. K., ed. *The Letters of John Johnstone c.1565–1611 and Robert Howie c.1565–1645.* Edinburgh, 1963.

—. *The Political Thought of Martin Luther.* Sussex, 1984

Carlson Jr, C. P. *Justification in Earlier Medieval Theology.* The Hague, 1975.

Carsten, F. L. *Princes and Parliaments in Germany.* Oxford, 1959.

—. 'The Origins of the Junkers', *Essays in German History.* London, 1985.

Chadwick, O. 'The Making of a Reforming Prince: Fredrick III, Elector Palatinate', *Reformation, Confession and Dissent.* Ed. R. B. Knox. London, 1977.

Citron, B. *New Birth: A Study of the Evangelical Doctrine of Conversion in the Protestant Fathers.* Edinburgh, 1951.

Clanchy, M. T. *Abelard: A Medieval Life.* Oxford, 1997.

Clark, R. S. 'The Authority of Reason in the Later Reformation: Scholasticism in Caspar Olevian and Antoine de La Faye', *Protestant Scholasticism: Essays in Reassessment.* Ed. C. Trueman and R. S. Clark. Carlisle, 1999.

—. The Catholic-Calvinist Trinitarianism of Caspar Olevian', *Westminster Theological Journal* 61 (1999), 15–39.

—. 'Calvin and the *Lex Naturalis*', *Stulos Theological Journal* 6 (1998), 1–22.

— and J. R. Beeke, 'Ursinus, Oxford and the Westminster Divines', *The Westminster Confession into the 21st Century: Essays in Remembrance of* the *350th Anniversary of the Publication of the Westminster Confession of Faith*. Ed. J. L. Duncan. 3 vols. Fearn, Ross-shire, 2003-, 2.1-32.

Clasen, C. P. *The Palatinate in European History 1559-1660*. Oxford, 1963.

Clifford, A. C. *Atonement and Justification*. Oxford, 1990.

Clouse, R. G. s.v. 'Covenant Theology', *New International Dictionary of the Christian Church*. Second edition. Exeter, 1978.

Cochrane, A. C. 'Natural Law in Calvin', *Church-State Relations in Ecumenical Perspective*. Ed. E. A. Smith. Pittsburgh, 1966.

—, ed. *Reformed Confessions of the Sixteenth Century*. Philadelphia, 1966.

Coenen, L., ed. *Handbuch zum Heidelberger Katechismus*. Neukirchen-Vluyn, 1963.

Cohn, H. J. *The Government of the Rhine Palatinate in the Fifteenth Century*. Oxford, 1965.

—. 'The Territorial Princes in Germany's Second Reformation, 1559-1622', *International Calvinism 1541-1715*. Ed. M. Prestwich. Oxford, 1985.

Collins, G. N. M. s.v. 'Federal Theology', *Baker's Dictionary of Theology*. Grand Rapids, 1960.

—. s.v. 'Covenant Theology', *Baker's Dictionary of Theology*. Grand Rapids, 1960.

Collinson, P. 'England and International Calvinism 1558-1640', *International Calvinism 1541-1715*. Ed. M. Prestwich. Oxford, 1985.

—. *The Elizabethan Puritan Movement*. London, 1967.

—. 'The Elizabethan Puritans and the Foreign Reformed Churches in London', *Godly People: Essays on English Protestantism and Puritanism*. London, 1983.

—. 'The Reformer and the Archbishop: Martin Bucer and an English Bucerian', *Godly People: Essays on English Protestantism and Puritanism*. London, 1983.

Copleston, F. *A History of Philosophy*. 9 vols. New York, 1962.

Courtenay, W. J. *Covenant and Causality in Medieval Thought*. London, 1984.

Cranz, F. E. 'An Essay on the Development of Luther's Thought on Justice, Law and Society', *Justice and Law 1518 and Later*. *Harvard Theological Studies* 19. Cambridge, MA, 1959.

Cross, C. 'Continental Students and Protestant Reformation in England in the Sixteenth Century', *Reform and Reformation: England and the Continent c.1500- c.1750*. Ed. D. Baker. Oxford, 1979.

Cross, R. 'Alloiosis in the Christology of Zwingli', *Journal of Theological Studies* 47 (1995), 105-22.

Cunningham, W. *The Reformers and the Theology of the Reformation*. Edinburgh, 1967.

Cuno, E. W. *Blättër der erinnerung an Kaspar Olevianus*. Barman, 1887.

Darling, J. *Cyclopedia Bibliographica*. 3 vols. London, 1854-9.

Davies, C. '"Poor Persecuted Little Flock" or "Commonwealth of Christians": Edwardian Protestant Concepts of the Church', *Protestantism and the National Church in Sixteenth Century England*. Ed. P. Lake and M. Dowling. London, 1987.

Davies, R. E. *The Problem of Authority in the Continental Reformers*. London, 1946.

Davis, D. C. 'The Reformed Church of Germany: Calvinists as Influential Minority', *John Calvin: His Influence on the Western World*. Ed. W. S. Reid. Grand Rapids, 1982.

Davis, T. J. 'Images of Intolerance: John Calvin in Nineteenth-Century History Textbooks', *Church History* 65 (1996), 234–48.

de Greef, W. *The Writings of John Calvin: An Introductory Guide*. Trans. L. D. Bierma. Grand Rapids, 1993.

de Klerk, P., Ed. *Renaissance, Reformation, Resurgence*. Grand Rapids, 1976.

de Margerie, B. *The Christian Trinity in History*. Trans. E. J. Fortman. Still River, MA, 1982.

Dekker, E. 'Jacobus Arminius and His Logic: Analysis of a Letter', *Journal of Theological Studies* 44 (1993), 118–42.

—. 'Was Arminius a Molinist?', *Sixteenth Century Journal* 27 (1996), 337–52.

Dickens, A. G. *The Counter Reformation*. London, 1968.

Diener, R. E. 'Johann Wigand', *Shapers of Religious Traditions in Germany, Switzerland, and Poland 1560–1600*. Ed. J. Raitt. New Haven, 1981.

Disley, E. 'Degrees of Glory: Protestant Doctrine and the Concept of Rewards Hereafter', *Journal of Theological Studies* 42 (1991), 77–105.

Dobson, B. 'German History 911–1618', *Germany: Companion to German Studies*. Ed. M. Paisely. London, 1972.

Dohna, L. 'Staupitz and Luther: Continuity and Breakthrough at the Beginning of the Reformation', *Via Augustini: Augustine in the Later Middle Ages, Renaissance and Reformation*. Leiden, 1991.

Donagan, A. 'The Scholastic Theory of Moral Law in the Modern World', *Aquinas: A Collection of Critical Essays*. Ed. A. Kenny. London, 1970.

Donnelly, J. P. 'Calvinist Thomism', *Viator* 7 (1976), 441–55.

—. *Calvinism and Scholasticism in Vermigli's Doctrine of Man and Grace*. Leiden, 1976.

—. 'Immortality and Method in Ursinus's Theological Ambiance', *Controversy and Conciliation: The Palatinate Reformation, 1559–1618*. Ed. D. Visser. Pittsburgh, 1986.

—. 'Italian Influences on the Development of Calvinist Scholasticism', *Sixteenth Century Journal* 7 (1976), 81–101.

—. 'Peter Canisius', *Shapers of Religious Traditions in Germany, Switzerland, and Poland 1560–1600*. Ed. J. Raitt. New Haven, 1981.

Donnelly, J. P. and R. M. Kingdon. *A Bibliography of the Works of Peter Martyr Vermigli*. Kirksville, MO, 1990.

Dorner, I. A. *History of Protestant Theology*. Trans. G. Robson and S. Taylor. 2 vols. Edinburgh, 1871.

—. *History and Development of the Doctrine of the Person of Christ*. Trans. W. L. Alexander and D. W. Simon. 5 vols. Edinburgh, 1866–70.

Dowey, E. A. 'The Structure of Calvin's Theological Thought as Influenced by the Two-Fold Knowledge of God', *Calvinus Ecclesiae Genevenesis Custos*. Ed. W. Neuser. New York, 1984.

—. s.v. 'Heinrich Bullinger', *Encyclopedia of the Reformed Faith*. Louisville, 1992.

—. *The Knowledge of God in Calvin's Theology*. New York, 1952.

Dubbs, J. H. *Historic Manual of the Reformed Church in the United States.* Lancaster, 1885.

Duffield, G., ed. *John Calvin.* Grand Rapids, 1966.

Duke, A. G. Lewis and A. Pettegree, eds. *Calvinism in Europe 1540–1610: A Collection of Documents.* Manchester, 1992.

——. 'Perspectives on International Calvinism', *Calvinism in Europe, 1540–1620.* Ed. A. Pettegree, A. Duke and G. Lewis. Cambridge, 1994.

Ebeling, G. *The Study of Theology.* Trans. D. A. Priebe. London, 1979.

——. 'On the Doctrine of the *Triplex usis legis* in the Theology of the Reformation', *Word and Faith.* Trans. J. W. Leith. London, 1963.

Edwards Jr, M. U. *Luther and the False Brethren.* Stanford, CA, 1975.

Edwards, P., ed. *Encyclopedia of Philosophy.* 8 vols. New York, 1967.

Eire, C. M. N. 'Calvin and Nicodemism: A Reappraisal', *Scottish Journal of Theology* 10 (1979), 45–70.

——. *War Against the Idols: The Reformation of Worship from Erasmus to Calvin.* Cambridge, 1986.

Elazar, D. J. *Exploring Federalism.* London, 1987.

——. 'From Biblical Covenant to Modern Federalism: The Federal Theology Bridge', Unpublished paper. Center for the Study of Federalism, Temple University. Philadelphia, 1980.

Elert, W. 'The Third Use of the Law', *Lutheran World Review* 1 (1949), 38–48.

Elton, G. R. 'England and the Continent in the Sixteenth Century', *Reform and Reformation: England and the Continent c.1500– c.1750.* Edited by D. Baker. Oxford, 1979.

Emerson, E. H. 'Calvin And Covenant Theology', *Church History* 25 (1956), 136–44.

Erichson, A. *Bibliographia Calviniana.* 3rd edition. Nieuwkoop, 1965.

Evans, G. R. *The Language and Logic of the Bible: The Road to Reformation.* Cambridge, 1985.

Evans, R. J. W. 'The Wechel Presses: Humanism and Calvinism in Central Europe 1572–1627', *Past and Present Supplement* 2 (1975).

——. *Rudolf II and His World, A Study in Intellectual History 1576–1612.* Oxford, 1973.

——. *The Making of the Habsburg Monarchy 1550–1700.* Oxford, 1984.

Farthing, J. L. '*De Coniugio Spirituali:* Jerome Zanchi on Ephesians 5:22–33', *Sixteenth Century Journal* 24 (1993), 621–52.

——. 'Christ and the Eschaton: the Reformed Eschatology of Jerome Zanchi', *Later Calvinism: International Perspectives.* Vol. 22, *Sixteenth Century Essays and Studies.* Ed. W. F. Graham. Kirksville, MO, 1994.

——. '*Foedus Evangelicum:* Jerome Zanchi on the Covenant', *Calvin Theological Journal* 29 (1994), 149–67.

——. 'Holy Harlotry: Jerome Zanchi and the Exegetical History of Gomer' (Hosea 1–3), *Biblical Interpretation in the Era of the Reformation.* Ed. R. A. Muller and J. L. Thompson. Grand Rapids, 1996.

——. *Thomas Aquinas and Gabriel Biel: Interpretations of St. Thomas Aquinas in German Nominalism on the Eve of the Reformation.* Durham, NC, and London, 1988.

Fatio, O. 'Lambert Daneau 1530-1595', Trans. J. Raitt. *Shapers of Religious Traditions in Germany, Switzerland, and Poland 1500-1600*. Ed. J. Raitt. New Haven, 1981.

——. 'Présence de Calvin à l'epoque de l'orthodoxie reformée. Les abregés de Calvin à la fin du 16e et au 17e Siècle', *Calvinus Ecclesiae Doctor*. Ed. W. Neuser. Kampen, 1978.

Filiencron, F. R. *Allgemeine Deutsche Biographie*. 55 vols. Leipzig,1875-1910.

Finnis, J. *Natural Law and Natural Rights*. Oxford, 1984.

Fischer, R. H. 'A Reasonable Luther', *Reformation Studies: Essays Honoring Roland H. Bainton*. Ed. F. H. Littell. Richmond, VA, 1962.

Fleischer, M. P. 'Silesiographia', *Archive for Reformation History* 69 (1978), 219-47.

——. 'The Institutionalisation of Humanism in Protestant Silesia', *Archive for Reformation History* 66 (1975), 256-74.

——. 'The Success of Ursinus: A Triumph of Intellectual Friendship', *Controversy and Conciliation: The Palatinate Reformation, 1559-1618*. Ed. D. Visser. Pittsburgh, 1986.

——. *Späthumanismus in Schleisen*. Munich, 1984.

——. 'The Reception in Silesia', *Discord, Dialogue and Concord: Studies in the Lutheran Reformation's Formula of Concord*. Ed. L. W. Spitz and W. Lohff. Philadelphia, 1977.

Förstemann, K. E. s.v. 'Olevianus', *Allgemeine Encyclopädie der Wissenschaft und Künste*. Ed. J. G. Gruber. Leipzig, 1818-89.

Fraenkel, P. *Testimonia Patrum: The Function of the Patristic Argument in the Theology of Philip Melanchthon*. Geneva, 1961.

——. *De L'Écriture À La Dispute*. Lausanne, 1977.

Franklin, J. H. *Constitutionalism and Resistance in the Sixteenth Century: Three Treatises by Hotman, Beza, & Mornay*. New York, 1969.

——. *Jean Bodin and the Rise of Absolutist Theory*. Cambridge, 1973.

Friedlander, G., ed. *Beiträge zür Reformationsgeschichte: Sammlung ungedruckter Briefe des Reuchlin, Beza und Bullinger, nebst einem Anhange zür Geschichte der Jesuiten*. Berlin, 1837.

Gamble, R. C. 'Calvin's Theological Method: Word and Spirit, A Case Study', *Calviniana: Ideas and Influence of Jean Calvin*. Ed. R. V. Schnucker. Kirksville, MO, 1988.

Ganoczy, A. 'Observations on Calvin's Trinitarian Doctrine of Grace', Trans. K. Crim. *Probing the Reformed Tradition: Historical Studies in Honor of Edward A. Dowey, Jr*. Ed. E. A. McKee and B. G. Armstrong. Louisville, 1989.

——. *The Young Calvin*. Trans. D. Foxgrover and W. Provo. Edinburgh, 1977.

Geisendorf, P.-F. *Théodore de Bèze*. Geneva, 1967.

Gerl, Hanna-Barbara. *Philosophie und Philologie*. Munich, 1981.

George, R. P., ed. *Natural Law Theory*. Oxford, 1992.

George, T., ed. *John Calvin and the Church: A Prism of Reform*. Louisville, 1990.

Gerrish, B. A. 'John Calvin on Luther', *Interpreters of Luther*. Ed. J. Pelikan. Philadelphia, 1968.

——. 'Biblical Authority and the Reformation', *Scottish Journal of Theology* 10 (1957), 337-51.

—. 'John Calvin and the Reformed Doctrine of the Lord's Supper', *McCormick Quarterly* 22 (1969), 85–98.

—. *Grace and Gratitude*. Edinburgh, 1993.

—. *Grace and Reason. A Study in the Theology of Luther*. Oxford, 1962.

— and R. Bennedeto, eds. *Reformatio Perennis*. Pittsburgh, 1981.

—. *Tradition and the Modern World: Reformed Theology in the Nineteenth Century*. Chicago, 1978.

Gillet, J. F. A. *Crato von Crafftheim und Seine Freunde*. 2 vols. Frankfurt, 1860.

Gilmont, J.-Fr. s.v. 'Goulart, Simon', *Dictionnaire d' Histoire et de Geographie Ecclesiastiques*. Ed. R. Aubert. 25 vols. Paris, 1912–.

Gilson, E. *The Christian Philosophy of St. Thomas Aquinas*. Trans. L. K. Shook. London, 1961.

Göbel, M. 'Dr. Caspar Olevianus 1535–1587', Trans. H. Harbaugh. *Mercersburg Quarterly Review* 7 (1855), 294–306.

Godfrey, W. R. 'Back to Basics: A Response to the Robertson-Fuller Dialogue', *Presbyterion: A Journal for the Eldership, Covenant Seminary Review* 9 (1983), 80–84.

—. 'Biblical Authority in the Sixteenth and Seventeenth Centuries: A Question of Transition', *Scripture and Truth*. Ed. D. A. Carson and J. D. Woodbridge. Grand Rapids, 1983.

—. 'The Dutch Reformed Response', *Discord, Dialogue and Concord: Studies in the Lutheran Reformation's Formula of Concord*. Ed. L. W. Spitz and W. Lohff. Philadelphia, 1977.

—. 'Reformed Thought on the Extent of the Atonement to 1618', *Westminster Theological Journal* 37 (1975), 133–71.

—. 'Tensions within International Calvinism: The Debate on the Atonement at the Synod of Dordt 1618–1619', Ph.D. Diss., Stanford University, 1974.

Goeters, J. F. G. s.v. 'Olevian, Caspar', *Die Religion in Geschichte und Gegenwart*. 6 vols. Tübingen, 1960.

—. s.v. 'Föderaltheologie', *Theologische Realenzyklopädie*. Ed. G. Krause and G. Müller. 34 vols. Berlin. 1977–.

—. 'Caspar Olevian als Theologe', *Monatshefte für Evangelische Kirchengeschichte des Rheinlandes* 37/38 (1988–89), 287–344.

Good, J. I. *The Heidelberg Catechism in Its Newest Light*. Philadelphia, 1914.

—. *Historical Hand-Book of the Reformed Church*. Philadelphia, 1901.

—. *History of the Reformed Church in the United States in the Nineteenth Century*. New York, 1911.

—. *The Origin of the Reformed Church in Germany*. Reading, PA, 1887.

—. *The Reformed Reformation*. Philadelphia, 1916.

Graves, F. P. *Peter Ramus and The Educational Reformation of the Sixteenth Century*. New York, 1912.

Greaves, R. L. 'The Origins and Development of English Covenant Thought', *The Historian* 31 (1968), 21–35.

Green, L. C. 'The Influence of Erasmus upon Melanchthon, Luther and the Formula of Concord in the Doctrine of Justification', *Church History* 43 (1974), 183–200.

——. 'Faith, Righteousness, and Justification: New Light on their Development Under Luther and Melanchthon', *Sixteenth Century Journal* 4 (1973), 65–86.

——. 'The Three Causes of Conversion in Philip Melanchthon, Martin Chemnitz, David Chytraeus and the "Formula of Concord"', *Lutherjahrbuch* 47 (1980), 89–114.

——. 'Luther's Understanding of the Freedom of God and the Salvation of Man: His Interpretation of 1 Timothy 2:4', *Archiv für Reformationsgeschichte* 87 (1996), 57–73.

Grisilis, E. 'Seneca and Cicero as Possible Sources of John Calvin's View of Double Predestination: An Enquiry in the History of Ideas', *In Honor of John Calvin 1509–64*. Ed. E. J. Furcha. Toronto, 1986.

Gründler, O. 'From Seed to Fruition: Calvin's Notion of the *semen fidei* and Its Aftermath in Reformed Orthodoxy', *Probing the Reformed Tradition: Historical Studies in Honor of Edward A. Dowey, Jr.* Ed. E. A. McKee and B. G. Armstrong. Louisville, 1989.

——. 'Thomism and Calvinism in the Theology of Girolamo Zanchi', Th.D. Thesis, Princeton Theological Seminary, 1961.

Guggisberg, H. R. 'Castellio: Problems of Writing a New Biography', *The Emergence of Tolerance in the Dutch Republic*. Ed. C. Berkvens-Stevelinck et al. Leiden, 1997.

Haag, E. *La France Protestante, ou Vies des protestants français qui se sont fait un nom dans l'histoire*. 9 vols. Paris, 1846–59.

Hagen, Kenneth, 'From Testament to Covenant in the Early Sixteenth Century', *Sixteenth Century Journal* 3 (1972), 1–24.

——. 'Did Peter Err? The Text is the Best Judge', *Augustine, The Harvest, and Theology (1300–1650)*. Ed. K. Hagen. Leiden, 1990.

Hagenbach, K. R. *History of the Reformation in Germany and Switzerland Chiefly*. Trans. E. Moore. 2 vols. Edinburgh, 1879.

——. *A History of Christian Doctrines*. Trans. C. W. Buch et al. 3 vols. Edinburgh, 1883–95.

Hägglund, B. *The Background of Luther's Doctrine of Justification in Late Medieval Theology*. Philadelphia, 1971.

Hall, B. 'Calvin Against the Calvinists', *John Calvin: A Collection of Essays*. Grand Rapids, 1966.

——. 'The Colloquies Between Catholics and Protestants 1539–41', *Councils and Assemblies*. Ed. G. J. Cuming and D. Baker. Cambridge, 1971.

——. 'John Calvin, the Jurisconsults and the *Ius Civile*', *Studies in Church History*. Vol. 3. Oxford, 1966.

Hamm, B. *Promissio, pactum, ordinatio: Freiheit und Selbstbindung Gottes in der scholastischen Gnadenlehre*. Tübingen, 1977.

Harbaugh, H. 'Creed and Cultus', *Tercentenary Monument in Commemoration of the Three Hundredth Anniversary of the Heidelberg Catechism*. Chambersburg, PA, 1863.

——. *The Fathers of the German Reformed Church in Europe and America*. 2 Vols. Lancaster, PA, 1857.

Haremelink III, H. *Ecumenism and The Reformed Church*. Grand Rapids, 1968.

Harnack, A. *The Apostles' Creed*. Trans. S. Means. London, 1901.

Hastie, W. *The Theology of the Reformed Church in its Fundamental Principles.* Ed. W. Fulton. Edinburgh, 1904.

Hazlett, W. I. A. s.v. 'Rollock, Robert (c.1555–1599)', *Encyclopedia of the Reformed Faith.* Ed. D. K. McKim. Edinburgh, 1992.

Heckel, H. *Deutschland im konfessionellern Zeitalter.* Gottingen, 1983.

Heinz, J. *Justification and Merit: Luther vs. Catholicism.* Berrien Springs, MI.

Helm, P. 'Calvin and Natural Law', *Scottish Bulletin of Evangelical Theology* 2 (1984), 5–24.

—. 'Calvin and the Covenant: Unity and Continuity', *The Evangelical Quarterly* 55 (1983), 65–82.

—. *Calvin and the Calvinists.* Edinburgh, 1982.

—. 'Calvin (and Zwingli) on Divine Providence', *Calvin Theological Journal* 29 (1994), 388–405.

Henderson, G. D. *The Burning Bush: Studies in Scottish Church History.* Edinburgh, 1957.

Heppe, H. 'The Character of the German Reformed Church, and its Relation to Lutheranism and Calvinism', *Mercersburg Quarterly Review* 5 (1853), 181–207.

—. *Geschichte des Deutschen Protestantismus in den Jahren 1555–81.* 4 vols. Marburg, 1852.

—. *Geschichte des Pietismus und der Mystik in der Reformierten Kirche.* Leiden, 1879.

—, ed. *Theodor Beza: Leben und ausgewählte Schriften.* Elberfeld, 1861.

—. *Reformed Dogmatics Set Out and Illustrated from the Sources.* Trans. G. T. Thomson. Ed. E. Bizer. London. 1950.

Heron, A. I. C. 'Bund (Dogmatisch)', *Evangelisches Kirchen Lexikon.* 3 vols. Göttingen, 1986–92.

—, ed. *The Westminster Confession in the Church Today.* Edinburgh, 1982.

Hesselink, I. J. *Calvin's Concept of Law.* Pittsburgh, 1993.

—. 'Law and Gospel or Gospel and Law? Calvin's Understanding of the Relationship', *Calviniana: Ideas and Influence of Jean Calvin.* Ed. R. V. Schnucker. Kirksville, MO, 1988.

—. 'The Dramatic Story of the Heidelberg Catechism', *Later Calvinism: International Perspectives.* Ed. W. F. Graham. Kirksville, MO, 1994.

—. 'Luther and Calvin in Law and Gospel in Their Galatians Commentaries', *Reformed Review* 37 (1984), 69–82.

—. s.v. 'Natural Theology', *Encyclopedia of the Reformed Faith.* Ed. D. K. McKim and D. F. Wright. Louisville and Edinburgh, 1992.

Hillerbrand, H. J., ed. *The Oxford Encyclopedia of the Reformation.* 4 vols. New York, 1996.

—, ed. *Protestant Reformation.* New York, 1968.

—. *The World of the Reformation.* London, 1975.

Hinsburg, G. *Sayn-Wittgenstein-Berleburg: A History of the Counts of Wittgenstein.* Berleburg, 1920.

Hintze, O. 'Calvinism and Raison d'Etat in Early Seventeenth Century Brandenburg', *The Historical Essays of Otto Hintze.* Ed. F. Gilbert and R. M. Bergdahl. New York, 1975.

Hochstetter, E. 'Nominalismus?', *Franciscan Studies* 9 (1949), 370–403.

Hoekema, A. 'The Covenant of Grace in Calvin's Teaching', *Calvin Theological Journal* 2 (1967), 133–161.

Hoitenga Jr, D. J. *Faith and Reason from Plato to Plantinga: An Introduction to Reformed Epistemology*. New York, 1991.

Holborn, H. *A History of Modern Germany, The Reformation*. London, 1965.

Hollweg, W. *Neue Untersuchung zur Geschichte und Lehre des Heidelberger Katechismus*. 2 parts. Neukirchen, 1961–6.

Holmes, G., ed. *The Oxford History of Medieval Europe*. Oxford, 1992.

Holtmann, W. 'Caspar Olevian – 1536 bis 1587 – Ein evangelisch-reformierte aus Trier', *Monatshefte für Evangelische Kirchengeschichte des Rheinlandes* 37/38 (1988–89), 13–138.

Holtrop, P. C. s.v. 'Beza, Theodore', *Encyclopedia of the Reformed Faith*. Ed. D. K. McKim. Edinburgh, 1992.

——. *The Bolsec Controversy on Predestination from 1551 to 1555*. Vol. 1. Lewiston, NY, 1993.

Höpfl, H. *The Christian Polity of John Calvin*. Cambridge, 1982.

Hsia, R. P.-C., ed. *The German People and the Reformation*. London, 1988.

——. *Social Discipline in the Reformation: Central Europe 1550–1750*. London, 1989.

Hughes, M. *Early Modern Germany, 1477–1806*. London, 1992.

Hughes, P. E. *Lefèvre: Pioneer of Ecclesiastical Reform in France*. Grand Rapids, 1984.

——. 'Jacques Lefèvre d'Etaples (c.1455–1536)', *Calvinus Reformator: His Contribution to Theology, Church and State*. Pochestroom, 1982.

Isenberg, W. K., F. Loringhoven and D. Schwennicke, eds. *Europäische Stammtafeln, Stammtafeln zur Geschichte der Europäischen Staaten*. 15 vols. Marburg, 1961–92.

Iserloh, E. *Lexikon für Theologie und Kirche*. s.v. 'Olevian(us), Kaspar', 10 vols. Ed. M. Buchberger. Freiburg, 1957–65.

James III, F. A. 'A Late Medieval Parallel in Reformation Thought: Gemina Praedestinatio in Gregory of Rimini and Peter Martyr Vermigli', *Via Augustini: Augustine in the Later Middle Ages, Renaissance and Reformation*. Ed. H. A. Oberman, F. A. James. Leiden, 1991.

Jardine, L. 'Humanism and Dialectic in Sixteenth Century Cambridge: A Preliminary Investigation', *Classical Influences on European Culture A.D. 1500–1700*. Ed. R. R. Bolgar. Cambridge, 1976.

Jedin, H. *A History of the Council of Trent*. Trans. E. Graf. 2 vols. St Louis, 1957.

Jensen, K. 'Protestant Rivalry – Metaphysics and Rhetoric in Germany c.1590–1620', *Journal of Ecclesiastical History* 41 (1990), 24–43.

Jeon, J. K. *Covenant Theology: John Murray's and Meredith G. Kline's Response to the Historical Development of Federal Theology in Reformed Thought*. Lanham, 1999.

Jinkins, M. *Theodore Beza*: 'Continuity and Regression in the Reformed Tradition', *Evangelical Quarterly* 64 (1992), 131–54.

Johnson, M. S. 'Calvin's Handling of the Third Use of the Law and its Problems', *Calviniana: Ideas and Influence of Jean Calvin*. Ed. R. V. Schnucker. Kirksville, MO, 1988.

Jones, L. C. *Simon Goulart, étude biographique et bibliographique*. Geneva, 1917.

Kantzer, K. S. 'John Calvin's Theory of the Knowledge of God and the Word of God', Ph.D. Diss., Harvard University, 1950.

Karlberg, M. W. 'Covenant Theology and the Westminster Tradition', *Westminster Theological Journal* 54 (1992), 135–52.

——. 'The Mosaic Covenant and the Concept of Works in Reformed Hermeneutics: A Historical-Critical Analysis with Particular Attention to Early Covenant Eschatology', Ph.D. Diss., Westminster Theological Seminary, 1980.

——. 'Reformed Interpretation of the Mosaic Covenant', *Westminster Theological Journal* 43 (1980), 1–57.

Keen, R. *Sixteenth Century Bibliography: A Checklist of Melanchthon Imprints Through 1560*. St Louis, 1988.

Kelley, D. R. *Foundations of Modern Historical Scholarship*. New York, 1970.

——. *The Beginning of Ideology*. Cambridge, 1981.

Kelly, J. N. D., ed. *Early Christian Creeds*. Second edition. London, 1960.

Kelly, R. A. 'Tradition and Innovation: The Use of Theodoret's *Eranistes* in Martin Chemnitz' *De Duabus Naturis in Christo*', *Perspectives on Christology: Essays in Honor of Paul K. Jewett*. Ed. M. Shuster and R. A. Muller. Grand Rapids, 1991.

Kendall, R. T. *Calvin and English Calvinism to 1649*. Oxford, 1979.

Kickel, W. *Vernunft und Offenbarung bei Theodor Beza*. Neukirchen, 1967.

Kidd, B. J. *The Counter Reformation 1550–1600*. London, 1933.

——, ed. *Documents Illustrative of the Continental Reformation*. Oxford, 1911.

Kingdon, R. M. *Myths about the St. Bartholomew's Day Massacres 1572–1576*. London, 1988.

——. *Church and Society in Reformation Europe*. London, 1985.

——. *Geneva and the Coming Wars of Religion 1555–1563*. Geneva, 1956.

——. *Geneva and the Consolidation of the French Protestant Movement 1564–1572*. Geneva, 1967.

Kirk, J., ed. *Humanism and Reform: The Church in Europe, England and Scotland, 1400–1643*. Oxford, 1991.

Kittelson, J. M. 'Marbach vs. Zanchi. The Resolution of the Controversy in Late Reformation Strasbourg', *Sixteenth Century Journal* 8 (1977), 31–44.

——. 'The Confessional Age: The Late Reformation in Germany', *Reformation Europe: A Guide to Research*. Ed. S. Ozment. St Louis, 1982.

Klauber, M. I. 'Continuity and Discontinuity in Post-Reformation Reformed Theology: An Evaluation of the Muller Thesis', *Journal of the Evangelical Theological Society* 33 (1990), 467–75.

——. 'Between Protestant Orthodoxy and Rationalism: Fundamental Articles in the Early Career of Jean LeClerc', *The Journal of the History of Ideas* 54 (1993), 611–36.

——. 'The Use of Philosophy in the Theology of Johannes Maccovius (1578–1644)', *Calvin Theological Journal* 30 (1995), 376–91.

Klempa, W. 'The Concept of the Covenant in Sixteenth and Seventeenth-Century Continental and British Reformed Theology', *Major Themes in the Reformed Tradition*. Ed. D. K. McKim. Grand Rapids, 1992.

——. 'John Calvin on Natural Law', *John Calvin and the Church: A Prism of Reform*. Ed. T. George. Louisville, 1990.

Klooster, F. H. 'The Priority of Ursinus in the Composition of the Heidelberg Catechism', *Controversy and Conciliation: The Palatinate Reformation, 1559-1618*. Ed. D. Visser. Pittsburgh, 1986.

——. 'The Heidelberg Catechism: Origin and History', Unpublished syllabus. Calvin Theological Seminary, 1989.

——. 'Calvin's Attitude Toward the Heidelberg Catechism', *Later Calvinism. International Perspectives*. Ed. W. F. Graham. Kirksville, MO, 1994.

Knetsch, F. J. R. 'Church Ordinances and Regulations of the Dutch Synods "Under the Cross" Compared with the French (1559-1563)', *Humanism and Reform: the Church in Europe, England, and Scotland, 1400-1643*. Ed. J. Kirk. Oxford, 1991.

Knox, R. B., ed. *Reformation, Conformity and Dissent*. London, 1977.

Knudsen, R. D. 'Calvinism as a Cultural Force', *John Calvin: His Influence on the Western World*. Ed. W. S. Reid. Grand Rapids, 1982.

Koenigsberger, H. G. and G. L. Mosse. *Europe in the Sixteenth Century*. London, 1968.

——. 'The Empire of Charles V in Europe', *The New Cambridge Modern History*. Vol. 2, *The Reformation: 1520-1559*. Ed. G. R. Elton. Second edition. Cambridge, 1990.

——. 'The Politics of Philip II', *Sixteenth Century Essays and Studies*. Vol. 28, *Politics, Religion and Democracy in Early Modern Europe*. Ed. M. R. Thorp and A. J. Slavin. Kirksville, MO, 1994.

Kolb, R. 'Jacob Andrae 1528-1590', *Shapers of Religious Traditions in Germany, Switzerland, and Poland 1500-1600*. Ed. J. Raitt. New Haven, 1981.

——. 'Luther, Augsburg, and the Concept of Authority in the Late Reformation: Ursinus vs. The Lutherans', *Controversy and Conciliation: Reformation and The Palatinate, 1559-1583*. Ed. D. Visser. Pittsburgh, 1986.

——. *Martin Luther as Prophet, Teacher, and Hero*. Grand Rapids, 1999.

Korn, W. E. 'Die Lehre von Christi Person und Werk', *Handbuch zum Heidelberger Katechismus*. Ed. L. Coenen. Neukirchen-Vluyn, 1963.

Kouri, E. I. and T. Scott, eds. *Politics and Society in Reformation Europe: Essays for Sir Geoffery Elton on his Sixty-Fifth Birthday*. London, 1987.

Kretzmann, N. and E. Stump, eds. *The Cambridge Companion to Aquinas*. Cambridge, 1993.

Kristeller, P. O. *Renaissance Thought and its Sources*. Ed. M. Mooney. New York, 1979.

Krumm, J. M. 'Continental Protestantism and Elizabethan Anglicanism (1570-1595)', *Reformation Studies: Essays in Honor of Roland Bainton*. Ed. F. H. Littell. Richmond, 1962.

Kusukawa, S. *The Transformation of Natural Philosophy: The Case of Philip Melanchthon*. Cambridge, 1995.

Lake, P. and M. Dowling, eds. *Protestantism and the National Church in Sixteenth Century England*. London, 1987.

Lane, A. N. S. 'Calvin's Use of the Fathers and Medievals', *Calvin Theological Journal* 16 (1981), 149-205.

——. 'The Quest for the Historical Calvin', *The Evangelical Quarterly* 55 (1983), 95-113.

Lang, A. 'The Reformation and Natural Law', *Calvin and the Reformation*. Ed. W. P. Armstrong. New York, 1909.

——. *Der Heidelberger Katechismus zum 350 jährigen Gedächtnis seiner Entstehung*. Leipzig, 1913.

Lau, F. and E. Bizer, *A History of the Reformation in Germany to 1555*. Trans. B. H. Hardy. London, 1969.

Leithart, P. 'That Eminent Pagan: Calvin's Use of Cicero in Institutes 1.1.5', *Westminster Theological Journal* 52 (1990), 1–12.

——. 'Stoic Elements in Calvin's Doctrine of the Christian Life. Part I: Original Corruption, Natural Law, and the Order of the Soul', *Westminster Theological Journal* 55 (1993), 31–54.

——. 'Stoic Elements in Calvin's Doctrine of the Christian Life. Part II: Mortification', *Westminster Theological Journal* 55 (1993), 191–208.

——. 'Stoic Elements in Calvin's Doctrine of the Christian Life. Part III: Christian Moderation', *Westminster Theological Journal* 56 (1994), 59–85.

Leonard, E. G. *A History of Protestantism*. Ed. H. H. Rowley and trans. J. M. H. Reid and R. M. Bethell. 2 vols. London, 1965–7.

Letham, R. W. A. 'Faith and Assurance in Early Calvinism: A Model of Continuity and Diversity', *Later Calvinism. International Perspectives*. Ed. W. F. Graham. Kirksville, MO, 1994.

——. 'Saving Faith and Assurance in Reformed Theology: Zwingli to the Synod of Dort', 2 vols. Ph.D. Thesis. University of Aberdeen, 1979.

——. 'Amandus Polanus: A Neglected Theologian?', *The Sixteenth Century Journal* 21 (1990), 463–76.

——. 'The *Foedus Operum*: Some Factors Accounting For Its Development', *The Sixteenth Century Journal* 14 (1983), 457–67.

——. 'Theodore Beza: A Reassessment', *The Scottish Journal of Theology* 40 (1987), 25–40.

Lewis, C. S. *English Literature in the Sixteenth Century*. Oxford, 1954.

Lewis, G. 'Calvinism in Geneva in the Time of Calvin and Beza 1541–1605', *International Calvinism 1541–1715*. Ed. M. Prestwich. Oxford, 1985.

——. 'The Geneva Academy', *Calvinism in Europe, 1540–1620*. Ed. A. Pettegree, A. Duke and G. Lewis. Cambridge, 1994.

Lillback, P. A. 'The Binding of God: Calvin's Role in the Development of Covenant Theology', Ph.D. Diss., Westminster Theological Seminary, 1985.

——. *The Binding of God: Calvin's Role in the Development of Covenant Theology*. Grand Rapids, 2001.

——. 'The Continuing Conundrum: Calvin and the Conditionality of the Covenant', *Calvin Theological Journal* 29 (1994), 42–74.

——. 'Ursinus' Development of the Covenant of Creation: A Debt to Melanchthon or Calvin?', *Westminster Theological Journal* 43 (1981), 247–88.

Lindberg, C. *The European Reformations*. Oxford, 1996.

Linder, R. D. 'Calvinism and Humanism: The First Generation', *Church History* 44 (1975), 167–81.

——. 'Early Calvinists and Martin Luther: A Study in Evangelical Solidarity', *Regnum, Religio et Ratio: Essays Presented to Robert M. Kindon*. Ed. J. Friedman. Kirksville, MO, 1987.

Lindsay, T. M. *A History of The Reformation*. 2 vols. New York, 1922.

—. 'The Covenant Theology', *British a n d Foreign Evangelical Review* 109 (1879).

Little, D. 'Calvin and the Prospects for a Christian Theory of Natural Law', *Norm and Context in Christian Ethics*. New York, 1968.

Lobstein, P. *An Introduction to Protestant Dogmatics*. Trans. A. M. Smith. Chicago, 1902.

Lohff, W. 'Legitimate Limits of Doctrinal Pluralism According to the Formula of Concord', *Sixteenth Century Journal* 8 (1977), 23–38.

Lohse, B. *Martin Luther: An Introduction to His Life and Work*. Edinburgh, 1986.

Lortz, J. *The Reformation in Germany*. 2 vols. Trans. R. Walls. London, 1968.

Luscombe, D. E. 'Natural Morality and Natural Law', *The Cambridge History of Later Medieval Philosophy*. Ed. N. Kretzmann et al. Cambridge, 1982.

Lyall, F. 'Of Metaphors and Analogies: Legal Language and Covenant Theology', *Scottish Journal of Theology* 32 (1979), 1–17.

Maag, K. 'Education and Training for the Calvinist Ministry: the Academy of Geneva, 1559–1620', *The Reformation of the Parishes: The Ministry and Reformation in Town and Country*. Ed. A. Pettegree. Manchester, 1993.

—. *Seminary or University? The Genevan Academy and Reformed Higher Education, 1560–1620*. Aldershot, 1995.

Mackinnon, J. *Luther and the Reformation*. 4 vols. London, 1925–30.

Manschrek, C. L. *Melanchthon, the Quiet Reformer*. New York, 1958.

Marsden, G. 'Perry Miller's Rehabilitation of the Puritans: A Critique', *Church History* 39 (1970), 91–105.

Maruyama, T. *The Ecclesiology of Theodore Beza*. Geneva, 1978.

Marx, J. *Caspar Olevian oder der Calvinismus in Trier im Jahre 1559*. Mainz, 1846.

Mayer, L. *History of the German Reformed Church*. Vol. 1. Philadelphia, 1851.

McComish, W. A. *The Epigones*. Allison Park, PA, 1989.

McCoy, C. S. 'The Centrality of Covenant in the Political Philosophy of Johannes Althusius', *Politische Theorie des Johannes Althusius*. Ed. K.-W. Dahm et al. Berlin, 1988.

—. 'The Covenant Theology of Johannes Cocceius', Ph.D. Diss., Yale University, 1956.

—. 'Johannes Cocceius: Federal Theologian', *Scottish Journal of Theology* 16 (1963), 352–70.

McCoy, C. S. and J. W. Baker. *Fountainhead of Federalism: Heinrich Bullinger and the Covenantal Tradition with a Translation of De Testamento seu Foedere Dei Unico et Aeterno (1534)*. Louisville, 1991.

McGiffert, A. C. *A History of Christian Thought*. 2 vols. London, 1933.

—. *Protestant Thought Before Kant*. London, 1919.

McGiffert, M. 'From Moses to Adam: The Making of the Covenant of Works', *The Sixteenth Century Journal* 19 (1988), 131–55.

—. 'The Perkensian Moment of Federal Theology', *Calvin Theological Journal* 29 (1994), 117–48.

—. 'William Tyndale's Conception of Covenant', *Journal of Ecclesiastical History* 32 (1981), 167–84.

McGrath, A. E. '"Augustinianism"? A Critical Assessment of the So-called "Medieval Augustinian Tradition" on Justification', *Augustiniana* 31 (1981), 247–67.

—. 'The Anti-Pelagian Structure of Nominalist Doctrines of Justification', *Ephemerides Theologicae Louvanienses* 57 (1981), 107–119.

—. 'Forerunners of the Reformation? A Critical Examination of the Evidence for Precursors of the Reformation Doctrine of Justification', *Harvard Theological Review* 75 (1982), 219–42.

—. 'Humanist Elements in the Early Reformed Doctrine of Justification', *Archiv für Reformationsgeschichte* 73 (1982), 5–20.

—. *The Genesis of Doctrine*. Oxford, 1990.

—. *The Intellectual Origins of the European Reformation*. Oxford, 1987.

—. 'John Calvin and Late Medieval Thought: A Study in Late Medieval Influences on John Calvin's Doctrinal Development', *Archiv für Reformationsgeschichte* 77 (1986), 58–78.

—. 'Justice and Justification: Semantic and Juristic Aspects of the Christian Doctrine of Justification', *Scottish Journal of Theology* 35 (1982), 403–18.

—. 'Justification and the Reformation. The Significance of the Doctrine of Justification by Faith to Sixteenth Century Urban Communities', *Archiv für Reformationsgeschichte* 81 (1990), 5–19.

—. '*Mira et Nova Diffinitio Iustitiae*: Luther and Scholastic Doctrines of Justification', *Archiv für Reformationsgeschichte* 74 (1983), 37–60.

—. 'The Moral Theory of the Atonement: An Historical and Theological Critique', *Scottish Journal of Theology* 38 (1985), 205–20.

—. *A Life of John Calvin: A Study in the Shaping of Western Culture*. Oxford, 1990.

—. *Iustitia Dei: A History of the Christian Doctrine of Justification*. 2 vols. Cambridge, 1986.

—. *Luther's Theology of the Cross: Martin Luther's Theological Breakthrough*. Oxford, 1985.

—. *Reformation Thought: An Introduction*. Oxford, 1988.

McKee, E. A. and B. G. Armstrong, eds. *Preaching in the Reformed Tradition: Historical Studies in Honor of Edward A. Dowey*. Atlanta, 1990.

McKee, W. W. 'The Idea of Covenant in Early English Puritanism (1580–1643)', Ph.D. Diss., Yale University, 1948.

McKim, D. K., ed. *Encyclopedia of the Reformed Faith*. Louisville, 1992.

—. *Major Themes in the Reformed Tradition*. Grand Rapids, 1992.

—. 'William Perkins and the Theology of the Covenant', *Studies of the Church in History*. Ed. H. Davies. Allison Park, PA, 1983.

McNeil, D. O. *Guillaume Budé and Humanism in the Reign of Francis I*. Geneva, 1975.

McNeill, J. T. 'The Church in Sixteenth Century Reformed Theology', *Journal of Religion* 22 (1942), 251–69.

—. *The History and Character of Calvinism*. Oxford, 1954.

—. 'Natural Law in Luther's Thought', *Church History* 10 (1941).

—. 'Natural Law in the Teaching of the Reformers', *Journal of Religion* 26 (1946), 168–82.

McPhee, I. 'Conserver or Transformer of Calvin's Theology? A Study of the Origins and Development of Theodore Beza's Thought 1550–1570', Ph.D. Thesis, Cambridge University, 1979.

McWilliams, D. B. 'The Covenant Theology of the *Westminster Confession of Faith* and Recent Criticism', *Westminster Theological Journal* 53 (1991), 109–24.

Meijering, E. P. *Melanchthon and Patristic Thought: The Doctrines of Christ, Grace, the Trinity and the Creation*. Leiden, 1983.

Menk, G. 'Caspar Olevian während der Berleburger und Herborner Zeit (1577–1587)', *Monatshefte für Evangelische Kirchengeschichte des Rheinlandes* 37/38 (1988–89), 139–204.

—. *Die hohe Schule Herborn in ihrer Früzeit (1584–1660) ein Beitrag zur Hochschulen des deutschen Kalvinismus im zie alter der Reformation.* Wiesbaden, 1981.

Metz, W. *Necessitas Satisfactionis? Ein systematische Studie zu den Fragen 12–18 des Heidelberger Katechismus.* Zürich, 1970.

Midelfort, H. C. E. 'Curious Georgics: The German Nobility and Their Crisis of Legitimacy in the Late Sixteenth Century', *Germania Illustrata: Essays on Early Modern Germany Presented to Gerald Strauss.* Ed. A. C. Fix and S. C. Karant-Nunn. Kirksville, MO, 1992.

—. 'Toward a Social History of Ideas in the German Reformation', *Pietas et Societas: New Trends in Reformation Social History. Essays in Honor of Harold J. Grimm.* Ed. K. C. Sessions and P. N. Bebb. Kirksville, MO, 1985.

—. *Witch Hunting in Southwestern Germany 1562–1684: The Social and Intellectual Foundations.* Stanford, CA, 1972.

Miller, A. O. et al. *The Heidelberg Catechism with Commentary.* Philadelphia, 1962.

Miller, C. 'The Spread of Calvinism in Switzerland, Germany, and France', *The Rise and Development of Calvinism.* Ed. J. Bratt. Grand Rapids, 1959.

Miller, P. *The New England Mind: The Seventeenth Century.* New York, 1939.

—. '"Preparation for Salvation" in Seventeenth-Century New England', *Journal of the History of Ideas* 4 (1943), 253–86.

Moeller, W. *History of the Christian Church.* 3 vols. Trans. J. H. Freese. London, 1892–1900.

Möller, B. *Imperial Cities and the Reformation: Three Essays.* Trans. H. C. E. Midelfort and M. U. Edwards. Philadelphia, 1972.

Møller, J. G. 'The Beginnings of Puritan Covenant Theology', *Journal of Ecclesiastical History* 14 (1963), 46–67.

Moltmann, J. 'Covenant or Leviathan? Political Theology for Modern Times', *Scottish Journal of Theology* 47 (1994), 19–41.

—. 'Zur Bedeutung des Petrus Ramus für Philosophie und Theologie im Calvinismus', *Zeitschrift für Kirchengeschichte* 68 (1957), 295–318.

—. *Lexikon für Theologie und Kirche.* s.v. 'Föderaltheologie', 10 vols. Ed. Michael Buchberger. Freiburg, 1957–65.

Monter, W. E. *Enforcing Morality in Early Modern Europe.* London, 1987.

—. *Ritual, Myth and Magic in Early Modern Europe.* Brighton, 1983.

—. *Calvin's Geneva.* New York, 1967.

Müller, E. F. K. s.v. 'Piscator, Johannes', *The New Schaff-Herzogg Encyclopedia of Religious Knowledge.* 12 vols. Ed. S. M. Jackson. London, 1912.

Müller, G. 'Alliance and Confession: The Theological-Historical Development and Ecclesiastical-Political Significance of Reformation Confessions', *Sixteenth Century Journal* 8 (1977), 124–40.

Müller, K. 'Caspar Olevian – Reformator aus Leidenschaft Zum 400. Todestag am 15. März 1987'. *Monatshefte für Evangelische Kirchengeschichte des Rheinlandes*, 37/38 (1988-89), 13–138.

Muller, R. A. 'Arminius and the Scholastic Tradition', *Calvin Theological Journal* 24 (1989), 263–77.

Muller, R. A. and J. L. Thompson, eds. *Biblical Interpretation in the Era of the Reformation.* Grand Rapids, 1996.

—. 'Biblical Interpretation in the Era of the Reformation: The View from the Middle Ages', *Biblical Interpretation in the Era of the Reformation: Essays Presented to David C. Steinmetz in Honor of the Sixtieth Birthday.* Ed. R. A. Muller and J. Thompson. Grand Rapids, 1996.

—. 'Calvin and the "Calvinists": Assessing Continuities and Discontinuities Between the Reformation and Orthodoxy' (1), *Calvin Theological Journal* 30 (1995), 345–75.

—. 'Calvin and the "Calvinists": Assessing Continuities and Discontinuities Between the Reformation and Orthodoxy' (2), *Calvin Theological Journal* 31 (1996), 125–60.

—. *Christ and the Decree: Christology and Predestination in Reformed Theology from Calvin to Perkins.* Durham, NC, 1986.

—. 'Christ in the Eschaton: Calvin and Moltmann on the Duration of the *Munus Regium*', *Harvard Theological Review* 74 (1981), 31–59.

—. 'Covenant and Conscience in English Reformed Theology: Three Variations on a Seventeenth Century Theme', *Westminster Theological Journal* 42 (1979-80), 308–34.

—. 'The Covenant of Works and the Stability of Divine Law in Seventeenth-Century Reformed Orthodoxy: A Study in the Theology of Herman Witsius and Wilhelmus à Brakel', *Calvin Theological Journal* 29 (1994), 75–101.

—. 'The Debate over the Vowel Points and the Crisis in Orthodox Hermeneutics', *The Journal of Medieval and Renaissance Studies* 10 (1980), 53–72.

—. *Dictionary of Latin and Greek Theological Terms Drawn Principally from Protestant Scholastic Theology.* Grand Rapids, 1985.

—. 'Duplex Cognitio Dei in the Theology of Early Reformed Orthodoxy', *Sixteenth Century Journal* 10 (1979), 51–61.

—. 'The Era of Protestant Orthodoxy', *Theological Education in the Evangelical Tradition.* Ed. D. G. Hart and R. A. Muller. Grand Rapids, 1996.

—. 'The Federal Motif in Seventeenth Century Arminian Theology', *Netherlands Archief voor Kerkgeschiedenis* 62 (1982), 102–22.

—. 'Fides and Cognitio in Relation to the Problem of Intellect and Will in the Theology of John Calvin', *Calvin Theological Journal* 25 (1990), 207–24.

—. 'Giving Direction to Theology: The Scholastic Dimension', *Journal of the Evangelical Theological Society* 28 (1985), 183–93.

—. 'God, Predestination, and the Integrity of the Created Order: A Note on Patterns in Arminius' Theology', *Later Calvinism: International Perspectives.* Ed. W. F. Graham. Kirksville, MO, 1994.

—. *God, Creation, and Providence in the Thought of Jacob Arminius*. Grand Rapids, 1991.

—. 'Perkins' *A Golden Chaine*: Predestinarian System or Schematized *Ordo Salutis?*', *Sixteenth Century Journal* 9 (1978), 69–81

—. 'Scholasticism Protestant and Catholic: Francis Turretin on the Object and Principles of Theology', *Church History* 55 (1986), 193–205.

—. 'The Myth of "Decretal" Theology', *Calvin Theological Journal* 30 (1995), 159–67.

—. s.v. 'Orthodoxy, Reformed', *Encyclopedia of the Reformed Faith*. Ed. D. K. McKim and D. F. Wright. Edinburgh, 1992.

—. 'The Use and Abuse of a Document: Beza's *Tabula Praedestinationis*, the Bolsec Controversy, and the Origins of Reformed Orthodoxy', *Protestant Scholasticism: Essays in Reassessment*. Eds. C. R. Trueman and R. S. Clark. Carlisle, 1998.

—. '*Vera Philosophia cum sacra Theologia nusquam pugnat*: Keckermann on Philosophy, Theology, and the Problem of Double Truth', *Sixteenth Century Journal* 15 (1984), 341–65.

—. *Post-Reformation Reformed Dogmatics*. 2 vols. Grand Rapids, 1987–.

—. *Post-Reformation Reformed Dogmatics*. Second edn. 3 vols. Grand Rapids, 2003.

Murray, J. 'Calvin's Doctrine of Creation', *Westminster Theological Journal* 17 (1954), 21–43.

—. *The Collected Writings of John Murray*. 4 vols. Edinburgh, 1976–82.

—. *Calvin on Scripture and Divine Sovereignty*. Grand Rapids, 1960.

—. *The Covenant of Grace*. London, 1953.

Naphy, W. G. *Calvin and the Consolidation of the Genevan Reformation*. Manchester, 1994.

Nauert, C. G. 'The Clash of Humanists and Scholastics: An Approach to Pre-Reformation Controversies', *Sixteenth Century Journal* 4 (1973), 1–18.

Neuser, W. H., ed. *Calvinus Sacrae Scripturae*. Grand Rapids, 1994.

—. 'Calvin's Teaching on the *Notae Fidelium*: An Unnoticed Part of the *Institutio* 4.1.8', Trans. M. S. Burrows. *Probing the Reformed Tradition: Historical Studies in Honor of Edward A. Dowey, Jr*. Louisville, 1989.

Nevin, J. W. *History and Genius of the Heidelberg Catechism*. Philadelphia, 1847.

—. *The Heidelberg Catechism, in German, Latin and English: with an historical introduction*. New York, 1863.

—. *The Mystical Presence*. Philadelphia, 1867.

Newman, J. H. *Lectures on Justification*. London, 1838.

—. *An Essay on the Development of Christian Doctrine*. London, 1845.

Ney, J. s.v. 'Olevianus, Kaspar', *The New Schaff-Herzogg Encyclopedia of Religious Knowledge*. 12 vols. Ed. S. M. Jackson. London, 1912.

—. s.v. Olevianus, Kaspar', *Realencyclopädie für Protestantische Theologie und Kirche*. Ed. A. Hauck. Leipzig, 1896-1909.

—. s.v. 'Tremellius, Emmanuel', *The New Schaff-Herzogg Encyclopedia of Religious Knowledge*. 12 vols. Ed. S. M. Jackson. London, 1912.

Nichols, J. H. 'The Intent of the Calvinistic Liturgy', *The Heritage of John Calvin*. Ed. J. H. Bratt. Grand Rapids, 1973.

—. *History of Christianity 1650–1950: Secularization of the West.* New York, 1956.

—, ed. *The Mercersberg Theology.* New York, 1966.

Nicole, R. 'The Doctrine of Definite Atonement in the Heidelberg Catechism', *Gordon Review* 3 (1964), 138–45.

—. 'John Calvin's view of the Extent of the Atonement', *Westminster Theological Journal* 47 (1985), 197–225.

Niesel, W. *The Theology of Calvin.* Trans. H. Knight. Philadelphia, 1956.

Nijenhuis, W. 'Calvin and the Augsburg Confession', *Ecclesia Reformata: Studies on the Reformation.* Trans. M. Foran. Leiden, 1972.

—. 'Calvin's "*Subito Conversio*": Notes on a Hypothesis', *Ecclesia Reformata: Studies on the Reformation.* Vol. 2. Leiden, 1994.

—. *Adrianus Saravia [c.1532–1613].* Trans. J. E. Platt. Leiden, 1980.

Nischan, B. 'The Palatinate and Brandenberg's Second Reformation', *Conflict and Conciliation: The Palatinate Reformation, 1559–1618.* Ed. D. Visser. Pittsburgh, 1986.

—. '"The Fractio Panis": A Reformed Communion Practice in Late Reformation Germany', *Church History* 53 (1984), 17–29.

—. 'Reformation or Deformation? Lutheran and Reformed Views of Martin Luther in Brandenburg's "Second Reformation"', *Pietas et Societas: New Trends in Reformation Social History. Essays in Honor of Harold J. Grimm.* Ed. K. C. Sessions and P. N. Bebb. Kirksville, MO, 1985.

Norman, J. G. G. s.v. 'Olevianus, Kaspar', *New International Dictionary of the Christian Church.* Second edn. Exeter, 1978.

Nugent, D. *Ecumenism in the Age of the Reformation: The Colloquy of Poissy.* Cambridge, MA, 1974.

Oakley, F. *Omnipotence, Covenant and Order: An Excursion in the History of Ideas from Abelard to Leibniz.* London, 1984.

Oberman, H. A. and F. A. James, eds. *Via Augustini: Augustine in the later Middle Ages, Renaissance, and Reformation: essays in honor of Damasus Trapp.* Leiden, 1991.

— and T. A. Brady, eds. *Itinerarium Italicum. The Profile of the Italian Renaissance in the Mirror of its European Transformations: Dedicated to Paul Oskar Kristeller.* Leiden, 1975.

—. *The Dawn of the Reformation.* Edinburgh, 1986.

—. 'Europa Afflicta: The Reformation of the Refugees', *Archiv für Reformationsgeschichte* 83 (1992), 91–111.

—. 'The "Extra" Dimension in the Theology of Calvin', *Journal of Ecclesiastical History* 21 (1970), 43–64.

—. *Forerunners of the Reformation: The Shape of Late Medieval Thought.* Philadelphia, 1981.

—. *The Harvest of Medieval Theology.* Cambridge, MA, 1963.

—. 'The Impact of the Reformation: Problems and Perspectives', *Politics and Society in Reformation Europe: Essays for Sir Geoffery Elton on his Sixty-Fifth Birthday.* Ed. E. I. Kouri and T. Scott. London, 1987.

—. 'Initia Calvini: The Matrix of Calvin's Reformation', *Calvinus Sacrae Scripturae Professor.* Ed. W. H. Neuser. Grand Rapids, 1994.

—. *Luther and the Dawn of the Modern Era.* Leiden, 1974.

——. *Luther: Man Between God and the Devil*. Trans. E. Walliser-Schwarzbart. Repr. London, 1993.

——. *Masters of the Reformation: The Emergence of a New Intellectual Climate in Europe*. Trans. D. Martin. Cambridge, 1981.

——. *The Reformation. Roots and Ramifications*. Trans. A. C. Gow. Edinburgh, 1994.

——. 'Wir sein pettler. *Hoc est verum*: Bund und Gnade in der Theologie de Mittelalters und Reformation', *Zeitschrift für Kirchengeschichte* 78 (1967), 232–52.

Old, H. O. *The Shaping of the Reformed Baptismal Rite of the Sixteenth Century*. Grand Rapids, 1992.

Olsen, A. L. 'The Hermeneutical Vision of Martin Chemnitz: The Role of Scripture, and Tradition in the Teaching Church', *Augustine, The Harvest, and Theology (1300–1650)*. Ed. K. Hagen. Leiden, 1990.

Olson, O. K. 'The *Fractio Panis* in Heidelberg and Antwerp', *Controversy and Conciliation: The Palatinate Reformation, 1559–1618*. Ed. D. Visser. Pittsburgh, 1986.

——. 'Matthias Flacius Illyricus 1520–1575', *Shapers of Religious Traditions in Germany, Switzerland, and Poland 1500–1600*. Ed. J. Raitt. New Haven, 1981.

Ong, W. J. *Ramus: Method and the Decay of Dialogue*. Cambridge, MA, 1958.

Osterhaven, E. M. 'Calvin on the Covenant', *Readings in Calvin's Theology*. Grand Rapids, 1984.

Oxford University History Faculty. 'Calvin and Calvinists in Europe 1550–1620', History Faculty syllabus. Oxford University, n.d.

Ozment, S. E., ed. *Reformation Europe: A Guide to Research*. St Louis, 1982.

——. *The Age of Reform 1250–1550: An Intellectual and Religious History of Late Medieval and Reformation Europe*. London, 1980.

——, ed. *The Reformation in Medieval Perspective*. Chicago, 1971.

——. *The Reformation in the Cities. The Appeal of Protestantism to Sixteenth Century Germany and Switzerland*. London, 1975.

Packer, J. I. 'Arminianisms', *Through Christ's Word: A Festschrift for Dr. Philip E. Hughes*. Ed. W. R. Godfrey and J. L. Boyd III. Phillipsburg, 1985.

——. 'Calvin the Theologian', *John Calvin: A Collection of Essays*. Grand Rapids, 1966.

Pannenberg, W. 'Theology as Science in the History of Theology', *Theology and the Philosophy of Science*. Trans. F. McDonagh. Philadelphia, 1976.

Parker, T. H. L. *Commentaries on the Epistle to the Romans 1532–1542*. Edinburgh, 1986.

——. *The Doctrine of the Knowledge of God*. London, 1952.

Parker, T. M. 'Protestantism and Confessional Strife', *The New Cambridge Modern History*, vol. 3. Ed. R. B. Wernham. Cambridge, 1968.

Partee, C. 'Calvin and Experience', *Scottish Journal of Theology* 26 (1973).

——. 'Calvin's Central Dogma Again', *The Sixteenth Century Journal* 18 (1987), 191–9.

——. *Calvin and Classical Philosophy*. Leiden, 1977.

Pauck, W. *The Heritage of the Reformation*. New York, 1961.

Paulsen, F. *The German Universities*. Trans. E. D. Perry. New York, 1895.

Pearson, A. F. S. *Thomas Cartwright and Elizabethan Puritanism 1535–1603.* Cambridge, 1925.

Pelikan, J. *The Christian Tradition. A History of the Development of Doctrine.* 5 vols. Chicago, 1984.

—. *Historical Theology: Continuity and Change in Christian Doctrine.* London, 1971.

Peterson, R. A. *Calvin's Doctrine of the Atonement.* Phillipsburg, NJ, 1983.

Peterson, R. L. *Preaching in the Last Days: The Theme of 'Two Witnesses' in the Sixteenth and Seventeenth Centuries.* Oxford, 1993.

Pettegree, A. 'Coming to Terms with Victory: The Building of a Calvinist Church in Holland, 1572–1590', *Calvinism in Europe, 1540–1620.* Ed. A. Pettegree, A. Duke and G. Lewis. Cambridge, 1994.

—. 'The Struggle for an Orthodox Church: Calvinists and Anabaptists in East Friesland, 1554–1578', *Bulletin of the John Rylands Library* 70 (1988), 45–59.

Platt, J. E. *Reformed Thought and Protestant Scholasticism.* Leiden, 1982.

—. 'Sixtinus Amama (1593–1629): Franecker Professor and Citizen of the Republic of Letters', *Universiteit te Franeker, 1585–1811.* Ed. G. T. Jensma, F. R. H. Smit, F. Westra. Leeuwarden, 1985.

—. 'Eirenical Anglicans at the Synod of Dort', *Reform and Reformation: England and the Continent c. 1500–1750.* Ed. D. Baker. Oxford, 1979.

Poole, D. N. J. *History of the Covenant Concept from the Bible to Johannes Cloppenburg.* Lewiston, 1995.

Porter, C. W. *Reformation and Reaction in Tudor Cambridge.* Cambridge, 1958.

Porter, T. C. 'The Authors of the Heidelberg Catechism', *Tercentenary Monument in Commemoration of the Three Hundredth Anniversary of the Heidelberg Catechism.* Chambersburg, PA, 1863.

Postema, G. J. 'Calvin's Alleged Rejection of Natural Theology', *Scottish Journal of Theology* 24 (1971), 423–34.

Posthumus-Meyjes, G. H. M. 'Protestant Irenicism in the Sixteenth and Seventeenth Centuries', *The End of Strife.* Ed. D. Loades. Edinburgh, 1984.

—. 'Charles Perrot (1541–1608), His Opinion on a Writing of Georg Cassander', *Humanism and Reform: the Church in Europe, England, and Scotland, 1400–1643.* Ed. J Kirk. Oxford, 1991.

—. 'Jean Hotman's *Syllabus* of Eirenical Literature', Trans. J. C. Grayson. *Reform and Reformation: England and the Continent c.1500–c.1750.* Ed. D. Baker. Oxford, 1979.

Potter, G. R., ed. *The New Cambridge Modern History.* 14 vols. Cambridge, 1957–61.

Press, V. *Calvinismus und Territorialstaat. Regierung und Zentralbehorden der Kurpfalz 1559–1619.* Stuttgart, 1970.

Prestwich, M., ed. *International Calvinism 1541–1715.* Oxford, 1985.

—. 'The Changing Face of Calvinism', *International Calvinism 1541–1715.* Ed. M. Prestwich. Oxford, 1985.

Preus, R. D. 'The Influence of the Formula of Concord on the Later Lutheran Orthodoxy', *Discord, Dialogue and Concord: Studies in the Lutheran Reformation's Formula of Concord.* Ed. L. W. Spitz and W. Lohff. Philadelphia, 1977.

—. *The Theology of Post-Reformation Lutheranism: A Study of Theological Prolegomena.* 2 vols. St Louis, 1970.

Quere, R. W. 'Melanchthonian Motifs in the Formula's Eucharistic Christology', *Discord, Dialogue and Concord: Studies in the Lutheran Reformation's Formula of Concord*. Ed. L. W. Spitz and W. Lohff. Philadelphia, 1977.

Rainbow, J. *The Will of God and the Cross*. Allison Park, PA, 1990.

Raitt, J. 'Calvin's Use of Persona', *Calvinus Ecclesiae Genevenesis Custos*. Ed. W. Neuser. New York, 1984.

—. *The Colloquy of Montbéliard: Religion and Politics in the Sixteenth Century*. Oxford, 1993.

—. 'Elizabeth of England, John Casmir and the Protestant League', *Controversy and Conciliation: The Palatinate Reformation, 1559–1618*. Ed. D. Visser. Pittsburgh, 1986.

—. 'The French Reformed Theological Response', *Discord, Dialogue and Concord: Studies in the Lutheran Reformation's Formula of Concord*. Ed. L. W. Spitz and W. Lohff. Philadelphia, 1977.

—. 'Three Inter-Related Principles in Calvin's Unique Doctrine of Infant Baptism', *Sixteenth Century Journal* 11 (1980), 51–62.

—, ed. *Shapers of Religious Traditions in Germany, Switzerland, and Poland 1560–1600*. New Haven, 1981.

—. *The Eucharistic Theology of Theodore Beza*. Chambersburg, PA, 1972.

Rankin, W. D. 'Carnal Union with Christ in the Theology of T. F. Torrance', Ph.D. Thesis. University of Edinburgh, 1990.

Reid, W. S. 'Calvin and the Founding of the Academy of Geneva', *Westminster Theological Journal* 18 (1955), 1–33.

Rice, E. F. Jr, ed. *The Prefatory Epistles of Jacques Lefèvre d'Etaples and related texts*. New York, 1972.

Richards, G. W. *The Heidelberg Catechism. Historical and Doctrinal Studies*. Philadelphia, 1913.

Richter, A. L., ed. *Die evangelischen Kirchenordnungen des sechszehnten Jahrhunderts*. Leipzig, 1871.

Rist, J. M. *Stoic Philosophy*. Cambridge, 1969.

Ritschl, A. *Three Essays*. Trans. P. Hefner. Philadelphia, 1972.

—. *A Critical History of the Christian Doctrine of Justification and Reconciliation*. Trans. J. S. Black. Edinburgh, 1872.

Ritschl, O. *Dogmengeschichte des Protestantismus*. 4 vols. Göttingen, 1926.

Robertson, O. P. 'Current Reformed Thinking on the Nature of the Divine Covenants', *Westminster Theological Journal* 40 (1970), 63–76.

Rodriguez-Salgado, M. J. 'The Hapsburg-Valois Wars', *The New Cambridge Modern History*. Vol. 2, *The Reformation: 1520–1559*. Ed. G. R. Elton. Second edition. Cambridge, 1990.

Rogers Jr, E. F. 'Good Works and Assurance of Salvation in Three Traditions: *Fides Praevisa*, the Practical Syllogism, and Merit', *Scottish Journal of Theology* 50 (1997): 131–56.

Rogers, J. and D. K. McKim. *The Authority and Interpretation of the Bible*. San Francisco, 1979.

Rogness, M. *Philip Melanchthon: Reformer Without Honor*. Minneapolis, 1969.

Rolston III, H. 'Responsible Man in Reformed Theology: Calvin versus the *Westminster Confession*', *Scottish Journal of Theology* 23 (1970), 129–55.

—. *John Calvin versus the Westminster Confession*. Richmond, VA, 1972.

Rotondò, A. *Calvin and the Italian Anti-Trinitarians*. Trans. J. and A. Tedeschi. St Louis, 1968.

Rummel, E. *The Humanist-Scholastic Debate in the Renaissance and Reformation*. Cambridge, MA, 1995.

Rupp, G. *Patterns of Reformation*. London, 1969.

——. *The Righteousness of God*. London, 1953.

Sanbach, F. H. *The Stoics*. Bristol, 1989.

Schaefer, P. R. 'The Spiritual Brotherhood on the Habits of the Heart: Cambridge Protestants and the Doctrine of Sanctification from William Perkins to Thomas Shepard', D.Phil. Thesis. Oxford University, 1994.

Schaff, P., ed. *The Creeds of Christendom*. 3 vols. 6th edition. Grand Rapids, 1983.

——. *History of The Christian Church*. 8 vols. New York, 1910.

Scharlemann, R. *Aquinas and Gerhard: Theological Controversy and Construction in Medieval and Protestant Scholasticism*. New Haven, 1964.

Scheible, H. 'Olevian als Vereteidiger der reformierten Abendmahlslehre', *Bibliotheca Palatina*. Ed. E. Mittler et al. 2 vols. Heidelberg, 1986.

Schilling, H. 'Between the Territorial State and Urban Liberty: Lutheranism and Calvinism in the County of Lippe', Trans. T. A. Brady Jr. *The German People and the Reformation*. Ed. R. P.-C. Hsia. London, 1988.

——. *Civic Calvinism in Northwestern Germany and the Netherlands Sixteenth to Nineteenth Centuries*. Kirksville, MO, 1991.

——. *Religion, Poltical Culture and the Emergence of Early Modern Society: Essays in German and Dutch History*. Trans. S. G. Burnett. Leiden, 1992.

Schnucker, R. V. *Calviniana: The Ideas and Influence of John Calvin*. Kirksville, MO, 1988.

Schrenk, G. *Gottesreich und Bund im älteren Protestantismus, vornehmlich bei Johannes Cocceius*. Gütersloh, 1923.

Schweizer, A. *Dei Glaubenslehre der Evangelisch-Reformierten Kirche*. 2 vols. Zürich, 1844–47.

Scott, J. L. 'The Covenant in the Theology of Karl Barth', *Scottish Journal of Theology* 17 (1964), 182–98.

Scribner, R. W. 'Politics and the Institutionalization of Reform in Germany', *The New Cambridge Modern History*. Vol. 2, *The Reformation: 1520–1559*. Ed. G. R. Elton. Second edition. Cambridge, 1990.

——. *The German Reformation*. London, 1986.

——. 'Ritual and Reformation', *The German People and the Reformation*. Ed. R. P.-C. Hsia. London, 1988.

Seeberg, R. *Textbook of the History of Doctrines*. 2 vols. Trans. C. E. Hay. Philadelphia, 1905.

Shreiner, S. E. *The Theater of his Glory: Nature and the Natural Order in the Thought of John Calvin*. Grand Rapids, 1995.

Sinnema, D. 'Reformed Scholasticism and the Synod of Dort (1618-19)', *John Calvin's Institutes: His Opus Magnum*. Ed. B. J. Van de Walt. Potchefstroom, 1986.

——. 'The Discipline of Ethics in Early Reformed Orthodoxy', *Calvin Theological Journal* 28 (1993), 10–44.

Skinner, Q. *The Foundations of Modern Political Thought*. Cambridge, 1978.

Smeaton, D. D. 'The Wycliffite Choice: Man's Law or God's', *William Tyndale and the Law*. Ed. J. A. R. Dick, A. Richardson. Kirksville, MO, 1994.

Smith, H. B. and P. Schaff, eds. *The Creeds of the Evangelical Protestant Churches*. London, 1877.

Smith, M. H. 'The Church and Covenant Theology', *Journal of the Evangelical Theological Society* 21 (1978), 47–65.

Southern, R. W. *St. Anselm: A Portrait in a Landscape*. Cambridge, 1990.

—. *Western Society and the Church in the Middle Ages*. Harmondsworth, 1970.

Spitz, L. W. 'The Course of German Humanism', *Itinerarium Italicum: The Profile of the Italian Renaissance in the Mirror of its European Transformations*. Ed. H. A. Oberman and T. A. Brady. Leiden, 1975.

—. 'Headwaters of the Reformation: *Studia Humanitas, Luther Senior, et Initia Refomationis*', *Luther and the Dawn of the Modern Era*. Ed. H. A. Oberman. Leiden, 1974.

—. 'The Formula of Concord Then and Now', *Discord, Dialogue and Concord: Studies in the Lutheran Reformation's Formula of Concord*. Ed. L. W. Spitz and W. Lohff. Philadelphia, 1977.

—, ed. *The Protestant Reformation*. Englewood Cliffs, 1966.

—. *The Protestant Reformation 1517–1559*. New York, 1985.

—. *The Religious Renaissance of the German Humanists*. Cambridge, MA, 1963.

—. *The Renaissance and Reformation Movements*. 2 vols. St Louis, 1971.

Steinmetz, D. C. 'Calvin and Abraham: The Interpretation of Romans 4 in the Sixteenth Century', *Church History* 57 (1988), 443–88.

—. 'Calvin and the Natural Knowledge of God', *Via Augustini: Augustine in the later Middle Ages, Renaissance, and Reformation: essays in honor of Damasus Trapp*. Ed. H. A. Oberman and F. A. James. Leiden, 1991.

—. 'Calvin and the Absolute Power of God', *The Journal of Medieval and Renaissance Studies* 18 (1988), 65–79.

—. 'Calvin and His Lutheran Critics', *Lutheran Quarterly* 4 (1990), 179–94.

—. 'Luther and Augustine on Romans 9', *Luther in Context*. Bloomington, IN, 1986.

—. *Luther and Staupitz: An Essay in the Intellectual Origins of the Protestant Reformation*. Durham, NC, 1980.

—. *Misericordia Dei: The Theology of Johannes Von Staupitz in its Late Medieval Setting*. Leiden, 1968.

—. *Reformers in the Wings*. Philadelphia, 1971.

—. 'The Theology of Calvin and Calvinism', *Reformation Europe: A Guide to Research*. Ed. S. Ozment. St Louis, 1982.

—. 'The Scholastic Calvin', *Protestant Scholasticism: Essays in Reassessment*. Paternoster, 1997.

Stek, J. H. '"Covenant" Overload in Reformed Theology', *Calvin Theological Journal* 29 (1994), 12–41.

Stelling-Michaud, S., ed. *Le Livre Du Recteur de L'Académie de Genève (1559–1878)*. 2 vols. Geneva, 1959.

Stephens, W. P. *The Theology of Huldrych Zwingli*. Oxford, 1984.

—. 'Zwingli on John 6:63: "Spiritus est qui vivificat, caro nihil prodest"', *Biblical Interpretation in the Era of the Reformation*. Ed. R. A. Muller and J. L. Thompson. Grand Rapids, 1996.

Stoever, W. K. B. *A Faire and Easie Way to Heaven: Covenant Theology and Antinomianism in Early Massachusetts.* Middletown, CT, 1978.

Stoute, D. A. 'The Origin and Early Development of the Reformed Idea of the Covenant', Ph.D. Thesis. Cambridge University, 1979.

Strauss, G., ed. *Manifestations of Discontent in Germany on the Eve of the Reformation.* Bloomington, IN, 1972.

——, ed. *Pre-Reformation Germany.* London, 1972.

——. 'The Reformation and its Public in an Age of Orthodoxy', *The German People and the Reformation.* Ed. R. P.-C. Hsia. London, 1988.

Strehle, S. *Calvinism, Federalism and Scholasticism: A Study of the Reformed Doctrine of the Covenant.* Bern, 1988.

——. '*Imputatio iustitiae*: Its Origin in Melanchthon, its Opposition in Osiander', *Theologische Zeitschrift* 50 (1994), 201–19.

——. '*Fides aut foedus*: Wittenberg and Zürich in Conflict Over the Gospel', *Sixteenth Century Journal* 23 (1992), 3–20.

Strimple, R. B. 'St. Anselm's *Cur Deus Homo* and John Calvin's Doctrine of the Atonement', *Anselm, Aosta, Bec and Canterbury.* Ed. D. E. Luscombe and G. R. Evans. Sheffield, 1996.

Stroup, G. W. 'Narrative in Calvin's Hermeneutic', *John Calvin and the Church: Prism of Reform.* Louisville, 1990.

Strype, J. *Strype's Works.* 25 vols. Oxford, 1812–24.

Sudhoff, K. 'Sudhoff's Olevianus', *Mercersburg Quarterly Review* 8 (1856), 163–98.

——. *Leben und ausgewählte Schriften der Vater und Begründer der reformierten Kirche.* 10 vols. Ed. J. W. Baum et al. Elberfeld, 1857–63. Vol. 8: *C. Olevianus und Z. Ursinus*, 1857.

Tercentenary Monument in Commemoration of the Three Hundredth Anniversary of the Heidelberg Catechism. Chambersburg, PA, 1863.

Thelemann, O. *An Aid to the Heidelberg Catechism.* Trans. M. Peters. Grand Rapids, 1959.

Thomas, G. M. *The Extent of the Atonement: A Dilemma for Reformed Theology from Calvin to the Consensus.* Carlisle, 1997.

Thompson, B. and H. Berkhof, *Essays on the Heidelberg Catechism.* Philadelphia, 1963.

——. 'The Palatinate Church Order of 1563', *Church History* 23 (1954), 339–354.

Thompson, D. B. 'An Historical Reconstruction of Melanchthonianism and the German Reformed Church Based upon Confessional and Liturgical Evidence', Ph.D. Diss., Columbia University, 1953.

Thompson, J. *Modern Trinitarian Perspectives.* Oxford, 1994.

Thompson, W. D. J. Cargill, 'The Two Regiments: The Continental Setting of William Tyndale's Political Thought', *Reform and Reformation: England and the Continent c.1500– c.1750.* Ed. D. Baker. Oxford, 1979.

Toft, D. J. 'Zacharias Ursinus: A Study in the Development of Calvinism', M.A. Thesis. University of Wisconsin, 1962.

Töpke, G., ed. *Die Matrikel der Universität Heidelberg von 1386 bis 1662.* 7 vols. Heidelberg, 1884–6.

——, ed. *Die Matrikel der Universität Heidelberg von 1386 bis 1662.* 2 vols. Heidelberg, 1886.

Torrance, J. B. 'Calvin and Puritanism in England and Scotland – Some Basic Concepts in the Development of "Federal Theology"', *Calvinus Reformator: His Contribution to Theology, Church and Society.* Potchefstroom, 1982.

—. 'Covenant or Contract? A Study of the Theological Background of Worship in the Seventeenth Century', *Scottish Journal of Theology* 23 (1970), 51–76.

—. 'Interpreting the Word by the Light of Christ or by the Light of Nature? Calvin, Calvinism, and Barth', *Calviniana: Ideas and Influence of Jean Calvin.* Ed. R. V. Schnucker. Kirksville, MO, 1988.

—. 'The Concept of Federal Theology – Was Calvin a Federal Theologian?', *Calvinus Sacrae Scripturae.* Ed. W. H. Neuser. Grand Rapids, 1994.

—. 'The Covenant Concept in Scottish Theology and Politics and its Legacy', *Scottish Journal of Theology* 34 (1981), 225–43.

—. 'The Incarnation and Limited Atonement', *Evangelical Quarterly* 55 (1983), 83–94.

Torrance, T. F. *Calvin's Doctrine of Man.* Edinburgh, 1949.

—. *The Hermeneutics of John Calvin.* Edinburgh, 1988.

—. *The School of Faith: The Catechisms of the Reformed Church.* New York, 1959.

—. '"The Substance of the Faith": A Clarification of the Concept in the Church of Scotland', *Scottish Journal of Theology* 36 (1983), 327–38.

Tracy, J. D. 'Humanism and the Reformation', *Reformation Europe: A Guide to Research.* Ed. S. E. Ozment. St Louis, 1982.

Trevor-Roper, H. R. *Religion, the Reformation and Social Change.* Second edition. London, 1972.

Trinkaus, C. *The Scope of Renaissance Humanism.* Ann Arbor, 1983.

Trinterud, L. J. 'The Origins of Puritanism', *Church History* 20 (1951), 37–57.

Troeltsch, E. 'Calvin and Calvinism', *Hibbert Journal* 8 (1909), 102–21.

Trueman, C. *Luther's Legacy. Salvation and the Early English Reformers 1525–1556.* Oxford, 1994.

— and R. S. Clark, eds. *Protestant Scholasticism: Essays in Reassessment.* Carlisle, 1998.

Tuchau, K. H. 'The Problem of the Species in Medio at Oxford in the Generation After Ockham', *Medieval Studies* 44 (1982).

Turchetti, M. s.v. 'Olevianus, Kaspar', The Oxford Encyclopedia of the Reformation. 4 vols. Ed. H. J. Hillerbrand. New York, 1996.

Tyacke, N. *Anti-Calvinists: The Rise of English Arminianism c.1590–1640.* Oxford, 1987.

Tylenda, J. N. 'The Controversy on Christ the Mediator: Calvin's Second Reply to Stancaro', *Calvin Theological Journal* 8 (1973), 131–57.

Van Asselt, W. J. and E. Dekker, eds. *Reformation and Scholasticism: An Ecumenical Enterprise.* Grand Rapids, 2001.

—. *The Federal Theology of Johannes Cocceius (1603–1669).* Trans. R. A. Blacketer. Leiden, 2001.

—. 'The Doctrine of the Abrogations in the Federal Theology of Johannes Cocceius (1603–69)', *Calvin Theological Journal* 29 (1994), 101–16.

Van't Spijker, W., ed. *Calvin: Erbe und Auftrag. Festschrift für W. H. Neuser.* Kampen, 1991.

Venema, Cornelis P. 'Heinrich Bullinger's Correspondence on Calvin's Doctrine of Predestination', *Sixteenth Century Journal* 17 (1986), 435–50.

——. 'Recent Criticisms of the "Covenant of Works" in the Westminster Confession of Faith', *Mid-America Theological Journal* 9 (1993): 165–98.

——. 'The Twofold Nature of the Gospel in Calvin's Theology: The *Duplex Gratia Dei and the Interpretation of Calvin's Theology*', Ph.D. Diss., Princeton Theological Seminary, 1985.

——. *Heinrich Bullinger and the Doctrine of Predestination*. Grand Rapids, 2002.

Visser, D. 'The Covenant in Zacharias Ursinus', *Sixteenth Century Journal* 18 (1987), 531–44.

——. *Zacharias Ursinus: The Reluctant Reformer: His Life and Times*. New York, 1983.

——, ed. *Controversy and Conciliation: The Palatinate Reformation, 1559–1618*. Pittsburgh, 1986.

——. 'Junius. The Author of Vindicae Contra Tyrannos?', *Tijdschrift voor Geschiedenis* 84 (1971), 510–25.

von Rohr, J. *The Covenant of Grace in Puritan Thought*. Atlanta, 1986.

Vos, A. *Aquinas, Calvin and Contemporary Protestant Thought: A Critique of the Views of Thomas Aquinas*. Grand Rapids, 1982.

Vos, G. 'The Doctrine of the Covenant in Reformed Theology', *Redemptive History and Biblical Interpretation: The Shorter Writings of Geerhardus Vos*. Trans. and ed. R. B. Gaffin. Phillipsburg, 1980.

Wallace, R. S. *Calvin's Doctrine of Word and Sacrament*. Edinburgh, 1953.

Warfield, B. B. 'Hosea VI.7: Adam or Man?', *The Bible Student* 8 (1903), 1–10. Repr. in *Selected Shorter Writings of Benjamin B. Warfield*. 2 vols. Ed. J. E. Meeter. Nutley, NJ, 1970.

——. 'Calvin's Doctrine of the Trinity', *The Princeton Theological Review* 7 (1909), 553–652.

——. 'On the Literary History of Calvin's *Institutes*', *Calvin and Calvinism*. New York, 1931.

——. *Calvin and Augustine*. Philadelphia, 1956.

——. *Studies in Theology*. New York, 1932.

Watt, J. R. 'Women and the Consistory in Calvin's Geneva', *The Sixteenth Century Journal* 24 (1993), 429–39.

Wawrykow, J. 'John Calvin and Condign Merit', *Archiv für Reformationsgeschichte* 83 (1992), 73–90.

Weber, H. E. *Reformation, Orthodoxie und Rationalismus*. Gütersloh, 1951.

Weber, O. *Foundations of Dogmatics*. 2 vols. Trans. D. L. Guder. Grand Rapids, 1981–2.

Wedgewood, C. V. *William the Silent. William of Nassau, Prince of Orange 1533–1584*. London, 1944.

Weir, D. A. *The Origins of the Federal Theology in Sixteenth Century Reformation Thought*. Oxford, 1990.

Weisheipl, J. A. *The New Catholic Encyclopedia*. s.v. 'Scholastic Method', 18 vols. New York, 1967.

Weiss, R. *The Renaissance Discovery of Classical Antiquity*. Second edition. Oxford, 1988.

Wendel, F. *Calvin: Origins and Development of His Religious Thought*. Trans. Philip Mairet. London, 1965.

Wesel-Roth, R. *Thomas Erastus*. Lahr-Baden, 1954.

Whitney, J. P. *The History of the Reformation*. London, 1958.

Willis, D. 'Calvin's Use of *Substantia*', *Calvinus Ecclesiae Genevenesis Custos*. Ed. W. Neuser. New York, 1984.

—. *Calvin's Catholic Christology. The Function of the So-Called Extra Calvinisticum in Calvin's Theology*. Leiden, 1966.

Woolsey, A. A. 'Unity and Continuity in Covenantal Thought: A Study in the Reformed Tradition to the Westminster Assembly', 2 vols. Ph.D. Thesis, Glasgow University, 1988.

Yarnold, E. '*Duplex Iustitia*: The Sixteenth Century and the Twentieth', *Christian Authority: Essays in Honour of Henry Chadwick*. Ed. G. R. Evans. Oxford, 1988.

Zachman, R. C. *The Assurance of Faith in the Theology of Martin Luther and John Calvin*. Philadelphia, 1993.

Zeeden, E. W. 'Calvinistische Elemente in der Kurpfälzischen Kirchenordnung von 1563', *Existenz und Ordnung*. Frankfurt, 1962.

Zimmerman, G. 'Der Heidelberger Katechismus als Dokument des subjektiven Spiritualismus', *Archiv für Reformationsgeschichte* 85 (1994), 180–204.

Zuck, L. H. 'Heinrich Heppe: A Melanchthonian Liberal in the Nineteenth Century German Reformed Church', *Church History* 51 (1982), 419–33.

—. 'Melanchthonianism and Reformed Theology in the Late 16th Century', *Controversy and Conciliation: The Palatinate Reformation, 1559–1618*. Ed. D. Visser. Pittsburgh, 1986.

Zumkeller, A. 'Der Terminus "*sola fides*" bei Augustinus', *Christian Authority: Essays in Honour of Henry Chadwick*. Ed. G. R. Evans. Oxford, 1988.

INDEX